Regulating Cartels in India

This book presents a comprehensive assessment of anti-cartel enforcement and investigative procedures in India. It makes a case for enhanced sanctions for cartel conduct in India. Cartels are considered the most pernicious violation of competition law, referred to as "cancer to the free-market economy". While competition laws in most jurisdictions prescribe strict sanctions against cartels, Indian Competition Law provides only civil penalties, with an upper ceiling for proven cartel conduct.

This volume assesses the effectiveness of anti-cartel enforcement of the Competition Commission of India (CCI). It explores investigative procedures of the CCI through multiple qualitative and quantitative indicators and the extent to which enforcement of anti-cartel laws in India has led to cartel deterrence. Further, it also examines the priorities and processes of the CCI in terms of anti-cartel enforcement, their sanctioning mechanism and their dependency of computation of penalty on varied factors.

Featuring detailed case law studies and engaging data, this book will be an essential read for students and researchers of law and legal studies, competition law, corporate law, intellectual property law and business law.

Sudhanshu Kumar is an experienced academic and is currently working as an assistant professor of law at NALSAR University of Law, Hyderabad, India. He is also the coordinator for the Centre for Corporate and Competition Laws at NALSAR. He offers papers on corporate and competition law for both undergraduate and postgraduate students. Some of his publications include books on competition law, consumer protection law and capital market. He has worked on multiple government-sponsored projects and has been engaged in training professionals and administrative officers on corporate and commercial laws. Dr Kumar is also a member of the Network of Indian Competition Experts (NICE) of the Competition Commission of India.

Regulating Cartels in India

Effectiveness of Competition Law

Dr. Sudhanshu Kumar

Routledge
Taylor & Francis Group
LONDON AND NEW YORK

First published 2023
by Routledge
4 Park Square, Milton Park, Abingdon, Oxon OX14 4RN

and by Routledge
605 Third Avenue, New York, NY 10158

Routledge is an imprint of the Taylor & Francis Group, an informa business

British Library Cataloguing-in-Publication Data
A catalogue record for this book is available from the British Library

ISBN: 978-1-032-18731-0 (hbk)
ISBN: 978-1-032-38950-9 (pbk)
ISBN: 978-1-003-34765-1 (ebk)

DOI: 10.4324/9781003347651

Typeset in Sabon
by Apex CoVantage, LLC

Contents

Figures

Tables

Preface

Protection of a free-market economy is the bedrock of competition law across jurisdictions. The free market ensures that the allocation of resources is on the basis of demand and supply. Competition in such a market acts as an invisible hand to push market participants to work for their self-interest and, in turn, provide the consumers with the best possible options.

Market competition has been explained as having similar normative underpinnings as that of democracy in terms of "freedom of choice, decentralized decision making and adherence to rule of law"[1] and also having similar objectives of maximization of welfare. Competition law may be regarded as an effort by the state to "protect the process of competition"[2] and punish anti-competitive practices. Most of the countries of the world, irrespective of the nature of their economies, have realized the importance of a statutory safeguard in the form of competition law to protect the interests of consumers and increase the efficiency of the market.

India replaced its age-old law in the form of the Monopolies and Restrictive Trade Practices Act, 1969, with the Competition Act, 2002 (the Act), to respond to the changing economic environment of the country. However, due to the constitutional challenge, it took another nine years for the Act to become fully operational.[3] In the last 12 years, the Indian competition law has grown by leaps and bounds and has had a major impact on how the business entities operate in the market. The Competition Commission of India (CCI) has imposed previously unheard-of penalties to the tune of billions of rupees on corporations proved to be indulging in anti-competitive behaviour. Under the scheme of the Act, the CCI is vested with inquisitorial, investigative, regulatory, adjudicatory and to a limited extent, even advisory jurisdiction. The CCI is structured as an expert regulatory body acting as a watchdog for the economy.[4]

Competition law has to be applied rigorously and effectively and competition matters need to be dealt with expeditiously in order to prevent damage to any open market economy. The issue of cartelization in markets has been one of the major areas of concern for all competition regulators. Considered as "supreme evil" or "cancer to the market", cartels are supposed to be dealt with iron hands. Criminal sanctions and high monetary penalties in many competition jurisdictions are grounded in the theory of "deterrence" and are justified on the basis of their proven ill effects on the market and economy. Indian competition law, although inspired by antitrust legislations in countries like the US and the UK/EU, is not quite *in pari materia* with these legislations. Therefore, the Act in India does not envisage criminal sanctions for indulgence in cartel activities and is limited to civil penalties. In a time when we are rethinking the tenets of competition law, it is important to evaluate and assess the experience of the CCI in dealing with cartel cases in India. Reforms, if any, have to be in light of previous experiences and challenges to the effective enforcement of anti-cartel laws.

The main objective of the present work is to examine and assess the public enforcement of anti-cartel laws in India. Optimal enforcement leading to optimal deterrence forms the crux of the enquiry.

The present book, apart from Chapter 1, which provides a brief introduction to the underlying theme of the book, is divided into five core chapters. Chapter 2 lays down the theoretical underpinnings of competition law and, more specifically, anti-cartel laws in a larger market context. To understand cartels as a phenomenon, it is important to understand the determinants of cartels in the form of cartel conducive environment; the reasons for the formation of cartels; the establishment of, participation in and decision-making of cartels; and the mode and sector of operation of cartels and see how these factors have shaped the formulation of anti-cartel laws. It is imperative that the theories around cartels, which have led to the modern-day competition laws, are tested on Indian conditions. The theoretical understandings developed through wide-ranging literature are therefore juxtaposed with the incidences of cartels in India in order to assess whether theoretical assumptions apply to Indian markets as well. In order to provide scientific backing to the assumption of variance of both the nature of cartels and their treatment by the CCI, an investigation of the underlying determinants of cartels in India during the observation period has been undertaken to check for consistency in the empirical validation of theoretical assumptions.

A descriptive account of Indian cartels based on parameters like type, duration, number of involved entities (including trade associations), affected sectors, duration and involvement of executives is provided in Chapter 3. A similar investigation is done in Chapters 4 and 5 to examine the investigative procedures of the CCI to assess factors of anti-cartel enforcement, like duration of investigation and disposal, nature of detection, yield ratio, use of evidence, standards of proof and cartel sanctions. These acceptable and implementable parameters are based on information available in the public domain.

Finally, Chapter 6 examines the institutional design of the CCI in dealing with the issue of cartelization in Indian markets. The present work, in light of the existing evidence, tries to explore whether the CCI has been able to achieve optimal anti-cartel enforcement through detection, design and sanction parameters.

This book is a product of years of academic engagement in the classroom and interactions with subject experts, critics and policymakers. I take this opportunity to acknowledge the research assistance provided by my students Ms Garima Gupta, PhD (NALSAR), and Ms Rhea Reddy, BA LLB (NALSAR), and thank them for their excellent work, which helped me to complete the manuscript in a timely manner. I would also like to convey my sincere gratitude to the publisher and the editorial team at Routledge (Taylor & Francis Group) for their continuous assistance and input.

Notes

1 Balbir Chauhan, *Indian Competition Law: Global Context*, 54 (3) Journal of Indian Law Institute, 315 (2012).
2 House of Lords debate during the passage of the Competition Act, 1998 (Hansard (HL) 30 October 1997, col. 1156).
3 The conduct-related provisions of the Competition Act were enforced from 20 May 2009, and the merger control provisions were notified 1 June 2011.
4 *Mahindra and Mahindra Ltd. v. Competition Commission of India & Anr.*, (2019) SCC Online Del. 8032.

Cases

Indian cases

- *A & I C (P) Ltd., Bombay and Sulphur Mills (P) Ltd., Bombay*, Case No. RTPE 6/1981, decided on 23 February 1984 (MRTPC).
- *A Foundation for Common Cause & People Awareness v. PES Installations Pvt. Ltd. & Ors.* Case No. 43/2010, decided on 16 April 2012 (CCI)
- *A. N. Mohana Kurup and another v. CCI and others*, Appeal No. 5/2016, decided on 10 May 2017 (COMPAT).
- *Advertising Agencies Guild v. Indian Broadcasting Foundation & its members*, Case No. 21/2012, decided on 1 January 2013 (CCI).
- *AIMTC v. CCI*, Appeal No. 60/2015, decided on 18 April 2016 (COMPAT).
- *AIOCD v. CCI*, Appeal No. 21/2013, decided on 9 December 2016 (COMPAT).
- *AIOCD v. CCI*, Appeal No. 6/2014, decided on 9 December 2016 (COMPAT).
- *AIOCD v. CCI*, Appeal No. 7/2014, decided on 9 December 2016 (COMPAT).
- *AK Kraipak v. Union of India*, AIR 1970 SC 150.
- *Alkali and Chemical Corporation of India Ltd., Calcutta v. Bayer (India) Ltd., Bombay* (1984) 3 Comp L J 268 (MRTPC).
- *Alkali Manufacturers Association of India v. American Natural Soda Ash Corporation and Anr.*, (1998) 3 Comp LJ 152 (MRTPC).
- *Alkali Manufacturers Association of India v. Sinochem International Chemicals Co. Ltd. and Anr.*, RTP Enquiry No. 238/1997, decided on 24 April 1998 (MRTPC).
- *Alkem Laboratories Ltd. v. CCI*, Appeal No. 9/206, decided on 10 May 2016 (COMPAT).
- *All India Distillers' Association v. Haldyn Glass Gujarat Ltd. & Ors.*, Case No. 30 (146)/2008, decided on 18 June 2010 (CCI).
- *All India Organization of Chemists and Druggists v. CCI*, III (2015) CPJ 4 (COMPAT).

- *All India Tyre Dealers Federation v. CCI*, Appeal No. 2/2013, decided on 25 April 2013 (COMPAT).
- *All India Tyre Dealers Federation v. Tyre Manufacturers*, 2013 Comp LR 92 (CCI).
- *Amit Jain v. DLF Limited*, CA No. 01/2015, Appeal No. 20/2011, decided on 4 November 2015 (COMPAT).
- *Andhra Film Chamber of Commerce v. M/s Cinergy Independent Film Service Pvt. Ltd. & Ors.*, Appl No. 15/2013, decided on 14 October 2015 (COMPAT).
- *Andhra Pradesh Paper Mills Ltd.*, RTP Enquiry No. 5/1973, decided on 31 January 1976 (MRTPC).
- *Anil K Jain v. Yamuna Expressway Industrial Development Authority, Department of Stamp & Registration*, Case No. 48/2014, decided on 1 October 2014 (CCI).
- *Anonymous v. Bengal Greenfield Housing Dev. Co. Ltd.*, Case No. 103/2013, decided on 12 February 2014 (CCI).
- *Anticompetitive conduct in the Dry-Cell Batteries Market in India v. Panasonic Corporation, Japan & Ors.*, Suo Moto Case No. 03/2017, decided on 15 January 2019 (CCI).
- *AR Polymers Pvt. Ltd. v. CCI*, Appeal Nos. 34–43/2013 and Appeal No. 8/2014, decided on 12 April 2016 (COMPAT).
- *Arun Kumar Tyagi v. The Software Engineering Institute & Ors.*, Case No. 19/2011, decided on 30 September 2011 (CCI).
- *Arvind Sood v. Hyundai Motor India Ltd.*, Case 64/2015, decided on 29 September 2015 (CCI).
- *Association of Registration Plates Manufacturers of India v. Shimnit UTSCH India Private Limited & Others*, Case No. 58/2017, decided on 14 November 2017 (CCI).
- *Association of Third Party Administrators v. General Insurers (Public Sector) Association of India (GIPSA)*, Case No. 107/2013, decided on 4 January 2016 (CCI).
- *Automobiles Dealers Association, Hathras, UP v. Global Automobiles Ltd. and Pooja Expo India Pvt. Ltd.*, 2012 Comp LR 827 (CCI).
- *Balaji Chandra v. Shivdhari Yadav*, AIR 1978 SC 1062.
- *Balbit Singh Jamwal v. Paras Buildtech India Pvt. Ltd. & Bharti Airtel Limited*, Case No. 79/2014, decided on 29 January 2015 (CCI).
- *Bengal Chemist and Druggist Association v. CCI*, Appeal No. 37/2014, decided on 10 May 2016 (COMPAT).
- *Bengal Chemist and Druggist Association*, Suo moto Case No. 2/2012, decided on 11 March 2014 (CCI).
- *Bengal Tools Ltd.* (1988) 63 Comp Cas. 468.
- *Bharatpur Truck Operators Union*, RTP Enquiry No. 10/1982, decided on 24 August 1984 (MRTPC).
- *Bholanath Shankar Das v. Lachmi Narain*, (1930) 53 All.316.

- *BP Khare v. Orissa Concrete and Allied Industries Ltd.*, [2013] 114 CLA 208 (CCI).
- *Brahm Dutt v. Union of India*, (2005) 2 SCC 431.
- *Builders Association of India (Kerala Chapter) v. The State of Kerala & Ors.*, Case No. 42/2013, decided on 12 May 2015 (CCI).
- *Builders Association of India v. Cement Manufacturers Association*, 2012 Comp LR 629 (CCI).
- *Calcutta Discount Company Limited v. Income Tax Officer*, 1961 SCR (2) 241.
- *Cartelization in respect of zinc carbon dry cell batteries market in India v. Eveready Industries India Ltd.*, Suo moto Case No. 2/2016, decided on 19 April 2018 (CCI).
- *Cement Manufacturers Association v. CCI*, Appeal No. 122/2012, decided on 11 December 2015 (COMPAT).
- *Charging of differential rate of interest by banks*, MRTP Case No. DGIR/2007/IP104-RTPE Case No. 33/2007, decided on 7 June 2011 (CCI).
- *Chemist & Druggist Association, Baroda v. CCI*, Appeal No. 140/2012, decided on 18 November 2016 (COMPAT).
- *Chemist and Druggist Association v. Arora Medical Hall*, Appeal No. 21/2014, decided on 30 October 2015 (COMPAT).
- *Chemists & Druggists Association, Ferozepur v. CCI*, Appeal Nos. 21/2014 to 28/2014 and IA Nos. 31/2014 to 46/2014, decided on 30 October 2015 (COMPAT).
- *Chemists and Druggists Association of Baroda v. CCI*, Case No. C-87/2009/DGIR, decided on 18 November 2016 (COMPAT).
- *Chief Materials Manager – I v. M/s Milton Industries Ltd. & Others*, Case No. 2/2014, decided on 1 July 2015 (CCI).
- *Chief Materials Manager/Sales, Eastern Railway v. M/s Laxven Systems & other*, Case No. 06/2018, decided on 2 January 2019 (CCI).
- *Cinemax India Ltd. v. Film Distributors Association*, 2015 Comp LR 81 (CCI).
- *Cinergy Independent Film Services Pvt. Ltd. v. Telangana Telugu Film Distributors Association and Ors.*, Case No. 56/2011, decided on 10 January 2013 (CCI).
- *Coal India Ltd. v. CCI*, Appeal No. 81/2014 (COMPAT).
- *Cochin Port Trust v. Container Trailer Owners Coordination Committee*, Ref. Case No. 06 of 2014, decided on 1 August 2017 (CCI).
- *Colgate Palmolive India Pvt. Ltd. v. Union of India*, [1980] 50 Com Cas 456 (Del.).
- *Competition Commission of India v. Coordination Committee of Artists and Technicians of WB Film and Television*, [2018] 144 CLA 403 (SC).
- *Competition Commission of India v. Steel Authority of India Ltd. and Ors.* (2010) 10SC C 744.

- *Consumer Online Foundation v. CCI*, I.A. No. 7/2011 & I.A. No. 8/2011, decided on 14 July 2011 (COMPAT).
- *Consumer Online Foundation v. Tata Sky Ltd. & Ors.*, Case No. 2/2009, decided on 24 March 2011 (CCI).
- *Co-ordination Committee of Artist and Technicians of West Bengal v. EIMPA*, Appeal No. 131/2012, decided on 3 April 2014 (COMPAT).
- *Corporation Bank v. Navin J. Shah*, (2000) 2 SCC 628.
- *Crown Theatre v. Kerala Film Exhibitors Federation*, Appeal No. 16/2017 (COMPAT).
- *CSR Nanjing Puzhen Co. Ltd. v. Kolkata Metro Rail Co. Ltd. & Ors.*, Case No. 54/2010, decided on 24 November 2010 (CCI).
- *Daulat Ram v. Dharma Chand*, AIR (1934) Lah.110.
- *DDRS (G) -II, Railway Board, Ministry of Railways v. M/s RMG Polyvinyl India Ltd., New Delhi & Ors.*, Case No. RTPE 31/2008, decided on 6 April 2011 (CCI).
- *Deepak Panchamia v. Bombay Dyeing & Manufacturing Company Limited (BD), Confederation of Real Estate Developers Association of India (CREDAI), Maharashtra Chamber of Housing Industries-MCREDAI*, Case Nos. 10, 17, 18, 25, 26 and 27 of 2015, decided on 19 May 2015 (CCI).
- *Delhi Jal Board v. Grasim Industries Ltd. & others*, Ref. Case No. 03 and 04 of 2013, decided on 5 October 2017 (CCI).
- *Deputy Chief Materials Manager, Rail Coach Factory, Kapurthala v. M/s. Faiveley Transport India Ltd.*, Ref. Case No. 6/2013 decided on 8 September 2015 (CCI).
- *DG (IR) v. Sumitomo Corporation, Tokyo, Japan and others*, 2004 CTJ 26 (MRTP)
- *DG-IR v. M/s Bharti Airtel Limited*, RTPE 20/2007 (COMPAT).
- *DGS&D, M/o Commerce, Govt. of India v. M/s Puja Enterprises & Ors.*, Ref. Case No. 01/2012, decided on 6 August 2013 (CCI).
- *Dhanraj Pillay v. Hockey India*, 2013 Comp LR 543 (CCI).
- *Dilip Thakkar v. Maharashtra Industrial Development Corporation (MIDC) & Ors.*, Case No. 19/2012, decided on 30 May 2012 (CCI).
- *Director General (Investigation and Registration) v. Modi Alkali and Chemicals Limited and Ors.*, II (2002) C PJ19 (MRTP).
- *Director General (Investigation and Registration) v. Reliance Industries Ltd. and Anr.*, I (2003) C PJ80 (MRTP).
- *Director, Supplies & Disposals, Haryana v. Shree Cement Limited & Ors.*, Ref. Case No. 05 of 2013, decided on 19 January 2017 (CCI).
- *Director-General of Investigation and Registration v. Cement Manufacturers Association and Ors.*, [1991]71Comp Cas46.
- *Dr. Biswanath Prasad Singh v. Director General of Health Services & Ors.*, Case No. 20/2014, decided on 23 June 2014 (CCI).
- *Dr. Biswanath Prasad Singh v. Director General of Health Services & Ors.*, Case No. 20/2014, decided on 14 March 2017 (CCI).

- *Dr. Naveen Karnwal v. State of U.P., through Secretary, Department of Geology and Mines & Ors.*, Case No. 44/2012, decided on 19 September 2012 (CCI).
- *Dt Board Jhelum v. Hari Chand*, AIR (1934) Lah 474.
- *Dwarikesh Sugar Industries Limited v. Wave Distilleries & Breweries Ltd. & Other*, Case No. 47/2014, decided on 29 December 2017 (CCI).
- *Dy. Chief Materials Manager, Integral Coach Factory, Chennai v. M/s Celtek Batteries* (P) Ltd., Bangalore & Ors., MRTP Case No. C-57/09/DGIR (26/28), decided on 27 July 2011 (CCI).
- *Eros International Media Ltd. v. Central Circuit Cine Association, Indore and others*, 2012 Comp LR 20 (CCI).
- *Excel Crop Care Limited v. Competition Commission of India*, 2013 CompLR 799 (COMPAT).
- *Excel Crop Care Ltd. v. CCI*, (2017) 8 SCC 47.
- *Excel Crop Care Ltd. v. CCI*, Appeal No. 79/2012, decided on 29 December 2013 (COMPAT).
- *Excel Crop Care Ltd. v. CCI*, Civil Appeal No. 2480/2014, decided on 8 May 2017 (SC).
- *Exclusive Motors Pvt. Limited v. Automobili Lamborghini S.P.A.*, Case No. 52/2012, decided on 6 November 2012 (CCI).
- *Exclusive Motors Pvt. Ltd. v. Automobili Lamborghini SPA*, Appeal No. 1/2013, decided on 28 February 2014 (COMPAT).
- *Express Industry Council of India v. Jet Airways (India) Ltd.*, Case No. 30/2013, decided on 7 March 2018.
- *FICCI Multiplex Association of India v. United Producers/Distributors Forum*, 2011 Comp LR 79 (CCI).
- *Film & Television Producers Guild of India v. Multiplex Association of India (MAI) Mumbai & Ors.*, Case No. 37/2011, decided on 3 March 2013 (CCI).
- *Firestone Tyre & Rubber Co. of India (P) Ltd. (now changed to Bombay Tyres International Ltd.) and Others*, RTPE 13 of 1978, decided on 24 March 1983 (MRTPC).
- *Food grains and kirana Merchants Association, Indian Rayon Corporation, Gujarat*, RTPE 18 of 1981, decided on 22 February 1983 (MRTPC).
- *Ghai Enterprises Pvt. Ltd. and Quality Ice Creams*, RTPE 18 of 1983, decided on 25 April 1986 (MRTPC).
- *Ghanshyam Das Vij v. Bajaj Corp Ltd.*, Case No. 68/2013, decided on 12 October 2015 (CCI).
- *Ghaziabad Development Authority v. Balbir Singh*, (2004) 5 SCC 65.
- *Ghee Merchants Association*, RTPE 23 of 1976, decided on 14 February 1977 (MRTPC).
- *GKB Hi Tech Lenses Private Limited v. Transitions Optical India Private Limited*, Case No. 1/2010, decided on 16 May 2012 (CCI).

- *GlaxoSmithKline Pharmaceuticals Limited v. CCI*, Appeal Nos. 85, 86/2015, decided on 8 November 2016 (COMPAT).
- *Goods Truck Operators Union, Faridabad*, RTP Enquiry No. 13.13.1987, decided on 13 December 1989 (MRTPC).
- *Google Inc v. CCI*, 2015 Comp LR 391 (Del.).
- *Gujarat Guardian Limited v. The Competition Commission of India and Ors.*, 2011CompLR69 (Delhi).
- *Gulf Oil Corp Ltd. v. CCI*, 2013 Comp LR 409 (COMPAT).
- *Gulshan Verma v. Union of India*, 2012 Comp LR 812 (CCI).
- *Hari Das Exports v. All India Float Glass Manufacturers Association & Co.*, AIR 2000 (SC) 2728.
- *Haridas Exports v. All India Float Glass Manufacturers' Association*, (2002) 6 *SCC* 600.
- *Himachal Pradesh Society of Chemist & Druggist Alliance v. Rohit Medical Store* (201 6) CompLR 304 (COMPAT).
- *Hindustan Lever Ltd. and Tata Oil Mills Co. Ltd.*, RTP Enquiry No. 4/1978, decided on 22 July 1982 (MRTPC).
- *IATA Agents Association of India v. Federation of Indian Airlines and others*, Case No. 35/2012, decided on 7 November 2012 (CCI).
- *In re Excel Industries Limited* (1988) 64 Comp Cas 531.
- *In Re: Airlines*, Case No. 01/2011, decided on 11 January 2012 (CCI).
- *In Re: Alkali and Chemical Corporation of India Ltd. and Bayer (India) Ltd.*, RTP Enquiry No. 21/1981, decided on 3 July 1984 (MRTPC).
- *In Re: Alleged Cartelization in the matter of supply of spares to Diesel Loco Modernization Works v. Stone India Ltd., Faiveley Transport Rail Technologies India Ltd. and Escorts Ltd.*, 2014 Comp LR 170 (CCI).
- *In Re: Anti-competitive conduct in the dry-Cell batteries market in India v. Panasonic Corp, Japan*, Suo moto Case No. 2/2017, decided on 30 August 2018 (CCI).
- *In Re: Anti-Competitive Practices Prevailing in Banking Sector*, Case No. 1/2015, decided on 24 April 2018 (CCI).
- *In re: Bengal Chemist & Druggist Association*, 2014 Comp LR 221 (CCI).
- *In Re: Bengal Chemist and Druggist Association*, decided on 10 May 2016 (COMPAT).
- *In Re: Bharatpur Truck Operator's Union*, (RTP Enquiry No. 10 of 1982).
- *In Re: Cartelisation by broadcasting service providers by rigging the bids submitted in response to the tenders floated by Sports Broadcasters v. Essel Shyam Communication Limited & others*, Suo moto Case No. 2/2013, decided on 11 July 2018 (CCI).
- *In Re: Cartelization by Cement Manufacturers*, RTPE No. 52 of 2006, decided on 31 August 2016 (CCI).
- *In Re: Cartelization by public sector insurance companies in rigging the bids submitted in response to the tenders floated by the Government of*

Kerala for selecting insurance service provider for Rashtriya Swasthya Bima Yojna v. National Insurance Co. Ltd. and Others, Suo moto Case No. 2/2014, decided on 10 July 2015 (CCI).
- *In Re: Cartelization in respect of tenders floated by Indian Railways for supply of Brushless DC Fans and other electrical items*, Suo Moto Case No. 3/2014, decided on 18 January 2017 (CCI).
- *In Re: Cartelization in respect of zinc carbon dry cell batteries market in India, Suo moto* Case No. 2/2016, decided on 19 April 2018 (CCI).
- *In Re: Cartelization in the supply of electric power steering system*, Suo Motu Case No. 07 (01) of 2014, decided on 9 August 2019 (CCI).
- *In Re: Cartelization with respect to tenders floated by Pune Municipal Corporation for solid waste processing*, Case No. 50/2015, *Suo moto* Case No. 3/2016 (CCI).
- *In Re: Chloride India Ltd.*, RTP Enquiry No. 46/1977, decided on 15 May 1981 (MRTPC).
- *In Re: Cochin Port Trust and Container Trailer Owners Coordination Committee*, Case No. 6/2014, decided on 1 August 2017 (CCI).
- *In re: Collective boycott/refusal to deal by the Chemists & Druggists Association, Goa (CDAG), M/s Glenmark Company and, M/s Wockhardt Ltd.*, Suo-Moto Case No. 05 of 2013, decided on 27 October 2014 (CCI).
- *In Re: Deputy Chief Materials Manager, Rail Coach Factory v. M/s Faiveley Transport India Limited & Others*, Case 6/2013, decided on 8 September 2015 (CCI).
- *In Re: Domestic Air Lines*, Case No. 02/2010, decided on 10 January 2012 (CCI).
- *In Re: Excel Industries Ltd.*, [1988] 64 Comp Cas 531 (MRTPC).
- *In Re: Glass Manufacturers of India*, MRTP Case No. 161/2008, decided on 24 January 2012 (CCI).
- *In re: Hind Lamps Limited*, RTP Enquiry No. 13/1974, decided on 19 April 1984 (MRTPC).
- *In Re: Hyderabad Asbestos Cement Products*, RTPE No. 17 of 1979 (MRTPC).
- *In Re: Indian Jute Mills Association*, RTP Enquiry No. 80/1975, decided on 11 October 1977 (MRTPC).
- *In Re: Jugaldas Damodar Mody's*, [1983] 3 Comp L J 221.
- *In Re: Kannada Grahakara Koota v. Karnataka Film Chamber of Commerce*, Case No. 58/2012, decided on 24 March 2017 (CCI).
- *In Re: Kush Kalra v. Reserve Bank of India & Others*, Case No. 23/2017, decided on 23 August 2017 (CCI).
- *In Re: M/s Span Communications*, Case No. 3/2014, decided on 29 October 2014 (CCI).
- *In Re: Manufacturers of Asbestos Cement Products*, Case No. 1/2012, decided on 11 February 2014 (CCI).

- *In Re: Muthoot Mercantile Limited*, Case No. 81/2014, decided upon 30 December 2014 (CCI).
- *In Re: Nitesh Forest Hills Apartment Owners*, Case No. 11/2015, decided on 21 May 2015 (CCI).
- *In Re: NLC India Limited v. M/s. Phoenix Conveyor Belt India (P) Limited*, Case No. 42/2018, decided on 9 November 2018 (CCI).
- *In Re: Rise in Onion Prices*, Case No. 01/2011, decided on 10 April 2012 (CCI).
- *In Re: Rohtak Public Goods Motor Union*, RTP Enquiry No. 25/1983 (MRTPC).
- *In Re: Shri P.V. Basheer Ahmed v. Film Distributors Association, Kerala*, Case No. 32/2013, decided on 23 December 2014 (CCI).
- *In Re: Sugar Mills*, Suo-motu Case No. 1/2010, decided on 30 November 2011 (CCI).
- *In Re: Suo-moto case against LPG cylinder manufacturers*, Suo Moto Case No. 03/2011, decided on 24 February 2012 and 6 August 2014 (CCI).
- *In Re: Swastic Laminating Industries*, RTP Enquiry No. 81/1984, decided on 31 January 1986 (MRTPC).
- *In Re: The Air Cargo Agents Association of India*, Case No. 79/2012, decided on 4 June 2015 (CCI).
- *In Re: Truck Operators Union*, RTP Enquiry No. 32/1977 (MRTPC).
- *In Re: TTK Pharma Limited*, RTP Enquiry Nos. 157–185/1986, 179–185/1986, 148–149/1986, decided on 15 May 1986 (CCI).
- *India Glycols Limited v. Indian Oil Corporation Ltd. & Ors.*, Case No. 14/2012, decided on 26 July 2012 (CCI).
- *India Glycols Ltd. v. Indian Sugar Mills Association & others*, Case Nos. 21, 29, 36, 47, 48 & 49 of 2013, decided on 11 May 2018 (CCI).
- *Indian Foundation of Transport Research & Training v. Sh. Bal Malkait Singh, President and Ors.*, Case No. 61 of 2012, decided on 16 February 2015 (CCI).
- *Indian Jute Mills Association v. CCI*, Appeal No. 73/2014, decided on 1 July 2016 (COMPAT).
- *Indian Sugar Mills Association v. Indian Jute Mills Association*, 2014 Comp LR 225 (CCI).
- *Indian Woolen Mills Federation and others*, RTPE 32 of 1976, decided on 25 April 1977 (CCI).
- *Interglobe Aviation Limited v. The Secretary, Competition Commission of India and Ors.*, 173 (2010) DLT581.
- *Interglobe Aviation Ltd. (IndiGo Airlines) v. CCI*, Appeal No. 07/2016, decided on 18 April 2016 (COMPAT).
- *International Air Transport Association (IATA) v. Air Cargo Agents Association of India (ACAAI) & others*, Case No. 29/2017, decided on 12 September 2017 (CCI).
- *ISPAI v. DoT*, Case No. 10/2009, decided on 29 June 2010 (CCI).

- *J.K. Industries Ltd.*, RTP Enquiry No. 28/1984 (MRTPC).
- *Jay Engineering Works Ltd. and others*, RTPE 17/1980, decided on 6 April 1983 (MRTPC).
- *Jet Airways Limited v. CCI*, Appeal No. 102/2016, decided on 18 April 2016 (COMPAT).
- *Johnson & Johnson Ltd.* v. *Maharashtra State Chemists & Druggists Associations & others.*, 2002 CTJ 265 (MRTP).
- *Jupiter Gaming Solutions Private Limited v. Government of Goa & Ors.*, Case No. 15/2010, decided on 12 May 2011 (CCI).
- *Kelvion India Private Limited v. Apollo Industrial Corporation & others*, Case No. 33/2018, decided on 9 November 2018 (CCI).
- *Kerala Cine Exhibitors Association v. Kerala Film Exhibitors Federation*, 2015 Comp LR 666 (CCI).
- *KFCC v. CCI*, Appeal No. 13/2016, decided on 10 April 2017 (COMPAT).
- *Krishna Mohan Hospital & Ors. v. The Secretary, Ministry of Agriculture & Cooperation, New Delhi & Ors.*, Case No. 75/2011, decided on 28 December 2011 (CCI).
- *Kshitij Ranjan v. Indian Newspaper Society*, Case No. 34/2011, decided on 11 October 2011 (CCI).
- *Lafarge India Ltd. v. CCI*, Appeal No. 105/2012, decided on 11 December 2015 (COMPAT).
- *Lodestar Slotted Angles Ltd. v. Rockline Construction Company & Ors.*, Case No. 4/2011, decided on 22 March 2011 (CCI).
- *M. K. Shrivastava v. M/s Bharti Airtel Limited, M/s Vodafone Mobile Services Limited, M/s Idea Cellular Limited*, Case 55/2013, decided on 16 January 2014 (CCI).
- *M.P. Mehrotra v. Kingfisher Airlines Ltd. & Ors.*, Case No. 4/2009, decided on 11 August 2011 (CCI).
- *M/s Applesoft v. The Chief Secretary to the Government of Karnataka & others*. Case No. 8/2017, decided on 5 May 2017 (CCI).
- *M/s Arora Medical Hall, Ferozepur v. Chemists & Druggists Association, Ferozepur & Ors.*, Case No. 60/2012, decided on 5 February 2014 (CCI).
- *M/s Ashtavinayak Cine Vision Ltd. v. PVR Picture Limited & Ors.*, Case No. 71/2011, decided on 28 July 2016 (CCI).
- *M/s Bio-Med Private Limited v. Union of India & others*, Case No. 26/2013, decided on 4 June 2015 (CCI).
- *M/s Cinemax India Limited (now known as M/s PVR Ltd.) v. M/s Film Distributors Association (Kerala),* Case No. 62/2012, decided on 23 December 2014 (CCI).
- *M/s Dhanvir Food Product v. Bank of Baroda*, Case 21/2015, decided on 2 June 2015 (CCI).
- *M/s Dipak Nath v. M/s Oil and Natural Gas Corporation Ltd.*, Case No. 23/2013, decided on 5 July 2013 (CCI).

- *M/s DLF Limited v. Competition Commission of India & Ors.*, Appeal No. 20/2011, decided on 19 May 2014 (COMPAT).
- *M/S India Glycol Ltd. v. Indian Sugar Mills Association*, Appeal No. 119/2012, decided on 9 December 2013 (COMPAT).
- *M/s Indiacan Education Pvt. Ltd. v. M/s Aldine Ventures Pvt. Ltd. & Others*, Case No. 71/2016, decided on 10 November 2016 (CCI).
- *M/s K Sera Sera Digital Cinema Pvt. Ltd. v. M/s NBC Universal Media Distribution Services Pvt. Ltd. & Others*, Case 24/2015, decided on 4 June 2015 (CCI).
- *M/s Kyal Agencies Pvt. Ltd. v. Utkal Chemists and Druggists Association (UCDA) & Ors.*, Case 79/2015, decided on 17 November 2015 (CCI).
- *M/s Metalrod Ltd. v. M/s. Religare Finvest Ltd.*, Case 28/2010, decided on 23 May 2011 (CCI).
- *M/s National Insurance Company Limited v. CCI*, Appeal No. 48/2014, decided on 26 August 2015 (COMPAT).
- *M/s Oberoi Cars Pvt. Ltd. v. M/s Imperial Housing Ventures Pvt. Ltd.*, Case No. 60/2016, decided on 21 August 2016 (CCI).
- *M/s Pankaj Gas Cylinders Ltd. v. Indian Oil Corporation Ltd.*, Case 10/2010, decided on 22 June 2011 (CCI).
- *M/s Paper Merchants Association, Delhi & Ors. v. Vijay Gupta*, Appeal No. 13/2013, decided on 16 May 2013 (COMPAT).
- *M/s Royal Agency v. Chemists & Druggists Association, Goa & Others*, Case 63/2013, decided on 27 October 2015 (CCI).
- *M/s Royal Energy Ltd. v. M/s Indian Oil Corporation Ltd. & Ors.*, MRTP Case No. 1/28, decided on 9 May 2012 (CCI).
- *M/s Swastik Stevedores Private Limited v. M/s Dumper Owner's Association*, Case No. 42/2012, decided on 21 January 2015 (CCI)
- *M/s United Phosphorus Ltd. v. CCI*, Appeal No. 81/2012, decided on 29 October 2013 (COMPAT).
- *M/s Voltas Ltd., Bombay v. Union of India*, AIR 1995 SC 1881.
- *M/s. Bull Machines Pvt. Ltd. v. M/s. JCB India Ltd. & Anr.*, Case No. 105/2013, decided on 11 March 2014 (CCI).
- *M/s. FCM Travel Solutions (India) Ltd., New Delhi v. Travel Agents Federation of India & Ors.*, RTPE 09/2008 (C-31/2009/DGIR) decided on 17 November 2011 (CCI).
- *M/s. K. Sera Sera Digital Cinema Pvt. Limited v. Digital Cinema Initiatives, LLC & Ors.*, Appeal No. 42/2016, decided on 1 February 2017 (COMPAT).
- *M/s. Knorr Bremse India Pvt. Ltd.*, Appeal No. 10/2016 decided on 17 February 2016 (COMPAT)
- *M/s. National Insurance Company Ltd. v. CCI*, Appeal Nos. 94, 96, 97/2015, decided on 9 December 2016 (COMPAT).
- *Madhya Pradesh Chemists and Distributors Federation (MPCDF) v. Madhya Pradesh Chemists and Druggist Association (MPCDA) & Others*, Case No. 64/2014, decided on 15 January 2019 (CCI).

- *Madras Rubber Factory Ltd., Goodyear India Ltd., Dunlop India Ltd. and Bombay Tyres International Ltd.*, RTPE 6/1978, decided on 2 February 1983 (MRTPC).
- *Mahadhiraja v. Yasin Khan*, (1937) 17 Pat.255.
- *Maharashtra State Power Generation Company Ltd. v. Nair Coal Services Pvt. Ltd. & Ors.*, Compensation Application (AT) No. 02/2018 (COMPAT).
- *Major English Newspapers and Indian and Eastern Newspaper Society*, RTPE 46/1975, decided on 18 December 1975 (MRTPC).
- *Manaklal v. Prem Chand Singhvi*, AIR 1957 SC 425.
- *Manappuram Jewellers Pvt. Ltd., Thrissur, Kerala v. Kerala Gold & Silver Dealers Association, Thrissur, Kerala & Ors.*, Case No. 13/2011, decided on 23 April 2012 (CCI).
- *Maneka Gandhi v. Union of India*, AIR 1978 SC 597.
- *Manju Tharad v. Eastern India Motion Pictures Association (EIMPA) and Others*, [2012] 110 CLA 136 (CCI).
- *Maruti & Co., Bangalore v. Karnataka Chemist and Druggist Association (KCDA),* Case No. 71/2013, decided on 28 July 2016 (CCI).
- *MCX Stock Exchange Ltd. v. National Stock Exchange of India Ltd.*, Compensation application No. 01/2014, order dated 5 December 2016 (COMPAT)
- *MDD Medical Systems India Pvt. Ltd. v. Foundation for Common Cause and People Awareness*, 2013 Comp LR 327 (COMPAT).
- *Ministry of Tourism v. Span Communications & Ors.*, Appeal No. 80/2015, decided on 16 July 2015 (COMPAT).
- *Mohammed Tariq Sultan, Hyderabad v. Hongkong Shanghai Banking Corporation Ltd. & Ors.*, Case No. 39/2011, decided on 21 November 2011 (CCI).
- *Motion Picture Association v. Sunshine Pictures Pvt. Ltd.*, Appeal No. 19/2010, decided on 28 July 2011 (COMPAT).
- *Motion Pictures Association v. Reliance Big Entertainment Pvt. Ltd. & Ors.*, Appeal No. 66, 67, 69, 71, 73, 78, 96, 97, 102/2012, decided on 17 May 2013 (COMPAT).
- *MP Mehrotra v. Jet Airways (India) Ltd. and Kingfisher Airlines Ltd.*, Case No. Misc. 1/2010, decided on 9 January 2012 (CCI).
- *Mr Vijay Gupta v. M/s. Paper Merchants Association, Delhi*, Case No. 7/2010, decided on 3 February 2011 (CCI).
- *Mr. Ashok Kumar Vallabhaneni v. Geetha SP Entertainment LLP & Others*, Case No. 17/2018, decided on 1 August 2019 (CCI).
- *Mr. G. Krishnamurthy v. Karnataka Film Chamber of Commerce (KFCC) & Others*, Case No. 42/2017, decided on 30 August 2018 (CCI).
- *Mr. Kalyan Chowdhary v. Cipla Limited. & Other*, Case No. 43/2018, decided on 10 May 2019 (CCI).
- *Mr. Kuntal Chowdhary v. Macleods Pharmaceuticals Limited. & Other*, Case No. 44/2018, decided on 10 May 2019 (CCI).

- *Mr. Mir Jawwad Ali, California v. Standard Chartered Bank Ltd. & Ors.*, Case No. 35/2011, decided on 21 November 2011 (CCI).
- *Mr. Nadie Jauhr v. Jalgaon District Medicine Dealers Association (JDMDA),* Case No. 61/2015, decided on 20 June 2019 (CCI).
- *Mr. P. K. Krishnan v. All Kerala Chemists and Druggist Association & Ors.*, Case No. 28 of 2014, decided on 1 December 2015 (CCI).
- *MRF Ltd. v. Ministry of Corporate Affairs*, 2018 Comp LR 313 (Mad.).
- *Muthoot Mercantile Limited v. CCI*, Appeal No. 48/2015, decided on 6 April 2015 (COMPAT).
- *N Sanjeeva Rao and Mrs. Fatima Tahir v. Andhra Pradesh Hire Purchase Association and 162 Others*, Case 49/2012, decided on 7 February 2013 (CCI).
- *Nagole Auto Drivers Welfare Association v. M/s. Abhinandan Motors (P) Ltd. & Ors.*, Appeal No. 35/2014, decided on 14 July 2014 (COMPAT).
- *Nagole Auto Drivers Welfare Association v. M/s. Abhinandan Motors (P) Ltd. & Ors.*, Case 85/2013, decided on 5 February 2014 (CCI).
- *Nagrik Chetna Manch v. Fortified Security Solutions & Others*, case 50/2015, decided on 1 May 2018 (CCI).
- *Narayana v. State of Andhra Pradesh*, AIR 1958 AP 636.
- *National Insurance Co. Ltd. v. CCI*, Appeal No. 94–97/2015, decided on 9 December 2016 (COMPAT).
- *National Insurance Company Ltd. and Ors. v. Competition Commission of India*, 2017CompLR1 (COMPAT).
- *Neeraj Malhotra v. Deustche Post Bank Home Finance Ltd. & Ors.*, Case No. 5/2009, decided on 2 December 2010 (CCI).
- *Nirmal Kumar Manshani v. Ruchi Soya Industries Ltd.*, Case No. 76 of 2012, decided on 21 June 2016 (CCI).
- *Nitin Radheshyam Agarwal v. Nitin Radheshyam Agarwal*, Appeal No. 108/2015, decided on 14 December 2015 (COMPAT).
- *Organo Chemical Industries v. Union of India*, (1979) 4 SCC 573.
- *Oriental Rubber Industries v. Competition Commission of India* (2016), CompLR 611 (Delhi).
- *P. V. Basheer Ahamed v. Film Distributors Association (Kerala) & Other*, Case No. 7/2017, decided on 3 October 2017 (CCI).
- *P.E.C. Usha Furniture v. Military Engineer Services, Officials working under CE (Navy),* Case No. 113/2015, decided on 28 June 2016 (CCI).
- *PES Installations v. Foundation for common cause*, Appeal No. 94,95/2012, decided on 25 February 2013 (COMPAT).
- *Pitambara Books Private Limited, Delhi v. Primary Education Department, Office of the Director, Andhra Pradesh Open School, Andhra Pradesh & Ors.*, Appeal No. 14/2012, decided on 21 November 2012 (COMPAT).
- *Pitambara Books Private Limited, Delhi v. Primary Education Department, Office of the Director, Andhra Pradesh Open School, Andhra*

Pradesh & Ors., Case No. 53/2011, decided on 30 November 2011 (CCI).

- *Pravahan Mohanty v. HDFC Bank Ltd., Chennai*, Case No. 17/2010, dated 23 May 2011 (CCI).
- *Prints India v. Springer India Private Limited & Ors.*, Case No. 16/2010, decided on 3 July 2012 (CCI).
- *Puja Enterprises v. CCI*, Appeal No. 8/2014, decided on 12 April 2016 (COMPAT).
- *Quadrant EPP Surlon India Ltd. v. INA Bearings India Pvt. Ltd. & Ors.*, Case No, 19/2013, decided on 27 May 2013 (CCI).
- *Raipur Development Authority v. Chokhamal Contractors*, AIR 1990 SC 1426.
- *Rajasthan Cylinders and Containers Limited v. Union of India and Ors.*, [2018] 150 SCL 1 (SC).
- *Rajesh Kumar v. CIT*, (2007) 2 SCC 181.
- *Rambir Singh v. M/s Puri Constructions Pvt. Ltd.*, Case 19/2015, decided on 24 June 2015 (CCI).
- *Rangi International Ltd. v. Nova scotia Bank*, (2013) 7 SCC 160.
- *Ravi Pal v. All India Sugar Trade Association (AISTA) & Anr.*, Case No. 25/2018, decided on 22 March 2018 (CCI).
- *Raymond Woollen Mills Ltd. v. MRTP Commission*, (1979) 49 Com Cases 686 (Bom.).
- *RC Cooper v. Union of India*, (1970) 1 SCC 248.
- *Re Aluminum Phosphide Tablets Manufacturers*, 2012 Comp LR 753 (CCI).
- *Re Anti-competitive conduct in the dry-Cell batteries market in India v. Panasonic Corp, Japan*, Suo moto Case No. 2/2017, decided on 30 August 2018 (CCI).
- *Re: Alleged cartelization in the matter of supply of spares to Diesel Loco Modernization Works, Indian Railways, Patiala, Punjab*, Suo Moto Case No. 03 of 2012, decided on 5 February 2014.
- *Re: Tyre cartel*, RTPE/1971, decided on 19 April 1976 (MRTPC).
- *Reliance Agency v. Chemist and Druggist Association, Baroda*, case No. 97/2013, decided on 4 March 2018 (CCI).
- *Reliance Big Entertainment Ltd. v. Karnataka Film Chamber of Commerce*, 2012 Comp LR 269 (CCI).
- *Reprographics India v. Hitachi Systems Micro Clinic Pvt. Ltd. & Anr.* Case No. 41/2018, decided on 9 November 2018 (CCI).
- *Rohit Medical Store v. Macleods Pharmaceuticals Limited*, 2015 Comp LR 451 (CCI).
- *Rohtak Public Goods Motor Union*, RTP Enquiry No. 250/10983, decided on 25 August 1984 (MRTPC).
- *Royal Agency v. Chemist and Druggist Association*, Case No. 63/2013, decided on 27 October 2017 (CCI).

- *RRTA v. Hyderabad Asbestos Cement Products Ltd.*, RTP Enquiry No. 17/1979, decided on 20 December 1982 (MRTPC).
- *Sai Wardha Power Ltd. v. Coal India Ltd. & Ors.*, Transfer C.A. (AT) (Compensation) No. 01/2017 (COMPAT).
- *Sajjan Khaitan v. Eastern India Motion Picture Association*, 2012 Comp LR 914 (CCI).
- *Samir Agrawal v. ANI Technologies Pvt. Ltd. & others*, Case No. 37/2018, decided on 6 January 2018 (CCI).
- *Sandhya Organic Chemicals Pvt. Ltd. v. CCI*, Appeal No. 80 of 2012, decided on 29 October 2013 (COMPAT).
- *Santuka Associates Pvt. Ltd. v. Al Indian Organization of Chemists and Druggists and Others*, 2013 Comp LR 223 (CCI).
- *Sarv Prakash Developers v. Phantom Films & Others*, Case No. 65/2017, decided on 8 March 2018 (CCI).
- *Sateyendra Singh & Ors. v. Ghaziabad Development Authority*, Compensation Application (AT) No. 02/2018.
- *Schott Glass India Pvt. Ltd. v. CCI*, (2014) Comp LR 295 (COMPAT).
- *Sh. S.K. Sharma, Deputy CMM-IV, North Western Railway, Hasanpura, Jaipur v. M/s RMG Polyvinyl India Ltd., New Delhi & Ors.*, Case No. RTPE 31/2008, decided on 6 April 2011 (CCI).
- *Sh. Surinder Saini v. Delhi Metro Rail Corporation Ltd. & Ors.*, Case 89/2013, decided on 2 January 2014 (CCI).
- *Shailesh Kumar v. Tata Chemicals Ltd.*, 2013 Comp LR 509 (CCI).
- *Shamsher Kataria v. Honda Siel*, 2014 CompLR 1 (CCI).
- *Sheth & Co. v. CCI*, Appeal No. 102/2015, decided on 10 May 2016 (COMPAT).
- *Shib Sankar Nag Sarkar and another v. CCI and others*; Appeal No. 42/2014, decided on 10 May 2016 (COMPAT).
- *Shivam Enterprises v. Kiratpur Sahib Truck Operators Co-operative Transport Society Ltd.*, 2015 Comp LR 232 (CCI).
- *Shri Achintya Mukherjee v. Loop Telecom Pvt. Limited & Ors.*, Case No. C-125/2009/DGIR (22/28), decided on 20 January 2011 (CCI).
- *Shri Arun Mishra v. State of U.P. through Chief Secretary & Others*, Case No. 43/2017, decided on 24 January 2018 (CCI).
- *Shri D.K Srivastava v. M/s Faiveley Transport India Ltd., M/s Knorr Bremse India Pvt. Ltd.*, Case 5/2014, decided on 23 September 2014 (CCI).
- *Shri Gulshan Verma v. Union of India, through Secretary, Ministry of Health and Family Welfare & Ors.*, Case No. 40/2010, decided on 5 April 2012 (CCI)
- *Shri Kshitiz Arya & other v. Viacom18 Media Pvt. Ltd. & Others*, Case No. 3/2018, decided on 1 January 2018 (CCI).
- *Shri Nandan Kumar v. Association of Healthcare Providers (India) & Ors.* Case No. 55/2014, decided on 29 October 2014 (CCI).

- *Shri Neeraj Malhotra, Advocate v. North Delhi Power Ltd. & Ors.*, Case No. 5/2009, decided on 11 May 2011 (CCI).
- *Shri Sameer Agarwal v. M/s Bestech India Pvt. Ltd.*, Case No. 59/2016, decided on 6 September 2016 (CCI).
- *Shri Surendra Prasad v. M/s Maharashtra State Power Generation Co. Ltd. (MAHAGENCO) & Ors.* Case 61/2013, decided on 11 December 2013 (CCI).
- *Shri Tom Joseph v. Chairman, Steel Authority of India & Ors.*, Case 90/2013, decided on 5 February 2014 (CCI).
- *Shri Vijay Bishnoi v. M/s Responsive Industries Ltd. & Others*, Case No. 8/2014, decided on 21 September 2016 (CCI).
- *Shri Vipul v. All India Film Employee Confederation & Ors.*, Case No. 19/2014, decided on 31 October 2017 (CCI).
- *Siemens Engineering and Manufacturing Co. Ltd. v. Union of India*, AIR 1976 SC 1785.
- *Sirmur Truck Operator*, (1995) 3 CTJ 332 (MRTPC).
- *SN Mukherjee v. Union of India*, AIR 1990 SC 1984.
- *Somu Pillai v. Municipal Council, Mayavaram*, (1905) 28 Mad. 520.
- *South Gujarat Warp Knitters Association v. Prafful Overseas Private Limited & Others*. Case No. 24/2016, decided on 9 March 2017 (CCI).
- *Sponge Iron Manufacturers Association v. National Mineral Development Corporation*, Case No. 69/2012, decided on 19 February 2013 (CCI).
- *Standing Committee (S&C) Association of State Road Transport Undertaking v. Karmobiles Limited and Anr.*, II (2002) C PJ36 (MRTP).
- *State of Orissa v. D. Binapani Devi*, AIR 1967 SC 1269.
- *Sudeep P.M. & others v. All Kerala Chemists and Druggists Association*, Case No. 54/2015, decided on 31 October 2017 (CCI).
- *Sunil Bansal v. Jaiprakash Associates Ltd.*, Appeal No. 21/2016, decided on 28 September 2016 (COMPAT).
- *Sunshine Pictures Private Limited & Eros International Media Limited v. Central Circuit Cine Association, Indore & Ors.*, Case 52, 56 of 2010, decided on 16 February 2012 (CCI).
- *Suntec Energy Systems v. National Dairy Development Board*, Case No. 69/2016, decided on 10 November 2016 (CCI).
- *Suomoto v. North Delhi Power Ltd. & BSES & Ors.*, Case No. 19/2008, decided on 31 May 2011 (CCI).
- *Surendra Prasad v. CCI*, Appeal No. 43/2014, decided on 15 September 2015 (COMPAT).
- *Surendra Prasad v. Maharashtra State Power Generation Co. Ltd. & Others*, Case No. 61/2013, decided on 10 January 2018 (CCI).
- *Swapan Kumar Karak v. CCI and others*; Appeal No. 09/2016, decided on 7 December 2015 (COMPAT).
- *Tamil Nadu Film Exhibitors Association v. CCI*, AIR 2015 Mad 106.

- *Tarun Patel v. Haria Lakhamshi Govindji Rotary Hospital & Ors.*, Case No. 49/2015, decided on 18 November 2015 (CCI).
- *Telco v. Registrar of Restrictive Trade Agreements*, 2 SCC 55 (1977).
- *TG Vinay Kumar Bharathim and Association of Malyalam Movie Artitsts (AMMA), Film Employees Federation of Kerala (FEFKA),* Case No. 98/2014, decided on 24 March 2017 (CCI).
- *The Air Cargo Agents Association of India v. CCI and Others*, Appeal No. 98/2015, decided on 15 November 2016 (COMPAT).
- *The Air Cargo Agents Association of India v. International Air Transport Association (IATA) & other*, Case No. 79/2012, decided on 4 June 2015 (CCI).
- *The Belgaum District Chemists and Druggist Association v. Abbott India Ltd.*, C-175/09/DGIR/27/28-MRTP, decided on 2 March 2017 (CCI).
- *The Board of Control for cricket in India (BCCI) v. CCI*, 2015 CompLR 548 (COMPAT).
- *Tirunerveli District Lorry Owners Association*, RTPE 14 of 1983, decided on 20 March 1984 (MRTPC).
- *Travel Agents Association of India v. Lufthansa German Airlines & Ors.*, Case No. 14/2009, decided on 31 October 2011 (CCI).
- *Travel Agents Association of India v. Lufthansa German Airlines. & Ors.*, Appeal No. 25/2011, decided on 7 December 2012 (COMPAT).
- *Truck Operators and Transport Operators Association, Rampur and Other* -RTPE 11/1987, decided on 14 August 1987 (MRTPC).
- *Truck Operators Union v. Mr. N.C. Gupta & Mr. Sardar*, (1995) 3 CTJ 70 (MRTPC)
- *Truck Operators Union*, RTPE 32 of 1977, decided on 20 February 1978 (MRTC).
- *Uniglobe Mod Travels Pvt. Ltd. v. Travel Agents Federation of India*, 2011 Comp LR 400 (CCI).
- *Unilazer Ventures Private Limited. v. PVR Ltd. & Others*, Case No. 10/2019, decided on 24 July 2019 (CCI).
- *Union of India v. Hindustan Development Corporation*, [1993] 3 SCC 499, 529.
- *Union of India v. PK Roy*, AIR 1968 SC 850.
- *Union of India v. Shiv Raj*, (2014) 6 SCC 564.
- *UTV v. Software Communications Ltd., Mumbai v. Motion Pictures Association*, 2012 Comp LR 20 (CCI).
- *Varca Chemist and Druggist v. Chemist and Druggist Association, Goa*, 2012 Comp LR 838 (CCI).
- *Vedanta Bio Sciences, Vadodara v. Chemists and Druggists Association of Baroda*, c-87/2009/DGIR, decided on 15 January 2019 (CCI)
- *Vinod Chopra, Prop. Vinod Chopra Productions* v. *Film Makers Combine (FMC),* 2001 CTJ 436 (MRTP).
- *Vodafone India Ltd. v. CCI*, (2018) 143 CLA 429 (Bom.).

- *Voltas Limited v. Union of India*, (1995) Supp 2 SCC 498.
- *Western Coalfields Limited v. SSV Coal Carriers Private Limited & others*, Case No. 34/2015, decided on 14 September 2017 (CCI).
- *XYZ v. Indian Oil Corporation Ltd. & Others*, Case No. 5/2018, decided on 4 July 2018 (CCI).
- *Yashoda Hospital and Research Centre Ltd. v. Indiabulls Financial Services Ltd.*, Case No. 12/2010, decided on 22 March 2011 (CCI).

Foreign cases

United States of America

- *American Column and Lumber Co v. US*, 257 US 377 (1921).
- *American Needle Inc. v. National Football League*, 560 U.S. 183 (2010).
- *American Tobacco Co. v. United States*, 328 U.S. 781, 66 S. Ct. 1125, 90 L. Ed. 1575 (1946)
- *Arizona v. Maricopa County Medical Society*, 457 U.S. 332 (1982) (Powell, J., *dissenting*).
- *AT &T Corp.*, 248 F.3d 131 (3rd Cir. 2001).
- *Bell Atl. Bus. Sys. Services v. Hitachi Data Systems Corp.*, 849 F Supp. 702 (N.D. Cal. 1994).
- *Broadcast Music, Inc. v. Columbia Broadcasting System, Inc.*, 441 U.S. 1 (1979).
- *Business Electronics Corp. v. Sharp Electronics Corp.*, 485 U.S. 717 (1988).
- *Clamp-All Corp. v. Cast Iron Soil Pipe Inst.*, 851 F 2d 478, 484 (Ist Cir. 1988).
- *Continental T. V., Inc. v. GTE Sylvania Inc.*, 433 U.S. 36 (1977).
- *Copperweld Corp. v. Independence Tube Corp.*, 467 US 752 (1984)
- *Federal Trade Commission v. Sperry & Hutchinson Co.*, 405 US 233, 241 (1972).
- *Federal Trade Commission v. Superior Court Trial Lawyers Association*, 493 U.S. 411 at 422 (1990).
- *FTC v. Superior Court Trial Lawyers Association*, 493 US 411 (1990).
- *IAZ International Belgium NV v. Commission* [1983] ECR 3369.
- *In re High Fructose Corn Syrup Antitrust Litigation*, 295 F 3d 651, 654.
- *Interstate Commerce Comm'n v. Louisville & Nashville RR Co*, 227 US 88, 93 (1913).
- *KieferStewart Co. v. Joseph E. Seagram & Sons*, 340 U.S. 211 (1951).
- *Matsushita Electronics Industries Co. v. Zenith Radio Corp.*, 475 U.S. 574, 588 (1986).
- *Montana v. Super America*, 559 F.Supp. 298, 303 (1983).
- *National Collegiate Athletic Association v. Board of Regents of the University of Oklahoma*, 468 U.S. 85 (1984).
- *Northern Pacific Railway Co. v. United States*, 356 U.S. 1 (1958).

- *Northwest Wholesale Stationers Inc. v. Pacific Stationery & Printing* Co. 472 US 284 (1985).
- *Pepper v. United States*, 562 US 476, 501 (2011).
- *Texaco Inc. v. Dagher*, 547 U.S. 1, 3; 126 S.Ct. 1276, 1277 (2006).
- *Theatre Enterprises, Inc. v. Paramount Film Distributing Corp.*, 346 U.S. 537 (1954).
- *U.S. v. Trenton Potteries Co.* 273 U.S. 392 (1927).
- *United States v. General Motor Corp.*, 384 U.S. 127, 142–143 (1966).
- *United States v. Andreas*, 216 F.3d 645 (7th Cir. 1999).
- *United States v. Blakely*, 542 U.S. 296 (2004).
- *United States v. Booker*, 543 US 220 (2005).
- *United States v. Citizens & S. National Bank*, 422 US 86 (1975).
- *United States v. Goodman*, 850 F.2d 1473, 1476 (11th Cir.1988).
- *United States v. Hayter Oil CO.*, 51 F.3d 1265, 1273 (6th Cir. 1995).
- *United States v. SKW Metals & Alloys Inc.*, 195 F.3d 83, 91 (2d Cir. 1999).
- *United States v. Socony-Vacuum Oil Co.*, 310 U.S. 150, 223 (1940).
- *United States v. Suntar Roofing, Inc.*, 897 F.2d 469 (10th Cir. 1990).
- *United States v. Topco Associates Inc.*, 405 US 596 (1972).
- *United States v. Yellow Cab Co.*, 332 U.S. 218 (1947).
- *United States v. Aluminium Co. of America*, 148 F.2d 416 (2nd Cir 1945).
- *US v. CHAS Pfizer Co.*, 217 F. Supp 199 (1963).
- *US v. Griffith*, 334 US 100.
- *US v. James P. Heffernan*, No. 94–1080, US Courts of Appeals, Seventh Circuit.

European Union

- *A Ahlstrom Osakeyhtio v. Commission (Woodpulp II)* (1993) ECR I-1307.
- *Aalborg Portland and Others v. Commission*, C-204/00 P (2004).
- *ACF Chemiefarma v. Commission*, 41/69, EU:C:1970:71.
- *AEG Telefunken v. Commission*, 1983 ECR 3151.
- *Akzo Nobel NV v. Commission* [2007] ECR II-000.
- *Amino Acids*, (2001) O.J. L 152/24.
- *Anic Partecipazioni v. Commission*, Case C-49/92 P (1999).
- *Archer Daniel Midland v. Commission*, [2006] ECR I-4429.
- *Archer Daniels Midland and Archer Daniels Midland Ingredients v. Commission*, [2003] ECR II-2597.
- *BASF v. Commission*, Case T-15/02, Judgment of the Court of First Instance (Fourth Chamber), 15 March 2006.
- *Beguelin Import v. GL Import Export Case* 22/71 1971 ECR 949.
- *BMW Belgium v. Commission of the European Communities* [1979] ECR 2435.

- *BPB PLC v. Commission*, [2008] ECR II-1333.
- *Brasserie nationale et al. v. Commission*, [2005] ECR II3033.
- Case C-322/81, *NV Nederlandsche Banden industrie Michelin v. Commission*, [1983] ECR 3461.
- *CB and Europay v. Commission*, [1994] ECR II-49.
- CMA *CGM v. Commission*, [2003] ECR II-913.
- *Compagnie maritime Belge Transports SA and others v. Commission*, Cases C-395y, 396/96P (2000).
- *Confederación Española de Empresarios de Estaciones de Servicio v. Compañía Española de Petróleos*, (2006) ECR I – 11997.
- *Consten and Grundig* Case 56 [1966] ECR 299.
- *Cooperatieve vereniging 'Suiker Unie' UA v. Commission*, Joined Cases 40–48, 50, 54–56, 111, 113'& 114/73, [1975] E.C.R. 1663, 1916, 26–27, [1976] 1 C.M.L.R. 295, 348.
- *Copper Plumbing Tubes*, 03.09.2004 [2006] OJ L192/21.
- *Daimler Chrysler AG v. Commission of the European Communities*, (2005) ECR II-3319.
- *Dow Chemical v. Commission*, Case T-77/08 EU:T:2012:47.
- *Dresdner Bank and Others v. Commission*, EU:T:2006:271.
- *DSM NV v. the Commission (Polypropylene)* T-8/89, [1991] ECR II-1833.
- *East India Company v. Sandys*, (1685) 10 St. Tr. 371.
- *Fine Papers* (Commission Decision 84/380, O.J.L 182/24).
- *Glass Containers v. Commission*, (1984) O.J. L 212/13.
- *Graphite Electrodes v. Commission*, (2002) O.J. L100/1).
- *Hoechst v. Commission v. Commission*, [2008] ECR II-881.
- *ICI v. Commission*, Case 48/69 [1972] ECR 619, [1972] CMLR 557.
- *Imperial Chemical Industries Ltd. v. Commission (Dyestuffs)* [1972] ECR 619.
- *Intel Corporation Inc v. European Commission*, Case T-286/09 EU:T:2014:547.
- *International Belgium v. Commission*, [1983] ECR 3369.
- *JCB Service v. Commission*, [2004] ECR II-00049.
- *Lafarge v. Commission*, EU:T:2008:255.
- *LRAF 1998 v. Commission*, (T-23/99) [2002] 5 CMLR 10.
- *Metsä-Serla Sales Oy v. Commission*, [2000] ECR I-10157.
- *Michelin v. Commission*, 20.06.2001 [2001] OJ L 143, 31.5.2002.
- *Minoan Lines SA v. Commission of the European Union*, (2003) ECR II-5515.
- *Municipality of Almelo and Others v. NV Energiebedrijf Ilsselmij*, Case C-393/92 (1994).
- *P ThyssenKrupp Stainless GmbH and ThyssenKrupp Acciai speciali Terni SpA v. Commission*, C-65/02 P and C-73/02 (2005).
- *P Archer Daniel Midlands v. Commission* [2009] ECR I-1843.
- *Pioneer Hi-Fi Equipment*, 80/256/EEC, (1980) O.J. L 60/28.

- *Quinine*, 69/240/EEC (1969) O.J. L 192/5.
- *S/V v. Commission* [1992] ECR-II 1403.
- *Shell Petroleum & Others v. Commission*, [2012] ECR II-000.
- *Siemens AG v. Commission*, EU:T:2011:68.
- *Slovak Telekom*, Case COMP/AT.39523–15.10.2014, C (2014) 7465.
- *SM NV v. the Commission (Polypropylene)* [1991] ECR II-1833.
- *Societa Italiana Vetro SpA, Fabbrica Pisana SpA and PPG Vernante Pennitalia SpA v. Commission of the European Communities*, T-68/89, T-77/89 and T-78/89 (1992).
- *Solvay Solexis v. Commission*, Case T-195/06 (2011).
- *SPO and Others v. Commission*, [1995] ECR II-289.
- *Suiker Unie UA and others v. Commission of the European Communities*, 1975 ECR 1663.
- *Sumitomo Metal Industries and Nippon Steel v. Commission*, C-403/04, EU:C:2007:52 (2007).
- *Synthetic Fibers*, Commission Decision 84/380, O.J.L 207/17 (1984).
- *T mobile Netherlands BV v. Raad van Bestuur van de Netherlandse Mededingingsautoritleil*, Case 8/08 (2009).
- T-148/89 *Trefilenrope SARL v. Commission* [1995] ECR II-1063.
- Team Relocations v. Commission [2013] ECR I-000.
- *Thyssen Stahl v. Commission*, [1999] ECR II-347.
- *Toshiba v. Commission*, Case T-113/07 (2011).
- *Total Marketing Services* v. *Commission*, C-634/13 P, EU:C:2015:614 (2015).
- *Trelleborg Industrie SAS and Trelleborg AB v. Commission*, T-147/09 and T-148/09 (2013).
- *United Brands Company v. Commission*, 27/76, EU:C:1978:22 (1978).
- *Van Landewyck SARL and Others v. Commission*, [1980] ECR 3125.
- *Verband der Sachversicherer v. Kommission*, [1987] ECR 405.
- *Vereeniging van Cementhandelaren v. Commission of the European Communities*, Case 8–72, ECLI identifier: ECLI:EU: C:1972:84 (1972).
- *Viho Europe BV v. Commission* [1995] ECR II-117.
- *Viho Europe BV v. Commission* [1996] ECR 1–5457.
- *Volk v. Vervaecke*, Case 5/69, [1969] ECR 295.
- *Westfalen Gassen Nederland v. Commission* [2006] ECR II-4567.
- *Zuchner v. Bayerische Vereinsbank AG* (1981) ECR 2021.

Abbreviations

1998 Guidelines	Guidelines on the Method of Setting Fines, 1998, European Union
2004 Act	The United States Antitrust Criminal Penalty Enhancement and Reform Act, 2004
2006 Guidelines	Guidelines for Setting Fines in 2006, European Union
2011 Regulations	Competition Commission of India (Manner of Recovery of Monetary Penalty) Regulations, 2011
2012 Bill	Competition (Amendment) Bill, 2012 (India)
2014 Directive	The European Union Directive on Private Damages, 2014
2019 Committee	Competition Law Review Committee, 2019 (India)
AAEC	appreciable adverse effect on competition
Act	Competition Act, 2002 (India)
CCI	Competition Commission of India
COMPAT	Competition Appellate Tribunal
CSI	commercially sensitive information
DG	director general
DIPP	Department of Industrial Policy and Promotion
DISCOMS	distribution companies
DOJ	Department of Justice
EC	European Commission
ECJ	European Court of Justice
EU	European Union
FSC	fuel surcharge
FTC	Federal Trade Commission
GC	General Court
GDP	gross domestic product
HC	High Court
ICN	International Competition Network
MOA	memorandum of association
MOU	memorandum of understanding
MRTP Act	Monopolies and Restrictive Trade Practices Act of 1969
MRTPC	Monopolies and Restrictive Trade Practices Commission
NCLAT	National Company Law Appellate Tribunal

NCLT	National Company Law Tribunal
NOC	no objection certificate
OECD	Organization for Economic Co-operation and Development
OEM	original equipment manufacturer
OMC	oil manufacturing company
PIS	product information service
PSU	public sector undertaking
Reg.	regulation
SC	Supreme Court
Sec.	section
SME	small and medium enterprises
TFEU	Treaty on the Functioning of the European Union, 2011
TPA	third-party administrators
US Guidelines	Federal Sentencing Guidelines, United States of America

1 Introduction

Antitrust laws prohibit unilateral or collective action that adversely affects competition and functions to set prices at appropriate levels at which markets can survive, largely without interference and in a way that cannot be done through central control. The rules of the market are simple. Prices should be determined honestly through market forces, and benefits should accrue to those who innovate and endeavour to provide the "best value for money". The competitive process should not be undermined by private understandings where market participants start working together instead of competing against each other.

Economy benefits through fair competition. It is only when entities decide to act together instead of competing does a cartel start to function, and actions like price fixing, market allocation, bid rigging, controlling the supply, and restricting the availability of products in the market emerge as a consequence. Competition laws in most jurisdictions prescribe strict sanctions against cartels. The success of enforcement of anti-cartel laws to cause adequate deterrence, however, has always been a matter of debate and inquiry. One of the standards for testing the usefulness of any system is its effectiveness in achieving the purpose for which it was created.

1.1 Assessment of the effectiveness of competition enforcement

Enforcement of competition law entails three aspects: a clear and precise delineation of law to avoid any confusion in the understanding among stakeholders; an unambiguous, consistent, non-arbitrary and adequate sanctioning mechanism; and undertaking pre-emptive steps, including active monitoring to prevent anti-competitive conduct in the market including advocacy initiatives to build the ethos for a "normative commitment" towards competition law. It is not enough to have a good doctrine; it is also necessary to have enforcement mechanisms that ensure, at reasonable costs, a judicious degree of compliance with the law.

Despite extensive work, there has been no consensus on a set of acceptable parameters to assess the effectiveness of competition enforcement. The

DOI: 10.4324/9781003347651-1

fundamental question to explore is whether the existing enforcement structure has been able to achieve its stated objectives.[1]

It can be done by examining the outcomes of such enforcement through the study of quantifiable data on factors like productivity, price variations, market efficiency and level of competition in the market. This approach, however, suffers from a lack of adequate data and a general difficulty of measurement to make any valid and objective assessment. Sometimes, these effects are only realized in the long run and are not reflected in the current data.[2] Alternatively, one can evaluate the process of achieving such outcomes. The scheme of examining the process will have to then take into account the quality of interventions and the use and management of given resources. A superior technique of intervention and resource allocation will have a greater likelihood of achieving a given set of objectives. After all, even a good law will fail in the absence of effective implementation.[3] Evaluation of competition enforcement activities may highlight the need for modifications which may bring in the consistent application of law, resulting in legal certainty.

1.2 Categorizing cartel study

Apart from general literature on the basis, importance and objectives of competition law,[4] different studies across jurisdictions have tried to assess either the enforcement of competition law in general or some of its aspects in particular. These studies, depending upon their objectives, have employed different methodologies with their own assessment parameters. There are also studies that evaluate and compare the competition law enforcement or level of compliance of one jurisdiction with another[5] in order to do a hierarchical evaluation. Certain studies try to examine the impact of particular cases on identified subject matters like markets, competitors, or competition enforcement in general. The common reference point for these assessments comes from the parameters generally chalked out in several publicly released OECD documents. Scholarly works have used these parameters to examine different aspects of law or its enforcement.[6]

Performance of the competition agency can be seen through substantive results in terms of economic performance and social welfare or through administrative efficiency to churn out better outcomes. Kovacic marks the difficulty in assessing substantive results in light of the difficulty in their actual measurement.[7] The second level of inquiry is not that complicated as it is limited to the examination of activities of the competition authority. Given the dynamic nature of competition policy, competition regulators are generally evaluated within a particular time frame.

Studies related to cartels have been broadly categorized as those investigating their internal composition or the implementation of anti-cartel laws through enforcement, sanction and design parameters.

1.2.1 *Anatomy of cartels*

Scholarly work on different aspects of cartels has become the backbone of any evaluation exercise of cartel enforcement. For instance, while scholars like Posner[8] (1970), Dick[9] (1996), De[10] (2010) and Levenstein and Suslow[11] (2011) have examined the aspect of cartel success through the usage of data set of decided cartel cases, researchers like Hellwig and Hushelrath[12] (2018) have not necessarily examined the factors determining cartel duration or cartel success but have studied firm participation and their departure as a determinant for cartel survival. While the former group of studies consider factors like the number of firms involved, type of cartel and involvement of trade association as variables for cartel duration, the latter set of studies examines tangential issues concerned with the success of cartels. Another set of literature studies the internal organization of cartels and their contracting patterns. The works of Posner[13] (1970), Dick[14] (1996), Haucap[15] (2010), Hyytinen[16] (2017) and Levenstein and Suslow[17] (2011) are examples of such studies. Questions like mechanism of internal compliance, rules of admission of new members, punishment for defection or cheating, frequency of meetings, and process of decision-making were the subject matters of inquiry. The answers to these questions may vary depending on the type of cartel, area and sector of operation. Lack of sufficient data, however, is an inherent problem to such anatomy of cartels. Some scholars have also studied the role played by trade associations in cartel activities.[18]

1.2.2 *Enforcement parameters*

There have been studies on the enforcement activities of competition authorities in a particular jurisdiction. For instance, Hellwig and Huschelrath (2017)[19] undertook a quantitative assessment of the cartel enforcement process in the EU from 2001 to 2015. Similar studies have been conducted in the US. For instance, Connor (2008)[20] and Sokol and Ghosal[21] (2016) have assessed the effectiveness of anti-cartel enforcement by the Antitrust Division of the Department of Justice (DOJ). Connor[22] (2016) has also assessed the degree of the international cartel enforcement regime under the Canada Competition Bureau on the basis of a data set of decided cases using quantitative benchmarks from 1990 to 2015. Duration of investigation, for instance, is an important measure of the effectiveness of cartel enforcement. Huschelrath et al.[23] (2012) empirically investigated the determinants of the duration of cartel investigation of the European Commission (EC) between 2000 and 2011.

1.2.3 *Sanction parameters*

Sanctions have always been studied alongside enforcement processes. The trends of imposition of penalties or jail terms have been examined through policy interventions at different points in time. Sanctions are one of the parameters for examining the issue of deterrence. Landes[24] (1983) examined the idea of optimal enforcement by any commission through optimal sanctions. Wils[25] (2006) did not discard the idea of "optimal fine" but argued that it is, in fact, impractical and wanted to project it as a reference for the imposition of fines. Veljanovski did a quantitative assessment of the fines imposed by the EC in cartel cases and also examined the value of fines imposed under the 1998 and 2006 Penalty Guidelines of the EC in terms of "consumer harm".[26] Connor used the resources at the disposal of the DOJ to study the rate of cartel detection, the number of investigations conducted, leniency programs and cartel fines on corporations and individuals; as parameters to evaluate the efficiency of the Antitrust Division. The study highlighted the decreasing number of convictions in cartel cases and pointed to the insufficiency of resources of the Antitrust Division as the reason for backlogs, delay in litigation and over-generous concessions.

Lack of clarity and inconsistency in the imposition of fines may cause litigations to increase. Prof. Geradin and Henry[27] highlights the factors that are taken into account by the competition authority and the appellate body in the imposition of fines. Further, the need for balancing corporate and individual sanctions has been stressed by many scholars. They further elaborate on the point as to why sanctions on corporations would not cause enough deterrence unless enough sanctions are imposed on individuals.[28]

1.2.4 Performance parameters

Assessment of the performance of competition authorities is incomplete if not clubbed with the study of quality of such activity and consistency in decision-making. Treatment of a competition authority's decisions at the appeal stage or in the judicial review, then becomes an important parameter for assessment. Similar work has been done by Geradin and Petit[29] (2010) through an empirical study of the General Court's (GC) review of the EC's decisions. Specific aspects of appellate proceedings have also been studied. For instance, Smuda, Bougette and Huschelrath[30] (2014) studied the duration of proceedings in the appellate court as a marker for the efficiency of courts. The duration was statistically assessed in light of parameters like workload, nature of the case, cooperation by involved entities, the experience of judges and certainty of applicable rules and regulations to highlight that a lengthy appellate process can have serious implications on the deterrent effect of anti-cartel enforcement.[31]

1.2.5 Design parameters

Often, the effectiveness of competition policy is equated with the number of and visibility of cases pursued. Experience with competition policy shows that this focus ignores the need to evaluate an agency's commitments in light of its institutional capabilities[32] through important markers like budget allocation, the strength of the staff and the expertise of the investigators. An activity- or case-driven approach sometimes misses out on the non-litigation activities of the competition regulator. Advocacy initiatives might have a better outreach than cases which generally take years before they reach finality. These may become bridges between the industry and the competition authority as the agency will be more attuned to changing dynamics of the market, and enterprises will have better access to the agency. Non-litigation activities might also generate foundations for policy interventions for a problem which does not have a clear solution in enforcement per se. The attempt of these studies is to examine the priorities and processes of the competition authority with respect to system, structures, processes and procedures.

1.3 Scheme

This book presents a quantitative assessment of cartels and investigative procedures in India and tries to assess whether the Indian competition authority has been able to achieve "optimal enforcement". A mix of assessment parameters has been applied to the data gathered from all the decided cartel cases in India to provide an overall assessment of the performance of the Competition Commission of India (CCI). The comprehensive review of all the cartel cases decided by the CCI has led to the appraisal of substantive and procedural issues. Further, the success of the enforcement regime has been analyzed through appeals, leniency application, the deterrence value of fines and instances of recidivism. The performance of the CCI has been evaluated on the basis of three broad parameters, which in turn have been further divided in to points of reference.

a Enforcement parameters.
   - i Administrative activity.
   - ii Investigative procedures.
   - iii Appreciation of evidence in cartel cases.
   - iv Success of the CCI's orders (appeals).

b Sanction parameters.
   - i Fine structure.
   - ii Imposition of fines on enterprises, individuals and/or trade associations.
   - iii Use of aggravating and mitigating factors.
   - iv Effectiveness of amnesty program.

c Design parameters.
   - i Recovery mechanism.
   - ii Non-litigation activities.
   - iii Resources and their utilization (institutional capabilities).

1.3.1 Selection bias

As common with studies on cartels, the present assessment is also based on the information that has been ascertained from detected cases of cartelization in India between 2009 and 2021. Since cartels are considered to be clandestine, most of the cases of cartels remain undiscovered or undetected. Therefore, it may be possible that cartels that exist outside the zone of discovery depict a much more complex internal structure than what the data depicts. Further, the data set does not include cases pending investigations. It covers only type 1, or "hard-core", cartels. The present work, therefore, is not a comment on all operating cartels in the market but is limited to the critique of the enforcement of anti-cartel laws.

Notes

1 Evaluation of the Actions and Resources of the Competition Authorities, *Policy Roundtables, OECD* (2005) www.oecd.org/daf/competition/prosecution-andlawenforcement/35910995.pdf (last accessed on July 1, 2021).
2 William A. Kovacic, *Rating the Competition Agencies: What Constitutes Good Performance?,* 16 George Mason Law Review 903 (2009). *Also see*, William A. Kovacic, *Speech, Twelfth Annual Symposium on Antitrust* (2008) www.ftc.gov/sites/default/files/documents/public_statements/rating-competition-agencies-what-constitutes-good-performance/2009rating.pdf (last accessed on July 1, 2021).
3 William Kovacic, Hugh Hollman and Patricia Grant, *How Does Your Competition Agency Measure Up?*, 7 European Competition Journal 125 (2011).
4 Roger D. Blair and Daniel Sokol, *The Goals of Anti-trust: An Economic Approach*, 78 (2) Antitrust Law Journal 471–504; H. J. Hoven Kamp, Distributive Justice and Consumer Welfare in Antitrust, *Faculty Scholarship at Penn Law* (2013) (March 2018) scholarship.law.upenn.edu/faculty_scholarship/1868; B.Y Orbach, *The Antitrust Consumer Welfare Paradox*, 7 (1) Journal of Competition Law & Economics 133–164.
5 Rob Van der Noll and Barbara Baarsma, *Compliance with Cartel Laws and the Determinants of Deterrence – An Empirical Investigation*, 13 (2–3) European Competition Journal (2017).
6 William E Kovacic, *Using Ex Post Evaluations to Improve the Performance of Competition Policy Authorities,* 31 Journal of Corporation Law 503 (2006); *Also see, Supra note* 2 (William E Kovacic); I. Bos, S. Davies, J.E. Harrington Jr., and P.L. Ormosi, *Does Enforcement Deter Cartels? A Tale of Two Tails,* 59 International Journal of Industrial Organization 372–405 (2018); Kail Huschelrath and Nina Leheyda, *A Methodology for the Evaluation of Competition Policy*, 10 (81) ZEW Discussion Paper, Center for European Economic Research (2011), ftp://ftp.zew.de/pub/zew-docs/dp/dp10081.pdf (last accessed on July 10, 2021).
7 *Ibid.*
8 Richard Posner, *A Statistical Study of Antitrust Enforcement*, 13 Journal of Law and Economics, 365–419 (1970).
9 Andrew Dick, *When are Cartels Stable Contracts*, 39 Journal of Law and Economics 241–283 (1996).
10 Oindrilla De, *Analysis of Cartel Duration: Evidence from EC Prosecuted Cartels*, 17 International Journal of the Economics of Business 33–65 (2010).

11 Margaret Levenstein and Valerie Suslow, *Breaking up is Hard to do: Determinants of Cartel Duration*, 54 Journal of Law and Economics 455–492 (2011).
12 Michael Hellwig and Kai Huschelrath, *When do Firms Leave Cartels? Determinants and the Impact of Cartel Survival*, 54 International Review of Law and Economics 68–84 (2018).
13 *Supra note* 8.
14 Andrew Dick, *When Are Cartels Stable Contracts?*, 39 Journal of Law and Economics 241–283 (1996).
15 Justus Haucap, Ulrich Heimeshoff and Luis M. Schultz, *Legal and Illegal Cartels in Germany between 1958 and 2004*, 8 Dice Discussion Paper, Heinrich-Heine-Universität Düsseldorf, Department of Economics, Düsseldorf Institute for Competition Economics (DICE), (2010) www.dice.hhu.de/fileadmin/redaktion/Fakultaeten/Wirtschaftswissenschaftliche_Fakultaet/DICE/Discussion_Paper/008_Haucap_Heimeshoff_Schultz.pdf (last accessed on July 10, 2021).
16 Ari Hyytinen, Frode Steen and Otto Toivanen, *Anatomy of Cartel Contracts*, The Economic Journal (2018) https://academic.oup.com/ej/advance-article abstract/doi/10.1111/ecoj.12633/5280844 (last accessed on July 10, 2021).
17 *Supra note* 11.
18 Spencer W. Waller, *Trade Associations, Information Exchanges and Cartels*, 30 (2) Loyola Consumer Law Review 163 (2018).
19 Michael Hellwig and Kai Huschelrath, *Cartel Cases and the Cartel Enforcement Process in the European Union 2001–2015: A Quantitative Assessment*, 62 (2) The Antitrust Bulletin (2017).
20 John Connor, *Cartel Enforcement at the Antitrust Division, US Department of Justice, 1990–2007*, 9 Competition Policy International (2008).
21 Daniel Sokol and Vivek Ghosal, *Policy Innovations, Political Preferences and Cartel Prosecutions*, 48 Review of Industrial Organization 405–432 (2016).
22 John M. Connor, *Canada's International Cartel Enforcement: Keeping Score*, 39 (4) World Competition 557–592 (2016). See also, John M. Connor, The Private International Cartels (PIC) Data Set: Guide and Summary Statistics, 1990-July 2016 (Revised 2nd Edition (2016) https://papers.ssrn.com/sol3/papers.cfm?abstract_id=2821254 (last accessed on July 10, 2021); John M. Connor and Claes G. Helmers, *Statistics on Modern International Cartels – 1990–2005*, 7 (1) AAI Working Paper, The American Antitrust Institute, www.antitrustinstitute.org.recent2/567.pdf (last accessed on July 10, 2021).
23 Kai Hushelrath, Ulrich Laitenberger and Florian Smuda, *Cartel Enforcement in the European Union: Determinants of the Duration of Investigations*, 12 (71) Discussion Paper, ZEW – Centre for European Economic Research Discussion Paper No., (2012) https://papers.ssrn.com/sol3/papers.cfm?abstract_id=2179037 (last accessed on July 10, 2021). *Also see*, Ali Massadeh, *An Empirical Assessment of the European Commission Enforcement of Competition Law*, Working Paper, University of East Anglia, Norwich (2011) https://ueaeprints.uea.ac.uk/52465/1 /2015MassadehAAMPhD.pdf (last accessed on July 10, 2021).
24 William M. Lande, *Optimal Sanctions for Antitrust Violations,* 50 The University of Chicago Law Review 652 (1983).
25 Wouter P. J. *Wils Optimal Antitrust Fines: Theory and Practice*, 29 (2) World Competition 183 (2006).
26 Cento Veljanovski, *Cartel Fines in Europe – Law, Practice and Deterrence*, 29 World Competition, 65 (2007).
27 Damien Geradin and David Henry, The EC fining policy for violations of competition law: An empirical review of the Commission decisional practice and the Community courts' judgments, The Global Competition Law Centre Working Papers Series, GCLC Working Paper 03/05 (2005) www.coleurope.eu/system/files_force/research . . ./gclc_wp_03-05.pdf? (last accessed on July 10, 2021).

28 Priit Mändmaa, *Assessing the Effectiveness of Competition Law Enforcement Policy in Relation to Cartels*, 3 (11) Journal of Arts and Humanities 33 (2014)
29 Damien Geradin and Nicolas Petit, *Judicial Review in European Union Competition Law: Quantitative and Qualitative Assessment,* Tilburg Law and Economics Center (TILEC), 2011–008 Law and Economics Discussion paper and Research Paper No. 1/2011, Tilburg Law School Legal Studies, https://papers.ssrn.com/sol3/papers.cfm?abstract_id=1698342 (last accessed on July 10, 2021).
30 Florian Smuda, Patrice Bougette and Kai Huschelrath, *Determinants of the Duration of European Appellate Court Proceedings in Cartel cases,* WP No. 2014–25, GREDEG, Universite Nice Sophia Antipolis, www.zew.de/en/publikationen/determinants-of-the-duration-of-european-appellate-court-proceedings-in-cartel-cases/?cHash=f9af8a39096b044bb79d1913ffc15c90 (last accessed on July 10, 2021).
31 Christopher Harding and Alun Gibbs, *Why go to court in Europe? An Analysis of Cartel Appeals 1995–2004*, 30 European Law Review 349 (2005).
32 Timothy J. Muris, *Principles for a Successful Competition Agency*, 72 University of Chicago Law Review 165–181 (2005).

2 Conceptualizing cartels

2.1 Introduction: "Economy benefits through fair competition"

Competition law defends the practice of fair competition[1] and acts as a catalyst in promoting innovation and economic growth along with the social progress of the nation. A legal framework for competition in the market remedies those instances where the actions of one or more individuals or economic entities cause the collapse of a free-market system. It is important to lay down the rules of the market so that every participant has a fair and equal chance of flourishing.[2] With the growth of both the volume of transactions and the complexity of economies, jurisdictions across the globe have come to realize the benefits of having a well-defined competition policy. This is probably the reason that competition law regimes have seen the fastest growth when compared to other economic regulations. Competition policies are framed to ensure that competition is not restricted to the prejudice of both market and society.[3]

2.2 Market and market competition

Market, derived from the Latin word *mercatus*, is a medium that facilitates interaction between buyers and sellers.[4] This medium can be physical or virtual, local or global, and the persons who interact include not just individuals and corporations but also the government. The objective of this meeting is commercial in nature, largely related to buying and selling of products or services at a rate governed by the laws of supply and demand. Subsequent to the changes brought about by globalization, liberalization and privatization in an increasingly capitalist world, there has been a growing consensus that markets result in better outcomes than state planning.[5] Central to this idea of a market is that of competition, defined as a "process of rivalry between firms . . . seeking to win customers' business over time".[6] Thus, it is important to understand the relationship between markets, the level of competition that exists within them and how to preserve or protect any such competition.

DOI: 10.4324/9781003347651-2

The market can be classified on the basis of geographical area, the subject matter of sale or product, the volume of business, the level of governmental control, the delivery of goods and points of sale. The nature of the market has an impact on the level of competition that exists within it. Markets in which a few players account for a large percentage of the total (i.e. highly concentrated markets) have lower levels of competition due to which firms have greater market power.[7] In contrast, a competitive market is one in which many firms operate and the rivalry between sellers ensures competition between them.[8] On a scale from most to least competitive, the four prevalent types of market structure are (i) perfect competition, (ii) monopolistic competition, (iii) oligopoly and (iv) monopoly. Perfect competition is an ideal situation as most of its characteristics like the unlimited number of vendors and consumers, homogenous products, no asymmetry of information, and costless entry and exit are not commonly seen. Similarly, it is rare to find a true monopoly unless it is created by the state itself. Even if there is an ideal situation, questions may be raised on the assumptions themselves, like all sellers having a similar objective of making profits, which may not be the case. Moreover, while prices are theoretically kept minimum in perfect competition, it does not consider social costs.[9] The assumptions in true monopoly also do not consider the dynamic nature of markets. Noting the theoretical nature of perfect competition and the problems in the underlying assumptions, alternative models are used to frame competition policies. A practical theory that has thus been forwarded is that of "workable competition".

2.2.1 *Defining competition*

Competition, derived from the Latin word *competere* (meaning to "strive for") or *competio* (meaning "rivalry"), means the process of competing. In business parlance, it is an endeavour of two or more enterprises to win more customers. There is a vast amount of literature that attributes competition to a range of benefits, like low prices, better products, increased choices for customers and enhancement of innovation. This is the reason that policymakers across jurisdictions have taken steps to protect, preserve and promote competition. The prime objectives of competition law across jurisdictions are promoting/protecting the competition process and attaining greater economic efficiency, leading to allocative, productive and dynamic efficiency.[10] Competitiveness also enhances consumer welfare,[11] as it ensures that consumers retain a greater variety of choices in price, selection and service.[12] It has also been stated to be the key to strengthening economies.[13]

2.2.2 *Economics of competition*

The economics of competition is simple: economic resources will be allocated in the most efficient manner when any product market is challenged by rivals. The more the number of rivals, the better the allocation. The threat of loss of business will increase the efficiency of individual firms. Firms will be forced to bring in new and better products through technology and innovation in order to win customers, benefiting the consumers and society as a whole. The chance of optimal outcome (low prices and better and wider options) increases as the economy moves closer to perfect competition. The availability of options lowers the prices of the products when compared to markets with no competition.

The idea of modern-day inter-firm competition can be traced to the writings of Adam Smith, who advocated that it is ultimately self-interest that drives every action and that economic welfare can be achieved through competition between self-interested entities.[14] He pronounced competition as an exercise to enhance efficiency (allocating resources to their most high-valued uses). This was supported by the liberal economists of that time. His idea of free competition (free market and free entry) gave way to the law of competition – that is, competition pushes prices to equilibrium levels – in the 19th century.

2.2.3 Theoretical foundations of competition

Most jurisdictions of the world have realized the importance of market forces and have moved from the stage of a centrally planned economy with state ownerships to more liberalized and privatized economies. Competition is the fulcrum on which these market forces operate. Clark argued that competition policy should aim at creating workable competition rather than perfect competition.[15] The three key factors emphasized were inter-firm rivalry, the free option of the buyers to buy from alternative vendors and efforts by sellers to equal or exceed the attractiveness of others' offerings. While there is no consensus on the criterion to be used to assess if competition is workable, these factors are used to measure the level of competitive performance of markets.

There are two major schools of thought in the US which have had far-reaching effects in the approach towards competition law and policy. Per the Harvard School, stemming from the work done at Harvard University, particularly by scholars like Mason and Bain in the 1930s, the performance of a firm is guided by its conduct specific to the market structure, also called the structure-conduct-performance paradigm. This conduct would then have an impact on their market performance, including on parameters such as their profitability, growth, efficiency and technical progress.[16] To illustrate, an industry that is highly concentrated would result in a firm instituting higher (or monopolistic) prices and reduced output, due to which there would be poor economic performance.[17] This link between market structure and performance led to the conclusion that competition law should be concerned with structural remedies instead of behavioural remedies.[18] Such structural analysis was developed through empirical studies and led to the findings that most industries were more concentrated than necessary, that entry barriers were high and that monopoly pricing began to occur at relatively low levels of concentration.[19]

The Harvard School's correlation between market concentration and market power, along with its assumption that firms with market power would act in an anti-competitive manner, led to the presumption that any merger, joint venture, or agreement that allowed firms to obtain, gain, or exercise market power was illegal, irrespective of whether the conduct could potentially benefit consumers by lowering prices or increasing output.[20] This strict approach was due to the belief that firms may then leverage their market power in one market to gain market power in another, thus placing greater emphasis on State intervention.

The Harvard School has evolved since this initial conception. It is now less reliant on presumptions, more relaxed about conduct and mergers and less interventionist.[21] However, its initial conception influenced many judges to presume the illegality of any conduct by firms with market power. For example, in *United States v. Aluminum Co. of America*,[22] the court penalized Alcoa for merely expanding its manufacturing capacity to meet increasing demand, even though it was then able to take advantage of economies of scale to deliver quality products to customers at lower prices. As a result, the Harvard School had the effect of deterring consumer-friendly mergers.[23] Its presumption of illegality of certain conduct without an analysis of the economic circumstances in the relevant market led judges to find fault with an aggressive competition that could benefit consumers.[24] Thus, though it brought certainty to antitrust analysis, it was criticized for its flawed empirical studies and for wrongly equating market concentration with anti-competitive outcomes.[25]

The Chicago School, part of a school of neoclassical, libertarian and free-market economics known as Chicago economics developed around the 1970s, advocated that competition law has to strive for efficiency. It presumed that market actors are rational beings and that markets were likely to correct any competitive imbalances on their own without state intervention.[26] As a result, it emphasized free-market and monetarist economics.[27] Bork defined the requisite economic efficiency in terms of conditions that maximized wealth, thereby equating wealth enhancement with consumer welfare (i.e. reduced prices and increased output).[28] Consumer welfare, in turn, was seen through the lens of allocative and productive efficiency, which together were stated to make up the requisite overall efficiency. Thus, the goal of competition law was to promote consumer welfare by preserving, improving and reinforcing efficiency and economic mechanisms that compel businesses to respond to consumers.[29] Contrary to the Harvard School, it argued that concentrated markets are in a position to exploit economies of scale due to which greater efficiency was achieved. Further, it claimed that high or monopolistic prices signal unmet demands, which would act as an incentive for other firms to enter the market and render it competitive in the long run. Thus, it placed greater emphasis on long-term impacts.[30] Due to this, courts and regulatory agencies preferred not to prohibit competitive conduct on its face but to engage in an extensive factual enquiry to confirm the effects of a particular conduct on consumers before finding it illegal.[31] There was also increased leniency in allowing firms to acquire and exercise market power. For example, in *Broad. Music. Inc. v. CBS*,[32] the US Supreme Court refused to presume the illegality of a price fixing agreement among a group of musical composers. In 1979, the US Federal Trade Commission permitted the acquisition of McDonnell Douglas Corporation by the Boeing Company, which gave it a duopoly in the worldwide market for the manufacture of commercial airlines.[33]

Though the Chicago School had a profound influence on competition law across the world, critics state that it ultimately overreacted to the shortcomings of the *Harvard School*. Their rejection of a presumption of illegality of certain conduct resulted in a need to confirm specific economic effects of competitive conduct on consumers. This went beyond the competence of judges, juries and administrative agencies who now had an increased responsibility to decide complex economic issues on which they had received no training.[34] Unlike the Harvard School, there was also no certainty as to whether conduct would be anti-competitive, due to which antitrust laws lost their deterrent effect.[35] Some scholars argued that the neoclassical market efficiency model of the Chicago School was too simplistic to predict business behaviour in the real world.[36] The criticisms against the Chicago School also led to the Neo-Chicago School, which follows the core tenets of its predecessor but includes post-Chicago insight in designing rules that are to be assessed on their consequences in terms of their efficiency.[37]

The Post-Chicago School tempers extreme Chicago ideas with new insights.[38] It is founded on the belief that economics can indicate what questions to ask but does not always yield definitive answers. It is similar to the Chicago School in its belief that the goal of competition law is consumer welfare, but it diverges in its realization that the Chicago School relied on simplified assumptions that led to leniency and under-enforcement of competition law.[39] It focuses on the goal of allocative efficiency and emphasizes quantifiable, short-run welfare effects[40] and argues that certain market structures and conducts are more likely to have anti-competitive consequences than imagined by the scholars of the Chicago School. This is because markets are not always perfect, either due to entry being hampered for some firms, or competitive information not being available to all participants, or even firms gaining a dominant position that is hard to dislodge. Thus, it advocates for competition intervention to correct imbalances arising out of anti-competitive outcomes in imperfect markets[41] and places greater demands on authorities as opposed to the other schools.[42]

The Post-Chicago School focuses on solving emerging issues and provides for the realization of real-life complexities that are necessary for devising competition policy. To deal with such issues, the school is immensely informed by economic theories, such as the theory of contestable markets, game theory, the theory of raising rivals' costs and the theory of transaction cost analysis. Law and policy are influenced by the application of such theories.[43] However, it has been criticized for its theory-based analysis and the demand it places on competition authorities and regulators due to the abundance of theories on which it relies. It also offers little by way of empirical verification, making it of limited practical utility.[44]

Competition law in Europe, on the other hand, has mostly been influenced by the German Ordoliberal School, or the Freiburg School, which internalizes competition as a necessary concomitant for economic welfare and thus does not support the concentration of economic power in private hands.[45] It states that the goal of competition law is protecting individuals from the restraints of their freedom to compete.[46] The Freiburg School in Germany developed an ordoliberal theory that both highlighted intervention-free markets and offended private market power. Initially, there was an emphasis on freedom of economic action that allowed for any voluntary arrangements, including hard-core cartels, between enterprises. This resulted in a massive cartelization of the economy in the 1910s–1920s, due to which there was a shift in the location of decision-making power from individual enterprises to associations or syndicates. The insight that a free-market economy can "become incrementally transformed into a centrally-planned economy by allowing cartels to take-over and increasingly centralize economic decision-making . . . is decisive for the notion of Ordoliberalism".[47]

The core concept of the ordoliberal theory is the idea of the competition order – that is, a policed order – because the tendency of self-termination is inherent in market competition. To avoid the pressure of competition, market participants are individually incentivized to incrementally transform competitive markets into more centralized variants, such as cartels or syndicates. Ordoliberal theorists warn against the consequences of increased market power that results from the tendency of market participants to centralise because there is a danger of lobbyism that results from such accumulated market power, which can potentially lead to the long-term weakening of the state to protect competition. Thus, instead of state intervention, the focus is on the institutional framework of competitive markets.[48]

2.2.4 *Role of competition in the market*

Although different schools of thought diverge either on how competition plays out or on the very objectives of competition law, they agree that competition in itself is good.[49] Adam Smith considered competition and self-interest as the key factors that steer an economy and called them "invisible hands".[50] The driving force of each market participant is the pursuit of their specific objectives or self-interest. Unregulated pursuit of self-interest may lead to cheating, corruption, or restrictive actions. Competition forces participants to work harder and checks the negative effects of the unregulated pursuit of self-interest. Therefore, if the self-interest is to earn money, it can only be legally achieved by the production of goods or services, which, in turn, benefits society. To make money or survive in a market where different entities are producing similar goods or services, entities must make an effort to differentiate themselves, whether in terms of price, quality, or some other factor. A business entity will be able to increase its productivity by becoming more efficient by reducing its costs or developing new products. This rivalry between similarly placed entities that forces them to innovate and enhance their product or service or cut costs by giving the best possible price to increase sales, capture more customers, or gain more market share is competition, thereby benefitting customers. Robust competition results in both increase in productivity and efficient allocation of resources.[51]

Competition is also a catalyst for the growth of business units, both internally and externally. Internally, it acts as a disciplining force for the officers or managers of the company to strive towards greater efficiency. Externally, competition eventually leads to the exit of less efficient firms, thereby increasing the market share of more efficient firms. Competition brings dynamic efficiency as it causes firms to bring in new technology for production and increases innovation.

Competition thus has a positive impact both at the macro- and micro-economic levels. At the macro level, it helps in building a steady macroeconomic setting,[52] improves the efficiency of markets and enhances economic growth. At the micro level, it increases the quality of products and services, reduces the costs of products and increases the choices for the consumers.

2.3 Cartels

Competition is both desirable and essential. It ensures that market players compete with each other so that consumers get the best quality of product and/or service at the most affordable price. Cartel is a scenario wherein these players, in order to raise profits, join hands to actually "not compete with each other".

The Harvard School advocated for a *per se* rule for horizontal cartels on account of having clear anti-competitive effects (such as raised prices, reduced output and limited range of choices for consumers) and lack of any efficiency justifications. It argued that cartels were incapable of producing any economic benefits as they did not involve any integration of the parties' resources. In addition, cartels among buyers created oligopsonies and prevented competition among buyers on input prices, thereby increasing costs.[53] The Chicago School, on the other hand, did not consider oligopolies, oligopsonies, or price fixing as serious problems. Though it agreed that sellers have the propensity to collude, there was a reluctance to impose legal sanctions on this collusion as it believed that cartels are highly unstable and members were likely to cheat in the absence of legal sanctions. Moreover, it felt cartels were futile in the long run in the absence of substantial barriers to entry, especially in the context of rejection of the notion of barriers to entry.[54] Although G. Stigler did focus on collusion, he too stated that tacit collusion would only be a problem at very high levels of concentration and doubted the necessity for draconian antitrust measures.[55] In contrast, the Post-Chicago School argued that since cartels block new entrants through the practices like predatory pricing and would hence be able to hike prices, cut wages and increase profits,[56] strict state intervention was required. Similarly, the ordoliberal thinkers considered cartelization as problematic, as cartels, with the exception of those arrangements that demonstrably promote competition (for example, by increasing alternative market products and services), were thought to abolish competition and increase the power of lobbyism. Economic freedom was also thought to be threatened by cartel members as they rendered private individuals dependent on modern private power structures.

2.3.1 *Oligopoly and cartels*

Oligopolistic markets are characterized by firm interdependence. Due to a smaller number of firms, a change in the price or output of one firm affects the profits of other firms in the market. This interdependence causes uncertainty in the demand of the market at different price levels. Prices tend to be stable, though higher than in a perfectly competitive market. This is because if one firm reduces its price, other firms tend to follow, leading to reduced profits for all.

2.3.1.1 *Cartel as a special case of oligopoly*

In an oligopoly which is characterized by few producers/sellers, there are some players with such a large market share that their actions on output impacts market price. These sellers can sometimes also act like monopolists. In that situation, sellers can coordinate their actions or collude in a manner such that they operate like a single enterprise. This arrangement is called "cartel". Members of the cartel then sell at the same price and each firm agrees to a certain produce volume. Firms in an oligopoly enter the cartel arrangement to increase their market power. The profit maximizing decision of the cartel is similar to that of a monopolist.

2.3.2 *Cartel versus tacit collusion*

Guerrin and Kyriazis[57] classify cartels on the basis of their form and object.[58] On the basis of form, cartels have been classified based on whether they involve agreement or tacit understanding. Cartels based on agreement are either publicly known institutional cartels or are secretive in nature. Both, however, are based on an agreement, the terms and object of which are clear. These types of cartels are operationalized through a central mechanism which takes the responsibility of cartel management, dissemination of information and disciplining. The publicly known institutional structures are more in the form of associations which have been created to achieve certain objectives. Decisions taken by these institutions are covered within the definition of "agreement" and can be brought within the ambit of competition law. Secretive cartels characterized by secret meetings are also based on "agreement", but the structure of their operation is not publicly known.[59]

Collusion is the term used for behavioural coordination between firms with respect to price or quantity to maximize profit. Collusion is expressed either as "tacit" or "explicit". Tacit collusion is reached through mutual understanding and operationalized by price leadership, price signalling, exchange of price information and so on. The anti-competitive outcome, if any, in tacit collusion is the result of unilateral action. The nature of the market (high concentration, homogenous product, transparent market)[60] is such that the firms consider the actions of their competitors to decide on their own actions. Tacit collusion is mostly seen in oligopolistic markets as the conditions are favourable. Bishop and Walker tried to show the oligopoly problem through a version of the prisoner's dilemma.[61] In such a market, firms are conscious of their interdependency and take their decisions accordingly, leading to an outcome which is similar to a cartel. However, this outcome is the result of the rational business decisions of each firm. Contrastingly, explicit collusion is a more overt form of coordinated behaviour achieved through direct communication between firms regarding market variables like price, output, quotas and the like. The idea of agreement is the differentiating wall between the two. Insistence on the presence of some sort of agreement between firms for the applicability of anti-cartel provisions proves that the emphasis is on the process of reaching a coordinated behaviour and not just the outcome of it. This is the reason that conscious price parallelism is not illegal under competition laws.

There is a need to differentiate a cartel with tacit collusion. In economics, both forms might result in the same consequences. Even cartel screens do not differentiate between them. However, laws in most jurisdictions penalize cartel activity and not tacit collusion, which means that there is a requirement to produce evidence of a prior meeting of minds (agreement) between players. This is the reason that price parallelism is not *per se* bad and is only treated as evidence to prove cartels. Explicit collusion, where firms coordinate their behaviour through communication to maximize profits, is bad in law and heavily penalized.[62] Motta considers this legal distinction desirable to prevent sanctions on competitive behaviour.[63] Economic techniques or models do not really factor in the requirement of communication in their role in predicting the market conditions likely to harbour collusive behaviour.

The role of communication, however, cannot be discarded as the firms generally use communication to sustain cartels. Communication helps in price coordination and resolving disputes. Therefore, it may be possible that cartels with certain modes of communication exist in an environment where cartels are naturally unsustainable.[64] For instance, while the established economic assumption is that collusive behaviour is likely and stable in an environment which has a lesser number of symmetric firms, there have been multiple cases across jurisdictions where the average cartel membership is much higher.[65] This is either a result of selection bias due to the under-representation of undetected cartels in total prosecuted cartels[66] or because there is no need to communicate in a concentrated market (tacit collusion).[67] Garrod and Olczak have tried to provide an explanation for the occurrence of cartels in markets with larger asymmetric firms. They question the structural screens used to identify markets conducive to the cartel as such screens are most likely to flag markets with high chances of tacit collusion rather than markets where explicit collusion will occur.[68]

Whish and Bailey characterize tacit collusion as parallel behaviour of firms in the market "without a concerted practice in the legal sense".[69] This behaviour of firms to consider the decisions or strategies of the competitors in their own business does not mean that there is collusion between firms. While Turner believed that tacit collusion or conscious parallelism has to be differentiated from explicit collusion based on an "agreement" between parties and thus should not be treated as anti-competitive itself,[70] Posner argues that tacit collusion should be punished as parallelism in the market is similar to the concerted action of business units to charge monopoly prices. This is because elements of an agreement are present – that is, an offer in the form of restrictive conduct by one firm is accepted by the rival to follow the same.[71] As it would be extremely difficult to prove tacit collusion without proof of agreement, Posner lists the following pieces of evidence that can be adduced:[72]

a Pattern of systematic price discrimination.
b Prolonged excess of capacity over demand.
c Reduction of changes in the market price.
d Unusual profits and price leadership.
e Fixed market shares for a substantial period of time.
f Refusal to offer discounts despite substantial excess capacity.
g Announcement of price increases far in advance, without justification for doing it.
h Public statements in consideration of what should be considered the right price that the industry should maintain.

The cartel provisions in competition law of different jurisdictions are premised on proving the existence of an agreement. The European Court of Justice (ECJ) has held that parallel behaviour in itself cannot be considered as concerted practice but is taken as strong evidence of concerted practice if "it leads to conditions of competition which do not respond to the normal conditions of the market, having regard to the nature of the products, the size and number of the undertakings, and the volume of the said market".[73] Therefore, in the absence of evidence of direct or indirect contact between firms, parallel behaviour will be seen as individual choice.[74] The burden of proof will be on the enforcement agency to prove concerted practice. While the concept of "parallelism plus" has been advanced to counter tacit collusion (parallel behaviour along with facilitating factors to prove collusion), the application of the same has not been consistent.

2.3.3 Impact of cartels on competition and other stakeholders

Cartels contradict the principles of free-market economy as their operators attempt to eliminate or limit competition in the market.[75] As cartels prevent their members from being subjected to full market exposure, it results in a reduction of pressures on cartel members to control costs and innovate. Cartel agreements lead to deadweight loss (due to allocative inefficiency), productive inefficiency (due to the creation of barriers to entry) and dynamic harm (due to reduced incentives to innovate and strive for efficiency).[76] There is a loss in efficiency when a cartel either prevents the exit of inefficient firms from the market or locks in excess capacity, as the capital that could have been employed elsewhere in the economy would now be tied up.[77] There are also costs associated with the formation and enforcement of cartels.[78] In this manner, cartels result in a reduction in social welfare[79] and total welfare.[80]

2.3.3.1 Impact of cartels on consumers

Cartels have a direct impact on the consumers when they face increased prices and reduced supply of the product and/or services.[81] Consumers end up paying more for the desired product/service or have to forego the use of the product/service.[82] The average increase in the sale price due to a price-fixing cartel has been estimated to be around 10%, and the average decrease in output is close to 20%.[83] The freedom to choose the product and/or service per their desires is taken away. Cartels also eliminate the idea of competition that forces market participants to work towards the betterment of the product/service or reduction of costs. There is no incentive to innovate or use modern technology.[84] Consumer harm (loss in consumer surplus) has been talked about in terms of either cartel overcharges or loss of opportunity in terms of non-purchase due to high prices.[85] Assessment of cartel damages is not an easy task, especially in complex market scenarios where a final product in one market can be input in another. Cartelization in one market will then have ripple effects on other markets. Consumers will end up paying high prices not just in the cartelized market but in other markets as well. An example of this is upstream market product cartelization (less output and high price) having effects on the downstream market. Economic literature suggests that consumers do face substantial harm due to cartels in vertically related markets.

2.3.3.2 *Impact of cartels on the poor*

The poor in a country can be seen both as consumers of essential goods and services and small business owners and workers. UNCTAD (2013)[86] noted that cartels have the most harmful effect on the poor when cartelization occurs in the supply of essential goods and/or services. The general impact of cartels on consumers becomes multifold in context to the poor and their access to goods and/or services as they end up either reducing their consumption or substantially reducing their expenses on other products/services to get the cartelized product. Buyers' cartels again have a huge negative impact on the rural and poor agrarian economy. In agricultural products like cotton, cocoa and milk, the supply of which comes from small dispersed agriculturists, buyers' cartels have been reported, especially in underdeveloped economies. These cartels benefit from the lack of bargaining power of the suppliers. The impact of cartelization on the poor worsens in times of market slowdowns. Higher prices and reduced supply hit the poor with reduced incomes even more gravely and also cause small units to go out of business. Data from the Word Bank (2003),[87] S. Evenett et al. (2006),[88] and the OECD (2008)[89] regarding anti-competitive practices from developing countries show a high prevalence of anti-competitive practices (mostly cartel) in the markets for essential goods and services. Further, the supply of essential goods and services (medical facilities [medicines, hospitals], infrastructural facilities [road, transport, schools]) is often tendered out by the government to private contractors (public procurement contracts). The UNCTAD report highlights the high incidence of bid rigging in these tenders. Bid rigging leads to an increase in the cost of a product or service as the riggers will extract cartel profit from the consumers.[90] Cartels also reduce competition in the market, which adversely affects market efficiency, dynamism and innovation and has a long-term impact on the health of a country's economy.

2.3.3.3 *Impact of cartels on small and medium enterprises (SMEs)*

SMEs are organizations that contribute to creativity, enhance the options available to consumers and increase competition, thereby bringing dynamism to the market. Cartels also impact the growth and development of SMEs. A cartelized market creates high barriers to entry for these units. Further, if the units use the cartelized product or service as their own input, increased prices increase the cost of production and thus reduce the profit margin. If the units enter the space of supply of cartelized products or services as inputs to cartel members, reduced output decision by the cartel causes the sales of the SME units to decline. This impact of cartels on SMEs has a direct effect on growth factors like employment and generation of wealth, which in turn adversely affect the poor.[91]

2.3.4 *Defining a cartel*

The usage of the word "cartel" for anti-competitive agreements between horizontal players is a recent phenomenon. History of the term "cartel" can be traced back to 19th century when it was understood to mean "a written notice or letter". It began to be used to denote alliances of firms in the 1800s. Its meaning changed from being used to refer to trade associations or unions and even trade agreements in the early 20th century. The word "cartel" derives its origin from the Latin term *carta*, which literally means "paper" or "letter".[92] *Carta* was used to signify a military arrangement between two fighting nations on issues like handling of prisoners. It was only later that the term assumed its meaning as a business term for an arrangement for the exchange of sale or price information. "Cartel" today has a negative understanding of something which is frowned upon by the law. It is seen as an agreement to restrain trade for the mutual benefit of the parties entering into it.

US antitrust laws do not provide a definition of a "cartel", and it is covered within the wide ambit of Section 1 of the Sherman Act, 1890. Hard-core cartels have been treated as illegal *per se* by the US Supreme Court. It has been accepted by the US courts that cartels have a restrictive nature and cause considerable harm to the overall health of the market. The EU has a more comprehensive definition of cartels and encompasses the element of it being entered into between competing firms with an objective to maximize profits at the cost of consumers' interest.[93] The governing law – the Treaty on the Functioning of the European Union (TFEU) – contains a general prohibition under Article 101 (1) on

> any agreement or concerted practice between undertakings, or decision of an association of undertakings, which has its object or effect the prevention, restriction or distortion of competition, and which has an effect on trade between European Union (EU) Member States.

Certain cartels are not likely to be granted the benefit of exemption under Article 101 (3) of the TFEU. These agreements are price fixing, output restrictions, division of the market, discriminatory treatment of equivalent transactions and making the conclusion of contracts subject to acceptance by other parties of irrelevant supplementary obligations. The UK Competition Act of 1998 closely resembles Article 101 of the TFEU and represents the civil enforcement regime of the country.[94]

The Organization for Economic Co-operation and Development (OECD) categorizes horizontal agreements into general horizontal agreements and hard-core cartels.[95] The OECD recognizes that some horizontal agreements like agreements between competitors on research and development, marketing, production and sharing of technology are actually beneficial for consumers and have beneficial effects. The 1998 Recommendations exclude certain agreements that "are reasonably related to the lawful realization of cost-reducing or output-enhancing efficiencies" from the ambit of hard-core cartels. Therefore, these agreements need not be dealt with on a *per se* basis, and the anti-competitive effects, if any, have to be seen in the light of the pro-competitive effects. In other words, a reasoned assessment needs to be done. However, hard-core cartels will not have any pro-competitive effects and are *per se* illegal. They are seen as the most serious form of violation of competition law. The OECD treats the prosecution of "hard-core cartels" as a priority policy objective as they lead to a reduction in output and an increase in prices.[96] The International Competition Network (ICN)[97] uses the same terminology of "hard-core cartels" as advanced by OECD and conforms with the definition. ICN has also highlighted the common thread across 18 jurisdictions in their understanding of "cartel" as form (an agreement exists), party (competitors are involved) and object (competition is restricted).

While there is consensus on the definition of "cartel" across international organizations, it has been noted that the definition as such does not provide the direction of enforcement and implementation of anti-cartel law. Thus, there is a difference in approach in the detailing of anti-cartel provisions across jurisdictions. While some jurisdictions like India prefer to lay down illustratively the list of actions prohibited in clear, unambiguous terms, others have a more generalized version that states an overarching rule to not indulge in arrangements that prevent them from competing with competitors. Whether a particular conduct falls within the ambit of cartel prohibition will then be decided by enforcement agencies. In the long run, these jurisdictions will develop a list of prohibited conduct that are condemned on a repeated basis to act as reference points. The second level of divergence in anti-cartel laws is seen in terms of exemptions. These exemptions, on the one hand, are guided by the general economic understanding of certain benefit-generating horizontal agreements and, on the other, by larger policy calls of the country. Therefore, while exemptions for efficiency-enhancing joint ventures and research and development agreements are common, exemptions may also be extended to agricultural cooperatives and SMEs.

2.3.5 Cartel conducive environment

Cartels tend to exist and thrive more frequently in certain environments that possess factors like homogeneity of product or service, high concentration, stable demand, high entry barriers, low countervailing buying power and information symmetry. The stability of a cartel, once formed, will then depend on its management. Therefore, the strictness of punishment for cartel cheating, the likelihood of detection by competition authorities, and the efficiency of the leniency regime are necessary to be examined to comment on the stability of a cartel. It is important to look at factors that facilitate collusion and contribute to their stability so that a more robust and targeted anti-cartel policy can be crafted. Different scholars categorize the facilitating factors in different ways. These factors may be categorized as structural (number of competitors, entry barriers and information exchange between competitors), supply related (maturity of the industry with the level of technology, product and capacity symmetry) and demand related (growth of the market, stability of demand and buying power).[98]

- *Oligopolistic market*: The first factor is the presence of an oligopolistic market, with firms having significant market shares. There is a likelihood that these firms will join hands to decide on the price or output of the product or service. The following structural factors facilitate collusion.[99]
- *Product homogeneity:* When the product or service is homogenous, there is less uncertainty over demand and profits,[100] and it is easier to agree upon a particular price. Heterogeneity tends to make decision-making more complex as other variables like production, prices and division of profit come into the picture. Heterogeneity may also increase negotiation costs, which decreases the expected profit of collusion and increases the likelihood of defection,[101] thus lessening cartel stability.
- *High concentration:* The fewer the competitors in a relevant market, the easier it is to negotiate. When the market is highly concentrated, market participants realize their interdependence and the need to work closely to maximize profit. Further, a cartel is most stable when it is all-inclusive. An increase in the number of players outside the cartel, whether by new entry or otherwise, threatens cartel stability as it decreases the market share of the cartel and, in turn, reduces profits.[102] Thus, the popular conception is that the higher the number of cartel participants, the higher its instability.[103]
- *Low demand elasticity:* Lower demand elasticity increases the profit from the price increase above competitive levels.
- *High entry barriers:* High entry barriers to a market help in cartel stability as it would be difficult for new players to enter the market and undercut cartel price. It would prevent the aforementioned negative impact of new players outside the cartel. New conditions will also require re-negotiation.
- *Stable demand:* When the demand in the market is volatile, it will be very difficult to come to terms with any decision on output by the cartel. It will require firms to negotiate the terms of collusion on a regular basis. This increases the cost of cartel making. Volatile demand also affects stability as it makes the detection of cartel cheating very difficult.

- *Cartel participants:* Similarity in terms of capacity, market share and technological advancement of cartel members increase stability as it is easier to negotiate the terms of behaviour. It will be easier to come to an agreement on cartel price, output and profit sharing. On the other hand, some researchers argue that such differences are essential to avoid any power struggle between members.[104]
- *Entry and exit of players:* Late entry of new players has a destabilizing effect on cartels. Trust deficit leads to cartel cheating. However, an early exit of a player from the cartel has a binding effect.[105]
- *Established communication channels:* The presence of established communication channels, through either trade associations, regulatory frameworks that provide opportunities for discussions between competitors,[106] or privileged personal contacts between individual members of the market players, makes monitoring of compliance with the cartel agreement easier and ensures stability over a longer period of time. Similarly, if there is a higher frequency of interaction or communication, the incentives to deviate from a cartel are lower since retaliation would be more frequent.[107]

Cartels are also more prevalent when collusive business values exist in a specific sector.[108] For example, in the Austrian banks cartel, the sector was characterized by oversupply and a high level of public ownership. In this situation, market players saw cartels as a way to combat destructive competition.[109] In Calcium Carbide, collusive business practices were so deeply embedded in company strategy that the company did not even realize the illegality of the practices.[110] They could also result from exogenous trigger events such as considerable oversupply, fluctuation of crude oil prices, or even stagnation of demand triggered by abrupt changes or prolonged adverse conditions.[111]

2.3.5.1 Stability of cartels

Griffin provides the simplest categorization of factors that affect the stability of cartels.[112] He divides the factors into structural, behavioural and other factors. Structural factors are market induced. Therefore, conditions which make the cartel unprofitable will certainly affect the stability of the cartel. Behavioural factors are more in relation to opportunity costs that the cartel member's eye. Therefore, if the cartel members start to see more profit in deviating from cartel conduct, then it will destabilize the cartel as the instances of cheating increase. Other factors include non-economic factors, which are outside the control of cartel, like a change in government policy, war, or a change in market dynamics. Externally, cartel arrangements have to be adaptive to changing market conditions like changes in demand, entry of new players and new substitutable in the market. As Porter puts it, "an unobserved adverse demand shock might undermine cartel stability and induce opportunistic behaviour of cartel members".[113]

Consensus among cartel members is a crucial factor for the survival of a cartel. It is essential that the strategy is carefully negotiated to take everyone on board. The interests of a few cannot be ignored as they may create incentives to cheat, thus destabilizing the cartel. Factors like the size of players, market share and profit sharing have to be considered. A cartel will reach maximum stability when it starts functioning as a monopolist. There are both external and internal factors responsible for cartel stability.[114] While the high entry barriers and all-inclusive nature of the cartel form external factors that increase stability, the probability of detection and punishment for cheating form the internal factors behind cartel stability. There is always a temptation to cheat and increase individual profit. This is enhanced if there is a problem in the sharing of cartel gains.

Defection is another threat to cartel stability. The more robust the leniency scheme, the more likelihood there is of cartel defection. Levenstein and Suslow hold that the stability of a cartel can be enhanced if the sanctioning mechanism for cartel cheating is enhanced.[115] Threats of boycott, price war, or price cut by cartels are some of the measures used to deter cheating. In the presence of legal eyes, it is not always easy to sanction or punish cheating. As punishment for cartel cheating increases the chances of detection, cartels have moved from overt punishments, like price wars, to more sophisticated systems of coordination and management of cartels. Emphasis is then put on building mechanisms to prevent cheating itself. Many researchers have focused on the element of mutual trust as the binding force of a cartel. Mutual trust has been used to justify the existence of long-duration cartels that exist against the popular economic presumption about cartels being inherently unstable. Thus, in the absence of legal recognition of an arrangement between firms, trust plays the role of an adhesive. Communication between firms, reciprocity and reputation of credibility helps in the building of trust.[116]

The presence of a strict anti-cartel enforcement regime has a negative effect on cartel stability. The rising trend to criminalize cartel activity has made business participants act more secretively and reduce the frequency of communication to avoid being caught. The expectation of cartel profit must then overcome the sanctions and threat of being caught. This increased cost of secret collusion has an effect on deterring collusion. There are, however, doubts raised on the effect of the leniency provisions. As it is popularly understood, leniency schemes increase the chance of detection and increase the efficiency of anti-cartel policy even in situations when cartel members are allowed to join after the commencement of the investigation.[117] The success of the anti-cartel regime of any jurisdiction can, therefore, be gazed at by analyzing the leniency system.

2.3.6 Operation of cartels (cartel decision-making)

2.3.6.1 Organizational feature of a cartel

The administration of cartels involves the establishment of contacts and determination of behaviour in terms of price, output, quotas, bid price and monitoring of firm behaviour. The organization thus involves initiation, communication and compliance. Evidence suggests that cartels mostly have a starting time where one or more big players initiate the process to formalize a cartel followed by the induction of other players. This is more important in markets with a comparatively higher number of players. In a more concentrated market with comparable market shares, initiation is more of collective action. Explicit cartels do involve some mode of communication. Communication often happens through an exchange of information on the platform of trade unions. These trade unions also serve as monitors of unilateral behaviour and are responsible for highlighting defection. In case there is defection, punishment in the form of a boycott or price war is the consequence, which is the biggest binding element and, if designed well, trumps any benefit arising from cheating or leniency.

Communication is the trickiest part. Cartels have to do budget meetings to decide on differences, the future course of action and reporting on earlier actions. The whole premise of an anti-cartel enforcement structure is based on the establishment of some form of agreement. Cartel members, therefore, have to be extra cautious to prevent any detection. All attempts are made to minimize face-to-face meetings and avoid any written mode of communication, and mid-level executives are used rather than senior managers as buffers to administer cartels. The reduced involvement of key managerial personnel in the administration of cartels saves them from the eyes of the anti-cartel enforcement agencies.[118]

2.3.6.2 Decision-making structure of a cartel

A cartel, for its survival, has to create structures that facilitate decision-making, such as a mechanism to share information, induction of new members, use of trade associations as platforms, profit sharing and the decision to punish a cartel cheater. The internal organization of a cartel also depends on the type of cartel. A cartel has to consider external threats. Thus, the concealment of the structure is one of the prime considerations. To illustrate, in a price-fixing cartel where sharing of information is the essential requirement, the network for the flow of information has to be clear along with who will decide on the price and based on what parameters (implementation). To see that the members of the cartel adhere to the decided behaviour, the monitoring question has to be decided beforehand.

Direct mode of communication in the form of meetings or electronic communications, which leave a trail for enforcement agencies, is no more the preferred route of cartel members. Communication through information exchange, especially through an external third party, is more common. Marshall and Marx have elaborated on the role of trade associations as platforms for information exchanges playing a part in the communication chain.[119] The degree of communication varies with the type of collusion. In a bid-rigging cartel, communication is largely on who would win the bid. Once the winner is decided, the rest follows. The cartel can adopt a "phase of the moon" system (taking turns to win bids), bid suppression and complementary or cover bidding as the modality to execute the cartel decision. A price-fixing or production cartel usually sees a higher frequency of communication (may be in the form of meetings) to fix or set prices. The cartelists use various ways to communicate with each other to decide on prices, maximum discount limits, limitations of production and so on. Market-sharing cartel again does not require frequent communication after the initial decision has been taken to share the market on the basis of territory or customers.

On the basis of decision-making, the cartel structure can be categorized into two.[120] Democratic cartels are characterized by "democratic decision-making" by all the cartel members. This form of cartel mostly uses the platform of a trade association for cartel management and requires regular communication. A high detection rate induces decentralization in cartel decision-making.[121] Centralized cartels are where the decision as to price, quantity, bid, market and so on is taken by another party.[122] A centralized cartel is further categorized into the following:

a *Ring leader model:* there are cartel leaders, generally firms with the largest market shares, which decide on the terms of the cartel.
b *Committee model:* a committee is composed of a subset of cartel members.

2.3.6.3 Enforcement feature of a cartel

As cartelization is not legal, the law cannot be used to enforce arrangements or understandings between cartel members. The following of a cartel decision is premised on the fact that all members are set to gain from the arrangement and that there is a likelihood of punishment by other members of the cartel in case of cheating. Thus, implementation is based on mutual trust and reciprocity. In case of deviation from accepted behaviour, there is also an inbuilt mechanism of compensation. For instance, in a market sharing agreement, in fear of leaving a trail of easily detectable communication, if one firm finds it difficult to refer clients to the cartel members to whom that region or customer belongs, he can serve the client but would have to compensate the other cartel members. There is reciprocity to this behaviour as well. Many believe this mechanism based on mutual trust and reciprocity or a set of social rules is more effective for cartel stability than the fear of punishment.[123]

Social norms may be considered a binding force. However, it does not mean that monitoring cartel agreements do not happen. This monitoring can happen either in the form of information exchanges or through a third-party cartel administrator, such as a trade association. Monitoring of cartel activity can highlight instances of cheating by a member. There are again two ways to resolve this: either through punishment in the form of monetary compensation and threat of price war in case of non-compliance or through amicable negotiation and mediation. However, there is no guarantee that either of the modes will completely overcome the chance of repetition of cartel cheating. Growing disagreements and trust deficits will lead to the breaking up of the cartel. Members of a cartel will always have an incentive to cheat to maximize their individual profit or increase their market share by either pricing below the cartel price or selling beyond the agreed quota.[124] Since cheating is premised on its benefits in comparison with harm (punishment) from retaliation by cartel members, for cartels to survive, the gravity of punishment must exceed benefits, which in turn requires constant monitoring.[125]

In the Lysine cartel, in order to monitor compliance, one of the cartel members was assigned the task of preparing monthly "scorecards" for the cartel. Each company telephoned or mailed their sales volumes to Mimoto, who then prepared a spreadsheet that was distributed at the quarterly meetings of the cartel. To promote compliance, guaranteed buy-ins were used.[126] In another cartel, the market allocation was monitored through the reporting of sales. The setting of sales quotas with monitoring in terms of reported sales was also a practice deployed by cartels in the markets for carbonless paper, choline chloride, copper plumbing tubes, graphite electrodes, plasterboard, vitamins and zinc phosphate.[127]

2.3.7 Cartel agreement

Existence and proof of agreement are essential to prosecute cartels. However, it is an accepted fact that cartels are secretive, and cartel members will not enter into legally recognized formal agreements between themselves. Therefore, a wide interpretation is given to the meaning of the term "agreement" that considers both formal and informal modes of collaboration, understanding, arrangement, or action in concert. The inclusion of "concerted practice"[128] within the definition of "agreement" in some jurisdictions, including the EU,[129] widens the scope of the definition.[130] Even when the undertakings have expressed their intention to behave in a particular fashion, it is enough to bring it within the definition of "agreement".[131]

Direct evidence of a cartel agreement in the form of documents (electronic or non-electronic) or direct communication between competitors which lays out the material of understanding and identifies the members to the understanding is rare. Reliance is thus placed on circumstantial evidence to prove the existence of an agreement which refers to all other forms of evidence which do not refer to an agreement but occurrences from which the existence of an agreement can be inferred. It is a mix of factual occurrences, say, communication between competitors or their representatives and economic factors which facilitate collusion or conduct of the parties. Both circumstantial and economic pieces of evidence have some element of inconclusiveness; it is generally a combination of economic and circumstantial evidence of which a cumulative assessment is done.

Evidence of communication between competitors, which falls short of laying out the matter of communication, is also used by competition authorities. The OECD (2007) lists out a few forms of such communication evidence, such as telephone records, common travel plans, or participation in a meeting or trade circles. Minutes of meetings which indicate that issues of price, demand or supply, or tender were discussed are used as strong, convincing evidence.[132] Economic evidence can be either in the form of facilitating factors (market conditions that facilitate collusion) or conduct factors (factors which account for the behaviour of firms, like price parallelism, and stable and consistent market shares). It is not easy to draw a clear distinction between direct and indirect forms of evidence, especially in the case of communication evidence, and neither is the same insisted upon.

2.3.7.1 Single economic entity

Under the TFEU provisions, the term "undertaking" has not been defined. Whish notes that the ECJ has given the term a wide interpretation to include all types of business units irrespective of their legal character and financial sources.[133] However, as laid out in the EU guidelines on agreements, Article 101 applies to an agreement between "independent undertakings", so agreements between related parties will not be covered within its ambit.[134] Control or decisive influence over another has been taken as the criterion to check if two or more entities form a single economic entity.[135] Some of the obvious relations include that of wholly owned subsidiaries or sister companies[136] with a common parent.[137] But these presumptions are rebuttable. The assessment is factual and will vary from case to case as it will consider factors like shareholding pattern, composition of the board of directors, historical conduct and decision-making process.[138]

This also has a reverse implication, meaning that the parent company cannot be held jointly and severally liable for the fine imposed on account of the cartel activity of the subsidiary.[139] The presumption of decisive influence, of course, is rebuttable but, as *Wahl* notes, is extremely difficult.[140] The presumption has been applied for both wholly owned subsidiaries and nearly wholly owned subsidiaries. Decisive influence of minority shareholders by virtue of their contractual rights or otherwise can also be taken into account for establishing a single economic entity or imposition of liability. The same test can also be applied to a parent of a joint venture. Thus, two or more parents who have a decisive influence over the joint venture will be held to be a single economic entity, and conversely, the parents will be jointly and severally liable for the fines imposed for the cartelization of the joint venture. The presumption which exists in the case of parent and wholly owned subsidiaries does not exist here.[141] A single economic entity has another implication on the quantum of fines, which, if calculated on the basis of revenues, considers the revenue of the entire body rather than just the entity engaged in anti-competitive behaviour.

There is, however, no clarity on the tests to determine whether there is "unity of interest". Therefore, when the shareholding is less than 100% but the objectives of the two companies are common, do we treat them as a single entity? The US position on single economic entities is no different.[142] The US Supreme Court, in the *Copperweld* case,[143] reversed the earlier rulings[144] to hold the parent and its wholly owned subsidiaries as single economic entities.[145] In the *American Needle* case, it held that National Football League was not a single economic entity and laid down both structural and behavioural tests to determine a single economic entity.

2.3.7.2 Horizontal exchange of information

The exchange of information between competitors is not uncommon and happens through multiple channels. While it does bring transparency to the market, leading to an increase in market efficiency, it allows competitors to coordinate and collude and can be used as a mechanism to sustain a price-fixing or market-sharing cartel. Exchange of information may also be seen in efficiency-enhancing collaborations, like joint ventures, research and development arrangements, joint commercialization, and purchasing agreements, or as a simple means to enhance cooperation as a stand-alone practice.[146] Competition law across most[147] jurisdictions does not specifically include provisions for the exchange of information. If the exchange of information is part of a broader cartel scheme, it is treated in that fashion. However, there is confusion with respect to the stand-alone practice of sharing information.

The exchange of information is not *per se* bad and is mostly assessed from a rule of reason perspective. The object or reason for the exchange of information, nature of information, nature of the market, the timing of informational exchange and the conduct of the parties post-exchange are some of the factors that are looked into. Thus, information exchange in an oligopolistic market with a smaller number of players is likely to raise more eyebrows. The nature of information exchanged is the most important factor. The information can be categorized as follows:

a Highly risky exchanges, including competition-sensitive data exchanges (like current individualized pricing or quantities, future pricing, discounts, cost of production, quantities, distribution costs, individual sales data [sale volume, sale revenue, etc.], individual capacity utilization and supply stock); entity-specific strategic information or disaggregated data; future data on strategy, new products, innovation, or marketing initiatives.

b Exchanges with potentially low risk, like aggregated data on current pricing and quantities which does not identify individual members; historical data on aggregated pricing and quantities or general information on technology; sector promotion initiatives.

Exchange of information between competitors can happen directly or through a third party. In many cases, trade associations have played a crucial role. The direct exchange of sensitive information between competitors is seen as a mode to either establish or sustain a cartel. Third parties include the agencies which collect information and release reports on market development, market trends and so on. These third parties can also be hired by business units to provide industry data and market research. They mostly rely on information that is publicly available and obtain some via their personal effort. One of the major reasons that the exchange of information via independent third parties is not heavily scrutinized is that such information is publicly available, and hence, these do not constitute an "agreement" between competitors. The situation is different, however, where the collection of data is a joint exercise between competitors, only through a third party. The third party getting information at both ends can act like a trade association to channel this information. Information can also be disseminated by unilateral announcements.[148] Therefore, where an enterprise makes a public announcement of future price, the question is, is it anti-competitive? Per Kuhn,[149] the dissemination of CSI (commercially sensitive information) increases market efficiency and reduces the chances of coordination. However, the possibility of firms using announced information as an indication for future behaviour cannot be ruled out.

There is no clear-cut approach to informational exchanges between competitors. It can neither be banned because of its proven efficiency gains; nor can it be allowed freely as it creates a breeding ground for collusion. Then, sharing of information can take different routes (both direct and indirect [e.g. through a third party or a trade association]). Competition laws have not generally dealt with or given a statutory space to this aspect and left it to the enforcement agencies and courts to ascertain the pros and cons of informational exchanges. Certain jurisdictions have issued guidelines in the form of a list incorporating the acceptable and non-acceptable informational exchanges. Therefore, conditional exchange of CSI with respect to cost, sales, and production may be allowed to feed into larger industry statistics or benchmarking studies.

Some jurisdictions treat an agreement between competitors for the exchange of confidential information with an object to lessen competition as bad. However, the existence of an agreement in such situations has to be proved. But in case of jurisdictions like the EU and India, the definition is wide enough to include "concerted practice" (coordination between firms that falls short of an agreement). Debates around exchange of information can be summed up as follows:

- Treat certain information exchanges like data on future plans which do not have a positive effect on market efficiency as *per se* bad.[150] Other types of information to be treated on a case-to-case basis.
- Information sharing cannot be banned on a *per se* basis, and subjective assessment of the pro- and anti-competitive effects has to be done.
- Provide safe harbours to certain informational exchanges, which will be based on the market share of members (for instance, the *de minimis* principle, nature of information, or nature of the industry).
- Exchange of information can only be used as circumstantial evidence to prove the existence of cartels and cannot be treated as a violation in itself.

2.3.8 Cartels and the role of trade associations

"Association" is a common term used to signify cooperation between participating entities. It includes economic/social/cultural alliances of every form, such as unions, federations, or societies. It is composed of individuals or/and firms and is generally seen as a structure created by the players in the market for the means of collective bargaining and furtherance of common commercial goals. It is a means to advance common demands and objectives, like promotion of business, reduction in the asymmetry of information, collaboration in both innovation and research and adoption of common standards of business. Trade associations do serve a very important role in the market economy.[151] There is a long history of trade associations dating to the age of merchant guilds, playing a key role in development of the market economy. The problem arises when this collaboration is used as a device to lessen competition. On multiple occasions, trade associations have used their strength to impose restrictions, limiting the rights of market players to compete. It is not surprising that early competition laws[152] were framed as a response to these associations or trusts. The Treaty of Rome, for instance, specifically included "decisions by associations" within anti-competitive agreements under Article 81. Most jurisdictions today cover activities or decisions of trade associations within the definition of "agreement", thus making competition laws applicable to them. The application of competition law acts from two fronts: first, the by-laws of the association can be covered within the definition of "agreement" between members; and second, the decision of the association itself can be subject to competition law. There are multiple decisions of the European Commission (EC)[153] which have held decisions of trade associations, whether formal or informal – binding or non-binding – illegal if they had a negative effect on competition.

2.3.8.1 Role of trade associations in cartel formation

Trade associations can either act as cartels themselves or can facilitate them. Membership in such associations creates opportunities for competitors to meet and discuss. Even if the purpose of such a meeting called by the association was legitimate, it does create a breeding ground for collusion. Therefore, a practice guideline or a membership agreement or code of conduct for members that have the effect of fixing prices directly or indirectly or a decision of the trade association to limit the production or share the market is bad by law. For instance, where a trade association issues a voluntary or non-binding fee structure for its members, it may be treated as a decision of the members to coordinate prices.[154] Trade associations may also resort to collective boycott or discrimination in order to enforce the horizontal restriction. Decisions of a trade association in the form of recommendations, guidelines, voluntary standards, code of conduct and the like fall within the definition of "agreement", and their binding effect is generally of little significance.[155] Over the years, the trade associations have been found to be engaged in anti-competitive conduct of fixing minimum prices, discount rates and transportation fees; fixing levels of production or quotas for each member;[156] enforcing restrictive/selective or discriminatory membership or standardization systems;[157] allotting market on the basis of territory or type of customer; and deciding on the winner of the bids.

2.3.8.2 Trade associations and exchange of information

One of the primary activities of a trade association is to collect and disseminate information. This helps the members and the association to take coordinated action in pursuit of the larger objectives of the association. Availability of information or transparency in the market with respect to key variables like demand and supply information, trends in the market and growth of the sector on the whole is beneficial for the market players as it facilitates a better understanding of the market, helps in identification of problems and thus enables them to strategize. A high level of transparency, however, can also facilitate collusive behaviour as it enables the firms to coordinate their actions and, more importantly, monitor deviations from pre-decided behaviour. Thus, in an oligopolistic market where the trade associations act as channels for the dissemination of sensitive information, it results in a reduction in competition. Exchange of information related to cost, shipment details, sales data, discount and rebate plans, and information of credit have served as ways to enable the cartel to survive and also attain stability. The platform of the trade association is used to lobby, strategize and decide on common conduct, mostly initiated by the more influential members of the trade association. This reduces the dependency on more direct forms of coordination and thereby reduces the threat of detection. A trade association not just provides a platform for collusion and keeps a check on cheating members but also helps reduce the cost of managing the cartel. There is a very high rate of involvement of trade associations among prosecuted cartel cases across jurisdictions.

2.3.8.3 Single overall continuous agreement

Cartels are complex structures, and if continued for a long duration, they evolve and encompass multiple secret agreements and may involve different members. In long-term cartels, it is extremely difficult for enforcement agencies to identify and prove all agreements and involved members. Thus, the concept of single continuous agreement (SCI) was conceptualized in the 1980s by the EC.[158] The idea is to look at the cartel as a whole with a common objective and without the need to tie each agreement in the past with specific parties. It, therefore, bypasses the requirement to show continuous involvement of all the parties in day-to-day actions or decision-making of the cartel. The concepts of SCI and SOA (single overall agreement) have been devised keeping in mind the difficulties in identification and proof of agreements or concerted practices entered into at different times in long-term cartel cases and thus have wide procedural implications. When a series of agreements have a common objective to lessen or distort competition, they can be treated as part of a single chain and as one continuous violation.[159] Therefore, instead of treating the agreements as isolated violations of competition law, all the agreements are seen collectively as one system to distort competition in the market. The splitting up of these agreements, which show a pattern of continuity, is deemed artificial. What this does procedurally is that it enables the enforcement agencies to skip the hurdle of time limitation. Since the limitation period is counted from the date of conclusion of the SCI, it will not be applicable to old dated evidence and can be used to prove SCI, ensuring that violations are never time-barred. The punishment is not for multiple cartels but SCI. The concept allows one comprehensive assessment of all the evidence gathered. Similarly, per the concept of SOA, it is not necessary to show that each undertaking of the alleged cartel is part of every agreement or concerted practice. It is not necessary to adduce evidence to prove that the member was present in every meeting in which the decision took place, provided it is proved that all the members knew about the violation of competition law and had accepted the risk associated with it. There is no requirement to prove the existence of any written contract between parties, and an oral arrangement is enough.[160] In addition to the fact that the burden of proof will be on the enforcement agency, the conditions that are required to be proved for the application of SCI can be summarized as:

- *General plan with a common objective to distort competition:* Practices must have an identical nature of objectives.[161] The identical nature of the product or service is, however, not essential. Similarly, in a long-duration cartel, it is not necessary that the identity of members is intact. Participating members may vary both in terms of number and identity.

- *Willing participation of the members:* Willing participation of the members to the plan in furtherance of mutual objective has to be proved. Degree of participation is not a criterion but may be considered as a mitigating factor in the imposition of fines.
- *Awareness:* Awareness or foreseeability (reasonable presumption is also covered) of the prohibited conduct of other members has to be proved.[162]
- *Timeline:* Assessment of the timeline is a bit complex, and there has to be continuity of actions for the application of SCI. The implication of break in terms of time and the duration of break need factual assessment. The relevant question, therefore, is at what point (duration of time in which there is no evidence of cartel conduct) the SCI breaks. There is no clear answer to this. There are rulings where a break of a few months has been considered as the break point,[163] while in some cases, even a single meeting has been considered enough to sustain the cartel for years.[164]

If the factors stated earlier are satisfied, then each member of the cartel will be held liable for the entire infringement. It has generally been seen that the establishment of SCI invites the imposition of substantial fines. There is indeed a risk of bundling separate cartels into one SCI. This artificial bundling increases both the cartel duration and the fine imposed.

PUBLIC DISTANCING FROM CARTEL

Participation in the meeting in which discussions or decisions on anti-competitive conduct was taken is sufficient to prove that the member is part of the cartel. A member of a cartel can terminate its association with the cartel by public distancing, followed by non-participation in meetings post-distancing. Without publicly opposing the anti-competitive association, the defence of non-participation cannot be taken as there is a presumption of unlawfulness. Not distancing "is taken to be a tacit acceptance of an offer to collude".[165] It also reduces the chance of detection of a cartel. Another way to put it is that the non-participating members have no reason to not distance themselves. It cannot be argued by the member that it did not participate in any subsequent meeting. Break from the association can also be done by reporting the collusive association to the competition authorities. Public distancing is factual in nature and has to be examined on a case-to-case basis.[166] One of the prime considerations includes the "perception of other members".[167] Distancing has to be both "firm and unambiguous".[168] Other members of the cartel must be aware of the member's non-participation and the fact that the member disagrees with others. However, there have been narrow interpretations of this defence. If the firm is unable to prove that it did, in fact, distance itself publicly, it will be presumed that it was a part of the anti-competitive agreement.

2.3.9 Types of cartels

2.3.9.1 Horizontal price fixing

Price competition is good for the market because it allows prices to go down as competitors compete with each other for more customers. Competitors react to each other's action and act accordingly. Price fixing agreements eliminate this competition and allow the competitors to charge more without losing the customer base. Horizontal price fixing or an agreement by competitors in the same market to fix, raise, decrease or stabilize prices is considered one of the most pernicious forms of collusion and is thus considered a *per se* violation.[169] These agreements will have the effect of reducing both competition and output and are devoid of any redeeming features.[170] In price-fixing agreements, competitors "set prices above levels obtained in a competitive environment, thereby minimizing competition and reducing output".[171] The US Supreme Court categorizes price-fixing agreements more as a "naked restraint" which lacks any efficiency justification or a "restraint which is ancillary to some pro-competitive objective unrelated to price competition distortion and leading to enhancement of efficiency, output, consumer choice, etc." These tend to "reduce consumer welfare by restricting output and destroying the surplus value consumers place on lost production".[172] Posner also highlights the "social costs of cartels" to be higher than "deadweight welfare loss", if the competitors in the market do not compete on price.[173]

The expectation of a consumer to get the best possible product at the best possible price is affected if the enterprises selling those products decide to fix the prices. Neither can price fixing be reasonable nor be justified with reasons like market stability, enhancing consumer welfare or as an attempt to counter stiff competition as it comes at the cost of price competition. The fact that prices are fixed is enough to conclude that the consumer is not getting the best rates possible. Reasonableness of price fixed cannot be raised as a defence. In the words of the US Supreme Court, "the reasonable price fixed today may through economic and business changes become the unreasonable price of tomorrow. Once established, it may be maintained unchanged because of the absence of competition secured by the agreement for a price reasonable when fixed".[174]

The existence of an agreement is a necessary requirement to prove price fixing collusion, which, in turn, means that unilateral action or "intra-corporate decision-making" is not covered within its ambit and that there must be a plurality of actors. Technically, a joint venture which is controlled by two or more entities may be treated as a form of agreement for the purposes of investigation.[175] Similarly, a parent and its subsidiary company may be seen as conspirators.[176] However, it has now been settled that since the relationship between the parent company and its wholly owned subsidiary has a unity of interest with common objectives, they are not two distinct entities but one. The presumption, of course, is rebuttable. In the case of enterprises which are not wholly owned, decisional and economic independence will have to be checked. The same applies to any understanding or arrangement between two wholly owned subsidiaries *inter se* of a common parent company.[177] The test is economic integration and decisional dependence so as to eliminate the idea of competition between them.

Herbert Hovenkamp[178] provides a step-wise guide to characterize any agreement. Does the agreement fix prices in any way? Is the agreement "naked" (formed for the purpose of increasing prices or decreasing output) or ancillary to some other efficiency-enhancing agreement that might be beneficial to the consumers? If the agreement is "naked", *per se* rule applies; otherwise, an analysis of market power, concentration of market, entry barrier, or product quality has to be looked into. If there is evidence that the arrangement creates efficiency gains by a reduction in cost or improving quality of product or service, it has to be seen whether alternative ways to achieve the same are available. If there are alternatives present, then the present form of agreement may be termed illegal. The Australian and New Zealand courts have read the deeming *per se* rule in a similar fashion and have gone into the enquiry of surrounding circumstances.[179] Some scholars, however, have strongly argued against such an approach as it allows the defendants to submit detailed economic justification for their behaviour, thus seriously undermining the deterrence effect of a deeming provision.[180]

TYPES OF HORIZONTAL PRICE FIXING

Horizontal price-fixing agreements are not just those which actually set or fix prices but also include agreements that affect prices. The following may be different versions of price fixing:

- Any agreement to raise, lower, hold, peg, or stabilize the price.
- Any agreement to set minimum or maximum price.
- Any agreement to decide on discounts, terms of payment, commissions or warranties.
- Any agreement to not undercut prices.
- Any agreement to adhere to or adopt standard pricing formula.
- Any agreement to fix credit terms.
- Any agreement to impose fixed surcharges.
- Any agreement to fix the uniform pricing formula.
- Any agreement to fix any method to quote prices in a bid.
- Any agreement to standardize trade-in allowances.
- Any agreement to adhere to published prices.

- Any agreement to fix shipping or credit terms.
- Any recommendation of price by trade associations.

PRICE FIXING AND PRICE PARALLELISM

There is a need to differentiate price-fixing cartels from conscious parallelism. Proof that the parallel behaviour of firms in an oligopolistic market is the result of a pre-existing understanding, additional evidence, or "plus factors" will have to be produced. Turner raises three objections to treating conscious parallelism as collusion.[181] Firstly, he argues that since firms in an oligopolistic market are interdependent, they should be allowed to factor in the reaction or strategy of their rivals within their own business decisions. Secondly, if parallel pricing is considered bad *per se*, it will prevent the entry of new firms into the market. Thirdly, any rule prohibiting parallel pricing will be "tantamount to rule prohibiting supra-competitive pricing",[182] which in turn will make the judicial body the price regulators, an eventuality no one would want. Thus, Turner argued against the characterization of such parallel conduct as *per se* illegal, stating that they should instead be tested on the parameter of market monopolization. The US courts, while acknowledging the fact that such oligopolistic pricing is not desirable, accepted Professor Turner's idea more so because of the difficulty in devising a "remedy for interdependent pricing".[183] Scholars like Richard Posner[184] and Lewis Kaplow,[185] on the other hand, have argued that Section 1 of the Sherman Act, 1890, is wide enough to cover oligopoly pricing. Alan Devlin[186] tried to refute the argument of Professor Turner on the basis of modern game theory by arguing that business units, even in an oligopolistic market, are not compelled to price at supra-competitive levels and that, in most instances, market outcome is determined by conscious interaction between firms. Further, he argues that rules to prevent tacit collusion will not prevent the entry of new players as the market in question already has high entry barriers. Alan Devlin calls the oligopoly problem a failure of competition policy to address a situation which creates similar effects of explicit price fixing.[187] He thus argues that turning a blind eye towards parallel pricing, which in most cases is supra-competitive, will affect the allocative efficiency of the market. He highlights and extends the argument of Director and Levi[188] that parallel pricing in an oligopolistic market is not a compulsion but a choice. It is indeed a rational decision of firms but is not different from explicit coordination. Further, it is argued that most of these oligopolistic markets already have high entry barriers, which makes the argument of entry of new firms as a counter to supra-competitive pricing a bit redundant. Per Posner, since the firms chose to price at supra-competitive levels to maximize their profits with an understanding that their competitors will follow their actions, it should be enough to show concerted action. Similarly, it's argued that tacit collusion may be more harmful than explicit collusion as most markets today are oligopolies, and the problem of parallel pricing at supra-competitive levels is common.[189]

George Hay takes the example of two gas stations, more likely to create a situation of a duopoly, to prove that interdependence is real and there is natural parallelism that may occur without any prior communication. This, however, is premised on the structure of the market.[190] He also highlights the problem of lack of a yardstick to differentiate parallel pricing because of oligopolistic interdependence or because of tacit agreement.[191] He, therefore, argues in favour of problematizing "facilitating practices".[192]

Posner,[193] on the other hand, argues that even in oligopolistic markets, firms will compete against each other and will set prices that are competitive. To convert this competitive price into non-competitive monopoly pricing, express or tacit collusion is required. The firms choose, rather than being compelled to increase prices above competitive levels. Parallelism is, thus, evidence of express or tacit collusion and "that any supra-competitive price reached by firms acting in parallel may be capable of constituting an illegal price fix".[194] Per Posner, proof in the form of both market and economic evidence will have to be produced to prove collusion. Lopatka and Werden disagree about the teachings of game theory regarding whether "conscious parallelism" is a likely outcome in a concentrated market, while each acknowledges that Posner's use of "perfect competition" as a benchmark is unsupported by literature.[195] Piraino examines the behaviour of firms to conclude that business firms use signals like future price announcements as a mode of communication in the oligopolistic market, thus increasing the price to supra-competitive levels.[196] Lopatka, a game theorist, has criticized Posner's multi-factor approach as creating confusion for courts.[197]

The consensus seems to be that conscious parallelism cannot be equated with an agreement to conclude price collusion and can only be treated as circumstantial evidence.[198] Some of the popular plus factors that have been used include examination of the business rationale for parallel conduct, evidence of communication between parties, mismatch of demand and supply, assessment of self-interest of firms (whether there is a collective action which may not be in consonance to the habitual economic conduct of the individual enterprise) and the like.[199] The US courts have also looked into the motive of the enterprise to enter into concerted action. The plus factors or surrounding catalysts need not be illegal themselves.[200] The European courts have more or less followed a similar path and have insisted on evidence of collusion.

Insistence on plus factors prevents the courts from punishing unilateral or individual action rather than a concerted one. Price parallelism, however, is seen as strong evidence in markets where ordinarily such behaviour is not natural and which allows firms to attain price stability at a level that would not have been attained in a competitive market.[201] But in cases where parallelism can be explained due to narrow oligopolistic conditions of the market,[202] free availability of price information or due to price-leader phenomenon,[203] parallel behaviour will be treated as unilateral action only.[204] The burden of proof will be on the enforcement agency to adduce additional evidence (plus factors) along with the parallel conduct to prove concerted action. Further, there is no evidentiary hierarchy or conclusiveness of the plus factors, nor is there a detailed analysis of their economic merits. The struggle to produce plus factors is common across jurisdictions. It leaves enforcement agencies in a very difficult situation where the evidentiary standards are decided on a case-to-case basis.

Economists have tried to help in this pursuit by presenting an "economic interpretation of evidence". It is now accepted that in an ordinary market with multiple players and diffused market shares, without collusion, participants tend to have their own pricing strategies and are unaffected by the price decisions of competitors. They will thus act unilaterally to increase their consumer base and maximize profit. However, in an oligopolistic market, with a lesser number of players, participants are affected by the conduct of other players. Each player does consider the prices offered by other players.[205] This economic interdependence is the starting point or the platform on which price parallelism is checked. This means that the structural characteristics of the market have to be analyzed to check the level of interdependence.[206] Chang Shu highlights the factors considered by competition economists to assess the degree of concentration in a market and highlight the factors taken into account by market participants. These factors have two benefits. Firstly, they act as screens to investigate cartels in an industry as the presence of these factors will create the likelihood of cartel existence. Secondly, they also save the enforcement agency from wasting its resources on the allegation of collusion in a market, which has minimal likelihood of cartelized behaviour.[207]

Areeda[208] characterizes the evidence for price fixing as interdependence evidence (i.e. it takes into account the motive for agreement [the agreement will benefit the conspirators and that the act, if done alone, will harm the self-interest of individual parties]), evidence found under traditional conspiracy (i.e. if there is an opportunity to collude followed by an overt act which is consistent with the common action plan),[209] evidence of poor economic performance and evidence of facilitating practices. These factors will be taken into account to consolidate or weaken the claim of collusion. It is suggested that market features, as discussed in the previous paragraph, are not sufficient and that factors laid out as interdependence evidence are essential to prove the interdependency of firms.[210]

In spite of all the discussion, the fact of the matter remains that there is no uniformity in competition cases where a single or set of plus factors have been prioritized. The application of plus factors has varied from case to case. It is commonly seen that in the absence of direct evidence, a bundle of plus factors is applied to prove or disprove that parallel pricing is the result of collusion.[211] In other words, since there is no hierarchy on the basis of evidentiary value to any plus factor, enforcement agencies are left to themselves to pick and choose in their attempt to distinguish cartel from conscious parallelism. As has been rightly put forward by a few scholars,[212] this gap will allow the cases to be decided based on the intuition of the court. If the judges believe that parallelism is a sign of possible cartelization, it will reduce the range of actions, which, when combined with parallel behaviour, proves the existence of an agreement. However, if the judges see price parallelism as a natural outcome of interdependence, there will be greater reluctance to appreciate the plus factors.

2.3.9.2 Horizontal market-sharing cartel

Market-sharing arrangement is an agreement to not compete for the competitor's customers or not to expand in another competitor's territory. A market-sharing arrangement between competitors is another form of hard-core cartel and is considered a *per se* violation where the enforcement agency need not prove the anti-competitive effect of the agreement in the market. In an arrangement like this, market participants tend to divide the market on the basis of geographical operation, type or number of customers, sale quotas, or a combination of them. Another mode of cartelization may be market share allocation between competitors. Commenting on cartel organization, Posner notes that if in a market, there is little or no change in the market share of the major players for a good amount of time, there are chances that competitors have divided the market either geographically or by sale quotas or by customer division.[213]

Division of the market eliminates the idea of competition among market players and deprives the customers of their available choices, forcing them to buy the same goods and services from a specific seller at an increased price as players have no fear of being undercut by competitors. It will also disallow the business units to reduce their unit cost of production as there will be no benefit of economies of scale.[214] Further, if all the units want to reduce their distribution costs or do not sell outside a specific category of customers, there is nothing that stops them from doing so. It is certainly not necessary to enter into an agreement with other competitors. It has been generally argued that since it is easier to monitor defection and the confusion over fixing a particular price is avoided, market-sharing cartel arrangements are much easier to enter and thus more common. Most of the jurisdictions treat market-sharing agreements as bad.[215] These agreements are seen as an alternative to price-fixing cartels.

Market division is a more convenient choice for collusion and is easier to monitor. Trade associations play a big role in monitoring through the dissemination of information.[216] One can differentiate customer allocation, territory allocation and market share allocation on the basis of essential requirements for the operation of the arrangement, the monitoring of the cartel (monitoring gets tricky when customers have a global presence or when there is a fluidity of territorial limitations), market disruptions (they can change the set of existing customers and call for alterations) that affect market division and the effect of outside entry (it may or may not call for re-allocation). It is argued that a cartel involving market share division is the most stable as, firstly, it does not depend on pre-cartel requirements of either customer profile information or information on territorial sale, and secondly, it is not affected by market disruptions caused by either change in customer demography or territorial changes. No re-allocation within the cartel is thus required to meet the challenge of outside entry of new players. Further, market share division can be implemented and monitored through information exchange or "a reporting framework" on the platform of a trade association.[217] The stability of collusion has been studied to show a direct relation between transportation costs,[218] market size,[219] and market symmetry.[220]

2.3.9.3 Agreement to limit or control production or supply

Markets are guided by the economic principle of demand and supply, which basically determines prices. However, when market participants join hands to control production or supply in order to create artificial scarcity, prices can be pushed up. This is a profit maximization technique adopted by members of a cartel. The Organization of the Petroleum Exporting Countries (OPEC) is a prime example of an output-restricting cartel. Price is thus fixed by the "market demand curve at the level of output chosen by the cartel". In a cartelized market, the behaviour of a few players is akin to a monopolist to produce less and charge more. In terms of effect, these arrangements are similar to price fixing agreements where the reduction in output leads to an increase in prices. Cartels of this nature prevent the natural expansion of more efficient market players and do not allow them to achieve economies of scale. Competition is lessened, and consumers pay higher prices.[221] Restrictions with respect to input capital investment, installed capacity, or output with respect to quantity, fixed quota and so on are employed to achieve the desired result. Restriction may also be with respect to technical development, like the imposition of restrictions for the usage of a particular machinery or manufacturing process.

These types of cartels are generally not very stable as there is a strong incentive to cheat. Profit can be maximized if the output is increased beyond what is agreed. Thus, there is always an element of sanction associated with such arrangements. Further, the decision on output restriction is not simple. In a market with identical players, there may be a distribution of output. However, in markets with players of different sizes, which is mostly the case, output division is complex. While the smaller players may want output division equally, it may not be agreed by larger firms, relying on historical data of output, which again might not be agreeable to newer firms that would advocate division on the basis of productive capacity. The arrangement entered between players is in the form of pooling whereby the business units which sell in excess of their quota make payments to the pool to compensate the market players who sell below their quota.

2.3.9.4 Horizontal bid rigging

Procurement of goods or services through tender and bidding process is a widely accepted practice across both private and public sectors. The entire process is supposed to be closed and secret so that one bidder does not know about the price quoted by another bidder. This is done to achieve a maximum result (procurement at the lowest cost possible) as the market players are expected to compete with each other to win the tender.

Bid rigging or collusive bidding is one of the four recognized hard-core cartels.[222] It involves an understanding or arrangement or an agreement between horizontal players or competitors to rig the bidding process with respect to any tender for the procurement of any goods or services. Collusive bidding is a profit maximization effort on the part of the players. Collusive bidders (bidding ring) may consist of all the bidders or might compose a part of all the participants. Collusive bidding is more common than it is generally expected. There is a greater tendency to form bidding rings as bid rigging ensures the transfer of wealth from the procurement agency to the bidding ring, making the bidders better off.

Collusion in bidding results in an increase in procurement costs. Since there is no incentive to innovate or provide quality products or services, the market as a whole is affected. Considering that collusion can increase the median price by approximately 25%,[223] it is important that the enforcement agencies develop efficient tools to detect bid-rigging cartels and not just rely on whistle-blowers (OECD 2013). As has been discussed in price-fixing cartels, both structural and behavioural factors are used as screens to detect collusion. A survey of cases decided by different enforcement agencies shows specific conducts of parties which have been taken as evidence of collusion, such as similar bids (identical prices or same handwriting or similar errors in submitted bid document), small and repeated number of bidders where one firm wins the bid every time, some bids (in comparison to the winning bid) being priced unreasonably high, drop in bid price with the entry of new players, submission of a bid at the same time and evidence of subcontracting. Markets which see regular invitations of bids are more likely to attract collusive behaviour.

Bidding rings face similar challenges as a cartel in terms of fear of detection and internal control. The most common path taken by bidding cartels is that of quoting identical bids. While similar or identical bids are easy to be agreed upon, there is a strong possibility of any member quoting a bid lower than others to win the bid. If we take a sample of cases, most enforcement agencies have moved beyond simply looking at identical behaviour in terms of bids and are employing more sophisticated economic tests to detect cartelization. Phantom bidding is more difficult to achieve as it requires greater communication between bidders to decide on the winner and terms and conditions to be put in the losing bids. The distribution of surplus achieved through the winner who quoted the maximum price depends on the type of bidding ring members. Thus, if the members are the same financially, surplus is allocated equally. Otherwise, if some members are stronger than others, the distribution of collusive surplus shall depend on specific firm characteristics.[224] Subcontracting is a popular mode in procurement contracts to distribute surplus.

TYPES OF BID RIGGING

> "Colluding bidders suppress their rivalry through the elimination of meaningful bids by all colluding bidders except for the ring bidder with the highest value. All other details and logistics of bidder collusion flow from this foundational principle of the ring".[225] It may take various forms:

- *Cover bidding*: This entails bidding to ensure that one of the members/bidders wins the bid. Bidding is done in such a fashion that a pre-decided bidder emerges as the ultimate winner. This is achieved through other bidders quoting higher than the pre-decided winner or putting in such terms and conditions within their own bid that it becomes unacceptable for the procurement agency.
- *Bid suppression*: The cartel members decide one of the colluding members is the winner, and then other members do not submit any bid or withdraw any previously submitted bid. This ensures that there is no one but the pre-decided member who wins the bid.
- *Bid rotation*: It is a scheme agreed upon by members where they agree to take turns to win the bid through any of the modes discussed earlier. Bid rotation is seen in the market where floatation of bids by the procurement body is frequent.
- *Market allocation*: It is a type of bid rigging where the members of the cartel divide geographical territories among themselves and pre-decide the winner. In tenders that are floated on the basis of the region – for example, a gas distribution agency – colluding members pre-decide as to which player will win tenders of a specific region. This is achieved through either cover bidding or bid suppression.
- *Subcontracting*: It is generally seen that cartelized bidding is followed by a series of contracts that are entered between the winning bidder and other members of the cartel. As soon as the predetermined bidder is successful in obtaining the bid, it subcontracts the bid to other members of the cartel. This also incentivizes participation in the cartel as it ensures some sort of profit sharing.

DETECTION AND SCREENS

It is unlikely that one test is devised to detect bid rigging or collusive bidding. The common point of all the tests that have been utilized by different economists is the identification of differences between competitive and collusive behaviour, which ultimately depend on factors like the nature of the product, characteristics of the market, rules of tender and so on. Detailed information on economic returns data would be required.[226] For instance, an increase in the number of bidders or competitors decreases the chances of collusion as there is less likelihood of consensus. Even where consensus is reached, chances of defection are high. Therefore, markets with a fewer number of bidders are more likely to see collusive behaviour. Certain features of the market, such as the availability of public information on the identity of the bidders and multiple contacts (e.g. the same group of bidders bidding together in other bids of other projects), increase the propensity to collude.

The OECD prioritized the enforcement against bid rigging from 1998 itself.[227] The 2009 Guidelines attempted to create a structure for member states to detect and punish bid-rigging cartels. It consisted of methods of detection and recommended actions. In order to minimize bid rigging, it also put forward a checklist to design procurement bids.[228] In 2012, the OECD issued recommendations for the governments highlighting the issue of collusive bidding in public procurements and asked them to assess their rules related to public procurement to minimize the menace of bid rigging.[229] The 2012 recommendations asked the governments to ensure that their procurement officers are trained to suspect collusive behaviour of bidders. It also favoured the governments to establish coordination between the procurement agencies and the competition regulator. It further recommended that the member states consider making the detection of cartels a statutory duty of procurement officers. More importantly, it issued a "checklist for designing the procurement process to reduce risks of bid rigging".[230] The 2015 Council Recommendations emphasized on effective designing of procurement bids.

Per the OECD, public procurement constitutes the largest part of state spending. Therefore, any form of collusion in the bidding process results in the massive loss of wealth for the government that would have been otherwise spent on social welfare schemes.[231] The OECD, in its concept paper, has also highlighted the characteristics of markets prone to collusive bidding, having factors such as a small number of competitors, high entry barriers, homogenous products, stable demand, presence of active trade associations, high bidding frequency and low innovation.[232] The following list is a set of compiled "red flags" that have been identified by competition regulators across the world as a guide for procurement agencies.[233]

- Unusual pricing pattern of bidders. (Some bids are priced much higher than others or published price lists or their own bids in comparison to previous bids with similar specifications.)
- Unreasonable conditions in some bids.
- Signs of selective geographic bidding or non-bidding in certain locations.
- Fall in the number of bidders or dropping out of any prominent bidder.

- High regularity of one bidder winning the bid.
- Evidence of subcontracting.
- Evidence of exchange of price information or prior discussion/meeting of bidders.
- Identical bids.
- Joint tendering.
- Tender boycott.
- Similar appearance of the bids which can be identified by the usage of language, pricing, errors, miscalculations, last-minute adjustments and the like.
- Competitors submitting the bid together.
- References to suggested industry prices or industry price schedules.

The competition regulators also prescribe a list of dos for procurement agencies to minimize collusion in bidding.[234]

2.3.10 Treatment of cartels under law

2.3.10.1 Cartels and the per se *rule*

The *per se* rule is generally applied to hard-core cartels as they are considered to be the most pernicious violators of competition law with economically proven harmful effects. It simply means that the collusive action, if proven, will be enough to impose liability, and no harmful effects need to be proved. There are no redeeming virtues due to which the law does not require an enquiry into the reasonableness of the agreement. *Per se* rule has been advocated both on the basis of economic reliability and administrative or judicial convenience. On the one hand, it saves competition authorities from the detailed and expensive inquiry into the economic effects of the agreement. On the other hand, it brings the certainty of judicial action and consequences for the enterprises. The *per se* rule sends out a clear signal that certain behaviours would not be tolerated (also referred to as "bright line rule"[235]). Further, the rule minimizes type 1 (discouraging pro-competitive agreements) and type 2 errors (under-enforcement of anti-competitive agreements).[236]

HORIZONTAL AGREEMENTS AND RULE OF REASON

Not all horizontal agreements are *per se* bad. Anti-competitive agreements outside the four types of internationally recognized hard-core cartels have seen a "rule of reason" assessment.[237] There are some collaborative agreements, like joint marketing, joint purchasing and joint ventures, that may enhance efficiency and are good for the market and are thus tested under the "rule of reason" test. For instance, a joint-marketing agreement to sell, distribute, or market goods jointly may reduce the cost. However, marketing collaborations can involve agreements on price, output, or other competitively significant variables, resulting in competitive harm.[238] An assessment thus needs to be done if there is any net benefit to consumers. Similarly, joint purchasing might help in getting larger discounts from suppliers or reduction of transportation or distribution costs or may also facilitate collusion "through standardizing participants" costs.[239] The other type of horizontal arrangement is research and development collaboration, which will allow firms to learn from each other and produce better products. However, when these collaborations result in the imposition of restrictions on the exploitation of products or services, they have to be checked. Similarly, horizontal information sharing arrangements are not *per se* bad, but when used by firms to collude to maximize profit by entering into the domain of hard-core cartel activity, they will be held illegal. The exchange of sensitive information of variables like strategy, pricing, production and distribution data, and capacity utilization may be seen as means to collude. Similarly, while joint ventures are desired to achieve economies of scale and increase allocative and productive efficiency, the exemption will not be extended if the joint venture itself indulges in creating outcomes like hard-core cartels.

2.4 Development of Indian competition law and anti-cartel regime

India's economic policies post-independence were guided by the twin objectives of self-reliance and social justice. India chose a middle path for its economic model, which was neither a completely market-driven economy, like that of the USA, nor a socialist economy, like that of the then USSR. This model of mixed economy (referred to as Nehruvian socialism) was tilted more towards socialist ideas. While there was scope for private businesses, the government secured for itself strategic sectors like mining, heavy industries, electricity and railways. The state was both the regulator and a market participant.[240] The idea was to achieve inclusive growth and social justice.[241] The Industrial Policy of 1956 demarcated sectors where the public sector or the state would have prominence with minimal presence of the private sector. The government was the key driver for the flow of funds as it controlled all the major financial institutions. This phase saw both nationalization and the creation of important institutions. These institutions became instruments of state policies as they ensured that the capital flowed in the desired direction. This phase also saw legislative reforms to boost investor confidence. The Monopolies and Restrictive Trade Practices Act of 1969 (MRTP Act, 1969) was one of those legislations.

Financial and internal crises allowed the then prime minister Indira Gandhi to reinforce the public sector, a move which was then seen as pro-poor. The Appointment of the Monopolies Commission and the ban on the entry of multinational corporations in consumer goods can be understood in the same light.[242] Major aspects of the private businesses, like generation of capital, expansion, determination of price, foreign capital and ownership were heavily regulated. The permit system of the government (also called the License Raj) intended to channel resources towards sectors of priority actually resulted in slowing down the economy. Licenses acted as entry barriers to the market. The licenses were given to big corporations as they could secure better funding from financial institutions. With better funding options, resources, foreign collaborations and experiential knowledge, bigger corporations could bag most of the licenses, thus leading to a concentration of economic power in a few hands. High tariffs, limitations on foreign investment, and availability of funds added to the control mechanism, which also led "to the emergence of monopolistic industries and consequently to their indulging in restrictive trade practices".[243] The disproportionate growth and concentration of economic power were also highlighted by multiple committees formed by the government to review the industrial growth. The MRTP Act, 1969, in the later years, was one of the products of a controlled economy enacted to prevent the concentration of economic power. The report which led to the enactment of the MRTP Act, 1969, strongly believed that the concentration of market power was the root cause of market abuses and exploitative practices.[244] The Foreign Exchange Regulation Act (FERA) of 1973, which ensured an upper limit on foreign ownership, is another such example. The market did suffer as a lack of competition brought down its efficiency. The slow growth of the economy with depleting foreign reserves forced the government to introduce reforms.

India had to make changes to its existing economic policies in light of the impending financial crisis in the late 1980s. A string of changes brought in numerous policy shifts. The reform, otherwise known as the LPG model (liberalization, privatization, globalization), was starkly different from the "command and control" model followed until then. The new economic model increased the role of market forces and decreased the role of government. The reforms were market-oriented and included macroeconomic stabilization, de-licensing of industries, trade liberalization, currency reforms, reduction in subsidies, financial/capital/banking sector reforms, privatization and disinvestment in public sector units, tax reforms and corporate law reforms.[245] This led to the reorientation of the existing institutions and the creation of new organizations to respond to a reformed market scenario. Pre-reform legislations like the MRTP Act, 1969 (replaced by Competition Act, 2002); FERA, 1973 (replaced by the Foreign Exchange Management Act [FEMA] 1999); and Capital Issues (Control) Act, 1947 (replaced by Securities Exchange Board of India Act [SEBI], 1992) were found to be inadequate and were therefore replaced by newer legislations.

2.4.1 Treatment of cartels under the MRTP Act, 1969

The MRTP Act, 1969, was passed to address the issue of concentration of economic power in a few hands and to prevent certain restrictive and harmful business practices.[246] Its preamble outlined three objectives: prevention of concentration of economic power (which was not defined in the original format), control of monopolies and prohibition of monopolistic and restrictive trade practices. It was guided by "behavioural and reformist doctrines". The Monopolies Inquiries Commission Report (1965) considered the monopolies and restrictive trade practices as functions of "concentration of economic power", thus treating it as the central problem. The basic feature underlying the entire stature was prioritizing public interest, striving for the common good and keeping a check on the economic system to prevent the concentration of economic power.[247]

The MRTP Act, 1969, did not specifically define "cartel" but implicitly covered cartels under Section 33 (1) (d). The Indian Supreme Court, in the case of the Hindustan Development Corporation,[248] described cartels as an association formed to obtain monopolistic power. Considering the harmful effects of a cartel, the Apex Court categorized it as an "unfair trade practice". Cartels were declared to be *per se* against the public interest. The MRTP Commission (MRTPC) interpreted this decision to extend the definition of "cartel" to "entail all sorts of combinations, whether by producers or otherwise for the purposes of restrictive trade practices".[249] Three essential ingredients were insisted to prove the existence of cartels: parity of prices, specific agreement by way of a concerted action suggesting conspiracy and objective to gain monopoly or restrict or eliminate competition.[250] Per the MRTPC, "positive contact between parties" must be established to prove prior meeting of minds. Even though direct evidence is not generally available, circumstantial evidence must conclusively prove the existence of a cartel. Price parallelism in itself was held to be not problematic, and the same could be attributed to the economic forces of an oligopolistic market.[251]

Section 33 (1) (d) was wide enough to cover all types of collective agreements determining different aspects of trade activities, including determination of product or service, grant of discounts or commissions or warranties and market sharing. The existence of an express agreement between competitors was not particularly required to prove collusion, and the same could be inferred from the conduct of the parties and surrounding circumstances. Intention to collude in restraint of trade was required to be proved to take any action. Even though the statute did not define cartels, the idea of interpreting oligopolistic markets or oligopolistic interdependence existed.[252] Prices moved in parallel by smaller companies imitating the price leader in the standard market was not enough to conclude collusion.[253] Similarly, price movements were seen in the light of market factors. Therefore, where the price of the product synchronized with the price increase of the raw material, collusion was not inferred. Hence, mere price parallelism and simultaneous price increase, in the absence of concrete evidence, were not enough to prove a violation of the section.[254] Market factors that breed cartelization were taken into account by the MRTPC. A combination of behavioural, market and circumstantial pieces of evidence were required to prove cartelization. Most of the cartel cases between 1969 to 1991 related to price fixing, and there were very few cases of market sharing, bid rigging, or output restriction.[255] In *Bengal Tools*,[256] for instance, the MRTPC had to decide the case related to bid rigging. The parties in question had quoted identical bid rates despite there being differences in individual cost of production. Even though there was no concrete evidence to prove prior meeting of minds, there was enough circumstantial evidence to shift the burden of proof to the opposite side to disprove the existence of a cartel. A cease-and-desist order was passed by the MRTPC, which held that, while the burden to prove collusion is on the director general (DG), the burden shifts to the opposite party as soon as the DG produces evidence which *prima facie* gives rise to the presumption in his favour. Therefore, when it was reported that the parties had quoted identical rates despite the difference in cost of production, the burden shifted to the opposite side to rebut the presumption by producing evidence in justification of the identical price quoted.[257]

In *Excel Industries*,[258] the Food Corporation of India (FCI) alleged cartelization among the manufacturers of aluminium phosphide (ALP) tablets by quoting identical prices in the tender floated by it for procurement of ALP tablets. It was contended by the opposite parties that the peculiar conditions of the market, like there being only four manufacturers, the FCI being the biggest procurer and none of the manufacturers being as big enough to satisfy the entire tender quantity, necessitated cooperation among the bidders. Identical quotes were attributed to a history of joint meetings and the exchange of information with the government. The MRTPC, however, used the minutes of the joint meetings to conclude that the identical quotes were a result of a prior meeting of minds.[259] The MRTPC held the opposite parties to have entered into restrictive trade practices as envisaged under Section 2 (1) (o) and also guilty of violating Section 33 (1) (d) of the Act. Considering the negative impact of the cartel on the public benefit of gateways under Section 38 (1) was also refused despite accepting the fact that the FCI was the single largest procurer.

In *Newspaper* cases,[260] it was alleged that the companies had, in concert, increased the prices of newspapers despite the substantial reduction in the number of pages. Cease-and-desist orders were passed in all four cases. The MRTPC, in some cases, also looked at the commercial nature of the alleged collusion and let it pass as it was not prejudicial to public interest.[261]

The MRTPC only had the powers to pass cease-and-desist orders or to permit the defendants to amend the agreement so that it was no more prejudicial to public interest. The MRTPC, on occasions, deemed written statements from the parties alleged to be involved in cartelization sufficient to not proceed with inquiry.[262] The MRTP Act, 1969, can be argued as not being adequately armed to deal with the situation of cartels.[263] Only when the parties continued to indulge in restrictive practices could the MRTPC punish such members under Section 50 for contravention of its orders under Section 31 and 37 of the MRTP Act, 1969. It is not that the MRTPC was not able to have any effect. The breaking of the tyre cartel in the 1970s is a good example.[264] However, given the fact that the MRTPC did not have any power to punish, it had to be content with assurances from opposite parties even though the allegations post these assurances did not subside.[265] It was also able to pass orders against trade associations that were instrumental in anti-competitive practices, including fixing prices,[266] restricting supply, imposing commissions,[267] and allocating the market.[268] Further, the MRTP Act, 1969, did not confer extraterritorial jurisdiction to MRTPC which seriously impaired its powers to bust international cartels.[269] The Supreme Court of India in the *Glass Manufacturers* case categorically held that the MRTP Act, 1969, did not confer extraterritorial jurisdiction, and the MRTPC could only exercise jurisdiction when the goods were actually imported into India.[270]

Detection and punishment of cartels did not figure as one of the prime priorities of the MRTPC, which is also evident from the fact that between 1991 to 2007, there were only seven reported cartel cases. Most of the cases were dismissed for lack of evidence.[271]

2.4.2 Treatment of cartels under the Competition Act, 2002

The Indian Competition Act was passed in 2002 (Act) to replace the obsolete MRTP Act, 1969, which was found inadequate to meet the requirements of a new liberalized and globalized market. The Act has clearly laid out objectives and is centred towards preventing practices that cause an appreciable adverse effect on competition (AAEC) by regulating three aspects of market behaviour – anti-competitive agreements, abuse of dominant position and mergers and acquisitions.

Section 3 of the Act states that enterprises, persons or associations of enterprises or persons, including cartels, shall not enter into agreements in respect of production, supply, distribution, storage, acquisition, or control of goods or provision of services, which cause or are likely to cause an AAEC in India. Such agreements would consequently be considered void. The species of agreement which would be considered to have an AAEC would be those agreements which directly or indirectly determine sale or purchase prices; limit or control production, supply, markets, technical development, investment, or provision of services; or share the market or source of production or provision of services by allocation of *inter alia* geographical area of the market, nature of goods or number of customers, or any other similar way that directly or indirectly result in bid rigging or collusive bidding.

Cartels which were not defined under the MRTP Act, 1969, find a place under Section 2 (c) of the Act. There is no public interest gateway for cartels in the new statute. It remains an inclusive definition to include all such agreements between business units or associations that, through their agreement, limit or control production, fix prices and divide the market for the production, supply, distribution, or sale of goods or services. Cartels are prohibited under Section 3 (3) of the Act and are presumed to have an AAEC. The presumption stated in Section 3 (3) is a rebuttable one, and in instances where an inquiry is conducted by the Competition Commission of India (CCI), the burden of proof lies with the parties to such agreement to establish that there exists no possibility of such agreement of causing or the likelihood of causing an AAEC in India. Unlike the MRTPC, the CCI under Section 27 of the Act is empowered to impose a penalty on cartel members within the upper ceiling prescribed in the section. Indian law, unlike that of the US or the UK does not envisage criminal sanctions for cartel activity.

2.4.2.1 *Standard of proof and use of evidence*

CCI has on innumerable occasions held that as cartels are categorized as a civil offence under the Act, the standard of proving the violation beyond reasonable doubt does not apply to Section 3 violations. The definition of "agreement" is inclusive and is not restricted only to documented and written agreement among the parties. Thus, the CCI is not impeded from using circumstantial evidence for making inquiries into the act, conduct and behaviour of market participants.[272] In the *Sugar Mills* case,[273] the CCI laid down the standard of proof required in cartel cases and held that (i) conclusive proof of meeting of minds is required, (ii) there must be evidence of the alleged cartel participants having met and decided to take concerted action and (iii) the concerted action must have been implemented. Parallel behaviour in prices, dispatch and supply, accompanied by some other factors indicating coordinated behaviour among the firms, may become a basis for finding contravention or otherwise of the provisions relating to anti-competitive agreement of the Act.[274] Among a set of circumstantial pieces of evidence, evidence of communication among the participants to an anti-competitive agreement may give an important clue for establishing any contravention. Communication evidence might prove that contravening parties met and communicated with each other to determine their future or present behaviour. Price parallelism that is not the result of pure oligopolistic behaviour, but collusion will be held to be bad in law.[275]

Indian case laws do not seem to lay down a uniform approach when it comes to the appreciation of evidence. The degree of reliance on different sets of circumstantial evidence has varied. In the absence of direct evidence, the CCI has oscillated between unequivocal establishing of an agreement[276] and inference of an agreement based on evidence.[277] The next chapters of the book assess in detail the anti-cartel enforcement in India.

Notes

1 House of Lords Debate during passage of Competition Act, 1998 cited in Mark Furse, Competition Law of EC and UK (Oxford University Press, 6th ed., 2008).

2 Competition Commission of India v. Sail, (2010) 10 SCC 744, 1–7.

3 Massimo Mota, *Competition Policy: Theory and Practice* (Cambridge University Press, 2004).
4 Philip Kotler, *Principles of Marketing* (Pearson, 17th ed., 2017).
5 Richard Whish and David Bailey, Competition Law (Oxford University Press, 9th ed., 2018), p. 4.
6 Para 4.1.2, Merger Assessment Guidelines of the UK Office of Fair Trading and Competition Commission, CC2 revised and OFT 1254, September 2010.
7 Joe S. Bain, *Relation of the Profit Rate to Industry Concentration: American Manufacturing, 1936–1940*, 65 Quarterly Journal of Economics 293–324 (1951).
8 Dennis Carlton and Jeffrey Perloff, *Modern Industrial Organisation* (Addison-Wesley Longman Inc, 4th ed.) 1999.
9 Robert H. Bork, *The Antitrust Paradox: A Policy at War with Itself* (Basic Books, 1978).
10 *The Objectives of Competition Law and Policy*, OECD Global Forum on Competition CCNM/GF/COMP (2003) 3, p. 9.
11 Thomas J. Horton, *Unravelling the Chicago/Harvard Antitrust Double Helix: Applying Evolutionary Theory to Guard Competitors and Revive Antitrust Jury Trials*, 41 (4) University of Baltimore Law Review 51 (2012).
12 Competition Counts: How Consumers Win when Businesses Compete, US Federal Trade Commission, p. 6.
13 Philip Lowe, *Preserving and Promoting Competition: A European Response*, Competition Policy Newsletter of the European Commission 5 (2006).
14 Adam Smith, *An Inquiry into the Nature and Causes of the Wealth of Nations* (The Modern Library, E. Cannan ed., 1937).
15 John M. Clark, *Toward a Concept of Workable Competition*, 30 (2) The American Economic Review 241 (1940) cited in R. S. Khemani and David M. Shapiro, *Glossary of Industrial Organisation Economics and Competition Law*, Directorate for Financial, Fiscal and Enterprise Affairs, OECD, 1993, www.oecd.org/regreform/sectors/2376087.pdf (last accessed on Dec. 10, 2021).
16 Alison Jones and Brenda Sufrin, *EU Competition Law: Text, Cases, and Materials* (Oxford University Press, 7th ed., 2007), Section 4 (A).
17 Jonathan Faull and Ali Nikpay (eds.). *The EU Law of Competition* (Oxford University Press, 2nd ed., 2007) 173–189.
18 *Ibid.*
19 *Supra note* 16.
20 Thomas A. Piraino Jr., *Reconciling the Harvard and Chicago Schools: A New Antitrust Approach for the 21st Century*, 82 (2) Indiana Law Journal 346.
21 Herbert Hovenkamp, *The Antitrust Enterprise, Principle and Execution* (Harvard University Press, 2005) p. 35–38.
22 377 U.S. 271 (1964).
23 *Supra note* 20 at 349.
24 *Supra note* 20 at 350.
25 Harold Demesetz, *'Industry Structure, Market Rivalry, and Public Policy'*, 16 Journal of Law & Economics 1–3 (1973).
26 *Supra note* 24.
27 *Supra note* 16 at 21.
28 *Supra note* 20 at 350.
29 *Supra note* 9 at 90–91.
30 *Ibid.*
31 *Supra note* 20.
32 441 U.S. 1 (1979).
33 *In re Boeing Co.*, [1997–2001 FTC Complaints & Orders Transfer Binder] Trade Reg. Rep. (CCH) 24, 295 (July 1, 1997).

34 Arizona v. Maricopa County Med. Society, 457 U.S. 332, 343 (1982).
35 Thomas A. Piraino, Jr., *A Proposed Antitrust Approach to Collaborations Among Competitors*, 86 IOWA Law Review (2001) p. 709.
36 *Supra note* 20 at Section B (i).
37 David Evans and Jorge Padilla, *Designing Antitrust Rules for Assessing Unilateral Practices: A Neo-Chicago Approach*, 72 University of Chicago Law Review 73–75 (2005).
38 William Comanor, *Strategic Behaviour and Anti-trust Analysis,* 74 (2) The American Economic Review 372–376 (1984).
39 *Supra note* 20 at Section B (ii).
40 Oliver Budzinski, *Monoculture versus Diversity in Competition Economics*, Marburger Volkswirtschaftliche Beiträge 7 (2007).
41 *Supra note* 20 at 364.
42 Saif Ahmad Al Badwawi, *Does the New Competition Law Ensure Fair Competition in the UAE?*, Thesis Paper at the Southampton Solent University, 38.
43 *Ibid.*
44 Joshua Wright, *Abandoning Antitrust's Chicago Obsession: The Case for Evidence-Based Antitrust* 78 Antitrust Law Journal 241, 244 (2012).
45 Vinod Dhall, Competition Law and Consumer Protection – Insight into their Interrelationship, The effects of anti-competitive business practices on developing countries and their development prospects (Hassan Qaqaya & G. Lipimile ed.), UNCTAD, 2008, http://unctad.org/en/Docs/ditcclp20082_en.pdf. (last accessed on Dec. 10, 2021).
46 Ignacio Herrera Anchustegui, *Competition Law through an Ordoliberal Lens*, Oslo Law Review 160 (2015).
47 *Supra note* 40 at 15.
48 *Ibid* at 16.
49 Maurice E. Stucke, *Is Competition Always Good?* 1 (1) Journal of Antitrust Enforcement 162–197 (2013).
50 *Supra note* 14.
51 *Economic Growth and Productivity*, OECD www.internationalcompetitionnetwork.org/workinggroups/current/advocacy/benefits/messages/productivity.aspx. (last accessed on Dec. 10, 2021).
52 Marcin Przybyla and Roma Moreno, *Does Product Market Competition Reduce Inflation?* Working Paper Series, No. 453, European Central Bank, 2005 (July 2021) www.ecb.europa.eu/pub/pdf/scpwps/ecbwp453.pdf.
53 *Supra note* 20 at 379.
54 Richard A. Posner, *The Chicago School of Antitrust Analysis*, 127 UPENN Law Review 932 (1979).
55 George Stigler, *A Theory of Oligopoly*, 72 (1) Journal of Political Economy 44–61 (1964).
56 Adam Triggs and Andrew Leigh, *A Giant Problem: The Influence of the Chicago School on Australian Competition Law, Economic Dynamism and Inequality*, 47 (4) Federal Law Review 697 (2019).
57 Maurice Guerrin and Georgios Kyriazis, *Cartels: Proof and Procedural Issues*, 16 (2) Fordham International Law Journal 266 (1992).
58 *Ibid.*
59 The Court of Justice has defined concerted practice as 'a form of co-ordination between undertakings, which, without having been taken to the stage where an agreement properly so-called has been concluded, knowingly substitutes for the risks of competition, practical cooperation between them which leads to conditions of competition which do not correspond to the normal conditions of the market'. Cooperatieve vereniging 'Suiker Unie' UA v. Commission, Joined

Cases 40–48, 50, 54–56, 111, 113'& 114/73, [1975] E.C.R. 1663, 1916, 26–27, [1976] 1 C.M.L.R. 295, 348
60 *Supra note* 5 at 1–5
61 Simon Bishop and Mike Walker, *The Economics of EC Competition Law: Concepts Application and Measurement* (3rd ed., Sweet & Maxwell, 2010).
62 Article 101, TFEU; Section 1, Sherman Act, 1890.
63 *Supra note* 3.
64 Luke Garrod and Matthew Olczak, *Explicit v. Tacit Collusion: The Effects of Firm Numbers and Asymmetries*, 56 (C) International Journal of Industrial Organization 1–25 (2018).
65 Id. See also, Stephen Davies and Matthew Olczak, *Tacit versus Overt Collusion Firm Asymmetries and Numbers: What's the Evidence?* 4 (2) Competition Policy International 175–200 (2008).
66 Richard Posner, *A Statistical Study of Antitrust Enforcement*, 13 (2) Journal of Law and Economics 365–419 (1970).
67 George Hay and Daniel Kelley, *An Empirical Survey of Price Fixing Conspiracies,* 17 (1) Journal of Law and Economics 13–38 (1974).
68 *Supra note* 64.
69 *Ibid.*
70 Donald Turner, The Definition of Agreement under the Sherman Act: Conscious Parallelism and Refusal to Deal, 75 (N4) Harvard Law Review 661 (1962).
71 Richard Posner, *Oligopoly and the Antitrust Laws: A Suggested Approach*, 21 Stanford Law Review1564 (1969).
72 Jaime E.C. Mays, *The Limitations on the Punishability of Tacit Collusion in EU Competition Law*, 13 Rev. Derecho Competencia. Bogotá (Colombia) 195–240 (2017), https://centrocedec.files.wordpress.com/2018/03/7-castro-195-2401.pdf (last accessed on Dec. 10, 2021).
73 ICI v. Commission, Cases 48, 49, 51–57/69 [1972].
74 Zuchner v. Bayerische Vereinsbank AG (1981) ECR 2021.
75 Mario Monti, Fighting Cartels Why and How? Why should we be concerned with cartels and collusive behaviour?, Speech at the 3rd Nordic Competition Policy Conference, Stockholm 2000.
76 *Supra note* 16 at 643.
77 Cédric Argenton, Damien Geradin and Andreas Stephan, *EU Cartel Law and Economics* 28 (Oxford Competition Law, 2020).
78 Roger Van den Bergh and Peter Camesasca, *European Competition Law and Economics: A Comparative Perspective* 5.2.1.2 (Sweet & Maxwell, 2nd ed., 2006).
79 Commission, XXXIInd Report on Competition Policy (2002), part 26.
80 Ioannis Lionos, *Valentine Korah, and Paolo Siciliani, Competition Law: Analysis, Cases, & Materials* 696 (Oxford University Press, 2019).
81 *The Impact of Cartels on the Poor*, Intergovernmental Group of Experts on Competition Law and Policy, Thirteenth session, Geneva, July 2013, TD/B/C.I/CLP/24/Rev.1 http://unctad.org/meetings/en/SessionalDocuments/ciclpd24rev1_en.pdf (last accessed on Dec. 10, 2021)]
82 John M. Connor, *The Private International Cartels (PIC) Data Set: Guide and Summary Statistics, 1990–2013* (August 9, 2014) (June 2018) SSRN: https://ssrn.com/abstract=2478271 (last accessed on Dec. 10, 2021).
83 *Hard Core Cartels*, OECD Publications 2000, www.oecd.org/daf/competition/cartels/2752129.pdf (last accessed on Dec. 10, 2021). *See also*, Mario Monti, *Why Should we be Concerned with Cartels and collusive Behaviour?* In FIGHTING CARTELS, (Konkurrensverket, Swedish Competition Authority), 2001, www.konkurrensverket.se/globalassets/english/publications-and-decisions/fighting-cartels.pdf. (last accessed on Dec. 10, 2021)

84 Andrea Günster et al., *Do Cartels Undermine Economic Efficiency?* (unreported 2011), www.aeaweb.org/conference/2012/retrieve.php?pdfid=510 (last accessed on Dec. 10, 2021).
85 Martijn A. Han, Maarten P. Schinkel and Jan Tuinstra, *The Overcharge as a Measure for Antitrust Damages*, Amsterdam Center for Law & Economics, Working Paper 8 (2008) https://ec.europa.eu/competition/antitrust/actions-damages/schinkel.pdf (last accessed on Dec. 10, 2021).
86 *Supra note* 81.
87 *Global Economic Prospects and the Developing Countries*, The International Bank for Reconstruction and Development 101 (2003), http://siteresources.worldbank.org/INTGEP/Resources/335315-1257200391829/gep2003complete.pdf.
88 Simon Evenett, Julian Clark and Frederic Jenny, *Cartels and Collusion in Developing Countries: Lessons from Empirical Evidence*, 29 World Competition 109 (2006).
89 *Fighting Cartels in Public Procurement*, OECD (2008), www.oecd.org/daf/competition/cartels/41505296.pdf (last accessed on Dec. 10, 2021).
90 *Supra note* 81.
91 *Supra note* 81.
92 George Stocking and Myron W. Watkins, *Cartels in Action* (The Twentieth Century Fund 1946).
93 *Glossary of Terms used in EU Competition Policy, European Commission, Brussels 2002*, http://europa.eu.int/comm/competition/publications/glossary_en.pdf (last accessed on Dec. 10, 2021).
94 Chapter I, UK Competition Act, 1998.
95 *Recommendation of the OECD Council Concerning Effective Action against Hard Core Cartels*, OECD, March 1998, C (98) 35/FINAL – C/M (98) 7/PROV, www.oecd.org/daf/competition/2350130.pdf (last accessed on Dec. 10, 2021).
96 Sin Lai, *Defining and Regulating Hard Core Cartels in Hong Kong: Agency Reconciling the Divergence between Legislators and International Standard*, 20 (4) University of Pennsylvania Journal of Business Law (2018).
97 *Defining Hard Core Cartel Conduct Effective Institutions Effective Penalties, 1 Building Blocks for Effective Anti-Cartel Regimes*, Vol. 1, ICN Working Group on Cartels, ICN 4th Annual Conference, Germany 6–8 June 2005, www.internationalcompetitionnetwork.org/uploads/library/doc346.pdf (last accessed on Dec. 10, 2021).
98 Michael Hellwig and Kai Hüschelrath, *When do Firms Leave Cartels? Determinants and the Impact on Cartel Survival*, Discussion Paper No. 17–002, Centre for European Economic Research, ftp://ftp.zew.de/pub/zew-docs/dp/dp17002.pdf (last accessed on Dec. 10, 2021).
99 Paul Grout and Silvia Sonderegger, *Predicting Cartels,* Office of Fair Trading, Economic discussion paper (2005), https://research-information.bris.ac.uk/en/publications/predicting-cartels-oft-773 (last accessed on Dec. 10, 2021).
100 *Ibid.*
101 Margaret Levenstein and Valerie Y. Suslow, *What Determines Cartel Success?* 44 (1) Journal of Economic Literature 43–95 (2006).
102 *Supra note 99.*
103 Carl Shapiro, Theories of Oligopoly Behavior, in Richard Schmalensee and R. Willig (eds), *Handbook of Industrial Organization* 329–414 (Elsevier, 1st ed., 1989).
104 Olivier Bertrand and Fabrice Lumineau, *Partners in Crime: The Effects of Diversity on the Longevity of Cartels*, 59 (3) Academy of Management Journal 983 (2016).

105 Oindrila De, *Analysis of Cartel Duration: Evidence from EC Prosecuted Cartels,* 17 International Journal of the Economics of Business 33–65 (2010).
106 CCI (2006), Study of Cartel Case Laws in Select Jurisdictions, at 1, CUTS International, which details the importance of regular meetings, including chance meetings at a conference of industry executives, in evidencing communication and collusion; *See also*, R.R. Lokesh, *The Anti-Competitive Effect of Price Controls: Study of the Indian Pharmaceutical Industry*, 43 (2) World Competition 295 (2020), which looks at regular stakeholder meetings conducted by the government in relation to setting of a price-ceiling as a 'plus factor' for concluding that there was tacit collusion.
107 *Supra note* 80 at 1420.
108 Antoine Cplombani, Jindrich Kloub and Ewoud Sakkers, Part II: Specific Practices, in Faull and Nikpay (eds), *The EU Law Competition* (Oxford Competition Law, 3rd ed., 2014) 1073.
109 Commission decision relating to a proceeding under Article 81 of the EC Treaty, Case COMP/36.571, 2004.
110 Commission Decision relating to a proceeding under Article 81 of the Treaty and Article 53 of the EEA Agreement, Case COMP/39.396.
111 David Bailey and Laura Elizabeth John, Ch 5: Cartels, in Bellamy and Child (eds), *European Union Law of Competition* (Oxford Competition Law, 8th ed., 2018) para 5.005.
112 James Griffin, Previous Cartel Experience: Any Lessons for OPEC? in Lawrence R. Klein and Jamie Marquez, *Economics in Theory and Practice: An Eclectic Approach* (Kluwer Academic Publishers, 1989).
113 Edward J. Green and Robert H. Porter, *Non-cooperative Collusion under Imperfect Price Information,* 52 (1) Econometrica 87–100 (1984).
114 Joe Harrington, *Some Thoughts on Why Certain Markets are More Susceptible to Collusion*, OECD Global Forum on Competition – "Serial Offenders", U. of Penn. – Wharton (October 2015) www.oecd.org/competition/globalforum/Harrington_OECD_10%2015.pdf (last accessed on Dec. 10, 2021).
115 *Ibid.*
116 Jelle D. Jaspers, *Managing Cartels: How Cartel Participants Create Stability in the Absence of Law*, 23 European Journal on Criminal Policy and Research 319 (2017).
117 Massimo Motta and M. Polo, *Leniency Programs and Cartel Prosecution*, 21 (3) International Journal of Industrial Organization 347–379 (2003).
118 Regina Robson, *Crime and Punishment: Rehabilitating Retribution as a Justification for Organizational Criminal Activity*, 47 American Business Law Journal 109–144 (2010).
119 Robert Marshall and Leslie Marx, *The Economics of Collusion* (MIT Press, 2012).
120 Herbert Hovenkamp and Christopher R. Leslie, *The Firm as Cartel Manager*, 64 (3) Vanderbilt Law Review 813 (2011) in Sandra Marco Colino ed., *1 Cartels and Anti-Competitive Agreements* (Ashgate Publishing, 2012).
121 Emilie Dargaud and Armel Jacques, *Hidden Collusion by Decentralization: Firm Organization and Antitrust Policy*, Journal of Economics (2015) 153–176.
122 *Supra note* 120.
123 *Supra note* 116.
124 G. Stigler, *Price and Non-price Competition*, Journal of Political Economy 149–154 (1968).
125 *Supra note* 116.
126 Joseph E. Harrington and Andrzej Skrzypacz, *Private Monitoring and Communication in Cartels: Explaining Recent Collusive Practices*, American Economic Review 101 (October 2011) 1–25.

127 Id.
128 Imperial Chemical Industries Ltd. v. Commission (Dyestuffs) [1972] ECR 619.
129 Article 101 (1), TFEU.
130 C-32/78 and 36–82/78 BMW Belgium v. Commission of the European Communities [1979] ECR 2435.
131 T-148/89 Trefilenrope SARL v. Commission [1995] ECR II-1063.
132 *Prosecuting Cartels without Direct Evidence of Agreement*, OECD (2007), www.oecd.org/daf/competition/cartels/38704302.pdf (last accessed on Dec. 10, 2021).
133 *Supra note* 5.
134 Alison Jones, *The Boundaries of an Undertaking in EU Competition Law*, 8 (2) European Competition Journal 301 (2012).
135 Viho Europe BV v. Commission [1996] ECR 1–5457.
136 Para 11, Guidelines on the Applicability of Article 101 TFEU to Horizontal Cooperation Agreements, Official Journal C 11 of 14 January 2011.
137 Akzo Nobel NV v. Commission [2007] ECR II-000. See also, Wouter P. J. Wils, *The Undertaking as a Subject of EC Competition Law and the Imputation of Infringements to Natural or Legal Persons*, 25 European Law Review 103 (2000).
138 Case 107/82 AEG Telefunken v. Commission, 1983 ECR 3151.
139 Akzo v. Commission, Case C-97/08 P 2009 ECR I-8237.
140 Nils Wahl, *Parent Company liability – A question of facts or presumption?*, 19th St. Gallen International Competition Law Forum ICF (2012) (July 2018) https://papers.ssrn.com/sol3/papers.cfm?abstract_id=2206323## (last accessed on Dec. 10, 2021).
141 Dow Chemical v. Commission, Case T-77/08 EU:T:2012:47.
142 Nathaniew Grow, *American Needle and the Future of the Single Entity Defense under Section 1 of the Sherman Act*, 48 American Business Law Review 449 (2011).
143 Copperweld Corp. v. Independence Tube Corp., 467 US 752 (1984).
144 United States v. Citizens & S. National Bank, 422 US 86 (1975).
145 The lower Courts in US have extended the *copperweld* doctrine to partially owned subsidiaries (*Bell Atl. Bus. Sys. Services v. Hitachi Data Systems Corp.*, 849 F Su 702 (N.D. Cal. 1994) and sister companies (*AT &T Corp.*, 248 F.3d 131 (3rd Cir. 2001).
146 *Supra note* 136 at paras 111–149, 150–193, 194–224 and 225–256.
147 Some jurisdictions like Mexico do contain a reference to exchange of information within the statute.
148 Anna Kaczor, Warning: Exchange of Commercially Sensitive Information Between Competitors may result in an Infringement of Article 101 TFEU by Object, 85 Amicus Curiae (2011); See also, Information Exchanges Between Competitors under Competition Law OECD (2010), Policy Roundtables, DAF/COMP (2010) 37 www.oecd.org/competition/cartels/48379006.pdf (last accessed on Dec. 10, 2021).
149 Kai-Uwe Kühn, *Fighting Collusion by Regulating Communication Between Firms*, 32 Economic Policy 169–204 (2001).
150 *Supra note* 136.
151 Spencer Weber Waller, *Trade Associations, Information Exchange and Cartels*, 30 Loyola Consumer Law Review (2018).
152 The Sherman Act, 1890 (USA); Article 81 of Treaty of Rome (European Community).
153 IAZ international Belgium NV v. Commission, [1983] ECR 3369; Van Landewyck SARL and Others v. Commission, [1980] ECR 3125

154 Verband der Sachversicherer v. Kommission, [1987] ECR 405.
155 *Supra note* 153.
156 Id.
157 *Guidelines on the applicability of Article 81 of the EC Treaty to Horizontal Cooperation Agreements, European Commission Notice* (2011), Official Journal of the European Union, Chapter 6, https://eur-lex.europa.eu/legal-content/EN/TXT/PDF/?uri=CELEX:52011XC0114 (04) &from=EN (last accessed on Dec. 10, 2021).
158 SM NV v. the Commission (Polypropylene) [1991] ECR II-1833.
159 *Ibid.*
160 DSM NV v. the Commission (Polypropylene) T-8/89, [1991] ECR II-1833
161 Toshiba v. Commission, Case T-113/07.
162 'Constructive knowledge' test was emphasized by the European Court of Justice in *Anic Partecipazioni v. Commission,* Case C-49/92 P.
163 Trelleborg Industrie SAS and Trelleborg AB v. Commission, T-147/09 and T-148/09.
164 P ThyssenKrupp Stainless GmbH and ThyssenKrupp Acciai speciali Terni SpA v. Commission, C-65/02 P and C-73/02.
165 *Supra note* 16.
166 Case T-303/02 Westfalen Gassen Nederland v. Commission [2006] ECR II-4567; Case C-510/06P Archer Daniel Midlands v. Commission [2009] ECR I-1843.
167 Total Marketing Services v. Commission, C-634/13 P, EU:C:2015:614, paragraph 21
168 Westfalen Gassen Nederland BV v. Commission, Case T-303/02.
169 The *per se* rule of illegality in US originated in a price fixing case, Federal Trade Commission v. Superior Court Trial Lawyers Association, 493 U.S. 411 at 422 (1990), where the court refused to consider the social utility of the agreement. The US Supreme Court, however, has at times moved away from the strict application of *per se* rule with respect to horizontal price fixing. The court in the case of *Broadcast Music* paved way for a 'mini rule of reason' assessment when it was 'faced with an untested business practice which achieved pro-competitive goals'. *See*, Broadcast Music, Inc. v. Columbia Broadcasting System, Inc., 441 U.S. 1 (1979); Arizona v. Maricopa County Medical Society, 457 U.S. 332 (1982) (Powell, J., *dissenting*). *See also*, Joseph W. deFuria Jr., *Reasoning Per Se and Horizontal Price Fixing: An Emerging Trend in Antitrust Litigation?*, 14 (1) Pepperdine Law Review (1986).
170 Business Electronics Corp. v. Sharp Electronics Corp., 485 U.S. 717 at 723 (1988); United States v. Socony-Vacuum Oil Co., Inc., 310 U.S. 150 at 224 (1940).
171 Paul Gift, *Price Fixing and Minimum Resale Price Restrictions Are Two Different Animals*, 12 (2), Graziadio Business Review, (2009).
172 William H. Page, *A Neo-Chicago Approach to Concerted Action*, 78 Antitrust Law Journal 173 (2012), http://scholarship.law.ufl.edu/facultypub/584.
173 Richard A. Posner, *The Social Costs of Monopoly and Regulation*, 83 Journal of Political Economy 807, 820 (1975).
174 United States v. Trenton Potteries Co., 273 U.S. 392 at 397–98.
175 Indian Competition Act, 2002, creates an exception for the joint ventures from the application of S. 3 (3) – that is, horizontal anti-competitive agreements. 'Provided that nothing contained in this sub-section shall apply to any agreement entered into by way of joint ventures if such agreement increases efficiency in production, supply, distribution, storage, acquisition or control of goods or provision of services".

176 The US Supreme Court initially treated parent and subsidiary company as independent conspirators. (United States v. Yellow Cab Co., 332 U.S. 218 (1947); KieferStewart Co. v. Joseph E. Seagram & Sons, 340 U.S. 211 (1951). However, this changed after the 1984 decision in Copperweld Corp. v. Independence Tube Corp., 467 U.S. 752, 768 (1984) at 776–777, where the Court treated the parent and its wholly owned subsidiary as one on account of unity of interest.

177 The CCI initially held that any internal agreement between entities of the same group (as defined under S. 5) will not be considered as an agreement for the purposes of Section 3 of the 2002 Act (Exclusive Motors Pvt. Limited v. Automobili Lamborghini S.P.A., Case No. 52 of 2012; In Re: Association of Third Party Administrators, Case No. 107 of 2013; Shamsher Kataria v. Honda siel & Ors). However, in the case of *Delhi Jal Board* (In re: Delhi Jal Board, Ref. Case Nos. 03 & 04 of 2013), the commission rejected the argument since, because the parties belonged to the same group, there cannot be any agreement between them for the purposes of Section 3. The CCI considered that the bids of the two companies were treated as different and not collectively.

178 Herbert Hovenkamp, Federal Antitrust Policy: The Law of Competition and its Practice (West Publishing Company, 2nd ed., 1999).

179 Radio 2UE Sydney Pty. Ltd. v. Stereo F.M. Pty. Ltd. (1982), 62 F.L.R. 437.

180 Id.

181 Alan Devlin, *A Proposed Solution to the Problem of Parallel Pricing in Oligopolistic Markets*, 59 (4) Stanford Law Review, 1111–1151 (2007).

182 Id.

183 *Clamp-All Corp. v. Cast Iron Soil Pipe Inst.,* 851 F 2d 478, 484 (Ist Cir. 1988); George A. Hay, *Oligopoly, Shared Monopoly and Antitrust Law*, 67 Cornell Law Review 439 (1982). Same approach has been taken by the European Court as well. See, Joined cases C-89/85, C-104/85, C-114/85, C-116/85, C-117/85, C-125/85 to C-129//85 *A Ahlstrom Osakeyhtio v. Commission (Woodpulp II)* (1993) ECR I-1307 para 71.

184 In re High Fructose Corn Syrup Antitrust Litigation, 295 F 3d 651, 654 (7th Cir. 2002) dissent note.

185 Louis Kaplow, *An Economic Approach to Price-fixing*, 77 Antitrust Law Journal 343 (2011).

186 Id.

187 Daniel R. Shulman, *Proof of Conspiracy in Antitrust Cases and the Oligopoly Problem*, 4 The Sedona Conference TAR Case Law Primer 1 (2003).

188 Aaron Director and Edward H. Levi, *Law and the Future: Trade Regulation*, 51 Northwestern University Law Review 281 (1956).

189 Thomas A. Piraino, Jr., *Regulating Oligopoly Conduct Under the Antitrust Laws*, 89 Minnesota Law Review 9, 12–13 (2004).

190 George Hay, *Horizontal Agreements: Concept and Proof,* Cornell Law Faculty Publications, Paper 1142 (2006), http://scholarship.law.cornell.edu/facpub/1142 (last accessed on Dec. 10, 2021).

191 George A. Hay, *The Meaning of "Agreement" under the Sherman Act: Thoughts from the "Facilitating Practices" Experience*, 16 Review of Industrial Organization 113, 128 (2000).

192 Id.

193 *Supra note* 71.

194 *Supra note* 9.

195 Matthew M. Bunda, *Monsanto, Matsushita, and "Conscious Parallelism": Towards a Judicial Resolution of the "Oligopoly Problem"*, 84 Washington University Law Review 179 (2006).

196 Thomas A. Piraino Jr., *Identifying Monopolists' Illegal Conduct under the Sherman Act*, 75 New York University Law Review 809 (2000).
197 John E. Lopatka, *Solving the Oligopoly Problem: Turner's Try*, 41 Antitrust Bulletin 843, 845 (1996).
198 Theatre Enterprises, Inc. v. Paramount Film Distributing Corp., 346 U.S. 537 (1954).
199 Michael Vaska, *Conscious Parallelism and Price Fixing: Defining the Boundary*, 52 (2) University of Chicago Law, Article 10 (1985).
200 United States v. General Motor Corp., 384 U.S. 127, 142–143 (1966). See also, Matsushita Electronics Industries Co. v. Zenith Radio Corp., 475 U.S. 574, 588 (1986).
201 ICI v. Commission, Case 48/69 [1972] ECR 619, [1972] CMLR 557.
202 American Tobacco Co. v. United States, 328 U.S. 781, 66 S. Ct. 1125, 90 L. Ed. 1575 (1946).
203 Raghavan's Report on Competition Law, paragraph 4.3–3.
204 A Ahlstrom Oy v. Commission, [1993] ECR I-1307. See also, Van Gerven and Verano, T*he Wood Pulp Case and the Future of Concerted Practices*, 31 Common Market Law Review 575 (1994).
205 Phillip Areeda and H.J. Hovenkamp, *Antitrust Law: An Analysis of Antitrust Principles ad their Application* (Wolter Kluwer, 2nd ed., 2000).
206 Id.
207 Chang-Su Choe, *Antitrust Economics for Proof of Concerted Price-Fixing: Practical Points for U.S. and Korean Antiturst Jurisprudence*, 8 Brigham Young University International Law & Management Review 1 (2012).
208 *Supra note* 205.
209 Professor Turner although describes motive to collude and an overt act of collusion as factors under this category, does not demarcate them as plus factors.
210 *Supra note* 207.
211 Christopher R. Leslie, *Foreign Price Fixing Conspiracies*, 67 Duke Law Journal 556 (2017).
212 William E. Kovacic, Robert Marshall, Leslie Marx and H. White, *Plus Factors and Agreement in Antitrust Law*, 110 Michigan Law Review 393 (2011).
213 *Supra note* 71.
214 *Model Law on Competition,* Revised chapter III, Intergovernmental Group of Experts on Competition Law and Policy, UNCTAD, 12th Session Geneva, 9–11 July 2012, http://unctad.org/meetings/en/SessionalDocuments/ciclpL4_en.pdf (last accessed on Dec. 10, 2021).
215 Frederic M. Scherer and David Ross, Industrial Market Structure and Economic Performance, (Houghton-Mifflin, 3rd ed. 1990). *See, United States v. Suntar Roofing, Inc.*, 897 F.2d 469 (10th Cir. 1990), *United States v. Goodman,* 850 F.2d 1473, 1476 (11th Cir.1988).
216 *Supra note* 119.
217 *Ibid.*
218 Gross, J. and W. Holahan, *Credible Collusion in Spatially Separated Markets*, 44 International Economic Review 299–312 (2003).
219 Kai Andree and Mike Schwan, *Collusive Market Sharing with Spatial Competition*, Discussion Nr.105, University of Potsdam, 2012 https://publishup.uni-potsdam.de/opus4-ubp/frontdoor/deliver/index/docId/5991/file/vwd105.pdf (last accessed on Dec. 11, 2021).
220 Id.
221 *Model Law on Competition,* Revised chapter III, Intergovernmental Group of Experts on Competition Law and Policy, UNCTAD, 12th Session Geneva,

9–11 July 2012, http://unctad.org/meetings/en/SessionalDocuments/ciclpL4_en.pdf (last accessed on Dec. 11, 2021).

222 *Recommendation of the OECD Council Concerning Effective Action against Hard-core Cartels*, OECD, March 1998, C (98) 35/FINAL – C/M (98) 7/PROV, www.oecd.org/daf/competition/2350130.pdf (last accessed on Dec. 11, 2021). See also, *Guidelines on Fighting Bid-Rigging in Public Procurement* (OECD 2009).

223 John M. Connor and Robert H. Lande, *The Size of Cartel Overcharges: Implications for US and EU Fining Policies*, 51 Antitrust Bulletin 983 (2006).

224 John Asker, *A Study of the Internal Organization of a Bidding Cartel*, 100 American Economic Review 724–762.

225 *Supra note* 119.

226 Robert H. Porter and J. Douglas Zona, *Detection of Bid-rigging in procurement auctions*, 101 (3) Journal of Political Economy 518 (1993).

227 Recommendation of the OECD Council Concerning Effective Action against Hard Core Cartels, OECD, March 1998, C (98) 35/FINAL – C/M (98) 7/PROV (OECD 1998).

228 *Fighting bid rigging in public procurement* (OECD 2016) www.oecd.org/daf/competition/Fighting-bid-rigging-in-public-procurement-2016-implementation-report.pdf (last accessed on Dec. 11, 2021).

229 *Ibid.*

230 *Ibid.*

231 *Government at a Glance* (OECD 2015) http://dx.doi.org/10.1787/gov_glance-2015-en (last accessed on Dec. 11, 2021).

232 *Supra note* 228.

233 *The Detection and Prevention of Collusive Tendering*, The Competition Authority of Ireland, November 2009, www.ccpc.ie/business/wp-content/uploads/sites/3/2017/02/Booklet-The-Detection-and-Prevention-of-Collusive-Tendering.pdf (last accessed on Dec. 11, 2021); *Cartels Deterrence and detection a guide for government procurement officers*, Australian Competition and Consumer Commission (2011), www.accc.gov.au/system/files/308_Cartels_Deterence%20and%20detection_26-Feb-2016.pdf (last accessed on Dec. 11, 2021); *Detecting, Mitigating & Fighting Bid-rigging in Public Procurement*, Fair Trading Commission, www.ftc.gov.bb/library/2011-02-07_ftc_guidelines_checklist_procurement.pdf (last accessed on Dec. 11, 2021); *Diagnostic Tools for Procurement Officers – Towards Competitive Tenders*, Competition Commission of India, www.cci.gov.in/sites/default/files/whats_newdocument/Final%20Diagnostic%20Tool%2019032018-1.pdf (last accessed on Dec. 11, 2021); *Guidelines for Fighting Bid-rigging in Public Procurement*, OECD www.oecd.org/competition/cartels/42851044.pdf (last accessed on Dec. 11, 2021).

234 *Ibid.*

235 John Duns, Arlen Duke and Brendan Sweeney ed., Comparative Competition Law 92 (Edward Elgar 2017).

236 Matthew Bennett and Philip Collins, *The Law and Economics of Information Sharing: The Good, the Bad and the Ugly*, 6 European Competition Law Journal 311 (2010).

237 Northwest Wholesale Stationers Inc. v. Pacific Stationery & Printing Co., 472 US 284 (1985).

238 *Model Law on Competition,* Revised chapter III, Intergovernmental Group of Experts on Competition Law and Policy, UNCTAD, 12th Session Geneva, 9–11 July 2012, http://unctad.org/meetings/en/SessionalDocuments/ciclpL4_en.pdf (last accessed on Dec. 11, 2021).

239 Id.

240 Industrial Policy Resolution, 1948
241 Industrial Policy Resolution, 1956.
242 Ramachandra Guha, India after Gandhi, 433 (Picador, England, 2007).
243 Dr. S. Chakravarthy, *Why India adopted a Competition Law*, CUTS Center for Competition, Investment and Economic Regulation (2006).
244 Manas Kumar Chaudhuri, *MRTP Act to Competition Act: The Way Forward*, 41 (2) VIKALPA – The Journal for Decision Makers, 168–193 (2016).
245 MY Khan, Indian Financial System, 217 (McGraw Hill Education, 8th ed., 2014).
246 S. Chakravarthy, *India's New Competition Act 2002 – A Work Still in Progress*, 5 Journal of International Business and Law 240 (2004).
247 Raymond Woollen Mills Ltd. v. MRTP Commission, (1979) 49 Com Cases 686 (Bom.).
248 Union of India v. Hindustan Development Corporation, [1993] 3 SCC 499, 529.
249 Para 23–24, Alkali Manufacturers Association of India v. Sinochem International Chemicals Co. Ltd. and Anr., Restrictive Trade Practice Enquiry No. 238/1997, order dated 24 April 1998.
250 Director General (Investigation and Registration) v. Modi Alkali and Chemicals Limited and Ors., II (2002) C PJ19 (MRTP).
251 Standing Committee (S&C) Association of State Road Transport Undertaking v. Karmobiles Limited and Anr., II (2002) C PJ36 (MRTP).
252 *Hindustan Lever Ltd. and Tata Oil Mills Co. Ltd.*, RTP Enquiry No. 4/1978, order dated 22 July 1982; *RRTA v. Hyderabad Asbestos Cement Products Ltd.*, RTP Enquiry No. 17/1979, order dated 20 December 1982.
253 In Re: Chloride India Ltd., RTP Enquiry No. 46/1977, order dated 12 May 1981.
254 In Re: Alkali and Chemical Corporation of India Ltd. and Bayer (India) Ltd., RTP Enquiry No. 21/1981, order dated 3 July 1984.
255 In Re: Indian Jute Mills Association, RTP Enquiry No. 80/1975, order dated 11 October 1977; Andhra Pradesh Paper Mills Ltd., RTP Enquiry No. 5/1973, order dated 31 January 1976.
256 *In re* [1988] 63 Comp Cas 468 (MRTPC). See also, In Re: Excel Industries Ltd., [1988] 64 Comp Cas 531 (MRTPC).
257 In Re: Hyderabad Asbestos Cement Products, In re (RTPE No. 17/1979). Also see, In Re: Choloride India Ltd., (RTPE No. 46/1977).
258 In Re: Excel Industries Ltd., [1988] 64 Comp Cas 531 (MRTPC).
259 Para 23, Excel Industries Ltd., *In re* [1988] 64 Comp Cas 531 (MRTPC).
260 Major English Newspapers and Indian and Eastern Newspaper Society, RTPE 46/1975, order dated 18 December 1975, RTPE 47/1975, order dated 6/2/1976, RTPE 48/1975, order dated 27 February 1976, RTPE 49/1975, order dated 19 March 1976.
261 In Re: Swastic Laminating Industries, RTP Enquiry No. 81/1984, order dated 31 January 1986.
262 A & I C (P) Ltd., Bombay and Sulphur Mills (P) Ltd., Bombay, RTPE 6/1981, order dated 23 December 1984.
263 Divakara B. Chennupati and Rajasekhara M. Potluri, *A Viewpoint on Cartels: An Indian Perspective*, 53 (4) International Journal of Law and Management 252–261 (2019) https://doi.org/10.1108/17542431111147774 (last accessed on Dec. 1, 2021).
264 RTPE 1/1971, order dated 19 April 1976.
265 Madras Rubber Factory Ltd., Goodyear India Ltd., Dunlop India Ltd. and Bombay Tyres International Ltd., RTPE 6/1978, order dated 2 February 1983.

266 Alkali Manufacturers Association, RTPE 26/1984, order dated 29 March 1985; Indian Woollen Mills Federation and others, RTPE 32/1976, order dated 25 April 1977; Food grains and kirana Merchants Association, Indian Rayon Corporation, Gujarat, RTPE 18/1981, order dated 22 February 1983; Truck Operators and Transport Operators Association, Rampur and Other -RTPE 11/1987, order dated 14 August 1987; Ghee Merchants Association, RTPE 23/1976, order dated 14 February 1977.
267 Truck Operators Union, RTPE 32/1977, order dated 20 February 1978.
268 In Re: Truck Operators Union, (RTP Enquiry No. 32/1977); In Re: Bharatpur Truck Operator's Union, (RTP Enquiry No. 10/1982); In Re: Rohtak Public Goods Motor Union, (RTP Enquiry No. 25/1983).
269 Hari Das Exports v. All India Float Glass Manufacturers Association & Co., AIR 2000 (SC) 2728.
270 Sections Sections 1 (2), 2 (c) and 14 of the MRTP Act, 1969. Hari Das Exports v. All India Float Glass Manufacturers Association & Co., AIR 2000 (SC) 2728.
271 Aditya Bhattacharjea, India"s New Antitrust Regime: The First Two Years of Enforcement, 57 Antitrust Bull. 449 (2012).
272 All India Tyre Dealers' Federation Informant v. Tyre Manufacturers, 2013CompLR92 (CCI)
273 In Re: Sugar Mills, Suo-motu Case No. 1/2010, order dated 30 November 2011 (CCI).
274 Id.
275 Builders Association of India v. Cement Manufacturers' Association and Ors. 2012 Comp LR 629 (CCI)
276 *Supra note* 272.
277 *Supra note* 275. Also see, Express Industry Council of India v. Jet Airways (India) Ltd., Case No. 30/2013, order dated 7 March 2018.

3 Characterizing Indian cartels

3.1 Introduction

The second chapter discusses the theoretical underpinnings of the concept of cartels within the larger domain of market economics. Various empirical studies in different jurisdictions have helped us develop an idea of the external and internal functioning of cartels. These empirical results sometimes validate theoretical assumptions and sometimes oppose them. For instance, while it is theoretically asserted that cartels are inherently unstable and would not survive for long, there are pieces of evidence of cartels in many jurisdictions, including international cartels that have survived for decades. Similar studies have been done on various determinants of cartel formation in order to prove or disprove theoretical and legal assumptions. The present chapter entails an investigation of the underlying determinants of cartels in India during the observation period. The data set will thus provide an anatomy of cartels in India.

3.2 Categorizing cartels on the basis of type and sector of operation

3.2.1 Types of cartels in India

In the last 12 years of active enforcement of competition law, the CCI has investigated all forms of hard-core cartels. Examination of the data set with respect to the type of cartel can not just indicate the nature of the market (vis-à-vis cartels) and behaviour of participants but also highlight the focus area of the CCI in terms of detection and punishment of cartels. A large number of cases where the CCI has been able to successfully prove contravention are cases where there was direct evidence of infringement. There is a significant number of cases which involved anti-competitive behaviour of trade associations. These cases with primary involvement of trade associations usually had direct evidence of anti-competitive conduct in the form of diktats,[1] decisions of association,[2] code of conduct,[3] by-laws,[4] a charter of ethics, letter of intent,[5] circulars, minutes of meetings and advisories. A high

DOI: 10.4324/9781003347651-3

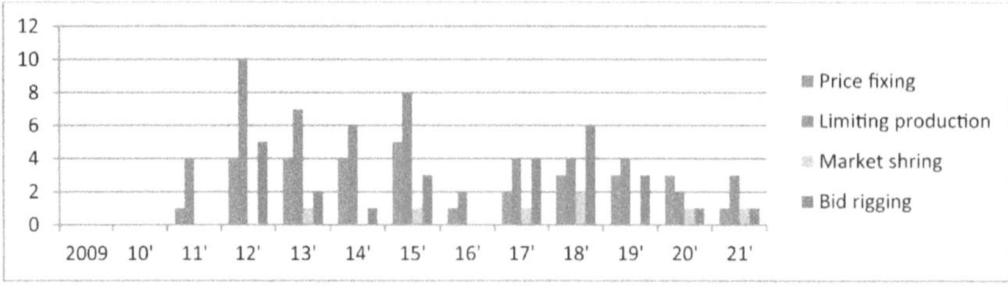

X Axis: Year of enforcement; Y Axis: Number of orders under section 27 of the Act.

Figure 3.1 Relative figures of types of cartels on a yearly basis for Section 27 orders.

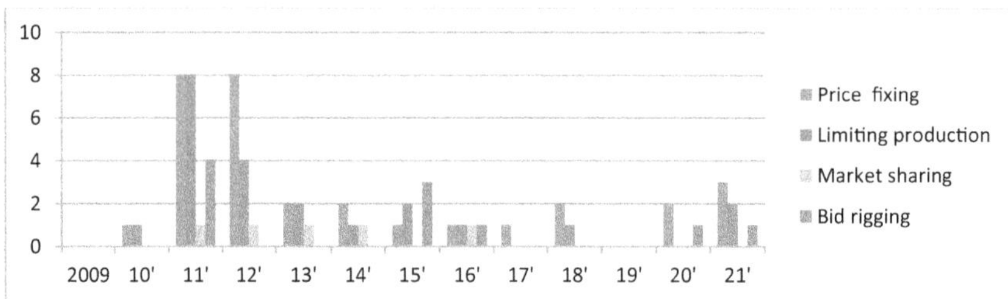

X Axis: Year of enforcement; Y Axis: Number of orders under Section 27 of the Act.

Figure 3.2 Relative figures of types of cartels on a yearly basis for section 26 (6) orders.

number of cases involved actions which limited or controlled the production or supply of goods or services in the market. The yearly activity of the CCI in terms of types of cartels has been shown in Figure 3.1.

Sometimes, cartel contracts are not restricted to one type of behaviour but cover other dimensions in order to avoid competition on non-contractual terms. For instance, a price-fixing cartel in a mass production product like cement which does not also simultaneously pre-decide on the utilization of the capacity of individual players is bound to fail. A common feature of these cases is the mixture of cartelized behaviour in a particular case. Almost 25% of cartel cases decided under Section 27 by the CCI involved more than one form of cartel behaviour.[6] Similarly, 44% of orders under Section 26 (6) involved allegations that pertained to more than one form of cartel (see Figure 3.2). Section 3 (3) of the Act also includes decisions or practices carried on by any association of enterprises or persons. Almost 60% of the cases in which a penalty was imposed by the CCI involved the behaviour of limiting or controlling production. Closer scrutiny of cases reveals that a bulk of these anti-competitive conducts were the result of decisions taken by sector-specific voluntary and dominant trade associations.

3.2.1.1 Horizontal price fixing

Prices of goods and services should be determined by market forces and not as a result of collusion between market participants who are expected to compete with each other. Pricing goods or services higher than the optimum cost brings down economic efficiency and overcharges consumers. Horizontal price fixing, be it in the form of increasing, decreasing, or stabilizing the price, is presumed to have an anti-competitive effect as it does not have any redeeming virtue. No justification will therefore be entertained for such an arrangement. Further, there is no requirement for the CCI to go into the aspect of harm caused by such an agreement. While price-fixing cartels have always been seen as being capable of reducing consumer welfare[7] and having social costs,[8] some believe that these forms of cartels are unsustainable and unstable and will break within a short span of time. The incentive to cheat and lack of punishment for defection makes the cartel vulnerable.[9]

Price fixing is not limited to mere overt actions. Section 3 (3) (a) of the Act does not describe in detail all types of price-fixing arrangements, but the same has been interpreted to be an inclusive provision encompassing all forms of horizontal price-fixing arrangements. Further, Indian courts have embraced the jurisprudence[10] around conscious parallelism and adopted the idea of plus factors that need to be produced to prove collusion. The Raghavan Committee Report notes,

> When a price leader alters the price of his goods or services due to factors such as increase in the cost of inputs, raw materials or other related costs, most other competitors will have no choice, but to follow him though the extent could vary. This cannot be said to be illegal because its behaviour is not based on any prior discussion or understanding, but on the sheer economic premise that any price increase taken by a small player ahead of the price leader would imply significant penalties in terms of loss of custom.[11]

Quantitatively, price-fixing cartels form the second most common form of anti-competitive behaviour in the observation period and are present in both direct and indirect forms of price fixing arrangements. The highest number of CCI orders related to price-fixing arrangements was in 2015. Orders under Section 26 (6) have the highest number of cases involving allegations of price fixing. However, in many such cases, there was not enough evidence to prove cartelization. In absolute numbers, in 28 out of 83 cases, an allegation of price fixing was proved. More than 50% of cases involved the primary role of a trade association. Incidentally, direct or naked price fixing has been proved in not more than 13 cases. Also, all cases of direct price fixing in the last four years with firms having a primary role have been leniency matters. Others involved primary action on the part of the trade associations in fixing rates of product or service or transportation costs.

Cases involving trade associations have revolved around the pharmaceutical, transport, or media sectors. In comparison, almost 50% of cases (24 out of 42 cases) under Section 26 (6) involved allegations with respect to price fixing arrangements, and the primary involvement of trade associations was identified in only seven cases. Allegations concerning collusive behaviour are also with respect to varied areas within the service sector. While the CCI, due to traceability of actions in the form of concrete evidence, has been able to detect and prosecute cartels where trade associations were involved as leaders, the same is not seen in other cases where allegations as to price fixing were made against firms. One reason for the same is the relative letdown of the leniency program. The CCI has been unable to acquire the trust of market participants who may want to defect from a cartel. The number of leniency applications has picked up only in the last couple of years.

Generally, price-fixing cartels are not easy to sustain for long durations of time as they require regular communication and monitoring. However, in India these cartels have been able to survive for long durations of time during the observation period. Even in cases where trade associations were not the primary actors/leaders, long durations of cartels have been seen. For instance, the cement cartel,[12] battery cartel[13] and beer cartel[14] survived for more than three years, eight years, and ten years, respectively. More than 60% of cases decided under Section 27 had an infringement duration of more than a year.

Different forms of price fixing have been seen across years, with the prominence of indirect price-fixing arrangements, mostly originating from the diktats of trade associations, which, by virtue of their command and authority in the market, were able to enforce them. This is the reason that none of these cartels has seen defections. There is always a credible threat of boycott for not towing the lines of the concerned trade association. There have also been cases of boycott, strike, picketing, non-supply, and non-dealing with any insider who tries to go outside the terms of agreed behaviour. However, apart from a few sectors, where certain trigger events spiralled into multiple cases on similar subject matters, there seems to be a general acceptance within large trade associations of mutually accepted anti-competitive behaviours which are passed off as market practice.

Different forms of price-fixing cartels seen in India with relative frequency have been highlighted in Table 3.1.

3.2.1.2 Agreement to limit or control production

When businesses switch to collusion and join hands to control production or supply to create artificial scarcity, it becomes a cartel. The behaviour of

Table 3.1 Types of cartels and their frequency in terms of the number of cases

Price fixing		*Limiting or controlling production or supply*		*Market sharing*	*Bid rigging*
Direct price fixing	*Indirect price fixing*	*Direct (as agreements between competitors)*	*Indirect (as diktats of trade associations)*		
Increase in prices (8); fixing rate of transport (2); fixing freight charges (2)	Fixing/imposing revenue sharing ratio/method (2); fixing trade margin (6); fixing amount of discount or zero discount policy (2); price fixing through identical bids with high quotes (3)	Withhold production or supply (4); reduced production (1)	Ban/refusal to supply (15); restricted supply (3); non-dealing with non-members (8); boycott (14); mandatory NOC (19); mandatory PIS (7); tender boycott (3); restricted quoting (1)	Territory allocation (1); imposition of geographical restrictions by association (1); mutual allocation in bidding (3)	Identical bid + bid sharing (11); bid rotation (6); subcontracting (2); complementary or cover bidding (5); tender boycott (1)

cartelists is akin to monopolists, which is to produce less and charge more and also affects the efficiency of the market. Per Section 3 (3) (b) of the Act, business entities who are supposed to compete with each other shall not enter into an agreement that "limits or controls production, supply, markets, technical development, investment or provision of services". Such agreements are presumed to have an AAEC, and by virtue of Section 3 (2) of the Act, such agreements are void *ab initio*. It also includes within its ambit all such decisions or practices carried on by any association of enterprises or persons.

Quantitatively, cartels limiting or controlling production are the most common form of anti-competitive behaviour in the observation period. This form of behaviour was found in 10% of cases in the manufacturing sector and 90% of cases in the service sector. In absolute numbers, this form of behaviour was proved in a total of 53 out of 83 (approx. 64%) cases. Out of these 53 cases, 47 cases involved the direct participation and action of trade associations spread across the manufacturing sector (5 cases), media and entertainment sector (17 cases) and wholesale and retail sector (25 cases). Only 7 cases of direct participation of enterprises were found, 4[15] of which included the primary allegation of bid rigging. Apart from the cement cartel case,[16] all others have been leniency matters (the zinc battery cartel,[17] cartelization in the supply of electric power steering systems,[18] automotive bearings[19] and the beer cartel[20]). In comparison, 22 out of 42 cases under Section 26 (6) involved allegations with respect to limiting production, with the primary involvement of trade associations in only 9 cases. Allegations were with respect to varied areas within the service sector and included electricity, insurance, transport, wholesale and retail, banking, media and entertainment, and publishing. Therefore, if we exclude all the cases with primary involvement of trade associations, we are not left with enough matters where the CCI's investigation has led to indictments. This may be for two reasons. Firstly, in light of low numbers of leniency applications, the quality of information has not been good, and due to lack of enough evidence, the matters get dismissed either at the preliminary stage itself – evidenced by the high number of orders under Section 26 (2) – or after investigation. Secondly, the investigative procedures at the CCI level are not strong enough to unearth enough evidence to support information about cartelization. There is a consistent presence of this form of anti-competitive behaviour across the years in the observation period, with the highest numbers in the years 2012 and 2015. Cases under Section 27 of the Act involving proven conduct of limiting or controlling production or supply constitute the highest number of cases across the years (except the year 2018) in comparison to other forms of hard-core cartels.

While direct or naked forms of limiting supply or production are rare, different forms of indirect restrictions have been seen in most of the cases involving trade associations. The greatest weapon in the hands of the trade associations, considering their size and strength, has been the practice of boycotting or refusing to deal. A simple resolution is enough to outcast any non-member or even an insider who digresses from the pre-decided form of conduct. It is, in fact, surprising that we have seen cases involving trade associations majorly across the previously mentioned three sectors. A majority of the cases in the wholesale and retail segment of the pharmaceutical industry are a result of a domino effect. Most of these have been guided by their respective by-laws or agreements of incorporation, which contain boycott or non-dealing as a common disciplining measure. Although the CCI has impressed on the trade associations the need for competition compliant behaviour, the same has not really been paid heed to, which is evident from the high incidence of cases of similar nature.

Different forms of restriction in supply or production have been highlighted in Table 3.1.

3.2.1.3 Market-sharing cartels

When collusion leads to division and sharing of market, it deprives the consumers of their available choices and forces them to buy the same goods or services from a specific seller at an increased price. It also disallows the business units to reduce their unit cost of production as there will be no benefit of economies of scale.[21] It has generally been argued that since it is easier to monitor defection and the confusion over fixing a particular price is avoided, market-sharing cartel arrangements are much easier to enter and thus more common. Most jurisdictions treat market-sharing agreements as *per se* bad.[22] These agreements are seen as an alternative to price-fixing cartels. Market sharing may be in the form of customer allocation or territory allocation or on the basis of market share. Market share division is argued to be more stable than others as it does not require pre-cartel arrangements in the form of customer or territory profiling. Further, it can be easily monitored through a simple reporting protocol or through a trade association. Per Section 3 (3) (c) of the Act, competitors shall not enter into an agreement that "shares the market or source of production or provision of services by way of allocation of geographical area of market, or type of goods or services, or number of customers in the market or any other similar way".

Quantitatively, market-sharing cartels are the least common forms of anti-competitive behaviour in India during the observation period, with only 8% of cases involving an allegation of market sharing, equally distributed between the manufacturing and service sectors. (See Figure 3.1.) Similarly, there are five orders under Section 26 (6) in the observation period where an allegation of market sharing was made. (See Figure 3.2.) As such, the numbers are too small to make any valid inference. One reason that can be attributed to such low numbers is the nature of the cartel with respect to its area of operation. Approximately, 65% of cartel cases during the observation period are localized either in their constitution or impact. Therefore, the scope of dividing the market on the basis of consumer or territory reduces to a great extent. Four out of seven cases involving market sharing involved mutual territory allocation through collusive bidding. There is just one case of imposition of geographical restriction by any trade association.[23] Another reason for such low numbers can be grounded in theory which argues that these forms of collusion are the most stable, which essentially means that it will be much tougher for the regulator to unearth such cartels. The CCI, therefore, is required to make an extra effort to collect and interpret market data to check if the particular markets have been shared between competitors on the basis of territory or consumer or product.

Different forms of market sharing seen in India with relative frequency have been highlighted in Table 3.1.

3.2.1.4 Bid rigging or collusive bidding

Collusion destroys the very purpose of a bidding exercise. It ensures that the bid is awarded not to the most appropriate bidder but to someone who has been pre-decided by the colluders. It has been recognized that some of such colluders are hard-core cartels,[24] and therefore, collusive bidding has been made illegal world over.[25] Placing identical bids is the most common form of collusive conduct. This minimizes the risk of undercutting by cartel members. It also saves everyone from having to decide on a particular price that suits everyone. These forms of collusion are most common in public procurements in sectors that witness repetitive bidding. While many advanced and old antitrust jurisdictions use econometric techniques[26] or econometric forecasting models to detect collusive behaviour, younger and less resourceful competition law regimes still rely on complaints and subsequent collection of evidence. Extensive information and data that is required to use these techniques are hardly present. Per Section 3 (3) (d) of the Act, competitors shall not enter into an agreement that "directly or indirectly results in bid rigging or collusive bidding".

Quantitatively, bid rigging or collusive bidding is the most common form of cartels in the least investigated sector of the country – the manufacturing sector. During the observation period, bid rigging was proved in more than 50% of cases in the manufacturing sector. In absolute numbers, out of total of 83 cases, bid rigging was found in 26 cases (manufacturing sector [21]; service sector [5]). In comparison, bid rigging was alleged in 10 cases out of total 42 cases under Section 26 (6) (manufacturing sector [8]; service sector [2]). Sharing of the bid or related information seems to be the most preferred route of collusion, which invites some sort of meeting of minds as it creates a possibility where no bidder suffers any loss. It is convenient, and cartelists can easily increase the quoted price uniformly to gain supra-competitive profits. In this situation, it really does not depend on whether the bid is repetitive. Most of the bid-rigging cases are all-inclusive, and therefore, chances of defection or complaint are minimal. There has been a consistent presence of bid rigging cartel cases across the observation period. (See Figure 3.1.) However, if we look at orders under Section 26 (6), cases where bid rigging was alleged are the least in number when compared to other types of cartels. The CCI has found it relatively easier to prove bid-rigging cases in the presence of direct and indirect evidence. The high success of bid rigging cases at the level of the CCI, however, has to be seen in the light of the success before appellate forums. Many of the decisions where the CCI, in light of indirect evidence, applied the "but for" test/analysis and were set aside by appellate forums because the CCI failed to take market realities into account.

Different forms of bid rigging seen in India with relative frequency have been highlighted in Table 3.1.

3.2.1.5 Additional cartel conditions

Apart from the primary agreement between cartelists with respect to types of cartel actions as indicated, the members also agree to additional obligations in order to ensure their sustenance. Cartel literature[27] categorizes such additional obligations, or additional cartel contracts, as obligations to maintain internal stability and organization, meet external threats, and face production-related issues. Therefore, clauses to maintain internal stability include clauses on monitoring as it is needed to ensure that no member cheats. Cheating destabilizes the cartel, and if it goes unpunished, it drives other cartel members to cheat as well. Regular exchange of information is essential for such monitoring. For instance, in the cement cartel case,[28] the association was used not just for discussion but also to monitor the cartel. The CCI observed that sharing of "Executive Summary – Cement Industry" and "Cement Statistics – Interregional Movement of Cement" gave details of production and dispatch of each company, which was problematic as it facilitated anti-competitive conduct. If trade associations act as a platform for the players to convey their market position and strategies, this might lead to the reduction or removal of uncertainty in the market, which in turn adversely affects competition in the market.[29] In most of the cases during the observation period, where the association itself acted as the primary cartelist, there was no need to have such arrangements. However, in other cases, especially in the manufacturing sector, enforcement was done by providing a convenient platform for sharing/discussing prices and other commercially sensitive issues on the pretext of discussing the market conditions and thus assisting the cartelists in monitoring cartel implementation.[30]

We have not come across any case in the observation period where defection or cheating led to any action being taken against any member of the cartel. Cartels in India appear to be more cohesive and stable, indicating some degree of mutual trust among the cartelists. However, cartel cases that had an active participation of trade associations had a clear stipulation of boycott or fine in case of non-compliance. There have been many cases in the last 12 years where a boycott, fine, expulsion, or other forms of punishment have been used by associations to discipline the participating members.

The second category of additional contracts caters for maintaining the internal organization of the cartel, which involves meetings, decision-making and dispute resolution. In most cases in India, the executive bodies of trade associations make decisions on behalf of the members. These cases have clear evidence of anti-competitive practices in the form of meetings of executive bodies that were done to issue diktats, resolutions, circulars and even press releases to disseminate decisions with an implicit threat for compliance. There are also cases where general body meetings were called to take decisions. Even in other cases, there is evidence of multi-level meetings to discuss the terms of behaviour. These meetings were either physically conducted at the platform of the association or indirectly as deciphered from individual conversations between participants. In the last 12 years, the CCI has not actually undertaken the exercise of figuring out the role of cartel leaders even though, in some cases, there were clear indications of such leadership.

The third category of contracts between members involves an understanding to ward off the external threat in the form of admission and removal policies for new members or on how to deal with non-members. Cartels in India have shown a high incidence of such understandings wherein dealing with non-members was heavily regulated within the cartel. The fourth category of additional contracts, which is almost absent in Indian cartels, is with respect to technology sharing or sharing of production enhancing efficiency techniques.

As is indicated from the data set, cartels with additional cartel contracts tend to survive for longer durations of time. During the observation, it is deduced that there is a very high incidence of category 1 and category 3 contracts. Category 1 contracts are more common among price-fixing cartels as they have to consistently respond to changing market scenarios, like demand fluctuations. Cartels to limit or restrict production or supply have shown more focus on decision-making protocols (category 2) and the ways to ward off external threats (category 3). Expulsion of any defector is also a common feature.

3.2.2 Sector-wise distribution of cartels in India

Characteristics of the market have a major role to play in the successful operation of cartels. Therefore, oligopolies with concentrated market shares, stable demand, homogenous products or services, high entry barriers and the presence of active trade associations tend to be more conducive to cartelization. Cartel figures, when juxtaposed with the industry or sector in which they operated, will highlight if any particular sector breeds any special type of cartel in India.

We can broadly divide the cartels in the observation period between the manufacturing and service sector. While more than 70% of the orders under Section 27 pertain to the service sector, indicating a higher level of cartelization as compared to the manufacturing sector, the numbers can be misleading if we do not subdivide the service sector into different areas of business. This is in sharp contrast to other jurisdictions. For instance, in the EU, between 2001 and 2015, more than 75% of cases (89 out of total 113 cases) belonged to the manufacturing sector.[31] Interestingly, 87% of cases in the service sector revolve around only three areas of business – wholesale and retail, media and entertainment, and transportation. These sectors (if air transport service, which is an oligopoly, is excluded) do not ordinarily breed cartelization as they do not have cartel-conducive environments. There can be two reasons for this imbalance – either the manufacturing sector and other areas in the service sector are truly competitive with a minimal level of cartelization or the CCI has gone only after low-hanging fruits. This gets substantiated by the fact that a very high percentage of cases in the service sector had a primary involvement of trade associations that acted as ring leaders. In these cases, the collection of evidence was comparatively easier than cartels between competitors who used platforms of trade associations only as conduits. While Section 3 (3) of the Act allows the CCI to look into anti-competitive behaviour not just as a practice or decision of a trade association but also as an agreement between members of a trade association engaged in a similar trade to hold individual members accountable for such decisions, most of the orders of CCI have stopped at penalizing only trade associations or their office bearers. One reason might be the large membership of the associations. However, even then, the role, if any, of any business unit as a ring leader could have been investigated. The CCI has not lifted the veil of the association to identify key decision-makers.

Further, if we look at another set of data from the orders under Section 26 (2) and Section 26 (6), while the service sector still surpasses the manufacturing sector (out of total 67 orders under Section 26 [2], 73% belonged to the service sector and 26% belonged to manufacturing sector), the areas in the service sector where the allegation of cartelization was made are much more diverse in nature. Most of these cases were either not pursued or were closed post-investigation because of a lack of evidence.

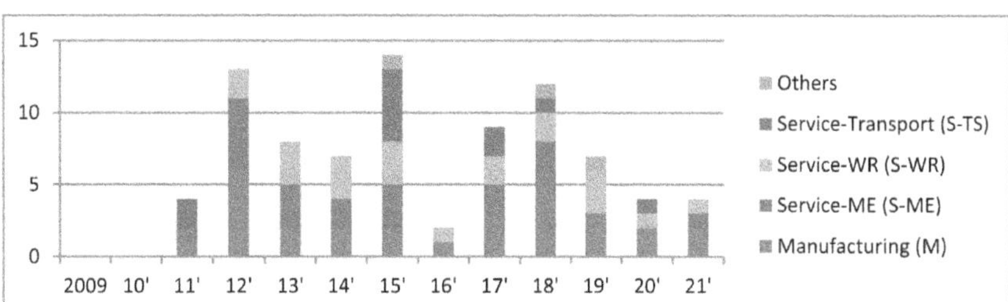

X Axis: Year of enforcement; Y Axis: Number of orders under section 27 of the Act

Figure 3.3 Year-wise distribution of cartels on the basis of sectors.

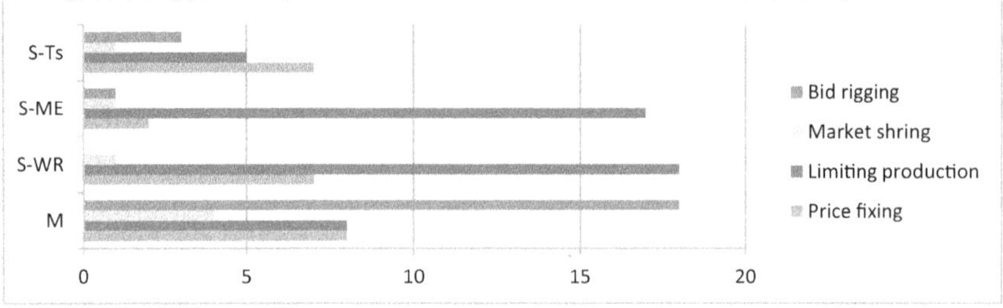

X Axis: Number of orders under Section 27 of the Act; Y Axis: Sector to which cartels belonged

Figure 3.4 Type and number of cartels in a specific sector (Section 27).

In comparison to orders under Section 27, cases belonging to manufacturing sector constituted 43% of total orders under Section 26 (6), and cases belonging to the service sector constituted 57% out of the total 36 orders. However, the cases in the service sector are not concentrated in a few areas but are distributed across sectors like banking, electricity distribution, lottery/gaming, transportation, wholesale and retail, media and entertainment, agriculture, supply, and publication. Similarly, in both the manufacturing and service sectors, allegations of price fixing have been the most common, followed by cartels to limit or control production (7 cases in manufacturing; 12 cases in the service sector). Bid-rigging cases are not the most common forms of allegation in the manufacturing sector (7 cases). Cases related to market sharing cartels are the least across both sectors.

3.2.2.1 *Manufacturing sector*

The manufacturing/industrial/production sector, which basically includes all those actions that convert raw material to usable goods, contributes around 16–17% of the GDP and employs around 12–14% of India's workforce.[32] It is one of the highest growth sectors in India, with an average growth rate of industry production of around 4.5%. This sector has also attracted large amounts of foreign investment.[33] Manufacturing cartels, in comparison to non-manufacturing cartels, sell less often to direct consumers and usually have a wider area of operation. Therefore, price fixing is more common in non-manufacturing areas as monitoring price is easier in comparison to manufacturing cartels. The data set supports Stigler's sectoral assessment of cartels where non-manufacturing cartels show higher strength in terms of participants producing undifferentiated products or services.[34] Market allocation is extremely difficult in such situations. However, the present data also diverges from Stigler's theory as even in the manufacturing sector where the products are sold not directly to the consumers, but in the downstream market with a level of differentiated products and a wider area of operation, very few cases of market allocation cases have been witnessed.

The distribution of cartel cases has not been seen across all the areas mentioned previously. Cases of cartelization are concentrated in the pharmaceutical sector. However, that too does not relate to manufacturing and is present in the distribution chain – wholesale and retail. Similarly, in the automobile sector, there is only one case of reported cartelization with respect to the supply of steel to original equipment manufacturers (OEMs).[35] Likewise, there are no reported cases in areas of textile and food processing. Even in the domain of electrical equipment, there is only one leniency case that was decided by the CCI in 2019.[36] There have been a couple of instances by chemical manufacturers of bid rigging in public procurements. The only sectors that have seen cartelization at the manufacturing level are cement and electronics. The cement cartel case[37] was among cement manufacturers to fix prices and limit supply in the market. In the battery cartel case,[38] cartelization was proved in the manufacture and supply of zinc-carbon dry-cell batteries. The cartel intended to control the distribution and price of zinc-carbon dry-cell batteries in India. The manufacturing sector has surprisingly not been investigated much. Experience in other countries has shown that the manufacturing sector is highly prone to cartelization.

Some of the areas where the allegation of cartelization was made but was not proven include glass, tyre, chemical, steel, and asbestos. In the glass manufacturers case,[39] it was alleged that float glass manufacturers had formed a cartel to increase prices and control supply. The increase in prices was due to the increase in price of raw materials, and price parallelism was held to be on account of prices moving in a band. The CCI held that there was no evidence to prove cartelization. Further, production had increased consistently, so no case was made out for controlling production. In the tyre cartel case,[40] the CCI did not concur with the DG that the tyre manufacturers had fixed prices. It held that there was no evidence to prove that the price change or capacity utilization was per a pre-decided agreement. In the *Tata Chemicals* case,[41] it was alleged that enterprises in the market of manufacturing and sale of soda ash in India had cartelized the market under the umbrella of the Alkali Manufacturers Association of India (AMAI). The CCI, in light of the absence of any concrete evidence, changing market share and capacity utilizations of participants, held that there was no cartel. In the steel case,[42] the DG noted price parallelism in four main products – HR coils, HR plates, wire rods, and TMT – and reported that data on demand and supply indicated periodic suppression of supply to prop up demand and prices. The CCI, however, did not find evidence of collusion and attributed price parallelism to the nature of the market and the tendency of the domestic producers to base their price movement per the landed import prices. There was no evidence suggestive of geographical allocations of territories or customers by the steel producers. In the asbestos case,[43] the CCI found no evidence to fix the price or share market. For the allegation of concerted shutdowns by top players to curtail production and limit supply, it was noted that possible justifications had been provided. Capacity utilization of major players was found to be optimum.

3.2.2.1.1 BID RIGGING IN PUBLIC PROCUREMENTS

Bid rigging in public procurement formed the bulk of cases in the manufacturing sector (more than 75%). Considering the fact that public procurement accounts for 30% of the GDP of India, with the state controlling major sectors like rail transport, defence, minerals, health, and so on, the number of cartel cases is not surprising. Cartel cases do not go into the examination of the behaviour of the procurement agency, and the fairness of the terms of the bid is not something with which the CCI is concerned. The CCI has not really explored the idea of examining the conduct of the procurer or issues of collusion between the procurer and the bidders under Section 3 (1) as anti-competitive in itself. For the CCI, an agreement needs to be established between bidders. There is always an option of scrutinizing the terms of the bid rolled out by the procurer if the procurement agency is dominant in the relevant market. However, it is not always feasible to go into the exercise of proving the dominance of the procurement agency. Thus, the CCI has looked into procurement contracts primarily from the lens of Section 3 (3), where unless an agreement is established between bidders showing the prior meeting of minds, cartelization cannot be proved.

While similarities in bids were the trigger points for investigation in most of the cases, the same has also been justified through economic factors, such as the nature of the market, the terms of the bid and the nature of the product. Although the CCI has emphasized that merely quoting high prices is not cartelization in itself, identical quoting has been considered strong evidence to prove cartelization.[44] The CCI looks for evidence to prove prior relation or meeting of bidders. In many cases, it has stressed the need for the bidders to explain or justify their quotations. In the absence of any economic, business or logical explanation for the quotation, a "but for" analysis is done to prove that the given conduct could not have been possible without collusion. There has been a major difference of opinion on the applicability of evidence to prove cartelization between the CCI and appellate forums. The CCI seems to have a lower threshold to conclude the existence of an agreement in comparison to appellate forums. For instance, in the LPG cartel case,[45] while the CCI found similarities in bid quotes in different states despite different production and transportation costs clubbed with evidence of meeting of some of the bidders before submission of bids as enough to prove cartelization, the Supreme Court in 2018 set aside the order on the grounds of lack of sufficient evidence.[46] Economic assessment of the market and reasons for behavioural patterns of the bidders is something that the appellate forums have examined and analyzed more in comparison to the CCI, leading to varying and different results.

Joint tendering has also not been held to be anti-competitive *per se*. In the *IOCL* case,[47] it was alleged that there was a cartel to procure biodiesel at fixed prices. The CCI noted that the oil manufacturing companies (OMCs) were not free in determining the prices of biodiesel as the prices were essentially to be fixed on the basis of guidelines and policies of the government of India.

Bid rigging has been reported and proved in the procurement of equipment,[48] machinery,[49] drugs[50] or chemicals[51] by government units,[52] hospitals, public sector enterprises and railways. The identical nature of bids and high quotes with subsequent bid sharing were found to be the common feature. Complementary bidding was proved in the matter of the case of the supply of spares to Diesel Loco Modernization Works to Indian Railways.[53] A collective boycott of any bidding process has also been held to be bad in law.[54]

3.2.2.1.2 MANUFACTURING CARTELS AND THE ROLE OF TRADE ASSOCIATIONS

Unlike the service sector, cases with primary action or leadership of trade associations are not so common in the manufacturing sector. Still, there have been cases where the trade associations were held guilty of violating Section 3 of the Act. For instance, in *M/s Paper Merchants Association, Delhi*,[55] the association was held guilty of asking members to boycott the informant as the latter failed to comply with the directions of the association. In the jute bags cartel case, the cartel pertained to the fixation of sale prices of jute packaging material by issuing the daily price bulletin (DPB) by the Gunny Trade Association (GTA) for jute bags for the members of the Indian Jute Mill Association (IJMA)/GTA.[56] Suppliers of ethanol (sugar mills) rigged the bids submitted pursuant to the tender floated by public-sector oil marketing companies (PSU OMCs) for the procurement of anhydrous alcohol by quoting an exorbitant price for the supply of ethanol to OMCs. This involved the participation of two trade associations. In the *India Glycols Ltd.* case,[57] it was alleged that the Indian Sugar Mills Association and the National Federation of Cooperative Sugar Factories Ltd. colluded to artificially raise the price of ethanol. The CCI, however, rejected the allegation and noted that the availability and supply of molasses in the country had a huge and decisive impact on the production and supply of ethanol, and opposite parties could not be said to be in collusion to create any artificial scarcity. In the cement cartel[58] and dry-cell[59] cases, the Cement Manufacturers Association and Association of Indian Dry Cell Manufacturers, respectively, were held to be guilty of facilitating the cartel. Similarly, in the beer cartel case,[60] while the three beer companies were held to be indulging in cartelization in the sale and supply of beer in various states and union territories in India, the All India Brewers' Association (AIBA) was found to be actively involved in facilitating such cartelization; therefore, the CCI held that AIBA violated the provisions of the Act.

3.2.2.1.3 MANUFACTURING CARTELS AND LENIENCY

Effectively, there are less than ten leniency applications across 12 years, all in the manufacturing sector. Cartelization was found in respect of tenders floated by Indian Railways for the supply of Brushless DC Fans and other electrical items.[61] Cartelization was also found post-leniency application in the manufacture and supply of zinc-carbon dry-cell batteries to control the distribution and price of zinc-carbon dry cell batteries in India.[62] The third leniency filing pertained to bid rigging in tenders floated by Pune Municipal Corporation (PMC) for the design, supply, installation, commissioning, operation, and maintenance of municipal organic and inorganic solid waste processing plants.[63] The year 2019 witnessed two cases decided under Section 27 on the basis of leniency applications, one concerning an ancillary cartel between Panasonic and Godrej Co. in the institutional sale of dry-cell batteries. Panasonic, having prior knowledge of the time of price increase through the primary cartel between Panasonic, Eveready and NIPPO to fix prices, used it as a leverage to increase the prices of batteries sold by it to Godrej.[64] The other concerned cartelization in the supply of electric power steering systems.[65] In the automotive bearings case (2020),[66] the CCI concluded that the four large auto-bearing firms colluded to mutually decide the bearings' price sold to OEMs. The colluded price increase was aimed at uniformly passing on the increase in raw material (steel) cost to the OEMs; otherwise, the OEMs were allegedly unwilling to abide by any individual price increase request. Interestingly, the CCI refrained from imposing any penalty, despite there being a long-duration pre-pandemic cartel without any special mitigating factors. The beer cartel case (2021)[67] was triggered when AB-InBev used CCI's leniency programme to disclose that it had detected a cartel while integrating SABMiller's operations in India. The CCI, on the basis of executives' conversations, WhatsApp messages, and emails, concluded that the companies regularly colluded to increase prices in several States, effectively forging a cartel. The companies also used the AIBA as a common platform to collectively decide prices. Giving the benefit of 100% reduction in penalty under the provisions of Section 46 of the Act to AB InBev and its individuals, 40% to UBL and its individuals and 20% to CIPL and its individuals, the CCI directed UBL and CIPL to pay penalties to the tune of approx. INR 750 crores and INR 120 crores, respectively, besides passing a cease-and-desist order. In the paper cartel case,[68] the CCI concluded that ten paper manufacturing companies had indulged in cartelization in fixing prices of writing and printing paper by participating in the meetings convened under the umbrella of the platform provided by their trade association and discussing prices and the roadmap for coordinated increase, besides monitoring the decisions taken in such meetings. A leniency application was made by one of the parties during the pendency of the investigation before the DG and was granted a 100% reduction in the penalty imposed.

3.2.2.1.4 MANUFACTURING CARTELS AND APPEAL RESULTS

Interestingly, until 2017, 71% of the cases decided by CCI have either been set aside or altered by appellate forums. This percentage is too high to ignore and raises questions on the quality of decisions of the CCI both in terms of collection of evidence and the appreciation of evidence. A huge disparity is seen in the imposition of fines, which in many cases have been modified by the appellate forums. Imposition of penalty in the absence of any penalty guidelines has left the entire domain of penalization at the discretion of the CCI. The exercise at the appellate level, similar to that of the CCI, is *ad hoc* and at the discretion of the forum.

3.2.2.2 *Service sector*

The service sector forms the most prominent part of India's GDP[69] and is composed of a wide array of business activities, including information technology, transport, entertainment, insurance, hospitality, banking, real estate, financing, and social and personal services.

As indicated earlier, cartels operating in the service sector constitute almost 70% of all decided cartel cases in India. Wholesale and retail, media and entertainment, and transport services form the bulk of these cases, constituting as high as 84% of all service cartels. Violation of Section 3 (3) (b) – agreement to limit or control production – forms the bulk of service cartels (60%), followed by agreements to fix prices (27%). Agreements to share the market and rig bids form a small percentage of all service cartels – 5% and 8%, respectively. In comparison, 58% of all orders under Section 26 (6) had allegations related to service sector cartels. The distribution of business areas is much wider in orders under Section 26 (6), and the three main business areas, as highlighted, constitute only 26% of all orders. A majority of orders under Section 26 (6) relating to the service sector had allegations of either price fixing agreements (53%) or agreements to limit or control production (33%).

3.2.2.2.1 TRANSPORTATION SERVICES

Transportation services constitute one of the three major service sector avenues where orders under Section 27 are concentrated. Most of these cases saw the primary involvement of trade associations with a mix of price fixing and supply restriction arrangements.

In the *Uniglobe* case,[70] information was filed by a market participant against a boycott call given by the Travel Agents Federation of India (TAFI) and the Travel Agents Association of India (TAAI). The boycott call was given on account of a shift from a commission-based fee structure to a transaction fee structure as it essentially cancelled the commission given by airlines on the sale of tickets. The informant defied the boycott call resulting in its expulsion from the membership of TAFI and TAAI. The DG, relying on the minutes of meetings, email communications for boycott, joint circulars of all associations, depositions of office bearers of associations and notice of expulsion sent to the informant, reported that the TAFI, TAAI and IATA had violated Section 3 (3) (b) of the Act. The CCI concurred with the findings of the DG and three other trade associations (IATO, ADTOI and ETAA) that participated in the meetings for the boycott were also held responsible. The penalty of one lakh was imposed on TAFI, TAAI and IATA, while a cease-and-desist order was passed against the other three trade associations. A similar stand was taken in the *FCM*[71] matter. The question of commission to travel agents was raised again in *Lufthansa*,[72] when the airline companies stopped paying commission to travel agents for the sale of tickets. The DG noted that the opposite parties were not competitors as they served different destinations. Further, there was no evidence of a meeting of minds. The CCI, too, did not find any violation and held that "the airlines had taken independent decisions to abolish the system of commission and there is no evidence of the meeting of minds".

The CCI investigated the allegation of price fixing by domestic airline carriers through the withdrawal of promotional offers and the hike in prices. It was found that although there was a price hike, it was not uniform across airlines. Further, there was no evidence that promotional offers were withdrawn simultaneously across all sectors.[73] In a related matter, the CCI found the price changes as a result of a dynamic pricing system common to all airlines. In another case,[74] it was alleged that the airline companies cartelized the fares of air tickets at the time of pilot strikes. The CCI, however, did not find evidence of an agreement between opposite parties and that the hike in price was an individual business practice followed everywhere. Per the CCI, the fare structure was based on supply and demand and was dynamic in nature.[75] In a recent matter[76] related to price collusion among airline companies, the CCI noted again that there was no pattern of stability or parallelism between the airlines. Moreover, it stated that parallel action would be actionable only if the changes were not made independently and were instead influenced by collusive conduct. However, since no such collusion was evidenced, the case was dismissed.

Actions or decisional practices of trade associations where they have restrained non-members of the association from operating in the market have also affected the transportation business. In *Swastik Stevedores*,[77] the association enabled only its own members in the market of transportation of goods and was also found to be enforcing the rate of transport on non-members in violation of Section 3 (3) (a) of the Act. A similar issue of restricting non-members from doing business freely in the *Kiratpur* region was held to be bad in law, and a penalty was imposed on the trade association.[78] The CCI, in *Indian Foundation of Transport Research*,[79] held the All India Motor Transport Congress (AIMTC) to be guilty of fixing freight charges. It relied on press releases and statements of spokespersons of AIMTC in the media to impose a penalty at a rate of 10% of the average receipts of the association. In *Cochin Port Trust*,[80] it was alleged that the trade association fixed prices by imposing a turn system on coastal operations, which indirectly fixed prices for hiring trailer services from the port. On the basis of evidence in the form of circulars and written communications sent by the trade association in favour of the alleged turn system, the CCI held the practice to be in violation of Section 3 (3) (a). In *Air Cargo*,[81] it was alleged that the trade associations, by determining the rate of cargo agents' commission in India through Resolution 016aa, violated Section 3 (3) (a) and that the implementation of CASS by IATA through Resolution 851 in India contravened the provisions of Section 3 (3) (b). It was held that the practice of 5% commission to cargo agents was continued due to the insistence of the informant and the Ministry of Civil Aviation, and the same could not be attributed to the opposite parties. Further, it was held that CASS was a "universally accepted system and was only in pilot stage in India". It noted that the "informant was part of negotiation before its implementation and also supported it". It was held that the clauses of Resolution 851 did not indicate that it would limit or restrict the international air cargo transportation services in India.

Indirect price fixing has also been held to be violative of Section 3 of the Act. In *Express Industry*,[82] it was alleged that the price for cargo transport was fixed through fuel surcharge (FSC). The CCI went against the opinion of the DG to hold the opposite parties guilty of collusion. It noted that the revenue from FSC could be forecasted, and no airline was able to give any data/costing study in support of the determination of FSC. Further, it was noted that FSC did not move per fuel price. A penalty at the rate of 3% of average turnover was imposed on all three opposing parties. In *M.P. Mehrotra*,[83] it was alleged that the strategic alliance for joint network and route rationalization done by airline companies was to limit market share. Further, it was alleged that the opposite parties were fixing prices, evident from the simultaneous increase of FSC. The DG, on the basis of a high degree of price parallelism and the announcement of alliance by opposite parties, held them to be in violation of Sections 3 (3) (a–c). The CCI did not concur with the findings of the DG and categorized the arrangement between airline companies as common trade practice and declared it to be pro-competitive as it reduced costs and facilitated passenger travel.

In *Western Coalfields*,[84] bid rigging was alleged in the tender floated by the informant for coal and sand transportation. The DG reported that there was no satisfactory explanation provided by the opposite parties for identical quotes. On the basis of behavioural evidence, like evidence of communication and prior financial dealings with each other, similar bidding patterns in earlier years, last-minute filing of tenders and the presence of trade associations for the exchange of information, the DG found the opposite parties to be in violation of Section 3 (3 (d) of the Act. The CCI concurred with the findings of the DG and imposed a penalty at the rate of 4%.

3.2.2.2.2 WHOLESALE AND RETAIL

Most of the cases in this subsection have revolved around the pharmaceutical sector. The wholesale and retail market in drugs is known for the strong presence of local and national trade associations. The activities of these trade associations have been questioned on multiple occasions by the CCI. Cease-and-desist orders along with penalties have been imposed when these trade associations went beyond their legitimate activities and indulged in anti-competitive behaviour. The highest rate of recidivism has been witnessed in this sector, and the penalty orders against trade associations and sometimes the office bearers do not seem to have created enough deterrence. The CCI in *Bengal Chemist and Druggist Association (BCDA)*[85] observes,

> When the trade associations indulge in taking commercially sensitive business decisions on behalf of the entire industry as to whether or not to offer discounts, 24x7 service, free home delivery etc., then competitive forces are not allowed to operate in the market for furtherance of one's business. Innovative business practices, superior services, consumer choice, lower prices, etc., take a back seat and do not become the guiding force for doing business. Consequently, not only the businesses suffer but irreparable harm is caused to the consumer.[86]

Most of the cases are similar in nature and revolve around questions of fixing margins, offering discounts by retailers, the requirement of mandatory NOC or product information service (PIS), refusal to deal with nonmembers and boycotting for non-compliance.

In *BCDA*,[87] it was alleged that the association issued circulars prohibiting retailers from giving any discount to consumers and that it compelled retailers to display "no discount" pamphlets. The system was controlled through a vigilance committee to enforce compliance. The CCI found that BCDA and its affiliates "took concerted action against retailers offering discounts by launching organizational movements, threatening them, picketing, imposing fines, forcing them to shut down or restricting supply". The penalty at the rate of 10% of the average receipts and income was imposed on BCDA and its office bearers, respectively. The COMPAT,[88] in appeal, reduced the penalty previously imposed, and the penalty on office bearers was revoked due to a lack of evidence to prove that they were in charge of and responsible to BCDA for the conduct of its business.

In *Varca Druggist and Chemists*,[89] it was alleged that the Chemist and Druggist Association of Goa (CDAG) forced all pharmaceutical companies to appoint their wholesalers only through the association by way of a mandatory NOC. The DG reported the cartel-like conduct of CDAG. It noted that the wholesalers could only supply to member retailers and that the association determined the maximum amount of discount that could be offered by the wholesalers and retailers. The association "*restricted the introduction of new drugs and pharmaceutical formulations into the market by requiring new stockists and distributors to pay sums of money to the CDAG under the guise of Product Information Service (PIS) fees*". The association had also warned of boycott in case of non-compliance. CCI, on the basis of evidences available in the form of MOA between the All India Organisation of Chemists and Druggists (AIOCD) and the Organization of Pharmaceutical Producers of India (OPPI), minutes of meetings and letters issued by the association to the pharmaceutical companies, held the association to be in violation of Section 3 (3) (a) and 3 (3) (b) of the Act and imposed a penalty at the rate of 10% of the average receipts. A similar order was passed against the Chemist and Druggist Association, Baroda, in the case of *Vedant Bio Sciences*.[90] The practice of mandatory NOC was held to be bad in law in *Rohit Medical Stores*[91] as well. In *Vinayak Pharma*,[92] the CCI held pharmaceutical companies guilty of colluding with the associations in order to enforce the NOC requirement. It examined the conduct of the companies under the generic language of Section 3 (1) of the Act. The tribunal, however, did not agree with this approach and held that the pharmaceutical company could not have acted with the association if it was coerced by it.[93] Recent cases of *KCDA*,[94] *CDAB*[95] and *Alis Medical Agency*[96] are indications that the practice of mandatory NOC still continues in the market. Three more cases in 2019 on the issue of mandatory NOC and PIS practice and fixing of trade margins for retailers were added to the long list of CCI orders against the pharmaceutical trade associations.[97]

In *Santuka Associates*,[98] while the CCI, similar to previous cases, held the practice of NOC and PIS facilitated by AIOCD as anti-competitive, the COMPAT set aside the order of the CCI. Per the COMPAT,[99] there was not enough evidence to prove that the NOC requirement was made mandatory or there was a boycott of any wholesaler at the instance of the association. Further, it was held that fixing of trade margins was done by the manufacturers and not by the association. The COMPAT took the same stand in *Peeveear Medical Agencies*[100] and *Sandhya Drug Agency*.[101]

In *Arora Medical Hall*,[102] the CCI held that decisions and practices of the Chemist and Druggist Association of Faridabad (CDAF) amounted to limiting and controlling supply in the market. It was alleged that the CDAF was enforcing the requirement of NOC for distributorship, and it had expelled the informant from the association when it objected to the practice. The tribunal, however, set aside the order of CCI and noted that the informant was expelled from the association because of its own unethical conduct of charging inflated bills and that a NOC was not mandatory.[103]

In another matter concerning trade associations with similar issues, it was alleged that the regulations of *Sonipat Distributors Association*[104] mandated membership for each distributor/retailer. Mandatory NOC was required to do business, and a fine was imposed in case of non-compliance. The association also prevented outsiders from operating in the region and enforced geographical area restrictions on members. The CCI, based on minutes of meetings, NOC records proving cancellation of membership due to sale in others' area and statements of office bearers of the association, held the association to be in violation of Sections 3 (3) (b) and 3 (3) (c) of the Act.

Cases in the pharmaceutical sector and the repeated nature of violations by the associations are perfect examples to demonstrate the lack of deterrence on the market participants and that associations seem comfortable paying fines instead of correcting their course of action. The CCI bases the quantum of penalty on the average of receipts of the association, which does not consider the turnover of the participating members. This makes the quantum of penalty small and ineffective.

Outside the pharmaceutical sector, there is only one case within the wholesale and retail sector where the CCI penalized anti-competitive behaviour. In 2021, the CCI held that the FPBAI[105] and its advisories, by restricting the quantum of discounts, indirectly determined sale prices of books and journals and indirectly limited and controlled their supply.

3.2.2.2.3 MEDIA AND ENTERTAINMENT

Similar to the pharmaceutical sector, the majority of the cases in the media and entertainment sector pertain to anti-competitive practices of trade associations that have the effect of limiting or controlling production or supply in violation of Section 3 (3) (b).

In *FICCI Multiplex*,[106] it was alleged that the opposite trade associations threatened to boycott multiplexes to force them to agree to the revised revenue-sharing formula. They issued notices to stop the screening of movies. The CCI, on the basis of minutes of meetings and notice sent by trade associations to their members not to screen movies, held them to be in violation of Sections 3 (3) (a) and 3 (3) (b) of the Act. Trade associations have commonly used their clout to force producers or distributors to mandatorily register their films with the association before their release in the territory of the association.[107] They have been found to put restrictions on the exhibition of films through restrictions on the number of screens for release.[108] Exhibitors have been forced not to exhibit movies of non-members. Instances of boycott,[109] strike and picketing have been reported to the CCI for non-compliance with the diktats of the associations.[110] The CCI has passed multiple orders in cases where the regional trade association restricted the supply or telecast of dubbed content.[111] In *Cinemax*,[112] the Film Distributors Association of Kerala directed the revenue-sharing pattern to the informant, which was also made binding for other members and exhibitors. The CCI held that the opposite party did not allow the informant to negotiate with individual distributors in violation of Section 3 (3) (a). It also held that the stoppage of screening for defying members was in violation of Section 3 (3) (b) of the Act.[113] Actions of trade associations to use their power to force various actors, technicians, producers and financiers not to associate with a particular person or entity has been held to be anti-competitive.[114]

In *FTGI*,[115] it was alleged that the opposite parties were acting in a concerted manner to decide the terms and conditions for the release of the films in multiplexes and had formed a cartel under the auspices of the Multiplex Association of India (MAI) in violation of Section 3 (3) (a) & 3 (3) (b) of the Act. The CCI held that there was enough evidence to suggest that such meetings were being used as a platform to carry out a scheme of concerted action by the opposite parties to extract more attractive terms from the producers/distributors of various Bollywood and Hollywood movies.

In one of the rare cases of leniency, bid rigging was alleged in the market for the provision of broadcasting services submitted in response to the tenders floated by sports broadcasters. The CCI, on the basis of evidence of exchange of commercially sensitive information related to bidding, such as bid prices and terms of offer, and emails signifying teaming arrangement for proposed quotations in such a manner that one party would win the bid, held the opposite parties to be in violation of Section 3 (3) (d) of the Act.[116]

The CCI, in *TFPC*,[117] reiterated that while the role of trade associations to further and espouse the cause of their respective members is undisputed, its conduct cannot transgress into a commercial thicket whereby collective decisions are taken which result, directly or indirectly, in the determination of prices. Similarly, if the impugned conduct limits or controls the value chain or results in sharing of markets, such conduct is presumed to have an AAEC by virtue of the provisions contained in Section 3 (3) of the Act and, unless rebutted, fall foul of the provisions of Section 3 (1) thereof.

3.2.2.2.4 BANKING SECTOR

There are limited cases related to the banking sector, all of which are under Section 26 (6) of the Act. In *Deustche Bank*,[118] it was alleged by the informant that the banks had entered into an agreement to levy pre-payment charges on the house loan. The DG, after the scrutiny of minutes of board meetings of the banking association, reported that there was a collective decision taken with respect to pre-payment charges in violation of Section 3 of the Act. The CCI, however, did not find any commonality across banks in the levy of charges and held that the meeting circular referred to by the DG was not mandatory in nature and did not constitute any agreement between parties. The CCI, going against the DG's report, took a similar stand in *Indiabulls*[119] and *Religare*.[120] In all these cases, the requirement of establishing an agreement between parties through concrete evidence was stressed. In another matter,[121] it was alleged that the banks had colluded to fix savings bank interest rates (SBIRs) and service charges on automated teller machines (ATMs) transactions. The DG examined ten banks and reported that the similarity in SBIRs offered by the banks was an outcome of their independent assessment of market conditions and not of any collusive arrangement. Further, it was reported that there existed a large variety and dissimilarity in different service charges levied by banks, which indicated that the same was decided independently and unilaterally. The CCI concurred with the findings of the DG.

3.2.2.2.5 ELECTRICITY DISTRIBUTION

There are only two reported cases related to this area of business, and both orders have been passed under Section 26 (6). In *New Delhi Power Limited (NDPL)*,[122] it was alleged that the power companies were overcharging consumers. Further, it was alleged that action on the part of DISCOMS to supply and install the electric meters themselves prohibited the consumers from purchasing and installing meters, which limited and controlled the production of electric meters in the market. The DG, on the basis of the survey conducted and responses from different organizations, reported that there was no evidence of any agreement or understanding between power companies. The CCI concurred with the findings of the DG. In another matter[123] related to electricity meters, it was alleged that the machines installed by the power companies were running faster. The DG, without doing any independent investigation, relied solely on the earlier case of NDPL to report that there was no evidence to prove concerted action between DISCOMS.

3.2.2.2.6 GAMING AND LOTTERY

There has been just one case related to cartelization in the gaming industry. In *Jupiter Gaming Solutions*,[124] it was alleged that the tender invited by the government of Goa for lottery services was rigged. The DG, based on circumstantial evidence, reported complementary bidding in the tender. The CCI, however, did not concur with the findings of the DG and held that there was not enough evidence to support the allegation of cartelization.

3.2.2.2.7 PUBLICATION

In *Prints India*,[125] it was alleged that Springer India and eight Indian institutes entered into anti-competitive co-publishing agreements in violation of Sections 3 (3) (a–c). Per the DG, such agreements were a usual norm in the field of science, technology and medicine (STM) journal publishing all over the world. The co-publishing agreement with one of the leading publishers of the world was, therefore, reported as an attempt to become free from the responsibility of marketing the journals which they were publishing. The CCI concurred with the DG's report. In 2021, the CCI held that the Federation of Publishers' and Booksellers' Associations (FPBAI),[126] by restricting the quantum of discounts, indirectly determined the sale prices of books and journals. FPBAI, by its advisories, indirectly limited and controlled the supply of books and journals.

3.2.2.2.8 INSURANCE

In this respect, there is one case each under Section 27 and Section 26 (6), respectively. In *National Insurance Co. Ltd.*,[127] it was alleged that the public sector insurance companies rigged the bids submitted in response to the tenders floated by the government of Kerala for selecting an insurance service provider for Rashtriya Swasthya Bima Yojna. The DG, on the basis of minutes of meeting between bidders, reported that the insurance companies colluded to rig the bid and raise prices in successive bids. The CCI agreed with DG's report and, considering the effect of anti-competitive behaviour of parties on the beneficiaries, imposed a penalty at the rate of 2% of their average turnover. The COMPAT, however, later reduced the penalty to 1% of their relevant turnover.[128] In another matter,[129] it was alleged that the insurance companies had colluded and agreed to share the group health insurance business among them. The DG, in light of insufficient evidence, reported that there was no attempt on the part of companies to determine the prices or limit or restrict the supply of services in the market of health insurance or provision of services relating to third-party administrators (TPAs). Further, it was reported that the formation of a new TPA would bring efficiency to the market and benefit the consumers. The CCI concurred with the findings of the DG.

3.3 Cartel market share

Market share of the cartel in comparison to that of cartel outsiders has a direct relation with its sustenance and longevity. The higher the market share of the cartel, the more stable it is, which in effect, increases the duration of the cartel. If there is an absence of outsiders or when the relative market share of the outsiders is insignificant, there is negligible risk of outsiders undercutting the cartel. There is also a lesser risk of breakdown of cartel due to defection as there is a very high risk of being outcast from the market or being forced into a price war. This, in turn, gives strength to cartels and also increases the cartel profit.

The data[130] from the observation period suggests that the combined market share of cartels is very high (close to 90%). One of the difficulties faced was the lack of data in the cases decided by the CCI. It is surprising that the CCI has penalized cartel members without looking at the market strength enjoyed by the cartel. The impact of a cartel on the market assessed though cartel market share could have been one of the criteria to impose the penalty. There is also a lack of data on the market share of cartel members during the period of cartelization, and this prevents any analysis of the effect of market share asymmetry within the cartel vis-à-vis the stability of the cartel. Since all the trade associations were in some manner either the most powerful organizations in terms of membership within a particular sector or were the only associations in the sector, the cases involving the practice of trade associations have been taken as all-inclusive cartels.

The majority of the cartels have been all-inclusive, which means they did not have to worry about non-cartel members. It can be said that the market participants have seen value in including all competitors to avoid any detection. This, when compared to cartel duration and death of cartels, may provide further insights into the factors that contribute to the stability of a cartel.

3.4 Area of operation of cartels

Sixty-five per cent of the detected cartels in India had a local character in terms of their impact or operation, and the rest can be said to have a pan-India impact or presence. This pattern reverses under Section 26 (6), where almost 70% of cases with allegations of cartelization were national in character. However, the CCI was unable to find enough evidence to conclude cartelization. In these cases, the evidence was more readily ascertainable. One of the reasons for this is that majority of the trade associations which the cases pertained to were localized and were operating specifically for a particular region or territory. For instance, apart from a few matters where the CCI penalized a national level trade association, the pharmaceutical wholesale and retail sector associations or the film exhibitors and distributors' associations have imposed their authority in the territory in which they operate.

3.4.1 Territorial concentration of cartels in India

There is a concentration of regional cartels in only a few Indian states. For instance, approximately 65% of cases of local cartels originated in the southern and eastern regions of India. The State of Kerala alone constitutes 25% of cases. This also indicates limited percolation of competition jurisprudence in the greater part of the country and gets strengthened when we look at the demography of informants filing information alleging cartelization. To make a limited illustration here, the state government in any state is the biggest contractor and the biggest procurement agency. However, if we look at the data, instances of state governments filing information to the CCI are the least among all categories. As high as 70% of all local cartels have come from just five states – Delhi, Haryana, Kerala, Karnataka and Maharashtra.

The high concentration of cartels in the southern and western parts of India may be attributed to a certain domino effect from the initial cases dealing with anti-competitive practices of the trade associations, especially in the wholesale and retail segments of the pharmaceutical sector and the media and entertainment sector and, therefore, have hovered around issues of boycott, non-dealing, mandatory NOC, PIS and fixing of rates for constituent members. The absence of similar trade association cases from other regions of the country may be attributed to low awareness of

State-wise distribution of localized cartels

North	Delhi + Haryana	7
	Madhya Pradesh	4
	Himachal Pradesh	1
	Punjab	1
	Uttar Pradesh	1
South	Karnataka	6
	Tamil Nadu	2
	Kerala	11
East	West Bengal	4
	Assam	1
	Orissa	1
West	Maharashtra and Goa	10
	Gujarat	2

competition law or due to the strong hold of the trade associations. There is a lesser likelihood of information where there is either a mutual acceptance of the anti-competitive practice or where the trade associations' practices have strong disciplining mechanisms which dissuade defection or complaints. Further, the lack of competition benches at the state level also has a negative impact on the rate of filing of information. Incidentally, the Raghavan Committee had recommended the Competition Authority of India have permanent benches in metropolitan cities. It also recommended the creation of the office of DG at regional levels who would investigate the matter and submit reports to the bench in that region. Its recommendations were adopted in the original text of the 2002 Act. Section 22 of the Act envisaged the creation of principal and regional benches. Unfortunately, the Competition (Amendment) Act, 2007, replaced the sections of the Act that laid out provisions for the creation and functioning of competition benches. Since the CCI was to act as an administrative body and not as an adjudicatory body, it was envisioned that it would function as a collegium and not as separate benches.[131] Considering that majority of cartel cases have in the last ten years originated at the local level clubbed with the fact that the majority of information against such anti-competitive practices has been concentrated in only certain regions of the country, it is time that the government reconsider its position on region-level enforcement of competition law. The presence of a competition bench or a competition/DG office will have a disciplining effect on market participants. It will be easier to track the activities of the regional trade associations both in terms of competition compliance and post-cartel tacit collusion. The Competition Law Review Committee, 2019,[132] also stresses the "need to increase the accessibility of CCI for corporates and other stakeholders that are not based in Delhi". The 2019 Committee Report recommends the creation of CCI offices in cities to advise and assist on competition-related concerns and issues.

3.5 Participation of firms/competitors and trade associations

3.5.1 Involvement of trade associations

Trade associations play a very important role in market economics as they are a means of collective bargaining for the furtherance of common commercial goals. They may be composed of either individuals or firms or a combination of both, and all legitimate activities are protected under law. However, when the collaboration leads to coordination between competitors, it becomes an issue for competition law. This is the reason that competition law does not exempt the practices and decisions of the trade associations. Trade associations can serve either as cartel facilitating structures or be engaged in anti-competitive behaviour through their decisions. Membership in such associations creates opportunities for competitors to meet and discuss common issues of concern. Many times, these associations adopt self-governing business codes to achieve synergy and prevent unfair practices. However, the platforms of trade associations have also been used to operate and maintain collusive arrangements. They are often used as mediums for the exchange of information. While the exchange of information is not in itself bad, when it is used to coordinate and sustain a cartel, it becomes a violation of competition law. The presence of an active and strong trade association in any business, therefore, increases the stability of the cartel.

The Indian experience is not very different from the understanding in developed jurisdictions, where the presence of an active trade association is considered one of the features of a cartel-conducive environment. Interestingly, apart from the presence of trade associations as facilitating structures in detected cartels, there is a very high number of cases where the decision of the trade associations has been held to be anti-competitive. While Section 3 (3) of the Act includes decisions of associations within its fold, the CCI has found it difficult to impose a penalty under Section 27. In most of the cases involving the primary action of the association, penalty has been imposed on the basis of the turnover/annual receipts of the association. The CCI has not yet calculated the penalty on the basis of the turnover of constituent members of the association, and thus, the penalty calculated on the basis of turnover of the association turns out to be less than optimal. One of the outcomes of this is the high rate of recidivism among trade associations.

Figure 3.5 gives a yearly trend with respect to participation in terms of the number of market participants and trade associations. In almost 60% of cases, the trade association has been the primary cartelist or leader, but only 9 out of a total of 42 cases (21%) had an allegation of such involvement under Section 26 (6). In comparison to prosecuted cartels in other jurisdictions, this is an astronomical figure. It is true that cartels tend to sustain longer when there is an active trade association to connect the cartel

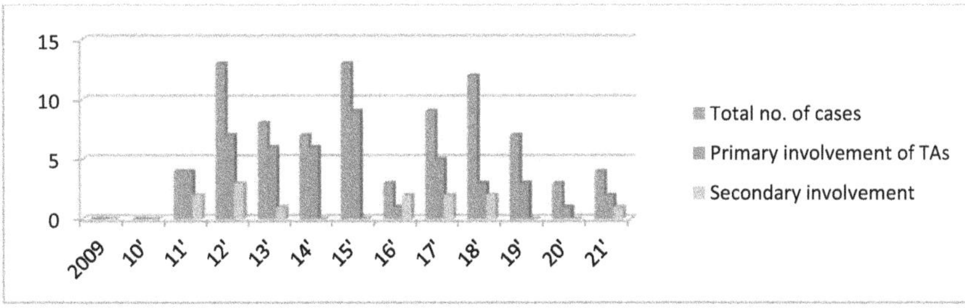

X axis: Years of enforcement; Y axis: Number of cases under Section 27 of the Act.

Figure 3.5 Yearly trend of participation of trade associations in all concluded cases of cartels.

members as they then do not have to communicate directly. However, that is seen in only 16% (14 out of total 84 cases) of all concluded cartel cases under Section 27. The fact that trade associations play an important role as conduits in high-duration cartels is not being discarded here, and this is evident from the bigger cartel cases in India, be it the cement cartel,[133] the LPG cartel[134] or the beer cartel.[135] However, this is not the general phenomenon. On average, there are four cases each year where the trade association is the primary player. Additionally, an average of one cartel per year involves a trade association on a secondary level, and this average excludes the cases in which the primary involvement of a trade association was there. On average, almost ten trade associations per year were involved in cartel cases during the observation period, but in contrast, an average of only 1.4 trade associations (out of a total of 17) were investigated for alleged cartelization under Section 26 (6).

The high bars showing direct participation of the trade association in the middle years can be attributed to the cluster of cases coming from anti-competitive behaviour in the sectors of media & entertainment and pharmaceutical wholesale and retail. If we remove all the cases where these trade associations were the primary actors, we are left with an average of less than four cartel cases per year, indicating towards a low rate of detection and prosecution of cartels in India.

3.5.2 *Involvement of firms*

The decline in the number of firms across the years can be attributed to the considerable decline in the number of orders under Section 26 (6). For instance, while the investigation was ordered against 127 firms (24 cases) in the first five years (2009–2013), it sharply declined to mere 36 firms

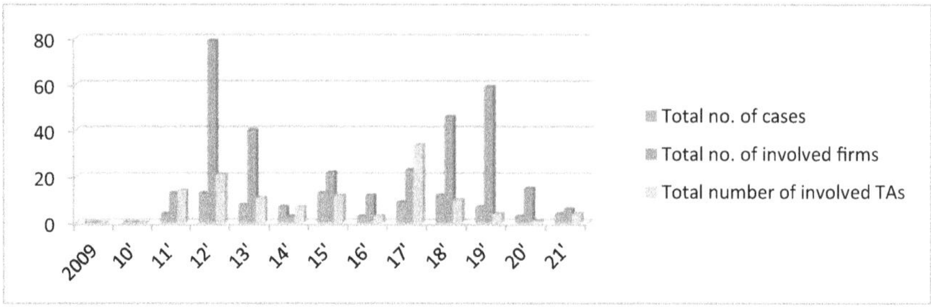

X axis: Years of enforcement; Y axis: Number of cases under Section 27 of the Act.

Figure 3.6 Yearly trends with respect to the total number of involved trade associations and market participants in all concluded cases of cartels.

(14 cases) in the next five years (2014–2018). If we compare this to orders under Section 27, cartelization was investigated and subsequently proved against 131 firms (23 cases) in the first five years, which dropped to 107 firms (45 cases) in the next five years. The numbers can be a bit misleading if we look closely at the nature of orders under Section 27. Of the 107 firms mentioned earlier, 77 firms were penalized in just two cases (48 in the LPG cartel case and 29 in the railway cartel case[136]). In the year 2019, there is not a single order under Section 26 (6) related to cartels. Out of the seven orders under Section 27 till August 2019, three cases related to anti-competitive practices of the regional trade associations in the pharmaceutical wholesale and retail sector. Out of 61 firms that were investigated and against whom orders were passed, 51 firms were involved in a single matter.[137]

Figure 3.6 further shows the yearly trend of the number of involved firms and trade associations. There is a high fluctuation in the numbers across years which range from 79 in 2012 to as low as 3 in 2014. The number of firms in individual cartels also fluctuates from as high as 51 (LPG 2019) to as low as 3.

On average,[138] 26 firms were involved in cartelization per year, and approximately eight firms were present per cartel.[139] Ten cases of cartelization involved cartels with ten or more members. In contrast, under Section 26 (6), 17.3 firms were investigated for cartelization per year, and on an average, 5.6 firms per cartel were investigated.

3.5.3 Observations

Per the data, anti-competitive behaviour has mostly revolved around associations. Decision-making associations with large memberships are mostly centralized and are taken by the office bearers/executive members. Further, there is a general acceptance of the anti-competitive conduct among the members who see such actions as general market practice. Therefore, complaints have only been filed with the regulator when either there is an insider who refuses to follow the diktats of the association or when there is a new entrant to the market who refuses to follow the business protocols set by the association and, in turn, faces resistance from the association in forms of boycott, strike or picketing. Enterprises that have to deal with the members of the association also end up following the practices of the association to avoid any form of confrontation. In fact, in some instances, they have helped the association to enforce the decisions of the latter by refusing to deal with business entities that go against the association. While these companies have been investigated by the DG whenever there has been information alleging their involvement or participation, they have largely escaped penalty because they were not in a horizontal relationship with the trade association, a prerequisite for the application of Section 3 (3). These companies, in the initial years, were also given the benefit of the doubt as the CCI believed that the companies operated under the pressure of trade associations. However, the CCI, seeing the high incidence and repetition of cases on similar subject matters, started expecting the companies to not follow the anti-competitive practices of the trade associations and report the same to it instead of involving themselves in the execution of such practices. The CCI has now started invoking Section 3 (1) of the Act to penalize these companies.[140] It has read Section 3 (1) in a generic fashion without it being subject to Section 3 (3) or 3 (4) of the Act. Therefore, agreements' need not necessarily be between horizontal or vertical players to be brought within the ambit of Section 3. Agreements which are not necessarily horizontal or vertical, like the one between trade associations and pharmaceutical companies, can be brought within the ambit of Section 3 (1) and scrutinized for their anti-competitive effect. This approach of the CCI, however, is yet to be approved by the appellate forums. Previously, all these companies escaped any liability under the Act for their complicity in the anti-competitive practice of the trade association.

Most of these trade associations also escape from the application of provision on abuse of dominant position as they fail to qualify as enterprise due to the absence of any economic activity. This also meant that the penalty imposed on them was calculated not on the basis of turnover but on annual receipts, which happens to be very low. There is no restriction within the Act to impose liability on the members constituting the association. Decisions of the trade association can be examined under Section 3 (3) of the Act as a practice in itself or as an agreement between constituent members. The CCI, over the years, has not applied the second level of scrutiny and has been content with penalizing the association as a separate person. It is only later, when it realized that the imposition of monetary penalty on associations was not having any effect on their activities, that it started penalizing the executive members of the associations. The CCI has not lifted the veil of the association to take into account the turnover of the members of the association to compute the penalty.[141]

Another set of cases is those where the trade associations were involved at the secondary level, meaning thereby that the platform of the association was used by the cartelists to implement and execute their cartel decisions. More often, these associations were used to disseminate strategic information to sustain cartels. Exchange of information, as discussed earlier, is used not just for the dissemination of information but also to monitor the actions of the participating members. In all these cases, the trade associations were penalized along with the cartelists, although at a different rate. Interestingly, the rate at which the associations were penalized in cases where they had a primary involvement is similar to cases where they did not. Theoretically, since penalty depends on the gravity of offence and degree of involvement, there should have been a natural gradation of penalty in these two types of cases. However, the same has not been witnessed in India.

3.6 Structural scheme of cartel

The structural or organizational scheme of any cartel can be examined through its decision-making practice during its lifetime. If we apply the Baker and Faulkner[142] categorization technique to the data set, Indian cartels can be broadly categorized as centralized and decentralized cartels. Centralized cartels have a clear hierarchy of decision-making and have one or more cartel leaders (also known as ring leaders) in comparison to decentralized cartels, where there is no identifiable ring leader, and decision-making is more of a collective nature. A decentralized or bureaucratic cartel is managerial in nature with multiple objects involving multilateral arrangements and group meetings. Such cartels generally require a monitor to see that the collective decision is followed by all necessitating exchange of relevant information at some level. Third-party monitoring reduces the risk of detection as there is no record keeping at the individual firm level. The platform of a trade association becomes a perfect conduit for such exchanges. However, such cartels have also proven to be less stable in nature due to a lack of trust in fellow cartelists. On the other hand, if the cartel has a strong sanctioning mechanism where there is credible economic fear, defections are lesser, and the cartel may survive for a longer duration of time.

The categorization of cartels may serve two purposes. Firstly, the data, when juxtaposed to data on cartel duration, may enable us to examine the stability of the cartels in the presence of a ring leader; secondly, to examine whether such identification has any role to play when the CCI decides on fines to be imposed in entities involved in cartelization. Logically, one who acts as a cartel leader should be imposed greater penalties when compared with one who only has a passive involvement. The USA, for instance, excludes ring leaders from the leniency program.

3.6.1 Cartel ring leaders

The concept of a ring leader of a cartel can be broken down into three forms: *originator* (an entity which takes the effort to establish the cartel and gets it going through its connection with other market participants), *instigator* (an entity which advances the objectives the cartel through its decision-making, monitoring and coordination), and *coercer* (an entity which pressured other business entities to join the cartel). The US Guidelines of Corporate Leniency, 1993, includes all these forms in its provision for exclusion from the leniency regime.[143] The leniency provisions of the EU, however, allows ring leaders to make applications for a reduction in penalty.[144] While the 1996 Commission Notice (EU) acted as a barrier to immunity from fines for cartel ring leaders, the 2002 and 2006 Commission Notice (EU) only banned immunity in case the undertaking coerced another undertaking to either join or stay in the cartel. These undertakings can still apply for a reduction in fines if they fulfil the relevant criterion. The commission notice does not prevent other forms of ring leaders from applying for immunity. Therefore, if an undertaking was instrumental in establishing the cartel (instigator) or was one who coordinated the cartel in its operation or played a determining role in its operation (leader), it would still be eligible for immunity if it has not coerced other undertakings into the cartel. One can be called a leader if it, in order to advance the objective of the cartel, was the first to voluntarily implement the cartel arrangement or takes active steps to sustain the cartel. Therefore, even without coercion, an undertaking can still be categorized as a cartel leader.

It is not necessary, however, that the competition policies differentiate between 'instigators' and 'leaders' and cartels are broadly characterized either with or without a 'ring leader'. The important aspect is the consequence of such characterization in terms of the imposition of fines, grant of immunity or even reduction in penalties. The presence of an anti-cartel enforcement regime that differentiates between ring leaders and others has an effect on the internal organization of the cartel. If the cartel members know beforehand that certain undertakings will not be eligible for immunity from fines, trust in these entities by others increases, thus increasing the stability of the cartel as there are minimal chances of self-reporting. Ring leaders can provide the best possible evidence to prove cartels. If, on the other hand, ring leaders and other cartel members have the same rights, there is a possibility that non-leaders might feel the risk of the ring leader defecting. On the other hand, it may be argued that in a non-differentiated regime, ring leaders are likely to get more penalty, thereby reducing the likelihood of establishing or operating the cartel in the first place. Undertakings would not like to take leadership roles for fear of high fines, thus impacting the creation and also the sustenance of the cartel. Identification of a ring leader is also tricky and may not be that simple in many cases. Therefore, a differentiated regime that excludes ring leaders may deter undertakings from reporting if their identity as a ring leader is unclear.

Essentially, a differentiated regime with no special treatment to ring leaders would be preferred in jurisdictions with low cartel prosecutions where the door to immunity or reduction in fines through leniency may induce some ring leaders to adduce relevant evidence to detect cartels. However, if the rate of cartel detection and prosecution is relatively high, ring leaders should not be allowed to take advantage of the system created for the purpose of destroying the structures that they built.

Leniency provisions under Section 46 of the Act or the CCI (Lesser Penalty) Regulation of 2009 do not provide any clarity on the aspect of cartel ring leaders. Neither does India have penalty guidelines which consider different factors, including cartel leadership to quantify fines for cartelization. It has to be mentioned here that nothing stops the tribunal or the appellate authority from taking into account cartel leadership as an aggravating factor to impose a penalty within the upper limit prescribed under Section 27 of the Act.

In the present book, all the cases decided by the CCI have been examined to identify the role of ringleaders, if any. The cases have been divided into two parts. One where there is evidence to indicate one or more firms as ring leaders and others where the CCI identified ring leaders in the given factual scenario. The next level enquiry is whether CCI considered 'leadership' as an element to determine the fine to be imposed. The CCI, in the last ten years, has rarely considered the aspect of leadership as a relevant factor in imposing a penalty.

In the observation period, there was no attempt to identify ring leaders within a cartel. This is common for both types of cases in India – one with a trade association as the central player and the other where the trade association either is absent or is present only as a conduit for cartelization. The identification of a ring leader, which leads to higher penalties for such actors, helps in developing the required deterrence value. Through non-identification, the CCI has taken an easier route by sidestepping the requirement to collect evidence against one or more central actors. It has, during the observation period, attempted to identify such leaders in just six cases over the last ten years. This necessarily means that since there is no attempt to identify ring leaders, there is no harm in establishing or coordinating cartels because, if detected, the cartel ring leaders would be treated in a similar fashion as compared to other participants who might have entered due to the coercion by the ring leaders. Even in these six identified cases, while the evidence suggests that the cartel has key or central figures, there is no sign of any effect on the resultant penalty imposed. In *Uniglobe*,[145] while the CCI identified three trade associations among six as taking the lead role and having a high degree of involvement, it did not reflect in the actual computation of fine. On the contrary, it acted as a mitigating factor for the other three associations that were left without any penalty. The three leader associations were handed over a penalty of one lakh each, something which was based neither on their turnover nor on annual receipts. In *Nagrik Chetna*

Manch,[146] while the managing director of one of the firms admitted to having established and operationalized the cartel of bid rigging, the CCI made no distinction in imposing the penalty, either individual or at the undertaking level.[147] A uniform penalty at the rate of 10% of average turnover and income was calculated for six firms and five individuals, including the ring leader. Interestingly, the CCI also granted a 25% reduction in penalty for the ring leader. Similarly, in the *Dry-cell batteries*[148] case, even though it was observed that Panasonic played a key role in the cartel and "was in a position to influence and dictate the terms" of the anti-competitive arrangement to Godrej, it was granted a 100% reduction in penalty in lieu of the leniency application. Non-appreciation of the fact that Panasonic played the role of a ring leader has made the outcome of the case a bit unfair.

This is very different from other jurisdictions where the concerned regulator takes the effort to identify ring leaders in order to either not extend to them any benefit of leniency or to impose higher penalties. When there is no threat of identification as the leader, the general trust within the cartel increases the overall life of the cartel.

We can see the entire picture from a different angle. If there has been no or limited identification of cartel ring leaders during the observation period, it might be possible that all the cartels in India were democratic in nature with an idea of collective decision-making. This can be held to be true for the 47 cases where trade associations played a key role. Therefore, when the cartel-like conduct flew from articles, memorandum of association or code of ethics of the association, it can be said that such conduct was the result of the collective decision-making of all the members of the association. However, it has been seen across the years that in most of these cases, the real exercise of cartel conduct happened in the form of diktats, circulars, calls of boycott or strikes done at the level of the executive body of the association. The decisions were majorly taken by executive bodies or office bearers, which clearly comes out in the evidence collected by the DG of investigation. The CCI, however, has not been keen to penalize the office bearers and rather has been content on fining the trade associations as a body.

It has to be remembered here that most of these trade associations are not engaged in any economic activity and thus have no turnover to show. Therefore, the penalty is based on the receipts of the association, which is generally a contribution by all the members. Since any penalty on the association can be very well recovered from the members of the association, non-identification of either ring leaders in the form of key members or key office bearers seriously undermines the deterrence effect of any penalty imposed. This may be the reason for recidivism among trade associations. The situation is not very different in other cases where trade associations are not the key players. Decisions in almost all these cartels are at the level of enterprises taken by directors, managing directors, CEOs or managers. However, this does not translate into fixing accountability for the decision-makers of enterprises. The basic rule of corporate governance is fixing accountability for decision-makers, which gets reinforced through Section 48 of the Act. Less than 30% of cases within the subgroup of cases outside trade associations in the observation period fix accountability for office bearers in the form of a penalty. In all the other cases, the CCI has stopped imposing a penalty on the enterprise involved in cartelization. Something that we have realized and understood in corporate jurisprudence is that unless accountability is fixed at an individual level, a change in decision-making at the board level will not be achieved. Positively, the CCI has, in recent years, started to impose liability on the office bearers of business units. In the last two years, individual liability has been imposed in 11 out of 14 matters.

3.7 Cartel duration and death

While there has been no study that examines the determinants of duration of cartels for Indian cases, there are studies that have done the exercise for cartels in the US or the EU.[149] Examination of the duration of cartels can provide us with possible evidence to back our general theoretical assumptions on cartels and can indicate the effectiveness of detection techniques of the competition regulator. Therefore, a high average cartel duration might break the myth of cartels being "inherently unstable". If, in general, cartels are able to survive and sustain themselves profitably for a long duration of time without any defection, the effectiveness of the anti-cartel enforcement structure will require to be revisited. Data on the duration of cartels can be juxtaposed with previous data on firms' and trade associations' involvement to check if the number of members in a cartel has any effect on the duration or stability of the said cartel. Also, data on causes of cartel death can be examined with data on cartel duration.

The determination of the duration of a cartel is in itself a contentious issue. While theoretically, cartel duration means the period from the time of the establishment of a cartel till the termination of a cartel, data is rarely available to reach an exact figure. Unless it is a leniency application where the informants may divulge the date on which a cartel was created, finding the beginning point of cartels becomes a real task as no cartel member, in fear of increased penalties, will reveal the information on the duration of a cartel. Termination of a cartel may be due to the natural breakdown (due to change in market dynamics; entry of new members into the market; or the cartel being no more profitable) or because of the investigation and detection by the competition authority (enforcement process). Legally, cartel duration is the period during which the cartel activity can be proved. Since the cartel members will never exactly expose the duration of cartels, it is more of a choice of a time period depending on the availability of information.[150]

Data suggests that more than 90% of detected cartels in India ceased to exist due to the intervention of the CCI. The factors that generally play a role in the breakdown of cartels have not really played out that well in India. Therefore, there are rare instances of cartels breaking down due to

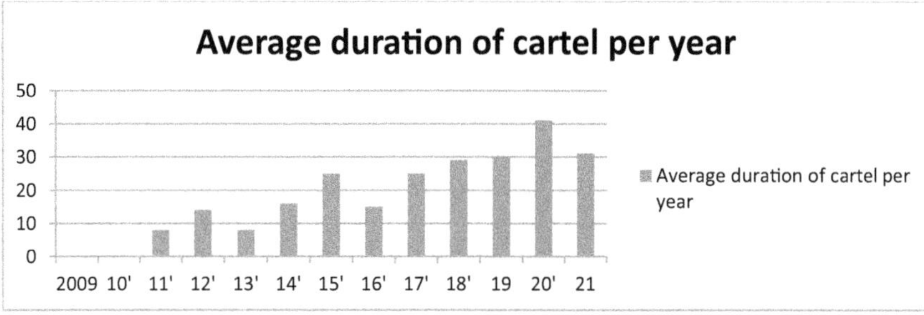

X axis: Years of enforcement; Y axis: average duration of cartel per year (in months)

Figure 3.7 Average duration of cartels per year.

Note: Around 40% of all the cases show evidence of cartel behaviour continuing from a period before the enforcement of Section 3 itself. Cartel duration in such cases has been counted from May 2009 – the month of enforcement of Section 3 of the act. Eleven cases that did not have a trade association as the primary actor existed prior to notification of Section 3.

economic factors, changes in market dynamics, entry of new players or even defection or cheating from cartels. Most of these cartels are all-inclusive with a high market share, which means that there is little possibility of cartel outsiders undercutting cartels. Of course, as indicated earlier, since more than 60% of these cases have trade associations as the key unit, cartels tend to remain stable for longer durations of time. While the lesser penalty regulations were notified as early as 2009, the first matter post leniency application was decided as late as 2017. Leniency cases comprise only 9% of total orders under Section 27 passed by the CCI.

The usual method for assessing cartel duration is the number of months the cartel operated before it was detected or died naturally. Figure 3.7 marks the cartel duration for all the detected cases in the observation period. The duration of the cartel where it did not die naturally has been counted from the month of the first instance of proven anti-competitive behaviour till the date investigation was ordered by the CCI. In case of multiple anti-competitive actions, first infringement has been taken as the starting point.

3.7.1 Duration of cartel vis-à-vis sector of operation

As indicated in the previous section, among the cases involving trade associations, there is a high concentration of cases in the service sector, primarily the media and entertainment sector and the wholesale and retail sector. The media and entertainment sector shows the highest average cartel duration, followed by the wholesale and retail sector. It is not surprising that these cartels have a high average cartel duration as most of these cases involve associations that have multiple level participation and comprise almost all the market participants. Since they are all-inclusive, there is rarely a case of any insider defecting from the general course of predetermined behaviour. These cases have only been detected when an outsider tries to enter the market or when there is an internal dispute between one or more members. Some cases also involve multiple trade associations which behave like one unit. These associations might be there in a hierarchical structure or exist as parallel organizations catering to different classes of members in the same sector. Arrangements between these parallel organizations have also been subject to scrutiny. However, what seems to be a departure from the general understanding is that a large number of participants in these associations do not seem to destabilize the cartel structure. Many of these cases existed prior to notification of Section 3, and therefore, such behaviour had continued for years before it was finally invalidated by the CCI under the Act.

The trade association cases are also concentrated around a few business areas, as one case spiralled into multiple cases with essentially the same subject matter or allegation but placed in a different territory. For instance, the practice of mandatory NOC from a regional trade association to do business was held to be having the effect of limiting or controlling the supply of medicines in the market as early as 2012. But this did not cause other similar trade associations in different regions to make a change in their respective charters, and they continued with their action till the same was informed to the CCI. A similar situation arose in the sector of media and entertainment where the local or regional associations of distributors or exhibitors were putting unfair conditions for the exhibition of films in their territory. The first case on this subject matter happened in 2012 and then spiralled into multiple similar cases. The beginning of such practices can be traced to either the charter documents or incorporation documents of these associations, which carried anti-competitive covenants through the years or can also be attributable to some memorandum of mutual understanding. The purpose of these restrictive clauses is not always to make a profit, and they also exist to exert market power of the associations. These cohesive units are strong and all-inclusive, and therefore, more often the information is not filed by an insider but by an outsider who wants to enter the market and is faced with restrictive or anti-competitive practices of associations. The depiction of the duration of these practices is, therefore, a bit tricky. Since the provision on anti-competitive practices was notified in 2009, the CCI has looked at evidence pre-2009 and restricted it only as an exercise to establish a continuation of practice rather than to impose any accountability for such actions. Any information to exclusively examine the practice which happened prior to 2009 has been considered to be outside the jurisdiction of the CCI. One thing that is certain is that anti-competitive practices are a common feature across the board and have continued for years. For instance, the practice of restricting dubbed content in any territory by a regional association of distributors or exhibitors has existed for decades.

Even if we consider cartel durations after 2009, the cases depict a high average duration of practice. One of the reasons, as indicated earlier, is the all-inclusive nature of such associations because any market participant cannot do business without their approval. What is interesting is that even when the CCI was unanimously, continuously and vehemently questioning the practices of trade associations, many did not alter their course of action.

Even in cases where trade associations are either absent or are present as conduits to cartels, the average cartel duration is remarkably high. The majority of these cases are in the manufacturing sector, with an average duration of over 24 months. These cartels are mostly all-inclusive or have a high combined market share. The majority of the cases in the manufacturing sector are bid-rigging cases. However, interestingly, cartel structures do not seem to break after the bidding process and continue for subsequent biddings as well. While case laws have not specifically examined individual cartel members' participation and involvement in the cartel, facts are still indicative of cartels retaining their integrity. We have not seen any case where membership within the cartel has fluctuated, making the average cartel member involvement duration close to the average cartel duration.

In ten cases, there was evidence to indicate that the cartel existed before May 2009 – the date of notification of Section 3. The duration of cartels in the manufacturing sector (25 cases in the observation period) was a minimum of 4 months (in *Lachs*) and a maximum of 108 months (in the beer cartel case[151]), followed by 84 months (in the battery cartel case[152]). The observation period has just one case related to the insurance sector, which lasted for 48 months. In the transport services, the average duration of a cartel was 22 months. Further, a high number of participants has not often destabilized the cartel.

The majority of cases in the service sector (approximately 84%) are in areas of media and entertainment and wholesale and retail, primarily in the pharmaceutical sector and transportation services. The fact that although these markets do not have the best environment for breeding cartels, they have formed and survived for long durations of time may be indicative of the fact that cartels can form in markets irrespective of the facilitating factors if they have an all-inclusive nature and the market has a presence of a strong trade association. Almost all the cases in the pharmaceutical wholesale and retail sector had a presence of trade associations. Similarly, 82% of cases in media and entertainment and 60% of cases in the transport sector had trade associations as the primary actor and a high average cartel duration. None of these sectors has the most conducive cartel breeding environment. These markets have the presence of small and diffused market concentration without any real identified market leader. In fact, the office bearers of such formal/informal associations become the decision-makers and are able to take decisions which are then followed by all. Since the business of these sectors operates internally and external dealings, if any, of the member is dependent on the approval of these self-regulatory bodies, any complaint of the anti-competitive practices of these all-inclusive organizations will invite the risk of boycott and serious impairment to the business objective of the individual firm. Cartels in the manufacturing sector have largely been detected in markets with cartel-conducive features.

3.7.2 Cartel duration vis-à-vis type of infringement

If we see the cartel duration data along with the type of cartel, it appears that market-sharing cartels have the longest lifespan. However, in India, they are rather rare (under ten cases in the span of ten years), and therefore, the numbers might not show the correct picture. Apart from market sharing cartels, bid-rigging cartels have the highest duration, with an average of 21 months per cartel. Considering the fact that bid-rigging collusions are relatively easier to detect, the high average duration is indicative of a low detection rate. This gets strengthened from another set of data on the demography of informants, which establishes that collusive-bidding reporting is not very common across central government, state government or public sector enterprises. Many cases involving price fixing and limiting or controlling production or supplies had existed for long durations of time without any fear of detection or penalty and were only detected when information was filed by victims of cartelization. Price-fixing cartels have a higher duration in comparison to cartels that control or limit production or supply goods or services.

Notes

1 Swastik Stevedores Pvt. Ltd. v. Dumper Owners' Association, 2015 Comp LR 212 (CCI); Varca Chemist and Druggist v. Chemist and Druggist Association, Goa, 2012 Comp LR 838 (CCI); Santuka Associates Pvt. Ltd. v. Al Indian Organization of Chemists and Druggists and Others, 2013 Comp LR 223 (CCI).
2 Uniglobe Mod Travels Pvt. Ltd., v. Travel Agents Federation of India, 2011 Comp LR 400 (CCI).
3 Dhanraj Pillay v. Hockey India, 2013 Comp LR 543 (CCI).
4 Manju Tharad v. Eastern India Motion Pictures Association (EIMPA) and Others, [2012] 110 CLA 136 (CCI).
5 Automobiles Dealers Association, Hathras, UP v. Global Automobiles Ltd. and Pooja Expo India Pvt. Ltd., 2012 Comp LR 827 (CCI).
6 George Stigler, *Price and Non-Price Competition*, 76 Journal of Political Economy 149. *See also*, 2 (1) Joseph Harrington, *How do Cartels Operate? Foundations and Trends in Microeconomics* 1 (Now Publishers 2006).
7 William H. Page, *A Neo-Chicago Approach to Concerted Action*, 78 Antitrust Law Journal 173 (2012), http://scholarship.law.ufl.edu/facultypub/584 (last accessed on Dec. 13, 2021).
8 Richard A. Posner, *The Social Costs of Monopoly and Regulation*, 83 Journal of Political Economy 807, 820 (1975).
9 Aaron Director and Edward H. Levi, *Law and the Future: Trade Regulation*, 51 Northwestern University Law Review 281 (1956).

10 Micheal Vaska, *Conscious Parallelism and Price Fixing: Defining the Boundary*, 52 (2) University of Chicago Law, Article 10 (1985).
11 Raghavan Committee Report on Competition Law 2000, paragraph 4.3–3.
12 Builders Association of India v. Cement Manufacturers' Association and Ors., 2012 Comp LR 629 (CCI).
13 Cartelization in respect of zinc carbon dry cell batteries market in India v. Eveready Industries India Ltd. & Ors., Suo-Moto Case No. 02/2016, order dated 19 April 2018 (CCI).
14 In Re: Alleged anti-competitive conduct in the Beer Market in India; Suo-Motu Case No. 06 of 2017; order dated 24 September 2021 (CCI).
15 Coal India v. GOCL, Case No. 6/2011, order dated 16 April 2012 [The COMPAT in April 2013 upheld the decision of CCI but took in to account mitigating circumstances to reduce penalty]; DGS&D, M/o Commerce, Govt. of India v. M/s Puja Enterprises & Ors., Ref. Case No. 01/2012, order dated 6 August 2013 (CCI) [The COMPAT on 12 April 2016 set aside the order of CCI]; In Re: Cartelization in the supply of electric power steering system, Suo Motu Case No. 07 (01) of 2014, dated 9 August 2019; In re: Chief Materials Manager, South Eastern Railway, Case No. 3/2016, order dated 10 July 2020.
16 *Supra note* 12.
17 *Supra note* 13.
18 In Re: Cartelization in the supply of electric power steering system, Suo Motu Case No. 07 (01) of 2014, order dated 9 August 2019 (CCI).
19 In Re: Cartelization in Industrial and Automotive Bearings, Suo-Moto Case No. 05/2017, order dated 5 June 2020.
20 *Supra note* 14.
21 *Model Law on Competition*, Revised chapter III, 2012, Intergovernmental Group of Experts on Competition Law and Policy, United Nations Conference on Trade and Development, TD/B/C.I/CLP/L.4, (July 2018) http://unctad.org/meetings/en/SessionalDocuments/ciclpL4_en.pdf (last accessed on Dec. 13, 2021).
22 Frederic M. Scherer and David Ross, *Industrial Market Structure and Economic Performance* (Houghton-Mifflin, 3rd ed., 1990). *See*, *United States v. Suntar Roofing, Inc.*, 897 F.2d 469 (10th Cir. 1990), *United States v. Goodman*, 850 F.2d 1473, 1476 (11th Cir.1988) [Agreement to divide market on the basis of customers between horizontal players is a per se violation of S. 1 of Sherman Act. *Also see*, *United States v. Topco Assocs., Inc.*, 405 U.S. 596, 608, 92 S.Ct. 1126, 1133, 31 L.Ed.2d 515 (1972).
23 Ghanshyam Das Vij v. Bajaj Corp Ltd., Case No. 68/2013, order dated 12 October 2015 (CCI).
24 *Supra note* 21 at para 31.
25 S.1, Sherman Act, 1890 (US); Article 1, TFEU; S. 188 (5), UK Enterprise Act, 2002; S. 3 (3) (d), Indian Competition Act, 2002.
26 Patrick Bajari and Lixin Ye, *Deciding between Competition and Collusion*, 85 (4) The Review of Economics and Statistics 971–989 (2003).
27 George Stigler, *A Theory of Oligopoly*, 72 Journal of Political Economy 44–61 (1964). See also, Margaret C. Levenstein and Valerie Suslow, *Breaking up is Hard to do: Determinants of Cartel Duration*, 54 (2) Journal of Law and Economics 455 (2011).
28 *Supra note* 12.
29 Case C-8/08 T-Mobile Netherlands BV & Others v. Commission ECJ [2009] ECLI:EU:C:2009:343.
30 In Re: Anticompetitive conduct in the Dry-Cell Batteries Market in India v. Panasonic Corporation (2018) SCC OnLine CCI 81.

31 Michael Hellwig and Kai Huschelrath, Cartel cases and the cartel enforcement process in the European Union 2001–15: A quantitative assessment, 62 (2) Sage – The Antitrust Bulletin (2017). See also, M. Carree, A. Günster and MP Schinkel, *European Antitrust Policy: An Analysis of Commission Decisions*, 1964–2004, 36 Review of Industrial Organization 97–131 (2010).
32 CII Research, *Confederation of Indian Industries* (March 2019) (June 2019) www.cii.in/Resources.aspx?enc=prvePUj2bdMtgTmvPwvisYH+5EnGjyGX-O9hLECvTuNvOiAyvvZ7D6DNA1ctlBENi5RyHSIfayFAi3tHXmMVccxKi7t-Fd3bWCSlRhqOu6yv0= (last accessed on Dec. 13, 2021).
33 Growth of manufacturing industries in India – info-graphic, *India Brand Equity Foundation* (March 2019), www.ibef.org/industry/manufacturing-sector-india.aspx (last accessed on Dec. 13, 2021).
34 *Supra note* 27 (Stigler).
35 *Supra note* 18.
36 *Supra note* 17.
37 Builders Association of India v. Cement Manufacturers' Association & Ors., 2012CompLR629 (CCI).
38 *Supra note* 13.
39 In Re: Glass Manufacturers of India, MRTP Case No. 161/2008 order dated 24 January 2012 (CCI).
40 All India Tyre Dealers Federation v. Tyre Manufacturers, MRTP Case: RTPE No. 20/2008, order dated 30 October 2012 (CCI).
41 Shailesh Kumar v. M/s Tata Chemicals Limited & Ors., Case No. 66/2011, order dated 16 April 2013 (CCI).
42 In In Re: Alleged cartelization by steel producers, Case No.: RTPE No. 09 of 2008, order dated 2 December 2014 (MRTP).
43 In Re: Manufacturers of Asbestos Cement Products, Suo-Moto Case No. 01/2012, order dated 2 December 2014 (CCI).
44 Dy. Chief Materials Manager, Integral Coach Factory, Chennai v. M/s Celtek Batteries (P) Ltd., Bangalore & Ors., MRTP Case No. C-57/09/DGIR (26/28), order dated 27 July 2011 (CCI).
45 In Re: Suo-moto case against LPG cylinder manufacturers, Suo Moto Case No. 03/2011, order dated 24 February 2012 and 6 August 2014 (CCI).
46 Rajasthan Cylinders and Containers Limited v. Union of India, Civil Appeal No. 3546/2014, order dated 1 October 2018 (SC).
47 Case No. 1/28 (C-97/2009/DGIR, order dated 9 May 2012 (CCI).
48 Ref. Case filed by Shri B P Khare, Principal Chief Engineer, South Eastern Railway, Kolkata. V. M/s Orissa Concrete and Allied Industries Ltd. & Ors. Ref. Case No. 05/2011, order dated 21 February 2013 (CCI); In Re: M/s Sheth & Co & others, Suo Moto Case No. 04/2013, order dated 10 June 2015 (CCI) [The COMPAT set aside the order of CCI on 10 May 2016]
49 A Foundation for Common Cause & People Awareness v. PES Installations Pvt. Ltd. & Ors. Case No. 43/2010, order dated 16 April 2012 (CCI) [The COMPAT upheld the decision of CCI but reduced the penalty on 25 February 2013]; Shri Gulshan Verma v. Union of India, through Secretary, Ministry of Health and Family Welfare & Ors., Case No. 40/2010, order dated 5 April 2012 (CCI) [the COMPAT in 2013 set aside the order of CCI for lack of evidence].
50 M/s Bio-Med Private Limited v. Union of India & others, Case No. 26/2013, order dated 4 June 2015 (CCI). [The COMPAT set aside the order of CCI on 8 November 2016].
51 In Re: Aluminium Phosphide Tablets Manufacturers, Suo-Moto Case No. 02/2011, order dated 23 April 2012 (CCI). [the COMPAT upheld the decision of CCI but reduced the penalty on 29 October 2013]; Delhi Jal Board v. Grasim Industries Ltd. & others, Ref. Case No. 04/2013, order dated 5 October 2017.

52 DGS&D, M/o Commerce, Govt. of India v. M/s Puja Enterprises & Ors., Ref. Case No. 01/2012, order dated 6 August 2013 (CCI). The COMPAT set aside the order of CCI on 12 April 2016.
53 Alleged cartelization in the matter of supply of spares to Diesel Loco Modernization Works, Indian Railways, Patiala, Punjab v. M/s Stone India Limited & Ors., 2014 CompLR 170 (CCI). The COMPAT set aside the order of CCI on 18 December 2015. In Sh. S.K. Sharma, Deputy. CMM-IV, North Western Railway, Hasanpura, Jaipur v. M/s RMG Polyvinyl India Ltd., New Delhi & Ors.; RTPE 31/2008, order dated 6 April 2011 (CCI), there was enough evidence to prove that a cartel existed; however, since the cause of action was pre-2009, no action could be taken. Allegation of cartelization was not proved in cases like Chief Materials Manager – I v. M/s Milton Industries Ltd. & Others, Ref. 2/2014, order dated 1 July 2015 (CCI); In Re: Deputy Chief Materials Manager, Rail Coach Factory v. M/s Faiveley Transport India Limited & Others, Ref. 6/2013, order dated 8 September 2015.
54 Coal India Limited vs GOCL Hyderabad & Ors., Case No. 6/2011, order dated 16 April 2012 [the COMPAT in April 2013 upheld the decision of CCI but reduced the penalty].
55 Vijay Gupta v. M/s Paper Merchants Association, Delhi, Case No. 7/2010, order dated 24 March 2011 (CCI).
56 Indian Sugar Mills Association & Ors. v. Indian Jute Mills Association & Gunny Trade Asso (GTA), Case No. 38/2011, order dated 31 October 2014. The COMPAT set aside the order of CCI on 1 July 2016.
57 India Glycols Ltd. v. Indian Sugar Mills Association & others, Case No. 94/2014 order dated 11 May 2018 (CCI).
58 *Supra note* 12.
59 *Supra note* 13.
60 *Supra note* 14.
61 Cartelization in respect of tenders floated by Indian Railways for supply of Brushless DC Fans and other electrical items, Suo moto Case 3/2014, order dated 18 January 2017 (CCI).
62 *Supra note* 13.
63 Nagrik Chetna Manch v. Fortified Security Solutions & Others, case 50/2015, order dated 1 May 2018 (CCI).
64 Anticompetitive conduct in the Dry-Cell Batteries Market in India v. Panasonic Corporation, Japan & Ors., Suo Moto Case No. 03/2017, order dated 15 January 2019 (CCI).
65 *Supra note* 17.
66 Case No. 05/2017, order dated 5 June 2020 (CCI).
67 *Supra note* 14.
68 In Re: Anti-competitive conduct in the paper manufacturing industry, Suo Motu Case No. 05/2016, order dated 17 November 2021 (CCI).
69 *Service Sector in India*, India Brand Equity Foundation, March 2019, (June 2019) www.ibef.org/industry/services.aspx (last accessed on Dec. 13, 2021).
70 *Supra note* 2.
71 M/s. FCM Travel Solutions (India) Ltd., New Delhi v. Travel Agents Federation of India & Ors., RTPE 09/2008 (C-31/2009/DGIR) order dated 17 November 2011 (CCI).
72 Travel Agents Association of India v. Lufthansa German Airlines & Ors., Case No. 14/2009, order dated 31 October 2011 (CCI).
73 In re: Domestic Airlines, Suo moto Case No. 2/2010, order dated 10 January 2012 (CCI).
74 Ref: Case No. 01/2011 (*Airlines*), order dated 11 January 2012 (CCI).

75 R.Prasad, J., gave a dissenting opinion. Per the dissent, there were enough plus factors to prove cartel. *Id.*

76 In Re: Alleged Cartelization in the Airlines Industry, Suo-Moto 03/2015, order dated 22 February 2021 (CCI).

77 M/s Swastik Stevedores Private Limited v. M/s Dumper Owner's Association & Ors., Case No. 42/2012 order dated 21 January 2015 (CCI).

78 M/s Shivam Enterprises v. Kiratpur Sahib Truck Operators Co-operative Transport Society Limited & Ors., Case 43/2013, order dated 4 February 2015 (CCI).

79 Indian Foundation of Transport Research & Training v. Sh. Bal Malkait Singh, President and Ors., Case No. 61/2012, order dated 16 February 2015 (CCI). [The COMPAT on 18 April 2016 set aside the order of CCI as the DG ignored replies from most of transport companies and also due to lack of evidence].

80 Cochin Port Trust v. Container Trailer Owners Coordination Committee & Others, Ref. Case No. 06/2014, order dated 1 August 2017 (CCI).

81 The Air Cargo Agents Association of India v. International Air Transport Association (IATA) & other, Case No. 79/2012, order dated 4 June 2015 (CCI).

82 Express Industry Council of India v. Jet Airways (India) Ltd. & Others, case 30 of 2013, order dated 7 March 2018 (CCI)

83 M.P. Mehrotra v. Jet Airways (India) Ltd. with Kingfisher Airlines Ltd., Case No. 04/2009, order dated 11 August 2011 (CCI).

84 Western Coalfields Limited v. SSV Coal Carriers Private Limited & others, Case No. 34/2015, order dated 14 September 2017 (CCI).

85 In Re Bengal Chemist and Druggist Association, Suo Moto Case No. 2/2012, order dated 11 March 2014 (CCI).

86 *Supra note* 85 at para 64.

87 *Supra note* 85.

88 BCDA v. CCI, Appeal No. 37/2014, order dated 10 May 2016 (COMPAT).

89 Varca Druggist & Chemist & Ors. v. Chemists and Druggists Association, Goa, MRTP C-127/2009/DGIR4/28, order dated 11 June 2012 (CCI).

90 Vedant Bio Sciences v. Chemists & Druggists Association of Baroda, C-87/2009/DGIR, order dated 5 September 2012 (CCI). (The COMPAT set aside the order of the CCI on 18 November 2016 and remanded the matter back for violation of principles of natural justice. The CCI passed another order on 16 January 2019, repeating its earlier order of imposition of penalty at the rate of 10% of average receipts of the association.)

91 Rohit Medical Store v. Macleods Pharmaceutical Limited & Ors., Case No. 78 of 2012, order dated 29 January 2015 (CCI).

92 Mr. P. K. Krishnan Proprietor, Vinayaka Pharma v. Mr. Paul Madavana, Divisional Sales Manager, M/s Alkem Laboratories Limited. & Others., Case No. 28/2014, order dated 1 December 2015 (CCI). See also, The Belgaum District Chemists and Druggists Association v. Abbott India Ltd. & Others, Case No. C-175/09/DGIR/27/28-MRTP, order dated 2 March 2017 (CCI).

93 M/s. Alkem Laboratories Limited v. CCI and Others, Appeal No. 9/2016, order dated 10 May 2016. Also see, M/s Maruti & Company v. Karnataka Chemists & Druggists Association & Others, Case No. 71/2013, order dated 28 July 2016 (CCI) with KCDA v. CCI order dated 20 September 2017 (NCLAT).

94 Sudeep P.M. and others v. All Kerala Chemists and Druggists Association, Case No. 54/2015, order dated 31 October 2017 (CCI).

95 Reliance Agency v. Chemists and Druggists Association of Baroda & Others, Case No. 97 of 2013, order dated 4 January 2018 (CCI).

96 M/s. Alis Medical Agency v. Federation of Gujarat State Chemists & Druggists Associations & Others, (71/2014) M/s. Stockwell Pharma v. Federation of Gujarat State Chemists & Druggists Associations & Others, (72/2014)

M/s. Apna Dawa Bazar v. Federation of Gujarat State Chemists & Druggists Associations & Others, (68/2015) M/s. Reliance Medical Agency v. The Chemists & Druggists Association of Baroda & Others, Case 65/2014, 71/2014, 72/2014 & 68/2015, order dated 12 July 2018 (CCI).

97 Vedanta Bio Sciences, Vadodara v. Chemists and Druggists Association of Baroda, Case No. c-87/2009/DGIR, order dated 15 January 2019 (CCI); Madhya Pradesh Chemists and Distributors Federation (MPCDF) v. Madhya Pradesh Chemists and Druggist Association (MPCDA) & Others, Case No. 64/2014, order dated 15 January 2019 (CCI); Mr. Nadie Jauhr v. Jalgaon District Medicine Dealers Association (JDMDA), Case No. 61/2015, order dated 20 June 2019 (CCI).

98 Santuka Associates Pvt. Ltd. v. All India Chemists and Druggists, 2013 Comp LR 223 (CCI).

99 AIOCD v. CCI, Appeal No. 21/2013, order dated 9 December 2016 (COMPAT).

100 AIOCD v. CCI, Appeal No. 7/2014, order dated 9 December 2016 (COMPAT).

101 AIOCD v. CCI, Appeal No. 6/2014, order dated 9 December 2016 (COMPAT).

102 M/s Arora Medical Hall, Ferozepur v. Chemists & Druggists Association, Ferozepur & Ors., Case No. 60/2012, order dated 5 February 2014 (CCI).

103 Appeal No. 21/2014 and I.A. Nos. 31 & 32/2014, order dated 30 October 2015 (COMPAT).

104 Shri Ghanshyam Das Vij v. M/s Bajaj Corp. Ltd. & Others, Case No. 68/2013, order dated 12 October 2015 (CCI).

105 Case No. 33/2019, order dated 23 February 2021.

106 FICCI – Multiplex Association of India v. United Producers/Distributors Forum & Ors., Case No. 1/2009, order dated 25 May 2011 (CCI).

107 Case No. with info filed on 25/2010 (14 June 2010), 41/2010 (10 August 2010), 45/2010 (19 August 2010), 47/2010 (25 August 2010), 48/2010 (30 August 2010), 50/2010 (30 September 2010), 58/2010 (27 October 2010), & 69/2010 (16 December 2010), order dated 16 February 2012 (CCI). *See also*, Sunshine Pictures Private Limited & Eros International Media Limited v. Central Circuit Cine Association, Indore & Ors., Case 52, 56 of 2010, order dated 16 February 2012 (CCI); UTV Software Communications Limited, Mumbai v. Motion Pictures Association, Delhi, Case No: 9 of 2011, order dated 8 May 2012 (CCI); Cinergy Independent Film Services Pvt. Ltd. v. Telangana Telugu Film Distributors Association and Ors., Case No. 56/2011, order dated 10 January 2013; M/s Ashtavinayak Cine Vision Ltd. v. PVR Picture Limited & Ors., Case No. 71/2011, order dated 28 July 2016.

108 Mrs. Manju Tharad & Ors. v. Eastern India Motion Picture Association (EIMPA), Kolkata & Ors., order dated 24 April 2012 (CCI).

109 Kerala Cine Exhibitors Association v. Kerala Film Exhibitors Federation, Case No. 45/012, order dated 23 June 2015 (CCI).

110 In Re: Shri P.V. Basheer Ahmed v. Film Distributors Association, Kerala, Case No. 32/2013, order dated 23 December 2014 (CCI).

111 Kannada Grahakara Koota v. Karnataka Film Chamber of Commerce & Ors., Case No. 58/2–12, order dated 27 July 2015 (CCI); Mr. G. Krishnamurthy v. Karnataka Film Chamber of Commerce (KFCC) & Others, Case No. 42/2017, order dated 30 August 2018 (CCI).

112 Case No. 62/2012, order dated 23 December 2014 (CCI).

113 Cinemax India Ltd. v. Film Distributors Association (Kerala), Case No. 62/2012, order dated 23 December 2014 (CCI).

114 Shri T. G. Vinayakumar (also known as Vinayan) v. Association of Malayalam Movie Artists & others, Case No. 98/2014, order dated 24 March 2017 (CCI).

115 Film & Television Producers Guild of India v. Multiplex Association of India (MAI) Mumbai & Ors., Case No. 37/2011, decided in 3 January 2013 (CCI).

116 In Re: Cartelization by broadcasting service providers by rigging the bids submitted in response to the tenders floated by Sports Broadcasters v. Essel Shyam Communication Limited & others, Suo moto Case No. 2/2013, order dated 11 July 2018 (CCI).
117 Case No. 7/2018, order dated 22 June 2020 (CCI).
118 Neeraj Malhotra v. Deustche Post Bank Home Finance Ltd. & Ors., Case No. 5/2009, order dated 2 December 2010 (CCI).
119 Yashoda Hospital and Research Centre Ltd. v. Indiabulls Financial Services Ltd., Case No. 12/2010, order dated 22 March 2011 (CCI).
120 M/s Metalrod Ltd. v. M/s. Religare Finvest Ltd., Case No. 28/2010, order dated 23 May 2011 (CCI).
121 In Re: Anti-Competitive Practices Prevailing in Banking Sector, Case No. 1/2015, order dated 24 April 2018 (CCI).
122 Shri Neeraj Malhotra, Advocate v. North Delhi Power Ltd. & Ors., Case No. 5/2009, order dated 11 May 2011 (CCI).
123 Suo moto v. North Delhi Power Ltd. & BSES & Ors., Case No. 19/2008, order dated 31 May 2011 (CCI).
124 Jupiter Gaming Solutions Private Limited v. Government of Goa & Ors., Case No. 15/2010, order dated 12 May 2011 (CCI).
125 Prints India v. Springer India Private Limited & Ors., Case No. 16/2010, order dated 3 July 2012 (CCI).
126 In re: M/s International Subscription Agency v. Federation of Publishers' and Booksellers' Associations in India, Case No. 33/2019, order dated 23 February 2021 (CCI).
127 In Re: Cartelization by public sector insurance companies in rigging the bids submitted in response to the tenders floated by the Government of Kerala for selecting insurance service provider for Rashtriya Swasthya Bima Yojna v. National Insurance Co. Ltd. and Others, Suo moto Case No. 2/2014, order dated 10 July 2015 (CCI).
128 M/s National Insurance Company Limited v. CCI, Appeal No. 48/2014, order dated 26 August 2015 (COMPAT).
129 Association of Third-Party Administrators v. General Insurers' (Public Sector) Association of India, Case No. 107/2013, order dated 4 January 2016 (CCI).
130 Detailed information on the market share is not available for many cases. For cases involving regional trade associations, cartel market share is taken as 100% as in all such cases it was clear that operation in the market was impossible without being a member of the association. In other cases, the market share of cartel and other members has been shown.
131 Competition (Amendment) Bill, 2006, 44th Report, Standing Committee on Finance (2006–07), 14th Lok Sabha, Ministry of Company Affairs, Lok Sabha Secretariat (June 2019) www.prsindia.org/sites/default/files/bill_files/bill73_2007050873_Competition_Bill__2006_standing_committee.pdf (last accessed on Dec. 13, 2021).
132 Report of the Competition Law Review Committee, Ministry of Corporate Affairs, Government of India (July 2019).
133 *Supra note* 12.
134 *Supra note* 45.
135 *Supra note* 14.
136 Ref. Case filed by Shri B P Khare, Principal Chief Engineer, South Eastern Railway, Kolkata. v. M/s Orissa Concrete and Allied Industries Ltd. & Ors., Ref. Case No. 5/2011, order dated 21 February 2013 (CCI).
137 In Re: Alleged cartelization in supply of LPG Cylinders procured through tenders by Hindustan Petroleum Corporation Ltd. (HPCL) v. Allampally Brothers Ltd. & Others, Suo-Moto-Case-No. 1/2014, order dated 9 August 2019 (CCI).

138 *Supra note* 14.
139 In comparison, an average of 5.6 firm groups per cartel has been reported in EU between 2001–2015.
140 Madhya Pradesh Chemists and Distributors Federation (MPCDF) v. Madhya Pradesh Chemists and Druggist Association (MPCDA) & Others, Case No. 64/2014, order dated 15 January 2019 (CCI).
141 Article 23, Regulation 1/2003 (EC) on the implementation of the rules on competition laid down in Articles 81 and 82 of the Treaty. Regulation allows taking in to account the turnover of members to determine fine. See also, Guidelines on the method of setting fines imposed pursuant to Article 23 (2) (a) of Regulation No. 1/2003 (2006/C 210/02). See, also *Potential pro-competitive and anti-competitive aspects of Trade/Business Associations*, Policy Roundtables, OECD (2007), DAF/COMP (2007) 45, (July 2018) www.oecd.org/regreform/sectors/41646059.pdf (last accessed on Dec. 14, 2021).
142 Wayne E. Baker and Robert Faulkner, *The Social organization of Conspiracy: Illegal Networks in the Heavy Electrical Equipment Industry*, 59 (6) American Sociological Review 837–859 (1993).
143 Para A (6), Corporate Leniency Policy, 1993, Department of Justice (March 2019), www.justice.gov/atr/corporate-leniency-policy (last accessed on Dec. 14, 2021).
144 The 1996 Commission Notice excluded entities who "compelled another enterprise to take part in the cartel" and which "acted as an instigator or played a determining role in the illegal activity" (See, Para B [e], *Commission Notice on the Non-Imposition or Reduction of Fines in Cartel Cases, Official Journal C 207, 18/07/1996 P. 0004–0006*, European Commission *[March 2019]*, https://eur-lex.europa.eu/legal-content/EN/ALL/?uri=CELEX%3A31996Y0718%2801%29 [last accessed on Dec. 14, 2021]). The 2002 Commission Notice in para A11 (c) retained the exclusion for undertakings that took "steps to coerce other undertakings to participate in the infringement". However, per section B, entities would be eligible for reduction of any fine if the undertaking provides "the Commission with evidence of the suspected infringement which represents significant added value with respect to the evidence already in the Commission's possession". (See, *Commission Notice on Immunity from Fines and Reduction of Fines in Cartel Cases, Official Journal C 045, 19/02/2002 P. 0003–0005*, European Commission *[March 2019]*, https://eur-lex.europa.eu/legal-content/EN/ALL/?uri=CELEX:52002XC0219 (02) [last accessed on Dec. 14, 2021]). Similarly, the 2006 Commission Notice excluded all undertakings from grant of immunity from fines if the undertaking "took steps to coerce other undertakings to join the cartel or to remain in it". However, such undertakings would "still qualify for a reduction of fines if it fulfills the relevant requirements and meets all the conditions therefor".
145 Uniglobe Mod Travels Pvt. Ltd. v. Travel Agents Association of India & Ors., Case No. 3/2009, order dated 4 October 2011 (CCI).
146 *Supra note* 63.
147 Nagrik Chetna Manch v. SAAR IT Resources Private Limited & Ors., Case No. 12/2017, order dated 9 August 2019 (CCI).
148 In Re: Anticompetitive conduct in the Dry-Cell Batteries Market in India, Suo Moto Case No. 03/2017, order dated 15 January 2019 (CCI).
149 Richard Posner, *A Statistical Study of Antitrust Enforcement*, 13 Journal of Law and Economics 365–419 (1970); Andrew Dick, *When Are Cartels Stable Contracts?*, 39 Journal of Law and Economics 241–283 (1996). *Also see*, Oindrila De, *Analysis of Cartel Duration: Evidence from EC Prosecuted Cartels*, 17 International Journal of the Economics of Business, 33–65 (2010); Jun Zhou, *Evaluating Leniency with Missing Information on Undetected Cartels:*

Exploring Time-Varying Policy Impacts on Cartel Duration, Discussion Paper Series of SFB/TR 15 Governance and the Efficiency of Economic Systems No. 353, Mannheim (2011); Margaret Levenstein and Valerie Suslow, *Breaking Up Is Hard to Do: Determinants of Cartel Duration,* 54 Journal of Law and Economics 455–492 (2011). Margaret Levenstein & Valerie Suslow, *What Determines Cartel Success?*, 44 Journal of Economic Literature (2006).

150 There are several economic studies that have tried to study the determinants of cartel duration by applying survival estimation techniques to their respective datasets. *See*, Margaret C. Levenstein & Valerie Suslow, *Breaking up is Hard to Do: Determinants of Cartel Duration*, Working paper no. 1150, Michigan Ross School of Business (September 2000); Michael Hellwig & Kai Huschelrath, *When do firms leave cartels: Determinants and the Impact of Cartel Survival*", ZEW-Discussion Papers, No. 17–002; (March 2019) http://hdl.handle.et/10419/148923 (last accessed on Dec. 14, 2021). These studies however study only the impact of certain organizational features along with structure of the market on the duration of the cartel. These studies do not study the implication of examining the duration of the cartel for the application of the law.

151 *Supra note* 14.

152 *Supra note* 13.

4 Investigation of investigative procedures of the CCI

4.1 Detection of cartels: screening and identification

The presence of a strict anti-cartel enforcement regime has a negative effect on cartel stability. With the advancement of both technology and resources clubbed with experiential knowledge, competition authorities across jurisdictions have become more efficient. But then, so have cartels. Cartel members now are extra cautious to camouflage their anti-competitive behaviour and, sometimes, even mimic competitive patterns.

Per an estimate, the average cartel detection rate in the US and the EU is between 12.9 to 15%.[1] Over-reliance of competition authorities on leniency programs has been argued to be a reason for the low rate of cartel detection. Competition regulators, thus, have to be more cautious of and receptive to the use of econometric techniques or cartel screens to identify areas of concern and behaviours most likely to be problematic and where they should concentrate their resources. Screening is

> [t]he ability to flag unlawful behaviour through economic and statistical analyses. Cartel screens are economic tools designed to analyse observable economic data and information, such as information on various product and market characteristics, data on costs, prices, market shares, various aspects of firm behaviour, etc. and flag markets which may either have been affected by collusion, or which may be more susceptible to collusion.[2]

Detection of cartels is approached from multiple angles ranging from leniency applications, direct complaints, *suo moto* enquiries based on external information and references from other regulators (traditional tools of cartel detection) to the use of econometric techniques or screens (economic 'complimentary tools'[3]). Detection mechanisms centre around either communication or information about a cartel or through observance of suspicious patterns in the market like simultaneous price rise or identical bidding.

Husschelrath[4] puts cartel detection methods into two categories: reactive and proactive. Some of the methods listed earlier, which are based on

DOI: 10.4324/9781003347651-4

information provided by cartel members (leniency applicants), complainants or external whistle-blowers, constitute the reactive methods of detection. Methods based on observation of behaviour constitute the proactive methods. They include the use of economics, case analysis, monitoring of industry (including infiltration, tracking individuals, industry representatives, press and internet) and inter-agency cooperation. Many scholars have advocated the use of proactive methods for the detection of cartels instead of waiting for external sources of information.[5] The screens provide an indication of the likelihood of cartel behaviour in a given set of parameters (cartel markers) like price, quantity, costs or market share. These markers are used to differentiate a competitive market from a cartelized market. Cartel screens can help competition authorities identify markets with possibilities of cartel conduct and potential participants of collusion and estimate cartel duration. The timely application of screens can increase the detection rate of at least hard-core cartels. A high detection rate will, in turn, increase the harm quotient of cartel participation in comparison to an increase in profits and will deter the participants from entering into cartel arrangements.

Screens can also be categorized as structural (dentification of markets that are prone to cartelization) and behavioural (identification of already present cartel behaviour). Therefore, once the market which is likely to have collusive behaviour is identified, further detailed behavioural assessment can be done. Industries in a particular jurisdiction can be screened using structural screens to identify the markets most likely to witness collusion (flagging exercise). Flagging is the first step in the screening exercise. It allows the identification of markets conducive to cartelization. The structural screens such as a small number of competitors, the high entry barriers, frequent interaction between firms and market transparency can be used for such identification. Grout and Sonderegger used econometric techniques clubbed with structural factors to note that certain industries like telecommunication, automobile, cement and chemicals are prone to cartelization. Similarly, the Dutch Competition Authority developed a competition index based on structural factors to detect cartel-prone industries. Accordingly, the index examined nine factors to do the exercise (number of trade associations, price comparison with other jurisdictions, market concentration based on HHI, number of market participants, import rate, market growth, churn rate, survival rate, and research and development rate).[6]

Flagging is followed by identification, which is essentially the application of behavioural screens to see if a cartel exists in the market in question. Behavioural screens are the economic tests that are used for cartel detection based on market data of price, market share, margin and output. Data from the market in question is then compared with data from a competitive market. This may also be called a benchmarking exercise based on historical data. Benchmarking in itself is tricky. For instance, if a price screen has to applied, there must be the availability of data on price from an alternate product or geographic market or from a time when the market was competitive. This again is dependent on the time and duration of a cartel. Further, to use price increase as a determinant, one must have the data on demand and supply clubbed with the idea of margins. Even otherwise, price fluctuations, in fear of detection, are rarely seen in a cartelized market. Therefore, stable prices over a long duration of time may indicate towards cartelization. Price parallelism, price uniformity across enterprises despite the difference in cost of production, stable market share, price rise with declining imports, low price variance, periodic switching between high and low price levels (structural shifts) and disappearance of discounts that previously existed are some of the markers used to identify cartelized market. Non-price markets like stable market share, exponential increase in profits with the same demand in the market, reduced production or capacity utilization even when demand increases can also be used. Assessment can be either on a "but for" analysis, which means there is no other reason for a particular behaviour but for a cartel or on a comparative assessment of similarly situated markets. Different time zones of the same market with and without the collusive participants can also be examined. The OECD has come out with a full-fledged recommendation entailing a checklist to detect bid rigging.[7]

Identification is then followed by prosecution. Economic literature in the last few years has identified structural features of a market that will attract collusion. The OECD Report[8] identifies these factors as both supply-related (such as product homogeneity, limited innovation, cost symmetry, structural links and multi-market contacts) and demand-related (such as stable demand, low demand elasticity and buying power). Different jurisdictions have approached the structural factors in their own ways to find sectors with a high probability of cartels.[9]

Some of these behavioural screens have been explained in the following list:

a *Price screens*: Most cartels have an effect on the resultant price of the good or service. Cartel members tend to maximize profit by increasing the price above the competitive level and then share the profits gained. The rise in prices can be used as a marker if a comparative data set on price is available. However, the price of a product is determined by the cost of inputs and by the demand in the market. Therefore, to say that prices are high due to a cartel will require the data on inputs and demand with an idea of margin. This becomes difficult in the absence of information on the time and duration of the cartel. Screening of average prices at different times may, although it seems to be a logical marker, is not easy to apply as it requires a comparison of data (from the cartelized market and competitive market) and further requires benchmarking of various kinds of data. Price volatility can be used as a price screen marker. It has been proved both theoretically and empirically that a cartelized market sees a low price fluctuation or variance as frequent communication on price, and its corresponding movement might attract detection.[10] Therefore, stable prices over a period of time might indicate a cartelized market. Changes in costs are not fully passed through to avoid any suspicion. Entry of new players is non-existent due to high entry barriers, or new players are co-opted in the cartel, thus preventing any price undercutting. Instability of demand can be pre-empted by an information-sharing mechanism. Avoidance of discount avoids price fluctuation between cartel members. Some of the price markers indicating a cartel are as follows:

- Sharp price decline followed by a steady increase in prices over a period of few years in non-seasonal markets.
- Parallel pricing.
- Price uniformity irrespective of the cost of production and firm size.
- Price stability for a long duration of time.

b *Market share*: In a competitive market, market shares of the participants see fluctuations, and hence, their high stability over a period of time may also indicate collusion. Stable market shares can be the result of players dividing either the market or customers. Another mode may be to limit the production of cartel members to control individual production capacities. Apart from price, there are other variables that can be used to detect cartels. Lorenz[11] was able to use variables like innovation in technology, market clearing, rate of return and innovation in the product to examine cartelized behaviour. Data on these variables of a particular market, when compared with a competitive market, might be able to highlight any differences.

c *Benchmarking*: Behavioural screens are data-intensive. This means that, firstly, it requires a collection of data on the market response to a particular variable over a period of time, and secondly, collected data needs to be compared to the data collected from a competitive market. This comparison of data to a reference point is called benchmarking. Benchmarking can be done on the basis of time (data is collected over different time periods, particularly before and after the collusion, to compare if the prices [considering general demand and supply changes] vary or remain the same), alternate product markets (comparison on prices can be made with a different product of the same industry) or geographic market (comparison with a comparable market in a different location).

d *Bid rigging*: Certain markers are also used to detect collusion in procurement bid cartels. Common patterns (such as identical bids, a high co-relation between bids, disconnect between bids and the underlying cost of the bidder, repetitiveness of bid winner, big difference in the bid of the winner and the rest of the bidders, withdrawal of a likely bidder and evidence of subcontracting) have been identified to indicate towards collusion. The features of the market that tend to increase the likelihood of collusion include similarity of products and the bidders,

> lesser number of bidders, the possibility of subcontracting and lot splitting. The underlying assumption is that bidders will act independently and submit independent bids reflecting the cost in competitive markets. Behavioural screens have been used quite frequently to detect bid rigging in public procurements. The OECD Recommendations[12] provide a checklist or a list of red flags to detect bid rigging.

Screening, however, only raises a suspicion derived from comparing a specific set of data with a competitive market model and does not establish collusive behaviour. Further, screens do not particularly differentiate between explicit and tacit collusion as the patterns are more or less similar. The differentiation is, however, very relevant legally as many competition authorities would require some evidence of prior agreement.

4.1.1 Screens are just smoke in the air

Screens used to detect cartel behaviour, or cartelized markets are never foolproof. They only show a likelihood of collusion and, therefore, can be best taken for identification purposes. This is because screens can provide false positives (identifying cases which do not require further investigation) or false negatives (failing to identify collusion in a particular market) or fail to distinguish between explicit and tacit collusion.[13] Another challenge is the availability of extensive data, which is hardly present, especially with the competition authorities of developing countries. Some scholars[14] also question the assumption of cartel conducive environment for explicit cartels. If the law makes a distinction between explicit and tacit collusion, and rightly so, the assumption that the factors that are conducive to cartel will be applicable for both explicit and tacit collusion is problematic. In tacit collusion, there is no evidence of communication, and the behaviour can have economic justifications. Communication is, in fact, required for explicit collusion, particularly in environments where tacit collusion is not easy. Evidence from the US suggests that the conventional idea of factors that facilitate or destabilize cartels rests on shaky grounds.[15] The inability of the screens to differentiate between explicit and tacit collusion clubbed with a very low detection rate of cartels worldwide raises the question of the very usage of screens. It may even be possible that cartels exist in markets that do not actually conform to the structural screen parameters. For instance, the inverse relation of the duration of a cartel with the number of involved firms or that the cartels can survive only in concentrated markets has been empirically disproved in many cases.[16] Similar doubts have been raised by scholars like Posner, Hay and Kelley as well as Fraas and Greer on the factor of the number of members of a cartel as having an inverse relation with the sustainability of cartels. Others have tried to explain this anomaly on account of selection bias and the non-detection rate of hard-core cartels with higher stability. Doubts have, therefore, been raised on the over-reliance on structural screens.

4.2 Rate of activities of CCI with respect to cartels and yield ratio

Over the years, cartel decisions have been an important part of Indian competition law enforcement. The first point of reference of any cartel study is to see the trend across the years with respect to the number of cartel cases that have come up. This can give us two starting points: firstly, the overall focus of the CCI in dealing with cartel cases when compared with the total number of orders, and secondly, an idea as to the overall infestation of markets with cartelization. It has to be noted that while enforcement activities of the CCI can be assessed by the number of investigation and penalty orders, a heightened activity does not necessarily indicate cartel deterrence. Therefore, if instances of recidivism are high, a high number of penalty orders does not mean much. In fact, a low number of cartel detections or decisions (in case of violations) might indicate the success of CCI in terms of creating an optimal level of deterrence.

Out of a total of 831 substantive orders of the CCI, including orders under Section 26 (2) (orders recording closure due to absence of a prima facie case), orders under Section 26 (6) (orders concluding absence of anti-competitive behaviour after considering the DG investigation report) and orders under Section 27 (orders declaring the existence of anti-competitive behaviour after considering the DG investigation report), orders relating to cartels constitute 36% of the total orders. This can be attributed to the low number of information filed with the CCI alleging cartelization and, therefore, leading to a low number of indictments. The CCI ordered an investigation for either Section 3 or Section 4 violations in only 26% of all the information filed with it, which also raises concerns about the quality of information. The number of matters related to cartels, however, form the bulk of these investigations, with 58% of matters having an element of cartelization.

The data indicates a high incidence of investigations leading to indictments in the form of orders under Section 27, which is 129 orders under Section 27 out of total of 219 orders. In a total of 219 investigations ordered by the CCI under Section 26 (1) of the Act, 125 matters related to cartels. The CCI declared the parties to be in violation of Section 3 (3) of the Act in approximately 68% of such investigations. While the success ratio of investigations leading to indictments is good, it is marred by a dismal number of

Table 4.1 Number of CCI orders related to cartels during the observation period (2009–2021)

Observation period	*Orders under Section 26 (2)*	*Orders under Section 26 (6)*	*Orders under Section 27*
Total no. of orders	612	90	129
No. of cartel matters	105	42	83

investigations. This gets even more troublesome when the data with respect to the nature of cases dealt by the CCI is analyzed. The similarity in the nature of violations and the area of operation shows some kind of domino effect of one or more penalty orders on the number of information filed. Therefore, clubbed with the fact that there are low numbers of information filed with the CCI, the success ratio of investigations leading to indictments may give a false impression of the CCI winning the war against cartels.

Orders of investigations are taken as important starting points in the anti-cartel enforcement structures, and the concerned date is taken as the date of detection of the cartel. The high success ratio of investigations leading to penalties indicates a better detection system. However, the focus must not be merely on the numbers but also on the quality of decisions. The average cartel detection rate has been calculated by dividing the total number of cartel cases across years by the number of years. Resultantly, the average cartel detection rate[17] in India comes to around seven cartel cases per year (the rate of discovery has been calculated by dividing the total number of reported cartel cases in which the CCI ordered by the number of years). While close to 70% of investigations have led to indictments in the form of cease-and-desist or penalty orders, the general approach of the CCI towards cartel cases can at best be described as passive when compared to other competition regulators. Not a single case in the last 12 years pertains to international cartels, whereas in contrast, the number of foreign defendants in the US increased from 1% to 50% between the 1990s and 2000s.[18] The Department of Justice (DOJ) in the US, for instance, has launched 434 investigations with an average of 43.4 cartel investigations per year between 2008 and 2017.[19] Further, an average of seven international cartels have been investigated per year. Even the European Commission (EC), dealing primarily with multi-state activities, has an average of six cartel decisions (all such cases where a fine was imposed) between 2015 and 2018. The average has remained more or less the same in the last 20 years.[20] With respect to the CCI, there is also a gradual decline in the number of cartel investigations after the initial few years of anti-cartel enforcement.

Order of investigation under Section 26 (1) of the Act leads to the DG filing the investigation report with the CCI. The CCI, on the basis of the report, after giving due opportunity to the parties concerned to reply on the DG's report, examines the report vis-à-vis the responses and decides that the case is that of cartelization (or not). The total number of cases decided by the CCI gives a sense of its overall activities. However, as mentioned previously, numbers here would only indicate activeness and not the quality of such assessment. Over the entire period of 12 years, 36% of all the orders of the CCI (831 in total comprising orders under Sections 26 [2], 26 [6] and 27) are related to cartels. However, if we consider all the orders where an investigation was ordered after the CCI formed a prima facie opinion, 58% of total orders involve allegations with regards to violation of Section 3 (3) of the Act. Out of all the cases related to cartelization in one or the other

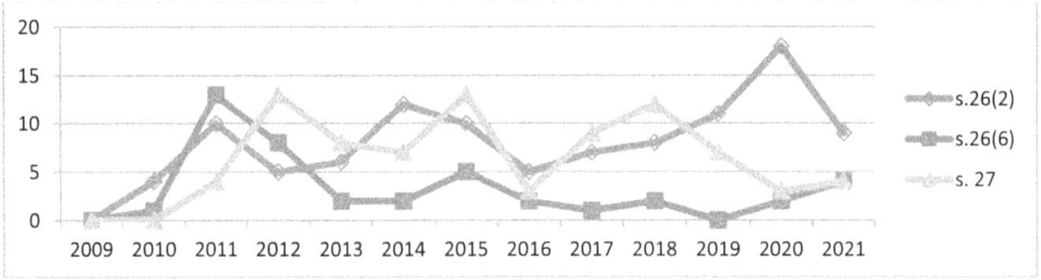

X axis: Year of enforcement; Y axis: Number of cases

Figure 4.1 Year-wise trend of all the orders passed by the CCI related to cartels.

form (125 in total), there have been indictments in approximately 67% of cases (yield ratio is calculated by dividing the total number of cases where cartelization was found by the total number of cases where the investigation was ordered by the CCI after forming a prima facie opinion under Section 26 [1] of the Act). This means that most of the investigations have led to penalties being imposed, which also means that the CCI was right in detecting cartels first-hand. On average, the CCI has detected and penalized seven cartels per year. Years 2012 and 2015 were the most active years in terms of the number of decided cases on cartels.

We see big fluctuations in the activity of the CCI across the observation period. For instance, the number of decided cartel cases after the most active years, 2012 and 2015, dropped drastically in the subsequent year. There is a general slag in the years following 2015, which only improves in 2018 due to leniency cases. The drop in the number of decisions post-investigation in the years 2020 and 2021 may be attributed to the pandemic situation in the country.

4.3 Cartel detection: Source of information/investigation

Detection of cartels has always been the most troubling part of cartel enforcement. Since cartels are secretive in nature, there are rarely any direct indications of cartelization. The competition regulator, therefore, has to act on two fronts. First, it has to be extra cautious and efficient to detect market irregularities. *Suo moto* investigative powers have been conferred on the CCI for this purpose only, which essentially means that the CCI, being an expert body, is expected to develop tools and processes to detect if any sector of the market is suffering from cartelization. The extent of the problem can be understood from the fact that the average detection rate of cartels in the US and the EU is between 12% and 14%, which in itself is low.[21] If, alongside this, enforcement agencies do not develop the expertise to detect cartel activities, it undermines the whole point of deterrence.

Cartel screening, thus, becomes an important aspect of enforcement activities. The second part of cartel detection is the enlargement of the source of information. Some older competition law jurisdictions rely heavily on leniency applications as a source of cartel information.[22] The DOJ in the USA does not annually report on the number of leniency applications received or granted each year. During 1993–2010, the Antitrust Division indicated that it received about 20 applications per year. Further, the Global Competition Review, in 2015, reported that most of the advanced jurisdictions received an average of 45 applications per year. Further, since the fiscal year 1998, over 90% of $5 billion in antitrust fines were tied to investigations assisted by leniency applicants, and of the 50 investigations the Antitrust Division typically opens at a time, more than half are initiated or are being advanced by the information received from a leniency applicant".[23]

The CCI, which does not have a very robust leniency regime yet, has to focus on other avenues for information. Cartel screening in this way can aid *suo moto* investigations, forming an important base for cartel information. Similarly, governmental and statutory bodies, being the largest procurers of goods and services, are in the best position to detect anti-competitive activities, especially in bid-rigging cases, and hence, their references can become a vital source of information. The present section deals with the traditional sources of information.

4.3.1 Sources of information under Section 19

Per Section 19 of the Act, the CCI may enquire into any alleged cartel activity on the basis of information received from "any person, consumer or their association or trade association". The CCI also has *suo moto* powers to order an investigation. Reference can also be made to the CCI by "the Central Government or a State Government or a statutory authority". It is important to study the source of information for two reasons: firstly, to check if the sources of information have any impact on the result of investigations in terms of duration and outcome; secondly, the source of information gives a picture of the level and percolation of awareness about competition law and its implications. For instance, if large numbers of information are coming from consumers, it indicates that the consumers of a jurisdiction understand how to assess anti-competitive behaviour and the recourse available to them in law. Figure 4.2 shows the comparative chart of the source of information during the observation period.

Section 19 refers to five categories of the sources of information – *suo moto*, consumer or consumer association, trade association, a reference from government or statutory authority or any person as defined under the Act. Unlike in the Consumer Protection Act, 1986, it is not necessary to qualify as a consumer to file information with the CCI. In the present analysis, the definition of person has been narrowed down to mean a competitor as a distinct category. This has been done to provide a clear picture of the

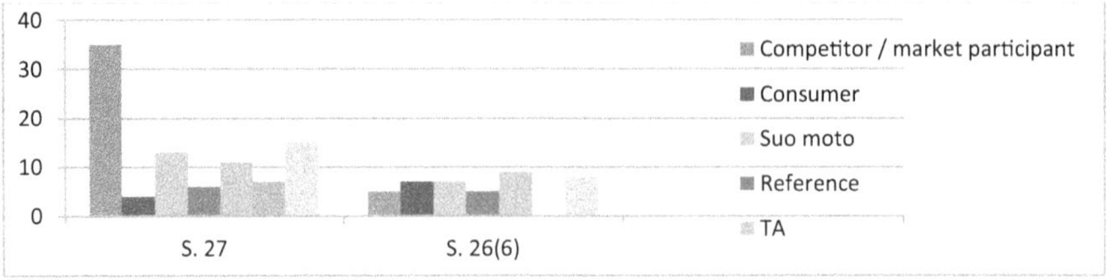

Figure 4.2 Section-wise source of information in cartel cases.

actual categories of persons filing information on cartel activity. The same has been presented, taking the type of order as the base.

4.3.2 Source of information and success rate

Different categories of sources of information of the CCI and their success rates are discussed here.

a *Competitor or market participant*: Of all the information filed with the CCI alleging cartelization, the ones filed by a competitor or existing market participant of the same relevant market shows the highest success rate. The bulk of information (approximately 45%) related to cartels has been filed by competitors, which is almost double the number of information filed by direct consumers of the affected market. It also constitutes the highest (38 out of a total of 83 cases) source of information under Section 27. In other words, 46% of cases in which the source of information was a competitor or market participant have resulted in an indictment from the CCI. These numbers are not surprising, considering that most of the cases under Section 27 are trade association cases where the boycott, non-dealing with non-members and mandatory authorization to operate are common forms of anticompetitive behaviour. Resultantly, the ones affected are not directly the end consumers but players who are trying to compete within the market and who are affected due to their refusal to join the association or follow the diktats of the association. They have the best evidence to file the information with the CCI to take necessary action. Competitors being the highest source of information holds true for orders under Section 26 (2) (34% of total orders) as well. Even for orders under Section 26 (6) quantum of information filed by the competitors does not lag behind considerably when compared to other sources of information.

b *Consumers or consumer association*: Consumers constitute a mere 4.8% of all orders under Section 27 (4 out of total 83 orders). In comparison, they constitute 33% of total orders under Section 26 (2) and 17% of total orders under Section 26 (6). In other words, information coming from consumers constitutes just over 18% of all the information related to cartels filed with CCI and has the least success rate in terms of getting an indictment order. As is evident from the data, consumers in India have not really used the law to their benefit. It is important to note here that, firstly, there is a very restricted form of private enforcement of competition law, and that too post-indictment orders from the CCI; and secondly, the matter at the CCI level is not actually between the informant and the opposite party but between the CCI and the opposite party. The penalties, therefore, flow to the CCI and not to the informant. Thus, there is no incentive as such for a consumer to file information against any anti-competitive behaviour. A consumer is happier to file for individual damages under the Consumer Protection Act, 1986, rather than filing information against anti-competitive behaviour of market participants. Even otherwise, cartelized products are generally of such "minor ingredient for the buyer that they have little economic incentive to invest in expert procurement managers".[24] In the data set too, the information as such is filed by institutional consumers who got affected due to collusive actions of the market players. Many of these are public procurement agencies. The second reason for the low numbers is the inability of consumers to adduce enough evidence for the CCI to form a *prima facie* opinion to launch an investigation. Thus, information filed by consumers gets rejected at the preliminary stage itself. The CCI has not, in a single instance, launched a *suo moto* inquiry based on any information filed by any consumer. Therefore, it is possible that consumers or their associations find it convenient to take recourse to consumer forums. Even otherwise, competition regulators do not generally bank on complaints from consumers as they lack the expertise and are unable to realize the harm that has been caused due to cartels and, thus, often delay in filing complaints.

c *Suo moto*: Per Section 19 of the Act, the CCI can on its own motion inquire into any alleged contravention under Section 3. When the baton was passed from the MRTPC to the CCI, it was envisaged that the latter would proactively exercise its powers to vet and screen business sectors and launch inquiries wherever there was a suspicion of anti-competitive behaviour. Per the available data, the CCI does not really fare well here. In total, the *suo moto* category constitutes 13% of total information related to cartels. While *suo moto* inquiries do constitute approximately 20% of all orders under Section 27 (17 out of 83 decisions), none of those inquiries originated due to any proactive effort by the CCI (eight *suo moto* inquiries were launched post a newspaper item alleging cartelization in a particular sector; four were launched after direct letters/emails were written by institutional consumers like the Food Corporation of India and Railways; seven *suo moto* inquiries were launched post leniency application; two investigations were initiated on CAG Report and information from CBI). Similarly, in only 7 out of 42 orders under Section 26 (6), an investigation was ordered on a *suo moto* basis. The CCI has largely ignored key industries, like construction, highways, education, health, manufacturing, and so on, where, even though information was not forthcoming, they had cartel-conducive environments. It is important to understand here that to launch an investigation, the CCI only has to form a *prima facie* opinion based on preliminary evidence, but it has not really used market screens to vet sectors and launch *suo moto* investigations. This goes a long way in creating an impression in the market that the CCI is not proactive in launching investigations. Therefore, if cartel members are successful in developing mutual trust, they can remain intact without fear of defection or cheating and can survive for long durations of time. The CCI, in such a situation, fails to create fear in the minds of existing cartelists to come out on their own and file leniency applications or to create any credible deterrence in the creation of new cartels. This is in stark contrast to the experience in other jurisdictions like the EU or USA, where a bulk of investigations have resulted from leniency applications which can be attributed to two reasons: first, the initial enforcement of anti-cartel laws by the competition regulator was able to create the level of fear whether in the form of very high monetary penalties or conviction that caused the cartel members to come out in the open; and second, the leniency regime is lucrative enough to convince the cartelists that the cartel profits will not be enough to offset the penalty that would be imposed when caught and the leniency structure in such situation provides a convenient and stress-free exit.

d *Reference under Section 19 (1) (b)*: The CCI may inquire into any alleged cartel activity on "a reference made to it by the Central Government or a State Government or a statutory authority". Similar to a *suo moto* inquiry as a basis to launch investigation, we have rarely seen references made by government agencies or statutory bodies alleging anti-competitive behaviour. During the observation period, mere 14 reference matters in a total of 125 orders related to cartels post-investigation. Only six reference matters have led to indictments under Section 27. Of these six cases, four cases are such where the referring authority was also the procurement agency and thus can be categorized as consumers. There are just two references that have been made by departments of the state governments (Haryana and Andhra Pradesh). Considering the fact that public procurements constitute 30% of the GDP,[25] both at the centre and state levels, it is highly unlikely that cartels have not formed, especially where there is repetitive bidding. A few union ministries – defence, railways and telecom – allocate approximately 50% of their respective budget for public procurement. We are differentiating here between anti-competitive bidding and bidding marred with corruption. Therefore, collusion between the procurement agency and one or more bidders is outside the scope of the present enquiry.

e *Trade association*: As discussed earlier, a bulk of cases under Section 27 have been filed against trade associations. We also witness cases where trade associations have filed information against anti-competitive practices. In a total of 32 cases, information has been filed by trade associations with a good success rate of 34% in terms of indictments.

4.4 Duration of enforcement

One of the common metrics that has been used in legal scholarship related to cartel enforcement is to study the duration of time to investigate a cartel and make a decision. For calculating the same, the date on which information or reference or leniency application was filed with CCI is taken as the starting point, and the date of the decision of the CCI is taken as the final point. This starting point is the least controversial as there is no clarity or availability of data on other options in the form of the date of dawn raids, opening of official proceedings and so on.

In India, the process, as shown in Figure 4.3, is simple. Information under Section 19 is filed with the CCI, which then forms a *prima facie* opinion of whether there has been a violation. If the CCI arrives at a conclusion that there is no *prima facie* case made out, it may close the matter and pass the necessary order under Section 26 (2) of the Act. Alternatively, the CCI may pass an order under Section 26 (1) directing the DG to conduct an investigation. If, based on the investigation report submitted by the DG, the CCI comes to a conclusion that there was no cartelization or there was not enough evidence to conclude cartelization, it may close the matter by passing an order under Section 26 (6) of the Act. Where the CCI concludes the existence of a cartel, it may pass orders of any nature as prescribed under Section 27 of the Act.

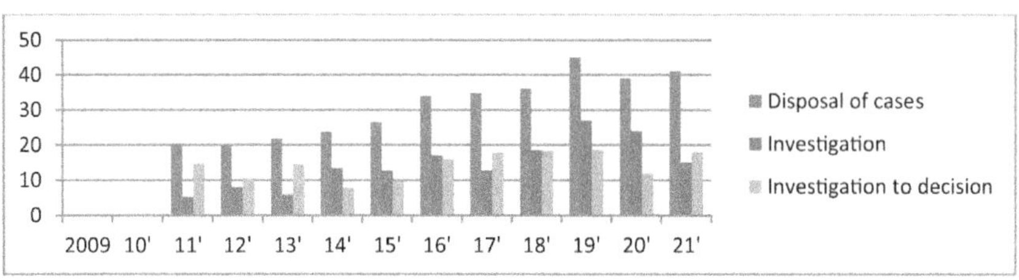

X axis: Year of enforcement; Y axis: Average duration of disposal (in months)

Figure 4.3 Average duration of disposal of cases; average duration of investigation and duration of decision from the submission of the investigation report (in months by year of decision under Section 27).

The entire enforcement process can be divided between detection (date on which investigation was ordered by the CCI), investigation (time taken by the DG to submit the investigation report) and decision by the CCI. The duration of investigation can only be considered for orders under Section 26 (6) and Section 27. The total time taken to decide a case can be calculated from the date of information till the date of the final decision by the CCI. An additional metric can be the duration to pass the final decision from the date of submission of the investigation report by the DG.

If we analyze the decided cases, the duration for disposal of a case fluctuates substantially, from the minimum of 4 months[26] to the maximum of 66 months (that too in a leniency application[27]). This fluctuation is not on account of the number of cartel members in the cartel leading to lengthy investigations or due to the complexity of the case that required time. There is also a considerable hike in the time taken by the CCI to dispose of cases in the last couple of years, where the average rate is 35 months. Per the data, there is no particular reason for this fluctuation, and similar fluctuation is also seen in the duration of the investigation and the gap between the submission of the investigation report and the order of the CCI.

The average duration for disposal of cases, as seen in Figure 4.3, has risen consistently, especially in the last five years (2014–2019). The average duration for disposal of cases has risen from 20 months in 2011 to 45 months in 2019. While there are fluctuations in the average duration of investigation time per year, the same also shows a considerable increase (from 5 months in 2011 to 27 months in 2019) which ordinarily, per the Indian position, must be completed within 60 days, saving a situation where the CCI grants extension to the DG.[28] Interestingly, the number of cases decided by CCI per year has not increased proportionately. This basically means that CCI is taking more time to investigate and dispose of cartel cases. Even in leniency cases, the average duration of disposal of cases is 35.4 months, and the average duration for investigation is 17.2, which is, in fact, higher than the average duration of ordinary cartel cases. Delay in the disposal of leniency cases may be counterproductive to the very idea of leniency, which in turn reduces the trust of market players in the legal structure. While cartel investigations in countries like the US may still take years, the same is not comparable to India. Cartel cases in the US are criminal in nature in comparison to civil nature in India. In the EU, the average duration of investigations between 2011 and 2015 was noted to be 48 months. The average number of cartels detected during the same period was 7.6 months, with the involvement of 35 firm groups.[29]

Another facet that can be seen is the high duration of time between the submission of the report and the final decision, which ideally should be made within 21 working days from the date of conclusion of arguments.[30] After the investigation report is submitted by the DG, the CCI forwards the report to all the concerned parties for their reply. It may also give them an opportunity to cross-examine any witness. As the data suggests, the CCI takes quite some time, with an average of almost 12 months. Similar trends are seen in orders under Section 26 (6).

At the cost of repetition, it is emphasized here that the duration of investigation or disposal of cases has a direct impact on the deterrence value of anti-cartel enforcement. A delayed procedure leading to deferred disposal of cases allows other cartelists to take preventive steps to avoid detection. As will be seen later in this chapter, the situation gets much more severe when the duration of disposal of cases by the CCI is clubbed with the time taken at the appellate stages or with the data on recovery of penalty. It takes years before cartel members are appropriately dealt with. For instance, in the cement cartel case,[31] while the case itself was decided in 2012 after two years of process at the CCI level, the case has not yet been finally concluded and is languishing at the appellate stage. Such delayed finality takes away the effect of the sting that any competition authority would intend to impose on cartelists. Another example is the LPG cartel case.[32] The case was decided in 2012, and a penalty was imposed by the CCI on more than 40 cartel members. The Supreme Court, in 2018, set aside the order of the CCI on the grounds of lack of enough evidence.

Long investigations create legal uncertainty on the fact, whether the alleged behaviour or action on the part of a few players constitutes an illegal action.[33] There is a possibility of firms being dragged into litigation for long durations of time for no fault of their own. Even when there is a likelihood of unfavourable order, there is uncertainty about the eventual imposition of fines. On the other hand, a prolonged investigation requires larger resource utilization by the CCI. One of the metrics to assess the efficiency of any competition regulator is to see the rate of disposal or investigations. A quicker process shows better internal procedures. Length of investigations or disposals also delays the recovery of penalties from the cartel participants. If the cartel members can foresee a lengthy process which may ultimately lead to penalty, they can devise better strategies to defend themselves and enables them to budget the prospective penalty in their yearly finances. Needless to say, it may take years before a final decision is given by the Apex Court. Resultantly, penalties fail to create the level of deterrence desired under anti-cartel enforcement regime. The backlog of cases at the investigation stage has been rising, for which complexity of cases and inadequacy of staff are certain reasons attributed to the CCI.[34]

This in no way discounts the importance of quality of decisions which withstand the scrutiny of appellate courts. Therefore, a high duration of investigative procedures with a high success rate is still tolerable. However, a high duration of enforcement with a poor success rate, as seen in the Indian context (elaborated further in the subsection dealing with appeal cases), is problematic. The appellate tribunal has set aside approximately 45% of all orders passed by the CCI between 2009 and 2017.

The duration of the investigation can be linked to the duration of the cartel itself. Theoretically, a long-surviving cartel takes a longer duration

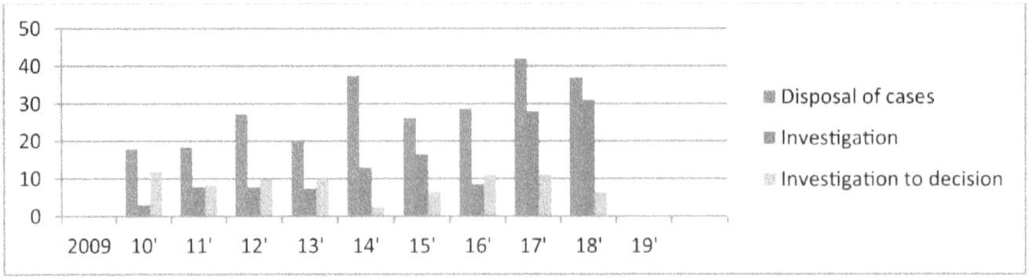

X axis: Year of enforcement; Y axis: Average duration of disposal (in months)

Figure 4.4 Average duration of disposal of cases; average duration of investigation and duration of decision from the submission of the investigation report (in months by year of decision under Section 26 (6).

to investigate. Therefore, a cartel such as the zinc dry-cell battery cartel[35] that lasted for more than seven years will take a longer time to investigate when compared to a cartel like the Pune Municipal Corporation bid-rigging cartel,[36] where the cartel only lasted for four months. Similarly, a cartel with the involvement of firms will take a longer duration of time to examine all parties. Certain types of cartels, like price-fixing cartels or those that limit or control production, to be successful have to run for longer durations of time in comparison to bid-rigging cartels, which are more or less bid-specific. Time taken to investigate, therefore, for a price-fixing or limiting cartel will be longer than that for a bid-rigging cartel.

4.5 Cartel screening and prediction

While it is true that competition regulators have advanced in terms of availability of resources and technology, which should have helped in better detection and prosecution of cartels, cartel detection rate is still very low, ranging from 13% to 15%, even in economies like the US and the EU[37] A logical reason for it may be a change in dynamics and sophistication of modern collusive arrangements. They have become more secretive and cautious. While direct evidence was always difficult in cartel cases, circumstantial evidence is harder to come by. Many jurisdictions across the world use econometric techniques or econometric forecasting techniques to predict cartel formation.[38] However, not many competition regulators have the wherewithal to engage in such exercises and have to rely on information or leniency applications as trigger points to start enquiry, which is followed by a collection of evidence. There is always a dearth of relevant information to apply prediction tools. Screening, which involves economic and statistical analyses to flag unlawful behaviour,[39] is therefore conducted. The CCI uses screens like the nature of the market and product and facilitating factors like evidence of communication or exchange or information in cartel cases.

The CCI has not particularly used cartel screens to vet and detect sectors prone to cartelization. While it has conducted or sponsored market studies[40] to check the competitiveness of different sectors, these studies have rarely led to investigations leading to any finding of cartelization. It has used structural and behavioural screens to build its case or reinforce its findings. The majority of cases under Section 26 (2), 26 (6) or 27 have used less than two screens. The majority of the orders (50%) under Section 27 have used one or two screens. Most of the orders under Section 26 (2) (more than 80%) used theoretically recognized and internationally employed structural screens to reach a finding that the market was not conducive to cartelization. Structural screens have also been used for orders under Section 27. Behavioural screens, on the other hand, have been heavily used by the CCI for orders under Section 26 (6), where almost 40% of orders used non-price behavioural screens.

Usage of screens by the CCI has been rudimentary, and it has been unable to develop, based on its experience, any country-specific screen which can then be applied to a different subject matter. The Cartel Report (2018) of the CCI mentions three India-specific structural screens, including the presence of active and strong trade associations used by it. The said report itself mentions the usage of the second India-specific structural screen, "informal service sector", at 0% across the CCI's orders. The last India-specific structural screen, "low value of individual transactions" has been used in just 2% of cases. As indicated earlier, the usage of structural and behavioural screens by the CCI has not been to take pre-emptive action but only to build the case of cartelization, if any. The CCI must move from passively applying cartel screens to taking proactive steps for detection. The large-scale exercise done by the Office of Fair Trading of the UK is an illustration. The agency used the data of price-fixing cases from the US (DOJ) since 1994 and the EC since 1990 to identify industry-level variables to predict cartelization. The agency "tried to predict the incidence of cartels with industry level data, and concluded that industry turnover, cost measures, concentration measures, entry barriers, and employee costs, among others, help explain the probability of collusion in an industry".[41] While in many countries today, the usage of screens for cartel prediction has been minimized due to the success of the leniency scheme. The same cannot be said for India. The failure of the CCI to create fear of detection and punishment in the minds of the cartelists has led to the limited success of the amnesty scheme. Even when the leniency scheme is successful, screening has its own benefits.

It may be argued that amnesty schemes are used by cartelists when the cartel is close to discovery or the cartel itself has become ineffective or non-profitable or is close to breaking up. Therefore, leniency is not attractive for profitable and stable cartels. In such a scenario, screening may come to the rescue as, unlike leniency, it is not based on insider information but on available market data to detect even the profitable cartels.

4.6 Evidence, standard and burden of proof in cartel cases

4.6.1 Standard of proof in cartel cases

Cartels are clandestine in nature and, therefore, while the definition of "agreement" under the Act includes both formal and informal agreements, there would rarely be any formal arrangement or written document which can be used to prove a cartel. The main reason behind this is the certainty of its illegality. Cartels are considered *per se* anti-competitive, and most jurisdictions across the world prescribe strict sanctions against them. Therefore, competitors who enter into such arrangements know that any overt form of engagement can be later used as evidence against them. As Adam Smith rightly said, "collaborators do not shout about their actions from the rooftop. Sometimes, all that is necessary is a 'nod' or a 'wink' ". What this means is serious work for enforcement agencies who generally have a hard time looking for evidence. In law, it has to be unequivocally established that there was an "agreement" between two or more players, and it will not be enough to say the market outcome is such that the participants must have colluded. Therefore, mere price parallelism is not enough to prove cartelization and, at best, can be treated as a starting point for investigation. Sometimes, parallel behaviour might be the result of the nature of the market[42] or an independent response to similar economic conditions.[43] For instance, in an oligopolistic market, competitors tend to mimic each other or follow a leader. While this might give the same result as cartelization, it is not *per se* bad in law. Unless parallel behaviour in the market is not because of a prior meeting of minds, it cannot be proceeded against. Therefore, proof of the existence of an agreement is a prerequisite for cartel investigation. This is also the most difficult part of the entire enforcement structure. Interestingly, the CCI has applied this basic principle of the evidentiary standard in allegations related to algorithmic collusions as well. In the airline case of 2021,[44] the CCI did not find any direct evidence to the effect that the common software was implemented by competing airlines with a view to fixing prices. Further, it observed that the involvement of a human element to decide the final prices indicated that the use of algorithms was only to facilitate genuine price determination in an industry that requires dynamic pricing and was not done with a view to implementing a price cartel.

For the purpose of application of Section 3 (3) of the Act, there must be evidence of the agreement between the competitors in question. As mentioned earlier, proof of the existence of an agreement is not generally available, and therefore, it has to be derived from a multitude of surrounding facts, called circumstantial evidence. These are also called plus factors, which, when clubbed with market behaviour of price parallelism, may lead to identifying a cartel. Per the CCI, "Plus factors are economic actions and outcomes, above and beyond parallel conduct by oligopolistic firms, that are largely inconsistent with unilateral conduct but largely consistent with coordinated action".[45] No single circumstantial evidence can be said to be conclusive of the existence of a cartel, and the enforcement agencies generally use a combination of multiple factors to prove its existence. The conduct of the parties can also be used as evidence to prove their involvement.

Per the procedure prescribed under the Act, the CCI may order the DG under Section 26 (1) to conduct an investigation and collect evidence to prove unequivocally that an agreement existed between the parties in question. Evidence may be direct or indirect. Per Section 41 of the Act, the DG has the powers of a civil court under the Code of Civil Procedure, 1908, which includes "summoning of a person and examining him on oath, requiring the discovery and production of documents, receiving evidence on affidavit, issuing commissions for the examination of witnesses or documents".[46] After the DG has collected all the necessary evidence, it submits the report to the CCI.

The most contentious part of cartel enforcement is the standard of proof. Simply speaking, since cartels under Indian law have been categorized as civil wrongs, cartel cases in India, unlike that in the USA or UK, are civil in nature. The standard of proof, therefore, is that of *preponderance of probabilities* and not of *beyond reasonable doubt*. Enforcement agencies have heavily relied on circumstantial evidence rather than direct evidence of collusion.

Cartel cases generally have to deal with a lot of indirect evidence and inferences. The European decisions started with a sense of high rigour in terms of establishing the standard of proof required in cartel cases. Certainty in terms of appreciation of evidence was stressed.[47] Courts refused to infer collusion unless it could be proved that the alleged conduct could not be explained but for collusion.[48] Therefore, there was recognition of *presumption of innocence*, which is taken into account in cartel cases.[49]

Benefit of the doubt: European courts soon realized that direct or concrete evidence would be hard to come by in cartel cases and, even if available, they would be fragmentary and sparse.[50]

> Accordingly, in most cases, the existence of an anti-competitive practice or agreement must be inferred from a number of coincidences and indicia which, taken together, may, in the absence of another plausible explanation, constitute evidence of an infringement of the competition rules.[51]

However, if plausible explanations are accepted, the standard of proof cannot be said to be low. Though the window of *benefit of the doubt* crept into some later judgments,[52] the ultimate test still lies in convincing the judge. Similar pieces of evidence, therefore, can be seen differently by different observers. We have come across multiple such examples in India as well, where a given set of evidence was looked at very differently by the CCI and appellate forums.

Plausible alternatives: The narrative of plausible alternatives is contentious. If the CCI holds that particular behaviour of parties cannot be explained except for collusion, it will be struck down in appeal if the parties are able to put the same facts in a different light and are able to provide another plausible explanation to the one adopted by the CCI. However, where the CCI relies on concrete evidence, be it documentary or otherwise, which is sufficient to show a prior meeting of minds, the defence of plausible alternatives cannot be taken. The only option available to the parties then is to question the sufficiency of the evidence.[53]

Perception of normality: It will not be open for alleged parties to claim that they were not aware of the illegality of the conduct or action in question, such as sharing of price-sensitive/secret information, participating in meetings with competitors or discussing bids with competitors before bidding. Enterprises are presumed to act rationally to further their own self-interests. The inferences drawn from situations, however, will have their own limitations and cannot be extended to behaviours which can be interpreted from both sides Therefore, it cannot be said, for instance, that the competitors would not have met regularly but for collusion.

4.6.2 Burden of proof in cartel cases

Per the Act, the 'burden of proof' to prove the existence of an 'agreement' is on the CCI. Section 3 (3) creates a presumption of anti-competitiveness of the 'agreements' of the nature prescribed under Section 3 (3). The CCI is not required to prove that such an agreement between competitors (horizontal agreements) related to fixing price, limiting or controlling the production of goods or services, market sharing or bid rigging causes an AAEC within India. This is similar to the *per se* treatment under the Sherman Act, 1890 (USA), or the "agreement by object" category (EU). The Act in India does not use the term "per se" or "object", but the implications of such agreements are the same. The presumption of an AAEC is, however, rebuttable. Hence, once the CCI establishes the existence of an agreement, the burden shifts to the opposite parties or the alleged cartelists. The opposite parties may then try and prove that there was no agreement of the nature provided under Section 3 (3) or that the agreement does not cause or has any AAEC. The parameters provided under Section 19 may be used to rebut such presumption.

To further elaborate on the previously mentioned aspects, we have divided the discussion into two parts. The first part is a quantitative assessment of the nature of evidence that has been used by the CCI in the last ten years. In the second part, we have picked up seven case studies from the last ten years to highlight the inconsistency in the appreciation of evidence at the level of both the CCI and the appellate forum.

4.6.3 Assessment of the use of evidence by the CCI

Evidence used in cartel cases can be best categorized as direct or circumstantial. Direct pieces of evidence are all those first-hand proofs that can be used to directly implicate the participants of the cartel. In contrast to circumstantial evidence, direct evidence is not based on inferential reasoning. They include documents, emails, and oral or written statements of cartel members. These are pieces of evidence that directly link one or more parties to an alleged conduct. However, as indicated, direct evidence is hard to come by in cartel cases. Therefore, circumstantial pieces of evidence have to be relied upon. They are all those facts that indicate or imply that a person committed an act. On the basis of the OECD document,[54] circumstantial evidence is further categorized into two types: communication evidence and economic evidence.

Communication evidence establishes prior meeting or association between different members of the alleged cartel. Such meetings are necessary to chalk out the details and modalities of the cartel and can be categorized into two types: first, where there is only evidence of meetings but the substance of the meeting is unknown, and second, where the CCI gathers information not just about the meeting but also the substance of the meeting. While the former relies upon pieces of evidence like telephone records, participation records of meetings, travel to common destinations and so on, the latter includes evidence of minutes or notes of meetings demonstrating, for instance, topics like price, demand or capacity utilization that were discussed. This may also include internal documents of an enterprise showing that it had knowledge of its competitors' pricing strategy, like future increases in prices of goods or services.

Economic evidence can also be categorized as market-related and firm-related evidence. Cartels tend to originate and sustain in a certain environment. Therefore, if in a particular market, factors that facilitate cartels are present, then such a market is more conducive to cartelization. Competition regulators generally tend to examine the market and see if there are conditions that facilitate cartelization. Cartel conducive environment includes situations like a high concentration in the market, homogenous product, stable demand, active trade association and high entry barriers. Firm-related evidence, or conduct evidence, is the most important type of economic evidence. Analysis of the conduct of parties is important to identify behaviours that can be categorized as contrary to a party's self-interest and which, therefore, support the inference of an agreement.[55] Conduct evidence can be further subdivided into behavioural evidence, industry performance and facilitating practices. Behavioural evidence includes actions of the enterprise in which it would not have indulged had there not been a cartel. This includes behaviours like parallel-pricing changes, reduction in output despite similar or increasing demand, and suspicious bidding patterns. Performance indicators generally include factors that show the standing of the enterprise in the market, like abnormally high profits and stable market share. Prior history of violation of competition law is also considered behavioural evidence. Facilitating practices are all such actions, which ease the formation or sustenance of cartels. Evidence related to the exchange of price-sensitive or strategic information, signalling of price by one or more enterprise and excessively restrictive product standards are taken into account.

It has to be mentioned here that none of the circumstantial evidence is conclusive proof of a cartel in itself. It is also possible that certain actions of an enterprise can be explained on the basis of market dynamics or have business justifications. Therefore, it is always a multitude of circumstantial evidence that is taken into account to prove cartelization. The assessment of such evidence will be subjective. Indian law does not provide for this classification, nor has it issued any guidelines on the usage and gravity of different types of circumstantial evidence. Therefore, reliance on these pieces of evidence has varied from forum to forum and also within the CCI.

In this section, all the decisions of the CCI under Section 27 have been studied to examine the kind of evidence that has been used by the CCI to decide cases related to cartels. Decisions of the CCI under Section 26 (6) where the DG found evidence of cartelization have also been covered.

4.6.4 *Case-wise usage of evidence by the CCI*

Interestingly, even though direct pieces of evidence are hard to come by in cartel cases, the CCI/DG, in a high percentage of cases (approx. 60%) in India, used direct evidence. Most of these cases are trade association cases, where direct evidence in the form of by-laws, memorandum of association, circulars, minutes of meetings, press releases and so on were readily available. Once the evidence was found, there was no reason for the CCI to go into the aspect of circumstantial evidence. In the rest of the cases, the CCI relied on circumstantial evidence to decide on the allegation of cartelization. For circumstantial evidence, a high percentage of cases looked at economic evidence (42% of cases) when compared to communication evidence (19% of cases). Conduct evidence was looked into in all the cases where economic evidence was examined or in 60% of cases where circumstantial evidence was examined. Facilitating evidence was found in just 14 cases out of the total cases.

4.6.5 *Inconsistency in the appreciation of evidence: illustrative case studies*

a *Neeraj Malhotra v. Deustche Post Bank Home Finance Ltd. & Ors.*, Case 5/2009, order dated 2 December 2010 (CCI)

This was one of the first orders of the CCI after the investigation into alleged anti-competitive behaviour. The case related to the allegation of indirect

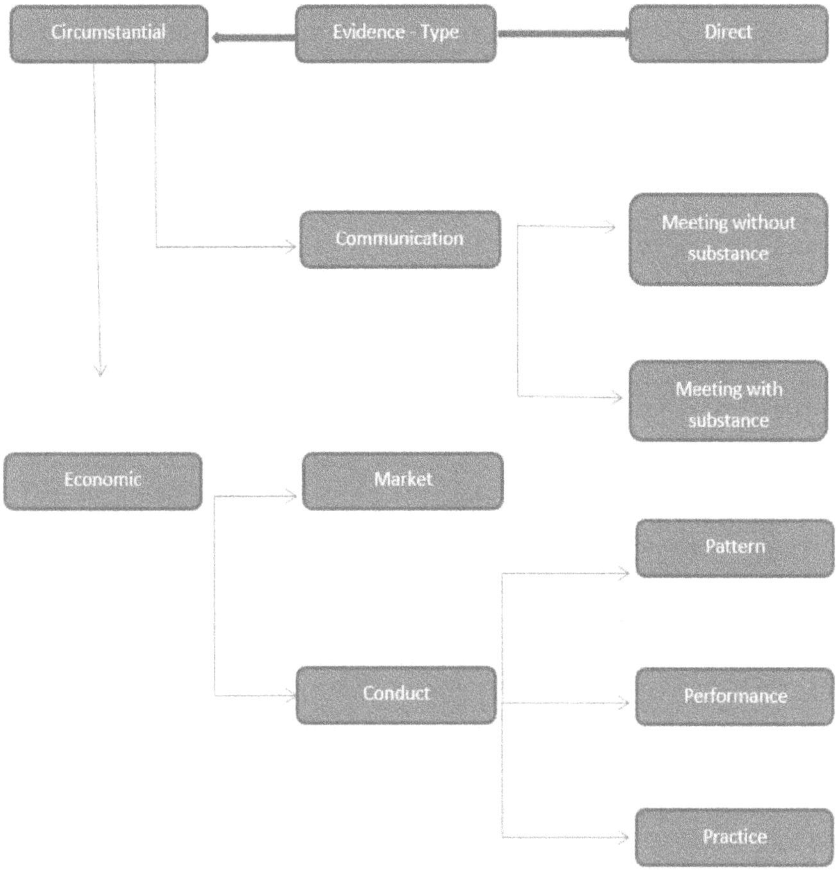

Figure 4.5 Types of evidence – pictorial representation.

price fixing of service of home loans by banking and non-banking financial companies. It was alleged that the opposite parties were charging pre-payment foreclosure charges at 1–4% of the outstanding loan amount, which prevented the buyers from shifting to another source of finance which offered a lower interest rate. It was alleged that banks and financial institutions had entered into an agreement or understanding to levy pre-payment charges, which effectively increased the rate of interest on which the loan was given. Information was filed against four entities. The CCI, after forming a *prima facie* opinion, ordered the DG to conduct an investigation on 10 September 2009, which submitted the report after three months of investigation. The DG expanded the scope of inquiry to 16 entities in total as the alleged practice was followed across the board. It scrutinized two meetings of the year 2003 of the Banking Association, which were related to the issue

Table 4.2 Detailing year-wise usage of types of evidence by the CCI

Case	*1*	*2*	*2A*	*2A1*	*2A2*	*2B*	*2B1*	*2B2*	*2B2a*	*2B2b*	*2B2c*
2010											
Neeraj – DG		✓	✓		✓	✓		✓	✓		
2011											
Tata sky – DG		✓				✓		✓	✓		
DDRS – DG		✓				✓		✓	✓		
SK Sharma – DG		✓				✓		✓	✓		
Jupiter – DG		✓				✓		✓	✓		
Metalrod – DG		✓				✓		✓	✓		
Kingfisher – DG		✓			✓	✓		✓	✓		
Sugar Mills – DG	✓	✓	✓		✓						
FICCI – DG/CCI	✓										
Uniglobe – DG/CCI	✓										
FCM – DG/CCI	✓										
Vijay – DG/CCI	✓										
2012											
Airlines – DG		✓				✓		✓	✓		
Tyre – DG		✓				✓	✓	✓	✓	✓	
25/10 – DG/CCI	✓										
Sunshine – DG/CCI	✓										
LPG – DG/CCI		✓	✓		✓	✓	✓	✓	✓	✓	
Coal – CCI		✓				✓		✓	✓		
PES – DG/CCI		✓				✓		✓	✓		
ALP – DG/CCI		✓		✓		✓		✓	✓	✓	
EIMPA – DG/CCI	✓										
Gulshan – DG/CCI		✓	✓	✓		✓		✓	✓		
UTV – DG/CCI	✓										
Varca – DG/CCI	✓										
Cement – DG/CCI		✓	✓	✓		✓		✓	✓	✓	✓
Shree – DG/CCI		✓	✓	✓		✓		✓	✓	✓	✓
Vedant – DG/CCI	✓										
2013											
FTPGI – DG		✓	✓	✓	✓	✓	✓	✓	✓		
Cinergy – DG/CCI	✓										
Santuka – DG/CCI	✓										
BP Khare – DG/CCI		✓	✓	✓		✓		✓	✓		
Ashtav – DG/CCI	✓										
Puja – DG/CCI		✓	✓	✓		✓	✓	✓	✓		✓
Reliance – DG/CCI	✓										
Peevear – DG/CCI	✓										
Sandhya – DG/CCI	✓										
2014											
Steel – DG (first report)		✓					✓	✓	✓		
Arora – DG/CCI	✓										
Diesel – DG/CCI		✓							✓	✓	
BCDA – DG/CCI	✓										
CDAG – DG/CCI	✓	✓	✓	✓							
ISMA – DG/CCI		✓				✓		✓	✓		✓
Basheer – DG/CCI	✓										
Cinemax – DG/CCI	✓	✓	✓	✓							

Case	*1*	*2*	*2A*	*2A1*	*2A2*	*2B*	*2B1*	*2B2*	*2B2a*	*2B2b*	*2B2c*
2015											
Faiveley – DG		✓				✓	✓	✓	✓		✓
Royal – DG	✓										
Swastik – DG/CCI	✓										
Rohit – DG/CCI	✓										
Shivam – DG/CCI	✓										
AIMTC – DG/CCI	✓										
Bo-Med – DG/CCI		✓				✓	✓	✓	✓		✓
Sheth – DG/CCI		✓				✓	✓	✓	✓		✓
KFEF – DG/CCI	✓										
Insurance – DG/CCI		✓	✓		✓						
KFCC – DG/CCI	✓	✓				✓		✓		✓	
Crown – DG/CCI	✓	✓				✓		✓		✓	
Bajaj – DG/CCI	✓										
Jet – DG/CCI		✓				✓		✓	✓		✓
Alkem – DG/CCI	✓										
2016											
Maruti – DG/CCI	✓										
2017											
DC Fans – DG/CCI	✓										
Shree – DG/CCI		✓	✓	✓		✓		✓	✓		
BDCDA – DG/CCI	✓										
Vinay – DG/CCI	✓	✓	✓		✓						
Cochin – DG/CCI	✓										
Coa – DG/CCIl		✓				✓		✓	✓		✓
DJB – DG/CCI		✓				✓		✓	✓		✓
KCDA – DG/CCI	✓										
Vipul – DG/CCI	✓										
2018											
CDAB – DG/CCI	✓										
MAHAGENCO – DG/CCI		✓	✓	✓		✓		✓	✓		✓
Dry cell – leniency	✓	✓	✓	✓							✓
Nagrik – leniency	✓										
Lachs Green – Leniency	✓										
Saara – leniency	✓										
Essel – leniency	✓					✓		✓	✓		✓
Alis – DG/CCI	✓										
KFCC – DG/CCI	✓										
Glycol – DG/CCI		✓	✓	✓		✓		✓	✓		✓
2019											
MP Chemist DG/CCI	✓		✓								
Dry-cell DG/CCI Leniency	✓	✓	✓	✓							✓
Nagrik DG/CCI Leniency	✓										
Jalgaon DG/CCI	✓										
Electric-supply DG/CCI Leniency	✓	✓	✓								
LPG 2019 DG/CCI		✓	✓		✓	✓	✓	✓	✓	✓	
EPS Systems 2019 Leniency	✓	✓	✓		✓	✓		✓	✓		✓

(*Continued*)

Table 4.2 (Continued)

Case	*1*	*2*	*2A*	*2A1*	*2A2*	*2B*	*2B1*	*2B2*	*2B2a*	*2B2b*	*2B2c*
2020											
BCDA	✓										
Automotive Bearings Leniency	✓	✓	✓		✓	✓		✓	✓		✓
Railways 2020	✓	✓		✓		✓	✓	✓	✓		✓
2021											
FPBAI	✓										
Usha International		✓	✓	✓		✓	✓	✓	✓		✓
TFPCA	✓	✓	✓		✓	✓	✓	✓	✓		✓
Beer Cartel	✓	✓	✓	✓	✓	✓		✓	✓		✓

1: Direct Evidence
2: Circumstantial Evidence
2A: Communication Evidence
2A1: Evidence of meeting without substance
2A2: Evidence of meeting with substance
2B: Economic evidence
2B1: Market Evidence
2B2: Conduct Evidence
2B2a: Pricing evidence
2B2b: Industry performance
2B2c: Facilitating practices

of a circular and noted that the collective decision taken with respect to pre-payment charges was in violation of Section 3 (3) (b). The DG reported that the alleged practice created barriers to new entrants, and the collective decision to "limit market competition and generate fee-based income" violated Section 19 of the Act. The CCI, after detailing and establishing the nature of the banking sector and, more specifically, the home loan segment, noted that while it was true that the entities charged pre-payment charges, the rate at which it was charged varied from one entity to another. Therefore, there was no uniformity in the practice. It emphasized the need to understand the market and economic principles to apply Section 3 of the Act. Per the CCI, it is essential to "pinpoint a specific point in time as the reference point of alleged agreement". It refuted the claim of the DG that the meeting of the Banking Association was used to form any such agreement, as according to the CCI, the discussion in the meeting with respect to pre-payment charges was only "consequential". Using the European Court of Justice's decisions, it was held that the existence of an agreement must be "unequivocally established" and that it cannot be "conjectured or even circumstantially adduced". The CCI, therefore, in light of the absence of any concrete evidence of an agreement between alleged the members, concluded that the action of pre-payment charges was not the result of any agreement but unilateral business decisions. The majority opinion seemed to be stressing the point of direct/concrete evidence of "conscious and congruous act" being a reference starting point.[56]

Two members of the CCI, Mr P. N. Parashar and Mr R. Prasad, in their dissenting opinion, held that the practice of pre-payment charges was a result of concerted action. They relied on the same Banking Association meeting of 2003 and the follow-up action of the entities to note that 12 out of 15 opposite parties started charging prepayment charges at 2% while the rest charged between 1% and 2%. The dissenting members did not apply the strict understanding of agreement as used by the majority opinion but were satisfied with the "factual existence of common approach". Mr Parashar noted the parties' conduct post-meeting to conclude that the decision of the meeting was actually given effect. The meeting of members was treated as a meeting of minds to take concerted action. Further, the internal circulars of some of the banks were examined to prove that the reason for prepayment charges was not asset-liability management as insisted in the majority opinion but to prevent consumers from switching to other banks. It was emphasized that for decisions under Section 3, it was not necessary that it is simultaneous and has common starting points for every party. "The concurrence of parties and the consensus among them can, therefore, be gathered from their common motive and concerted conduct".[57] Physical participation in the meeting need not be proved to say that the members were a part of the cartel, and the same can be inferred from preceding and subsequent behaviour. Per the learned judge, participation in a cartel can be proved through participation in decision-making. The dissenting opinion of Mr Parasahar clearly laid down the burden of proof in cartel cases, an aspect on which the majority opinion was completely silent.

b *In Re: Aluminium Phosphide Tablets Manufacturers*, Suo-Moto Case No. 02/2011, order dated 23 April 2012 (CCI)

The chairman and managing director of the Food Corporation of India (FCI) requested the CCI to conduct inquiries related to the rising cost of procurement of aluminium phosphide (ALP) tablets apprehending the existence of a cartel between manufacturing companies. It was further contended that in the last eight years, the four and the only manufacturing companies of the product in the country had quoted identical rates in all the tenders floated by the FCI. The CCI, taking *suo moto* cognizance of the matter and forming a prima facie opinion, ordered the DG to conduct an investigation on 24 February 2011, which submitted the report after eight months of investigation. The DG reported that the parties had been quoting identical prices in all the tenders and that, even in the last tender, all the parties had submitted bids at the same time and that there was a common entry at the visitor's gate of the FCI. The DG tried to establish that the parties had prior communication or association and that they had been quoting high prices even with different costs of production, which did not match with the trend of prices of the raw materials. The DG also reported that the parties had intentionally and collectively boycotted the global e-tender of FCI of 2011. The pattern of identical quoting was not just followed in FCI tenders but in other government procurements as well. The DG went for the "but for" assessment where the given conduct of consistent identical pricing could not have been possible without prior consultation. It was argued before the CCI that the reason for identical quotes was due to one reference point for quoting the price. The CCI rejected the arguments of the opposite parties and went with the reasoning of the DG. Unlike in *Neeraj Malhotra*, it did not insist on direct evidence and relied on circumstantial evidence to conclude that a cartel existed in the supply of ALP tablets to the FCI. Therefore, the identical prices, despite the difference in cost of production, clubbed with the possibility of a prior meeting as evidenced by the visitors' register, were taken as a primary factor to conclude cartelization. It is evident that the CCI considered the pattern of behaviour preceding the tender as evidence which goes more in line with Mr Parashar's opinion in the *Neeraj Malhotra* case. The CCI stressed that the standard of proof for anti-competitive agreements is "preponderance of probabilities" and not "beyond reasonable doubt".[58] It, however, unnecessarily tried to differentiate between a case of price parallelism and the present case of submission of identical bids. It is worthwhile to mention here that apart from the evidence of common entry in visitors' logbook, the CCI had no other evidence that the parties had met earlier to decide upon a course of action. The fact that the parties displayed a behaviour unlikely to be seen by competitors was considered good enough to conclude cartelization. The conduct of the parties, therefore, was held to be in violation of Section 3 (3) (d) and 3 (3) (b). Penalty at the rate of 9% of average of three years' turnover was imposed on three opposite parties.

Three appeals were preferred to the COMPAT[59] and were disposed of by a common judgment. The COMPAT largely accepted the reasoning of the CCI but rejected the argument that identical quotes or parallel behaviour could be explained on the basis of the nature of the market as there was nothing to show that the market in question was of such a nature. However, relying on the EU and the Office of Fair Trading Guidelines, it accepted the argument of relevant turnover to impose a penalty for multi-product companies. It re-emphasized the need for the imposition of a penalty, taking into account factual aspects like "financial health of the company, necessity of the product, likelihood of the company being closed down on account of unreasonable harsh penalty", thus highlighting the importance of aggravating and mitigating factors and the principle of proportionality. Considering all the factors, the COMPAT imposed a penalty at the rate of 9% calculated on relevant turnover for two companies. Second stage appeal was preferred from the decision of the COMPAT, dated 29 October 2013. The Supreme Court found no fault in the approach taken by the appellate forum and found the parties guilty of bid rigging. On the issue of penalty, the Apex Court, in the absence of any guidance from the section, held that "adopting the criteria of 'relevant turnover' for the purpose of imposition of penalty will be more in tune with ethos of the Act and the legal principles which surround matters pertaining to imposition of penalties".[60]

c *In Re: suo-motu case against LPG cylinder manufacturers*, Suo-Moto Case No. 03/2011, order dated 24 February 2012 (CCI)

The CCI took *suo moto* cognizance in the present case after the investigation report was filed by the DG in another case[61] where it was reported that in the procurement tender of the Indian Oil Corporation Limited (IOCL) for the supply of LPG cylinders, the manufacturers rigged the bids by forming a cartel. The CCI, after forming a *prima facie* opinion, ordered the DG to conduct an investigation on 9 March 2011, who submitted the report after two months of investigation. It was reported that the IOCL, having a market share of 48.2% in the LPG market, was a major procurer of cylinders. The DG reported that there was a similarity in the pattern of bidding by all the bidders for supply in different states. The bids for different states were found to be the same for different bidders, and resultantly, all of them got the IOCL contract. Characteristics of the market like active association, a small number of companies, little or no entry, homogenous product and repetitive bidding were reported to facilitate collusion between bidders. It was found that the bidders actually met in a hotel just before the date of submission of bids. A similar pattern of bidding was also reported by the DG in other procurement tenders as well. The CCI, making a slight departure from the earlier *Neeraj Malhotra* case, discarded the requirement of any unequivocal evidence in cartel cases and held that "circumstantial evidence that tends to exclude the possibility of independent action would be sufficient to give rise to an inference of an agreement".[62] The standard of proof required per CCI was a balance of probability and a liaison of intention. Taking a cue from the OECD document on public procurement,[63] the CCI examined the existence of facilitating factors like stable demand, repetitive tendering, a small number of suppliers, active trade associations, homogenous and standardized products and no substitute of the product to conclude that the facilitating factors for cartelization were present in the LPG cylinders market. The facilitating factors and identical bids despite different costs clubbed with evidence of a meeting of bidders prior to submission of bid to discuss the tender was held to be conclusive proof to conclude that the market was cartelized. The CCI specifically rejected the argument that since all the bidders did not participate in the meeting prior to the bid date, it cannot be used as evidence against all as a meeting of minds could be inferred from subsequent conduct. Further, it held that even though the final price of procurement was negotiated by the IOCL, a manipulated and inflated price would impact the negotiation as well. Consequently, a penalty was imposed on 48 bidders at the rate of 7% of their average turnover. Forty-four appeals made to the COMPAT were disposed of with a common order dated 20 December 2013, where the tribunal agreed with a major part of the CCI's order but remanded the matter back to it on the issue of penalties. The CCI, in its 2014 order, reconsidered the penalty in light of mitigating factors like the nascent stage of competition jurisprudence and first-time contravention.

It rejected the argument of relevant turnover as there was no evidence of the companies being multi-product companies. The CCI, considering the social cost of bid rigging and the cost to consumers, decided to retain the penalty at the original level. The COMPAT set aside the order on 1 March 2016 as the CCI did not consider relevant turnover and mitigating factors. In a surprising turn of events, while the CCI and appellate forum were jostling with each other on the question of penalty, the Supreme Court in 2018 set aside the order of the CCI on merits as it found the evidence used by it to be inconclusive and insufficient. Appeals were filed against COMPAT's order of 2013 by both sides. The Supreme Court found it important to consider the nature of the market and whether an agreement as recorded by both the CCI and COMPAT was possible within such market dynamics. The Apex Court took into account attendant circumstances – like the presence of only three buyers, the IOCL being the biggest procurer, prices being fixed after negotiation with the IOCL and entry of new players in the market – as relevant factors. It noted that the IOCL was in practice awarding bids to all the suppliers to keep them in the market as there were a limited number of suppliers. Further, the price at which cylinders were sold to the consumers was regulated by the government. The primary evidence used by the CCI to establish a prior meeting of minds was also refuted by the Apex Court because even though all bidders did not participate in the meeting, they quoted identical prices, which prove that quoting identical prices was not the result of the meeting. It saw the nature of the market (oligopsony) as the reason for identical pricing and observed that

> the situation of oligopsony can be both ways. There may be a situation where the sellers are few and they may control the market and by their concerted action indulge into cartelization. It may also be, as in the present case, a situation where buyers are few and that results in the situation of oligopsony with the control of buyers.

It finally held that the LPG cylinder manufacturers were able to discharge their burden of rebutting the presumption by proving that parallel behaviour was not a result of collusion but due to prevailing market conditions where the procurer had all the advantages.

The reasoning in the LPG case provided by the Supreme Court creates confusion when we read its earlier decision in *Excel Crop Care*.[64] The Apex Court in the LPG case seems to suggest that even when there is identical quoting clubbed with plus factors, like meeting before tender, similar pricing despite the difference in cost of production of individual bidders and locational differences, it may not still lead to an inference of cartel. In the previous case related to bid rigging, the Apex Court had, in fact, under similar circumstances rejected this line of argument to hold the bidders liable and had rejected the argument around price parallelism for bid rigging cases which it seems to do in LPG. The Apex Court seemed to miss an important point here, which was highlighted by Justice Parashar in *Neeraj Malhotra*[65] way back in 2010 – that it is not necessary in cartel cases that all members participated in the meeting or that they had a common starting point.

d *All India Tyre Dealers Federation v. Tyre Manufacturers*, order dated 30 October 2012 (CCI) *("Tyre Cartel Case")*

The All India Tyre Dealers Federation (AITDF) had in 2007 written to the Ministry of Corporate Affairs (MCA) against the anti-competitive practices of tyre manufacturers. The MCA forwarded the information to the MRTPC. However, after the repeal of the MRTP Act, 1969, the same was transferred to the CCI, which, after forming a *prima facie* opinion, ordered the DG to conduct an investigation on 22 June 2010. The DG relied on multiple pieces of evidence, like price parallelism, across the manufacturers related to the net weighted average dealer price of tyres and the percentage change in prices; positive correlation of data involving production, capacity utilization, cost analysis, cost of sales and margins to conclude cartelization. The DG reported that the tyre manufacturers did not pass on the benefit of reduced excise duty to the consumers. Further, the net dealer price of lug tyres was the same across manufacturers and the percentage "change of net dealer price whether upward or downward was showing close correlation among the five tyre manufacturing companies". The DG also examined the data relating to production, capacity utilization, cost analysis, cost of sales/sales realization/margin, cost of production and natural price movement, net dealer price and margin and market share to conclude that the companies had not reduced the net dealer price (weighted price) in proportion to the actual production. Further, the companies were not utilizing their capacity in full, thereby resulting in limiting the supply. Also, the change in the price of natural rubber had no impact on the cost of production, and therefore, it did not explain the possible reason for the increase in the price of tyres by companies. The companies also maintained a percentage of market share throughout the duration of the investigation, which indicated high concentration in the market, causing high dependence on original equipment manufacturers and the spare parts market. The CCI, however, did not agree with the findings of the DG and emphasized that there was no economic reason for the underutilization of the capacity, especially in light of increasing imports. Further, per the CCI, the DG failed to take into account the cost of raw materials other than natural rubber, and therefore, "in the absence of detailed analysis of changes in total cost and resulting changes in prices", the CCI did not agree with findings of DG that "the benefit of decline in excise duty and price of natural rubber was not passed on to the consumers". The CCI also held that since there was a price difference in the range of 6–12% among manufacturers, there was no price parallelism. It observed,

> lack of clear trend in figures suggest that variations in Capacity Utilization are company specific and not necessarily due to any concerted

> action. The increase in production has been muted because of increase in capacity and not due to reduction of output leading to supply suppression. Cost of sales and sales realization have shown increasing trend year after year. Different manufacturers are differently placed as far as Net Margins are concerned. The bigger the range between the margins of manufacturers, lower are the chances of sustaining a cartel.

The CCI also noted that four out of five companies who were investigated had lost market share which was gained by the fifth company, a pattern which is inconsistent with a cartelized market. In light of these facts, the CCI did not agree with the findings of the DG, and even the appeal to the COMPAT was dismissed on technical grounds.

It is interesting, when compared to the cement cartel case, to note that the CCI in this case acknowledged the dynamics of an oligopolistic market and did not find the meeting between tyre manufacturers as an indication of cartelization. The oligopolistic nature of the market and "similarity in demand and pricing of almost identical products" was seen as a sufficient justification. The CCI emphasized that due to the fairly transparent market structure of the tyre industry, price parallelism was dictated by economic necessity and independent strategic choices rather than concerted action.

e *Builders Association of India v. Cement Manufacturers' Association & Ors.*, Case 29 of 2010 order dated 20 June 2012 (CCI)

The Builders' Association of India filed information against the Cement Manufacturers' Association (CMA) and 11 cement manufacturing companies with the CCI in 2010 for alleged violation of Sections 3 and 4 of the Act (a case with similar issues and parties, except for Shree Cement, was transferred from erstwhile MRTPC to CCI wherein additional penalty was imposed only on Shree Cement Limited). It was alleged that the cement manufacturers, under the aegis of the CMA, controlled the prices by limiting production or supply against available capacity. The companies were alleged to be indulging in price fixing as well as market sharing. The CCI, after forming a *prima facie* opinion, ordered the DG to conduct an investigation on 15 September 2010. The DG submitted the report after eight months of investigation. Although the market comprised 49 companies, the DG focused its investigation on 12 companies who together had 75% of the market share along with the CMA. The DG observed that the price of cement was consistently on the rise since 2004–2005. Price movement was in bands but not entirely in sync with production costs. Although it was argued that the price was based on market feedback, there was no methodical documentation system to assimilate and process market data. The companies were utilizing high demands to increase the margins rather than competing to supply at competitive levels. The DG noted price parallelism despite the different costs of production and transportation costs. There was a downward trend in capacity utilization across companies despite growth in the market. Per the DG, the bigger players set the prices to be followed by others, and they used the press and media as a mode of price signalling. The platform of CMA was used for the collection and dissemination of price information. The publication of the CMA meant for internal circulation contained important strategic information on production and dispatch with respect to each plant of member companies. Rules of the CMA provided for the collection and dissemination of statistical and technical information to members. High-powered committee meetings on prices at the CMA was followed by common action of all the parties to increase prices. The DG and the CCI also examined the nature of the market in the form of an oligopolistic market, homogenous product, stable demand, active association and high entry barriers. The CCI, in light of the evidence, concluded that the cement manufacturers had cartelized the market and imposed a penalty at the rate of 0.25 times the profit in the relevant period. The CMA was penalized at the rate of 10% of average receipts. The CCI relied on the *Dyestuffs* case,[66] where the European Court of Justice observed,

> whether there was a concerted action can only be correctly determined if the evidence considered as a whole and not in isolation, bearing in mind the peculiar feature of the market in question. It further noted that given the clandestine nature of cartels, circumstantial evidence is of no less value than direct evidence to prove cartelization.

The tribunal in 2015 set aside the order of the CCI on the grounds of violation of principles of natural justice as the chairperson who was party to the final order was not present during the hearing.

The CCI, in a fresh order in 2016, reiterated its earlier finding that the cement manufacturers cartelized the cement market by increasing prices and restricting supply to create artificial scarcity. The manufacturers intentionally did not utilize their full capacity to restrict supply even when the demand was increasing. The appeal filed to NCLAT was dismissed in 2018 as it agreed with the findings of the CCI that the platform of the CMA was used to share price-sensitive information on capacity, production, dispatch and supply. The appellate forum observed that the justification provided that the information was collected to comply with the directions of DIPP was not adequate as such information could have also been given as confidential information by each company. The tribunal observed that the "information exchange can constitute concerted practice if it reduces strategic uncertainty in the market thereby facilitating collusion", and in the current case, information was collected in a manner that each company could access the sensitive information of other company, thereby eliminating any strategic uncertainty. Further, it was noted that the cement companies displayed price, production and dispatch parallelism. While the prices increased, production and dispatch decreased despite increased demand in the market. All the forums (CCI, COMPAT and NCLAT) have emphasized the use of circumstantial evidence in cartel cases where the standard of proof is only the balance of probabilities. An appeal is currently pending before the Supreme Court of India.[67]

f ***Indian Sugar Mills Association & Ors. V. Indian Jute Mills Association & Gunny Trade Association (GTA)***, dated 31 October 2014 (CCI) *("Sugar Mills Case")*

The Indian Sugar Mills Association (ISMA), National Federation of Co-operative Sugar Factories Ltd. (NFCSF) and All India Flat Tape Manufacturers Association (AIFTMA) filed information with CCI against the Indian Jute Mills Association (IJMA), Gunny Trade Association (GTA) and Ministry of Textiles (MoT) for alleged violation of Section 3. It was alleged that members of the IJMA and the GTA were fixing the sale price of jute packaging material. GTA was alleged to be issuing a daily price bulletin (DPB) for jute bags for the benefit of the members of the IJMA and the GTA. The government in 1987[68] mandated the use of jute bags as packaging material for certain commodities, like cement, food grains, sugar and fertilizers. It was alleged that the IJMA and the GTA used their market power to price jute bags excessively. The CCI, after forming a *prima facie* opinion, ordered the DG to conduct an investigation on 2 August 2011, and the DG submitted the report on 17 July 2012. Two supplementary reports were also filed consequently. The DG reported that the rate at which transactions took place was close to the DPB price, and it certainly affected the competition in the market as the sugar manufacturers lost the power to negotiate prices. This got aggravated by the Jute Packaging Material Act, 1987, which banned the import of jute bags and mandated the use of jute bags manufactured in India by sugar manufacturers. It was reported that the DPB price did not move with market price or with the price of raw materials but was artificially fixed by the GTA and its members. The IJMA was also found to be in conversation with the GTA as it used its influence to increase prices. It was noted by the DG that there was a mechanism to collect information or any scientific methodology to achieve DPB. Further, though there was high demand, production decreased. This was reported to be in violation of Section 3 (3) (a) and 3 (3) (b) of the Act. The CCI, relying on the DG's investigation report, held that the IJMA and the GTA fixed the prices of jute packaging material through DPB, which was followed by the members of the GTA and the IJMA. The CCI, therefore, in light of the evidence like the use of DPB to fix prices and decreased production despite high demand and capacity, the non-optimal use of capacity held the IJMA and the GTA to be in violation of Section 3 of the Act. Also, considering the fact that the jute industry was going through a rough phase, a penalty at the rate of 5% of average receipts of three years of the IJMA and the GTA was imposed. Office bearers of the two associations were also penalized at the same rate.

The COMPAT in 2016 set aside the order of the CCI on the grounds of violation of principles of natural justice, as one of the CCI's members,

Mr U. C. Nahata, who was not present at the time of the hearing participated in the decision-making process. The COMPAT also rejected the CCI's orders on merits and noted that the CCI failed to establish that there was an agreement between the IJMA and the GTA about fixing the price of jute bags. Further, the tribunal also noted that the penalty imposed by the CCI was disproportionate and without any reason.

g *In Re: Alleged Cartelization in Flashlights Market in India,* Suo moto Case No. 1 of 2017, order dated 6 November 2018

The CCI took *suo moto* cognizance of this matter after a leniency application was filed by Eveready Industries India Ltd., where it was revealed that there was an exchange of information with respect to sales and production of flashlights through the platform of the Association of Indian Dry Cell Manufacturers (AIDCM). Such informational exchange between AIDCM, Eveready, Panasonic Energy India Co. Ltd. and Indo National Ltd. continued for eight years between 2008 and 2016, while Geep Industries India Pvt. Ltd. left in 2012. It was revealed that "information in relation to intended price increase or market information in relation to prices, discount schemes, etc. was exchanged among them regarding the product 'flashlights' to monitor the activities of competitors in the market". The CCI, after forming a *prima facie* opinion, ordered the DG to conduct an investigation. The DG examined both documentary and electronic evidence to report that the parties used the platform of AIDCM to share sensitive information on the subject matter from a period prior to 2009. This facilitated collusion in the flashlight market. The report established the existence of an agreement to increase the prices of dry cell batteries and flashlights between opposite parties through email exchanges. The DG rejected the argument of the opposite parties that the intended press release for an increase in prices was never implemented. The DG, on the basis of documentary and electronic evidences, concluded that the opposite parties, through the association, shared price and production data in order to monitor the market share of each member. Further, per the DG, the email of March 2012 to announce a price increase through a press release established an agreement between the opposite parties to cartelize the market of flashlights, but no evidence against Geep was found. The CCI held that an exchange of price-sensitive information "only indicates possibility of collusion and can be considered as a plus factor". However, a mere exchange of information does not imply collusion. While the CCI in para 97 notes that the email exchanges and statements disclosed that opposite parties had arrived at an agreement, it interestingly notes that the price discussion among parties did not prove that "that the concerned persons agreed upon the actual terms of increasing or determining prices". It brings in the angle of implementation of an agreement, and per the CCI, since there was no evidence to show that the activities of the opposite parties did, in fact, fix the prices of flashlights or implement the proposed press release, violation of Section 3 (3) cannot be concluded. The CCI took into account, probably for the first time, the effect of the cartel rather than just the existence of a cartel. The reason given by the CCI aligns with its earlier decision in the *Sugar Mills* case, where even though the DG, on the basis of oral depositions, press releases and minutes of meetings related to sugar price stabilization reported that the sugar mills colluded to fix minimum prices and limit and control supply, the CCI did not agree. Per the CCI, there are three requirements in cartel cases: "a. the parties must have met and order dated the concerted action; b. implementation of concerted action and c. there must be conclusive evidence of meeting of minds".

Compare this to the fuel surcharge (FSC) matter.[69] The CCI relied on circumstantial evidence to conclude that there was an agreement between competitors to indirectly fix the price of cargo transport through fuel surcharge. Per the CCI, since FSC was not affected by factors like aircraft type/flight/distance/sector/timings, revenue from FSC could be forecasted. The parties could not provide evidence to prove that the determination of fuel surcharge was an independent exercise, and the FSC was found to not move with fuel price as it should have.

4.6.6 Observations

These cases suggest that there is still a lack of a uniform threshold to establish cartels. The CCI and appellate forums have used varying methodologies to reach different conclusions. The evidentiary value and the standard of proof required to establish cartels have been hazy and inconsistent. In initial cases, the CCI stressed direct or concrete evidence, and the cases of *Neeraj Malhotra,*[70] *In re: Glass Manufacturers*[71] and *Consumer Online Foundation*[72] are examples of such an approach. *In re: Sugar Mills,*[73] the CCI emphasized the requirement of "evidence of the fact that the alleged cartel participants met and decided to take concerted action". Further, it was to be proved that such concerted action was implemented and that there were conclusive evidence of a meeting of minds.

However, the CCI watered down that approach and relied heavily on circumstantial evidence in cases like the cement cartel,[74] *Coal India v. GOCL*[75] and *ALP*[76] cases. In the cement cartel case, the CCI used the "parallelism-plus approach" where it held that in cartel cases it does not require direct evidence or proof of explicit agreement. "Agreement", per the CCI, could be "inferred from the intention or conduct of the parties". The CCI held that it may also use only circumstantial evidence to prove cartels.

However, there are also cases where the CCI went back to looking for a more concrete form of evidence to establish cartels, as done in the tyre cartel. It re-emphasized that it would rely on evidence which establishes that a particular set of acts and conduct of the market participants cannot be explained but for some sort of anti-competitive agreement and action in concert among them. The CCI, while holding the position of the *Neeraj Malhotra* case as to the requirement of unequivocal evidence as correct, also laid down the importance of circumstantial evidence. It noted that "if direct evidences are not present, but circumstantial evidences do indicate harm to the competition at a market place, the Commission will certainly take cognizance of the same". However, factors like loss in market share to new entrants, capacity expansion and mixed trends in capacity utilization, which were ignored in the cement cartel case, were taken into account in the tyre cartel case to refute any allegation of cartelization.[77]

Similar inconsistency is observed at the appellate stage, where the COMPAT (now NCLAT) and the Supreme Court have not maintained uniform tests to examine cartel cases. Therefore, we can see that the COMPAT overruled the CCI's order in cases like the sugar cartel case because, according to it, the CCI did not produce enough evidence to prove an agreement. The COMPAT looked for some clinching evidence to establish the existence of a cartel instead of relying merely on market evidence. In other words, the COMPAT was hesitant to apply the "but for" analysis. Similarly, we see a level of inconsistency when we examine the Supreme Court decisions in the *Excel Corporation* and LPG cases. The Apex Court in the LPG case seems to suggest that even when there is identically quoting clubbed with plus factors like meeting before tender and similar pricing despite the difference in cost of production of individual bidders and locational differences, it may not still lead to an inference of cartel. In the previous case related to bid rigging, the Apex Court had, in fact, under similar circumstances rejected this line of argument to hold the bidders liable while also rejecting the argument around price parallelism for bid rigging cases which it seems to do in the LPG case.

The reliance on circumstantial evidence in India has not been consistent and has varied to a large extent in the last ten years. Indian competition law does not provide any guidance on this aspect. There is no clarity on the type of evidence and the gravity of evidence on which a case of the cartel will be built. Such haziness also comes from the fact that the CCI has not been consistent with appreciation of evidence". The situation worsens when the idea of circumstantial evidence or plus factors does not match with the understanding at the appellate forums. There have been multiple cases where the appellate authorities, be it the COMPAT (now NCLAT) or the Supreme Court, disagreed with the findings of the CCI as they looked at the same evidence differently and which then led to different outcomes. The recent case of the LPG cartel, decided by the Supreme Court in 2019, is a prime example. The CCI has been more focused on establishing the law rather than punishing cartels. High cartel penalties that form headlines of newspapers do not really create financial difficulties for the guilty enterprises. The decisions of the CCI or appellate forums have been more focused on the use of evidence and not precisely on creating normative standards for the evaluation of evidence.

4.7 Qualitative assessment of cartel decisions

4.7.1 *Performance of cartel decisions at the stage of appeal*

The objective of the appeal process (excluding "right-based" functional aspect of judicial review, which is the domain of high courts and the Apex Court) is twofold: first, to minimize the chance of legal errors[78] and, second, to help refine the application of law or highlight any loophole in the law for the lawmakers. For instance, the concept of relevant turnover for the imposition of penalty was introduced in India by the appellate forum and later followed by the CCI. This setting of the normative standard helps in bringing legal certainty and uniformity in future decision-making, which has also been linked to economic efficiency.

An appeal mechanism provides an opportunity for the losing party to seek redressal or reconsideration of the matter. There is a greater likelihood of appeals being filed if the decision at the lower forum was flawed. Thus, an appeal mechanism also pushes the judges of the lower forum to take all reasonable care to avoid any infirmity in the decision, as they know that any such infirmity will be highlighted in the appeal.[79] However, it is not always necessary that appeals are used by parties to prevent flawed decisions and thus have welfare-enhancing motivations.[80] Appeals may be used by parties strategically to delay or sometimes avoid the application of the decision of the lower forum. Therefore, if the appeal process in a jurisdiction takes a long duration of time for disposal, parties may file appeals and try to stay orders of recovery of imposed penalty, not because they believe that the decision of the lower forum was erroneous but for tactical reasons.[81] An examination of the duration of appeal is also important to understand the behaviour of the firms. The longer the duration of appeal, the larger the costs associated with it. Therefore, if an appeal process takes years, it will have an impact both on the private party in terms of costs and on the CCI, which has to utilize its resources to stand its ground in appeal. A long duration of appeal also increases the uncertainty around the case and also prevents the recovery of fines. Delay in the appeal process has a negative impact on private enforcement of competition law as well. On the other hand, a very short duration of the appeal process would tempt parties to file appeals even when it is not required.

Thus, the twin objectives of the appeal process are to "promote economic welfare through the elimination of decisional errors" and the setting of normative standards.[82] However, competition law matters are complex in nature, which gets aggravated due to the presence of different theories and schools of thought with varying conceptual bases. When enforcement agencies start to cherry-pick theories which are distinct and which rely on diverse assumptions to back their own ends, it creates confusion and causes errors. Damien Geradin emphasizes,

> Modern Competition Law regimes are no longer anchored in a firm, unitary conceptual framework. Rather they borrow influences from

> distinct, and sometimes contradictory, theories; rely on diverse assumptions; and apply heterogeneous evidentiary techniques. While theoretical diversity may be a source of richness, and avoid the pit-falls of relying on one-sided theories, it may also be a source of confusion, and thus of errors, both in terms of competition policy making, but also in terms of adjudication.

The use of evidence in cartel cases is one such example, as there is no clarity on it or on the degree of reliance of each kind of evidence. There is no clear answer as to what extent circumstantial evidence can be used for a "but for" analysis. Further, even in horizontal agreements between competitors, there is a chance of rebuttal where the other side can prove that the agreement did not have anti-competitive effect. Such appraisals require complex economic analysis with which most judges struggle.

Another way to look at the appeal process is to examine it through the lens of accountability. The CCI is a quasi-judicial body that has legislative, executive and judicial powers. In a way, it acts as a mini-state.[83] These powers, especially the legislative powers, flow from the delegation of powers done by the law-making body. The appeal process helps in keeping this exercise of delegated power in check and ensures that it stays within the boundaries of delegation.

4.7.2 Process of appeal for competition matters in India

Per Section 53B of the Act, specifically with respect to cartels, any person aggrieved from any decision made by the CCI under Sections 26 (2), 26 (6) or 27 may prefer an appeal to the appellate tribunal. The appellate forum, per the scheme under the Act, on receipt of appeal filed within the prescribed time limit of 60 days from the date of receipt of the decision unless condonation of delay has been permitted by it,[84] may pass orders confirming or setting aside the order of the CCI. It may also modify the decision or direction of the CCI.[85] Per the Act, the appellate tribunal shall try to dispose of the appeal within six months from the date of receipt of the appeal.[86] The Finance Act of 2017[87] repealed the erstwhile Competition Appellate Tribunal (COMPAT), and now the appellate forum for competition law matters is the National Company Law Appellate Tribunal (NCLAT). Interestingly, the COMPAT itself came into existence in 2007 through the Competition (Amendment) Act, 2007. The idea of the central government to rationalize and merge tribunals has led to the repeal of a specialized agency and the transfer of all the matters to an agency which is already looking at two very broad areas of law – company law and insolvency law.

A two-stage appeal process is followed in India. Therefore, a 'person', as mentioned earlier, aggrieved by any direction or decision of the CCI may prefer an appeal before the appellate tribunal (now NCLAT) to modify or set aside the order of the CCI. Further, any person aggrieved by the decision

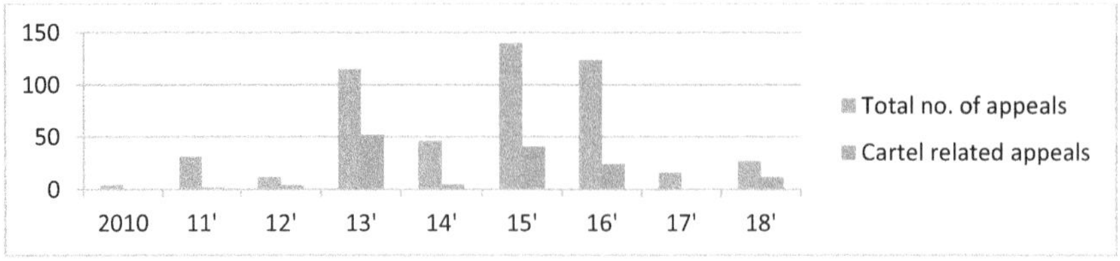

X axis: Years of enforcement; Y axis: duration of disposal of appeal (in months)

Figure 4.6 The total number of appeals related to cartels when compared to the total number of appeals.

of the appellate tribunal may prefer an appeal before the Supreme Court of India in accordance with Section 53T of the Act.

4.7.3 Duration of disposal of appeals (cartel cases) in India

The average rate of disposal of cases at the first appellate level in India is not that high. However, the number of appeals filed from orders under Section 27 is still very high. One of the possible reasons for such high figures may be the quality of the decisions of the CCI. We, therefore, in the later part of our discussion, focus on the nature of appeals and quality of the CCI's orders as a determinant for the high incidence of appeals in India. We have first charted the general activity at the appellate forum with respect to cartel cases across the years.

Appeals that were related to cartel decisions of the CCI have been used for representation. Therefore, other matters unrelated to cartels have been excluded. The high fluctuation in the figure across years is not surprising. The COMPAT was constituted through the Competition (Amendment) Act of 2007, but other provisions were only notified in 2009. Therefore, there were not many appeal cases in the initial years. The bulk of the activity happened between 2013 and 2017. As soon as the disposal rate of appeals started taking momentum, the Finance Act 2017 put the brakes and the COMPAT was repealed. The minimized activity related to appeals because a new appellate forum had to take over. Per Section 53B (5) of the Act, appeals filed before the appellate forum shall be dealt with "as expeditiously as possible" and "an endeavour shall be made by it to dispose of appeals within six months from the date of receipt of the appeal". Per the annual reports of the CCI, an average of 46% of cases remain pending for over a year. Clearly, the tribunal has been unable to follow the indicated timeline of Section 53B (5). Further, the COMPAT, over the years, had an average disposal rate of 42% per year with respect to all matters and not specifically pertaining to cartels. Timely adjudication of competition matters remained the desired objective under COMPAT.

Although the disposal rate of the COMPAT was merely 42%, as evidenced by annual reports of the CCI, the disposal rate at the NCLAT level is not very encouraging either.[88] On average, there have been 18 orders in the last four years related to competition law constituting less than 2% of the total NCLAT orders. On average, the NCLAT is passing 83 orders on a monthly basis, largely related to insolvency matters. Further, it can be seen that many of the orders of the NCLAT are related to Section 26 (2).

It seems that the idea of having a centralized appellate tribunal for all commercial matters is not really working because, presently, the priorities of the NCLAT appear to be skewed. Such utter disregard for competition matters seems to be also coming from the expertise of the panel itself. None of the members at the NCLAT have any prior experience in competition-related matters, and surprisingly, none of the erstwhile members in COMPAT were retained as a member of its successor.[89] This also goes against the recommendations of the 272nd Law Commission of India Report, which emphasized the need to appoint technical members with relevant and adequate experience in the field.[90] This is very different from the practice in other jurisdictions where specialized sectoral regulatory agencies have experts on their panel. Such need for expert assessment of competition law complexities has also been emphasized by various scholars from time to time.[91] Presently, the NCLAT has nine members, including the chairperson. There is no expert panel for competition law, and the same group is expected to look at all the matters related to the Companies Act, 2013; Insolvency and Bankruptcy Code, 2016; and the Competition Act, 2002. Section 411 of the Companies Act, 2013, which prescribes the qualification for appointment as chairperson or member of the appellate tribunal, does not require expertise in competition law as necessary eligibility. Further, per Section 410 of the Companies Act, 2013, the NCLAT can have a total strength of 11 members, while the present panel comprising nine members is struggling with an overload of cases, but the central government is taking steps to increase such strength.[92] The timely disposal of cases is crucial for the relevancy of competition law. The NCLAT Rules under the Companies Act, 2013, do provide a reduced time frame of three months to dispose appeals from the date of filing. However, it does not seem to be achieving the requirement, at least in competition matters.

4.7.4 *Analysis of decisions at the appellate stage*

The present data on appeals has been categorized per the CCI's decisions. Therefore, we trace the result of the CCI's decision in each year at the appellate forum. Cases during the observation period where the appeals were upheld have been categorized into four parts:

- a Appeals where the decision as to the level of fine was taken.
- b Appeals where the decision as to the procedure was taken.
- c Appeals where the decision as to the evidence or standard of proof was taken.
- d Appeals related to other substantive issues.

4.7.5 Outcome of the CCI's orders at the appellate stage

4.7.6 Success rate of orders under Section 27 for the years 2010–2016

As can be seen from the data, the CCI has not really fared well at the appeal stage, which is evident from the success rate of less than 40%; this, in turn, has hugely impacted the deterrence level that the CCI is trying to create. Successful anti-cartel regimes have been able to create deterrence through their tough decisions, which are able to withstand challenges at the appellate forums. The high chances of detection clubbed with a high success rate of orders of the enforcement agencies have also contributed to the success of their leniency programs. If, however, the parties alleged to have been involved in anti-competitive behaviour know that they might fare well at the appeal stage, the chances of which are more than 50% in India, they would not take the CCI's order very seriously. Appellate forums generally grant stays to the recovery of penalty, if any, ordered by the CCI. The cases get stuck at different stages of litigation. Delay in the recovery of penalty takes away the sting from the CCI's order. Data from the annual reports of the CCI suggests that although it has imposed an overall penalty of an amount close to 13,100 crores, only 43 crores have been recovered to date, which constitutes 0.3% of the total penalties imposed.[95] In comparison, the EC was able to recover a substantial portion of close to ten billion euros of the fine levied in the last five years.[96] Delay in the appeal process and the infinitesimal recovery of fines have also affected the recovery of damages by persons affected by anti-competitive conduct. Further, there has been no attempt by the CCI to check for post-cartel tacit collusion and see if the anti-competitive conduct is still continuing in the market.

Decisions of the CCI were set aside by the appellate forum either on substantive grounds or procedural grounds. Violation of principles of natural justice by the CCI was the main cause for setting aside the orders on the grounds of a faulty procedure. There are also cases where the tribunal upheld the decision of the CCI but reduced the penalty imposed on the parties. Reduction of penalty was ordered either because the CCI had wrongly considered average turnover instead of relevant turnover or because it failed to consider certain mitigating factors.

4.7.7 Case-wise assessment of the CCI's orders at the appeal stage

The present data on appeals has been categorized per the CCI's decisions. Therefore, we trace the result of the CCI's decision under Sections 26 (2), 26 (6) and 27 of the Act each year at the appellate forum. The year 2010 did not see any final decision at the appeal stage.

Table 4.3 A tabular representation of the outcome of the CCI's order at the appellate stage

Year	*Section 26 (2) orders*	*Appeal on Section 26 (2) orders*	*Section 26 (6) orders*	*Appeal on Section 26 (6) orders*	*Section 27 orders*	*Appeal on Section 27 orders*
2010	4	0	1	0	0	0
2011	10	2 (dismissed)	13	2 (dismissed)	4	4 (dismissed)
2012	5	2 (dismissed)	8	1 (dismissed)	14	2 (no appeal) 3 (dismissed) 5 set aside (2[93] on substantive grounds and 3 on procedure) 4[94] (reduction in penalty)
2013	6	1 (dismissed) 1 (allowed)	2	0	8	2 (no appeal) 6 (set aside on substantive grounds)
2014	12	2 (dismissed) 1 (allowed)	2	0	8	2 (no appeal) 1 (dismissed) 3 (set aside on substance and procedure) 1 (set aside on substance)
2015	10	1 (withdrawn) 1 (dismissed) 1 (allowed)	5	2 1 (dismissed) 1 (allowed)	13	3 (no appeal) 3 (dismissed) 2 (set aside on procedure) 2 (set aside on substance) 2 (set aside on procedure and substance) 1 (penalty reduced)
2016	5	2 (dismissed)	2	0	3	1 (set aside on substance) 1 (dismissed)
2017	7	2 (dismissed)	1	0	9	2 (dismissed)
2018	8	2 (dismissed)	2	0	12	**

Appeals made against orders under Section 26 (2) for the year 2011 were dismissed by the COMPAT. The COMPAT in *Pitambara Books Private Limited*[97] found the appeal to be infructuous as the tender in question was already withdrawn. Similarly, the appeal filed against the Consumer Online Foundation[98] was dismissed as no one appeared for the appellants, and the application for the condonation of delay in filing was rejected (14 July 2011). The COMPAT also approved the order of the CCI in *Lufthansa German Airlines & Ors.*[99] As there was no evidence to prove cartelization. The COMPAT accordingly held that "the airlines had taken independent decisions to abolish the system of commission and there was no evidence of the meeting of minds". Three out of four appeals to orders under Section 27 in 2011 got dismissed by the COMPAT, and one of the appeals was withdrawn.[100]

In the year 2012, out of five orders under Section 26 (2), three appeals were made, which were later dismissed by the CCI. While the *MIDC*[101] appeal was dismissed on procedural grounds (i.e. non-appearance), in the other two cases, the COMPAT agreed with the reasoning of the CCI. In *India Glycols Ltd.*,[102] it was alleged that the oil manufacturing companies had fixed the price for the procurement of ethanol (a kind of buyers' cartel). The minutes of the meeting of the Indian Sugar Manufacturers Association (ISMA) were produced as evidence to allege that prices for ethanol procurement were discussed at the meeting. The CCI, however, had concluded that there was no evidence of any agreement between the oil manufacturing companies after it noted that the price of ethanol was fixed by the Cabinet Committee of Economic Affairs (CCEA). The COMPAT, agreeing with the reasoning of the CCI, dismissed the appeal, holding that the demand for a high price by an association in itself does not amount to a cartel and will be wrong only if in pursuance of such demand something is done. In *Exclusive Motors*,[103] it was alleged that the agreement between the distributor company with its group company and its partner company was anti-competitive as it determined the purchase and sale price of the car. The CCI did not find the agreement between parent and subsidiary company to be subject of Section 3 as it was covered under the doctrine of "single economic entity". The COMPAT in 2014 affirmed the reasoning of the CCI. In April 2013, the COMPAT affirmed another decision of CCI in the *All India Tyre Dealers Federation*[104] under Section 26 (6). It was alleged that the tyre manufacturers had formed a cartel to fix the price of tyres. The DG relied on economic evidence, plus factors, market factors and other factors to conclude cartelization. The CCI, however, did not concur with the DG and noted that there was no wilful underutilization of capacity by the manufacturers. Further, it did not agree to consider only the cost of rubber and excise duty as the basis of input prices to infer price. Price parallelism reported by the DG was also found to be in the 6–12% range. The CCI noted that there was a fluctuation in the market share of the tyre manufacturers, which was not consistent with a cartelized market. The COMPAT, in April 2013, dismissed the appeal on technical grounds.

The COMPAT has been more critical of CCI's orders under Section 27. Out of a total of 14 orders, only three appeals preferred from the decision of CCI under Section 27 in the year 2012 were dismissed by COMPAT. Five orders of CCI were set aside by COMPAT either on substantive or procedural grounds. In four cases, the appellate forum ordered a reduction in the penalty imposed by the CCI.[105] In the *Motion Pictures*[106] case, eight matters were clubbed together as they had common issues. The information was filed against the practice of mandatory registration system of films practised by their respective film associations. It was further alleged that the associations were directing members not to deal with non-members and were threatening the film producers of boycott if the mandatory registration system was not followed. The CCI, in its decision, held the practice to be anti-competitive and in violation of Section 3 (3) (b) and thus imposed a penalty at the rate of 10% of the average receipts of the association for three years. The COMPAT in 2013 did approve the decision of the CCI but cautioned it to give reasons for the award of a penalty. The COMPAT remarked on the insignificance of the penalty in light of the gravity of contravention. A similar remark was given by COMPAT in *Sunshine Pictures Private Limited.*[107]

In the LPG cartel case, the CCI initiated a *suo moto* investigation for bid rigging in the tender floated by the IOCL. The DG found the market conducive to cartelization. There was a similarity in bidding pattern of all the 50 bidders who, despite being of different sizes and located at different locations, submitted identical bids. Further, there was evidence that the bidders had met in a hotel just before the submission of bids with an agenda to discuss the bids. The DG, on the basis of market, economic and behavioural evidence, concluded that bidders had rigged the bid. The CCI agreed with the findings of the DG and, therefore, in light of the absence of any mitigating factors, imposed a penalty at a rate of 7% of the average turnover for 47 companies, and one entity having failed to submit financial details was imposed a penalty of 2.1 times the net profit. The COMPAT approved the decision of the CCI but remanded the matter back on the issue of penalties. The LPG manufacturers then approached the Supreme Court against this finding. The CCI also filed a cross-appeal against the order to reduce fines, and then, in its 2014 decision, agreed to certain mitigating factors like the nascent stage of competition jurisprudence but also noted consumer and social harm as aggravating factors and thereby retained the earlier penalty. The CCI also rejected the contention of the parties that the computation of a penalty should be done on the basis of relevant turnover and not average turnover. The COMPAT in 2016 set aside the CCI's 2014 order as it did not consider relevant turnover and other mitigating factors. The Supreme Court,[108] finally in 2018, set aside the order of CCI on the grounds of insufficient evidence. It examined the market realities or the attendant circumstances and questioned the behavioural evidence in the form of prior meeting and held that the reason for quoting similarly was not meeting but "something else" as only 19 parties had attended the meeting, but the similarity of the quote was found in all bidders. The Supreme Court did agree that the nature of enquiry in cartel cases is "preponderance of probabilities". However, the assumption of an AAEC can be rebutted through evidence. It, therefore, went beyond a simplistic approach that was adopted by the CCI and examined the same market conditions of oligopsony from a different lens and noted that the CCI failed to discharge its burden of examining the defences made by opposite parties.

In another matter, the COMPAT dismissed the appeal against the order of the CCI in *Coal India*, where it was found that the opposite parties collectively boycotted the e-reverse auction. A penalty at the rate of 10% of turnover was imposed. The COMPAT, however, took into account certain mitigating factors like first-time contravention, uninterrupted supply of goods and participation of all parties in subsequent tenders and, thereby, reduced the penalty to only 10% of the penalty imposed by the CCI. Similarly, in the appeal made against the CCI's order in *PES*[109] for bid rigging in the supply of machinery to Safdarjung Hospital, the COMPAT reduced the penalty at the rate of 5% of turnover to 3%. Mitigating factors like first-time contravention, nascent stage of competition jurisprudence and good track record were taken into account. In a matter with similar facts as that of *PES*, the CCI held that the parties indulged in bid rotation. In light of the penalty imposed in *PES*, the CCI did not impose the penalty again as the contravention was in the same investigation period. The COMPAT set aside the findings of the CCI as the latter had unnecessarily relied on the evidence of a previous case.

In the bid-rigging case related to the procurement of aluminium phosphide tablets for Food Corporation of India, the CCI in 2012, on the basis of evidence like identical bids, common entries to visitor's register and similarity in bids despite the difference in cost of production, held the undertakings to be in violation of Section 3 (3) (d) and imposed penalty at a uniform rate of 9% of their average turnover of the preceding three years. The COMPAT[110] approved the decision of the CCI on the issue of bid rigging. However, it re-emphasized the need to give reasons for a particular penalty. The COMPAT imposed a penalty at the rate of 9% of the average relevant turnover. Further, it reduced the penalty for one of the undertakings to 1/10th of what was imposed by the CCI as owing to the fact that it dealt with only one product, its capacity was far lesser than others. The Supreme Court in 2017 upheld the decision of the COMPAT[111] and used purposive interpretation and the doctrine of proportionality to agree with the concept of 'relevant turnover' used by it to impose a penalty. Justice N. V. Ramana, in his separate opinion, noted that the discretionary power of the CCI under Section 27 (b) cannot be arbitrary.[112] As the law abhors absolute power and arbitrary discretion, this discretion provided under Section 27 needs to be regulated and guided so that there is uniformity and stability with respect to imposition of penalty. Very importantly, he noted,

> After such initial determination of relevant turnover, commission may consider appropriate percentage, as the case may be, by taking into

> consideration nature, gravity, extent of the contravention, role played by the infringer (ringleader? Follower?), the duration of participation, the intensity of participation, loss or damage suffered as a result of such contravention, market circumstances in which the contravention took place, nature of the product, market share of the entity, barriers to entry in the market, nature of involvement of the company, bona fides of the company, profit derived from the contravention etc. These factors are only illustrative for the tribunal to take into consideration while imposing appropriate percentage of penalty.

This sadly, as discussed later in the chapter, has not been followed or kept in mind by the CCI in the imposition of penalty leading to confusion and inconsistency.

The biggest penalty imposed on 12 cement manufacturers (including Shree Cement[113]) was set aside by the COMPAT[114] in 2015 on the ground of violation of principles of natural justice. The matter was sent back to the CCI for fresh adjudication. The COMPAT also noted that the CCI should have laid down comprehensive guidelines to conduct its proceedings in accordance with the principles of natural justice to ensure just and fair procedure. The CCI reheard the matter and passed fresh orders in 2016, reaffirming its earlier decision. The NCLAT in 2018 affirmed the decision of CCI, and the matter is now pending before the Supreme Court. *Vedant Bio Sciences*[115] was another decision of CCI that was set aside by COMPAT for violation of principles of natural justice. The matter related to the restrictive nature of the rules of the Chemist and Druggist Association of Baroda, where it was mandatory to get registered with the association to do any business as a stockiest or retailer in the relevant territory. Along with this, mandatory PIS and fixing of margins for wholesalers and retailers by the association were also challenged. Thus, the penalty imposed by CCI at the rate of 10% of average receipts was set aside. The CCI, in a fresh order in 2019, imposed the same penalty.[116]

The COMPAT set aside the order of CCI in *Eastern India Motion Pictures Association (EIMPA)*,[117] where it held the conduct of the association as anti-competitive. It was alleged that the by-laws of the EIMPA were restrictive in nature and were restricting the telecast of dubbed content. The CCI held that the trade associations, by their joint action, tried to stop the telecast of dubbed content. Since the EIMPA was already penalized in case 25/2010, a cease-and-desist order was passed against the Coordination Committee of Artist and Technicians of West Bengal Film and Television Industry. In an appeal filed by the coordination committee, the COMPAT set aside the order of the CCI but agreed with the minority opinion of the CCI to hold that Section 3 only covers agreements between competitors and since "*the members of the trade unions, being artists, technicians, etc., were not competitors in the market for 'telecasting of dubbed serials on the television in West Bengal*". Section 3 was not applicable. Further, there was no stoppage of the telecast of the dubbed content. Therefore, the COMPAT noted that there was no evidence to prove that the action of the trade association actually limited supply. The Supreme Court, however, in 2017 set aside the order of the COMPAT and affirmed the order of the CCI.[118] It held that the actions of the trade union could not be termed as pure unionism and their action hindered the exercise of choice of the consumers. Also, it read the term "market" in Section 19 (3) to mean "relevant market" and in the miscellaneous application clarified that delineation of the matter is not mandatory if the conduct falls within the statutory presumptions under Section 3 of the Act.[119]

In 2013, out of six orders of CCI under Section 26 (2), two appeals were made to the COMPAT. While the appeal in the matter related to *Andhra Pradesh Hire Purchase Association*[120] was dismissed, the appeal was allowed in the *MAHAGENCO*[121] case. In the former case, the allegation of cartelization was made against auto finance companies that had entered into an agreement to determine the rate of services by financiers in automobile finance. The COMPAT agreed with the finding of the CCI that there was no evidence to prove an agreement between the opposite parties. In the latter case, it was alleged that the bidders to the procurement tender of MAHAGENCO had colluded to divide the market among themselves across seven thermal power stations for liaison work. The CCI held that there was evidence to form a *prima facie* opinion as the quotes were not identical, and there was no other evidence to prove cartelization. It did not look into the question of market sharing. The COMPAT in 2015 relied on the observations of the Supreme Court in *BSN Joshi & Sons Ltd. V. Nair Coal Services Ltd.*[122] To allow the appeal and directed DG to conduct an investigation. The CCI in 2018 penalized and passed cease-and-desist orders against three undertakings for forming a hard-core cartel to rig the bids and dividing the market among themselves. No record of appeal was found against the 2013 orders of CCI under Section 26 (6).

The CCI faced an embarrassing outcome for its decisions made in 2013, as six out eight decisions were set aside for one or other reasons. In *Telangana Telugu Film Distribution Association (TTFDA)*,[123] information was filed against the film associations against their restrictive rules and practices, including mandatory registration, banning dealing with non-members, threat of boycott and restrictions on usage of satellite rights. The CCI, based on evidence gathered from circulars and notices, held the associations to be in violation of Section 3. Since the Karnataka Film Chamber of Commerce (KFCC) and TTFD were already penalized in previous cases, the CCI imposed a penalty at the rate of 10% of the average receipts on the Andhra Film Chamber of Commerce (APFCC). The COMPAT, however, questioned the evidentiary standards of the CCI to hold APFCC liable. It noted that APFCC only forwarded letters, and there was no evidence of it coercing anyone to restrict the release of films. Accordingly, the penalty imposed on APFCC by the CCI was set aside. In another matter related to media and entertainment, the CCI imposed a penalty at the rate of 10% on the

Tamil Nadu Film Exhibitors Association (TNFEA) for restricting supply as it issued directions to members to not screen the movie in question. The COMPAT[124] set aside the order of the CCI as it wrongly construed the facts in place. Relying on the by-laws of the association, the tribunal disputed the findings of the CCI that the boycott call was not given by the association but rather by the secretary in an individual capacity. The tribunal could not locate any resolution from the association to impute liability.

Similarly, the penalty imposed by the CCI on the All India Organization of Chemists and Druggists (AIOCD) in *Santuka*[125] was set aside by the COMPAT. The CCI, based on letters issued by the association with respect to NOC, stoppage of supply and MOU between AIOCD, IDMA and OPPI, held the conduct of AIOCD to be in violation of Section 3. The practice of mandatory NOC, PIS and fixing trade margins was held to be bad in law. The COMPAT, however, set aside the order of the CCI on the ground that there was no concrete evidence of AIOCD mandating NOC as there were companies who were appointed without an NOC as well. The COMPAT also held that PIS approval was meant to facilitate the implementation of the provisions of the Drugs (Prices Control) Order, 1995. Further, the implementation of trade margin was done by the drug manufacturers and not the association. It could not locate any evidence of a boycott call made by the association. The tribunal in 2016 also set aside the decision in *Peevear*[126] against AIOCD and AKCDA on similar grounds. The decision of the CCI in *Sandhya Drug Agency*[127] was met with a similar fate when the tribunal in 2016, on similar grounds, set aside the order of the CCI.

In another matter related to bid rigging in government procurement of polyester-based boot rubber soles,[128] The CCI, on the basis of market factors, economic factors and behavioural factors, held that the opposite parties had rigged the bid in their favour. And in light of the absence of any mitigating factors, the CCI imposed a penalty at the rate of 5% of average turnover. The COMPAT, however, overturned the decision of the CCI in 2016 on the grounds of insufficiency of evidence and faulty calculation of penalty on the basis of average turnover.

In 2014, an appeal was filed in four out of twelve orders of the CCI under Section 26 (2) but was withdrawn in two cases.[129] An appeal was allowed in the *Director General of Health Services (DGHS)*[130] matter where it was previously contended before the CCI that DGHS, in collusion with other opposite parties, had hiked up hospital rates through its differential rate of reimbursement based on accreditation with NABH. The CCI did not find it to be a fit case for investigation and noted that different rates, in fact, would act as an incentive to "to non-accredited hospitals to secure such accreditation and provide quality health care services". The COMPAT in 2016 remitted the matter back to CCI for fresh consideration after it held DGHS to be an 'enterprise'. The CCI in 2017 reiterated its earlier stand on the allegation of a cartel. An appeal to the NCLAT was then rejected in 2017. In *Span Communications*,[131] the CCI had closed the matter as it did not find any evidence that the opposite parties rigged the bid done by the Ministry of Tourism by quoting favourable rates "for releasing TV spots on the channels". An appeal made to the tribunal was dismissed on similar grounds as it did not find any evidence to prove that the bidders had colluded or that they belonged to the same family.

The year 2014 saw two *suo moto* investigations done by the CCI in the manufacturing sector related to steel and asbestos. In the steel matter,[132] the DG, in its first report, reported cartelization in the steel sector. However, in the supplementary report, the DG focused more on market factors to conclude against cartelization. The CCI agreed with DG's supplementary report and attributed price parallelism to oligopolist market realities (landed import prices, cost of production and the market demand and supply position). The CCI did not find any evidence of collusion and closed the matter. Similarly, in the asbestos case,[133] the CCI attributed price parallelism to market factors. No appeal was filed in either of the cases.

The CCI had to face another set of setbacks for its orders under Section 27 given in 2014. Four out of seven orders of CCI were set aside by the tribunal on both substantive and procedural grounds. *Arora Medical Hall*,[134] where the CCI had penalized the Chemist and Druggist Association of Ferozpur at the rate of 10% of the average receipts for mandating the NOC requirement and the office bearers at the rate of 10% of their average incomes, was set aside in 2015 by the tribunal. The tribunal noted that the informant was expelled from the association due to its own unethical conduct, and there was no evidence to prove that NOC was mandatory and also noted a violation of principles of natural justice. In the *Bengal Chemist and Druggist Association (BCDA)* case, it was held that the BCDA issued circulars prohibiting retailers from giving discounts to customers. The BCDA was found to be using coercive means to force retailers to comply with its diktats. The CCI, therefore, imposed a penalty at the rate of 10% of the average receipts and income on the association and office bearers, respectively. The tribunal[135] noted a few mitigating factors like the termination of anti-competitive conduct, no evidence of impact of action, to reduce the penalty on the association to 1% only. Further, the penalty on the office bearers was set aside on the ground of violation of principles of natural justice and that there was no evidence that they were responsible for the actions of the BCDA.

In another matter related to *Cartelization in the matter of supply of spares to Diesel Loco Modernization Works*[136] to Indian Railways, the CCI, based on identical quotes, had assumed that it was a case of cover bidding where few parties had intentionally made technical errors in their bids so that one of them could win. Further, per the CCI, the parties had quoted similarly despite the difference in cost of production and transportation. The COMPAT, however, set aside the order and remarked that it was "based on conjectures" and further noted that only a fraction of previous tenders had identical prices and that CCI had wrongly assumed tax to calculate rates.[137]

In the *Sugar Mills* case, the CCI had in 2014 held that the Indian Jute Mills Association (IJMA) and the Gunny Trade Association (GTA), as trade associations, fixed the sale price of jute packaging material by issuing of daily price bulletin. It held that there was no scientific basis for such prices as there was no concrete system to collect information, and the prices did not move per the movement in the prices of the raw materials. It thus penalized the IJMA and the GTA and their office bearers at the rate of 5% of average receipts and income, respectively. The tribunal,[138] however, in 2016 set aside the order of the CCI on the grounds of the violation of principles of natural justice. Further, the tribunal held that there was no evidence of an agreement between the two associations and also that the penalty imposed was disproportional.

In the year 2015, out of a total of orders under Section 26 (2) orders, three appeals were filed. While the appeal in the case of *Utkal Chemist and Druggist*[139] was withdrawn, the tribunal dismissed the appeal in the *Nitin Radheshyam Agarwal*[140] matter, where it was alleged that Bombay Dyeing, CREDAI and MCREDAI had colluded to incorporate "standard clauses in their respective apartment buyers" agreement resulting in directly or indirectly determining purchase or sale price of goods or services in violation of Section 3 (3) (a). The CCI, in the absence of any evidence that such practice was followed or that the clauses determined price, closed the matter. The tribunal in 2015 agreed with the reasoning of the CCI and dismissed the appeal. In *K Sera Sera*,[141] it was alleged that studios of opposite party companies had decided to release their films only through certain technical structure-compliant theatres. It was further complained that a revenue-sharing agreement was forced upon theatre owners. The CCI closed the matter without ordering for investigation as the market for Hollywood movies in India was too small, and there was no evidence to prove a cartel. It also noted the importance of technical specification. The tribunal in 2015, in light of insufficient evidence and over-reliance of the CCI on statements of the opposite parties, ordered fresh consideration. The CCI in 2016 rejected the application for investigation again, which led the tribunal in 2016 to order the DG to conduct an investigation.[142]

Out of a total of five orders under Section 26 (6) in 2015, records of two appeals were found in which one was dismissed and the other set aside. The CCI had, in *In Re: Deputy Chief Materials Manager, Rail Coach Factory*,[143] not agreed with the findings of the DG and held that there was insufficient evidence to prove cartelization in the procurement bid. It noted that the procurement policy of Railways was not conducive to healthy competition. The tribunal[144] in 2016 agreed with the reasoning of the CCI and reconfirmed its earlier position that mere quoting of identical prices does not mean cartelization and requires plus factors to prove otherwise. The COMPAT observed, "the players in a limited market are aware of the price quoted by each other in one or the other bid and it is a normal tendency to quote the same price in response to the next tender". The tribunal in the *IATA* case set aside the order of CCI as the DG had not investigated the allegation of abuse of dominance.

Out of total 13 orders under Section 27 in 2015, six orders were set aside by the tribunal, and the penalty was reduced in one case. In the *Rohit Medical Store* case,[145] the order of the CCI was set aside on the grounds of violation of principles of natural justice.[146] The matter was similar to earlier pharmaceutical association cases of mandatory NOC requirement. The CCI, on the basis of documentary evidence, found the association to be in violation of Section 3 and imposed a penalty at the rate of 10% of average receipts. The tribunal in 2016, in light of procedural irregularities, directed the DG to conduct a fresh investigation. In the *Vinayak Pharma* case,[147] the tribunal set aside the penalty imposed on the pharmaceutical company for its involvement in carrying out the practice of mandatory NOC. The tribunal, on both procedural grounds (violation of principles of natural justice and substance), set aside the penalty imposed on *Alkem*. The tribunal noted that Alkem could not have acted with the association if it was coerced by it, and the stoppage of supply was because the informant was not duly appointed and not because of the NOC requirement.[148]

In *All India Motor Transport Congress (AIMTC)*, it was alleged that AIMTC uniformly increased the truck freight by 15% across the country and asked its members to follow the decision. The CCI, based on the DG's report, held that AIMTC acted as a cartel by asking members to fix prices without actual regard to the effect of the hike in diesel prices. Statements made by the president, press releases and public announcements to increase freight were taken as evidence. The tribunal,[149] however, in 2016 set aside the order of the CCI as there was no evidence of any diktat or directive from the association to increase prices. Further, prices were not increased by 15% across the board. It also could not locate any evidence to prove that the association pressured its members to increase prices. It was also noted that the DG had ignored all the replies by the opposite parties.

The tribunal in 2016 set aside another decision of the CCI related to bid rigging. In *Bio-Med* case,[150] it was alleged that the opposite parties colluded to rig the bid for the supply of meningitis vaccine. The CCI analyzed the bids and concluded that the opposite parties had colluded to quote higher bids and share the total tender among themselves. It noted that the market was conducive to cartelization, and there was evidence of a prior meeting of the bidders. Interestingly, it used meeting visitors' register of government medical store depot to prove prior meeting. A penalty at the rate of 3% of average turnover was imposed on the opposite parties. The tribunal in 2016 set aside the order of the CCI and held that there was insufficient evidence to prove collusion. It noted that justification was "provided for reduced quantity in bid and price quoted", and there was nothing to prove that non-participation of one of the parties was part of the arrangement. It also reiterated that the penalty has to be imposed on 'relevant turnover'. The Supreme Court in 2017 affirmed the decision of the tribunal.

In another matter related to bid rigging in the supply of CN containers,[151] the CCI, in light of price parallelism, clubbed with the close association of the parties and similar pricing despite the difference in the cost of production, held them to be guilty of cartelization and imposed a penalty at a rate of 3% of average turnover. The tribunal, however, in 2016 set aside the order not just on violation of principles of natural justice but also on substantive grounds. It held that the "mere presence of some common features between some of the suppliers cannot lead to an inference that the market for CN Containers was conducive for reaching an agreement for bid-rigging among the bidders". Further, it was held that the bidders had quoted on the basis of the last purchase price available on the website of the procurer.

In *Express Industry*,[152] the CCI did not agree with the findings of the DG and imposed a penalty at a rate of 1% of turnover on three airline companies for fixing the rate of cargo transport through fuel surcharge (FSC). It noted that no company was able to provide any proof that the FSC was determined unilaterally. FSC was also not noted to move per the rate of fuel prices. The tribunal in 2016 set aside the order of the CCI on the grounds of violation of principles of natural justice and remanded the matter back to it. The CCI in 2018 reached the same conclusion, but it reduced the penalty to 3% of average relevant turnover instead of average turnover.

In the insurance case[153] that related to bid rigging by public sector insurance companies in response to calls for quotes by the government of Kerala, CCI, in light of the evidence of a prior meeting of bidders to discuss and share the bids, imposed a penalty at the rate of 2% of average turnover on four insurance companies. The tribunal did not agree with considering the effect on beneficiaries as an aggravating factor by the CCI and thereby reduced the penalty to 1% of relevant turnover – that is, revenue from "gross premium insurance provider under RSBY/CHIS scheme". The tribunal also upheld the order of CCI in *KFEF*,[154] *KFCC* and *Swastik Developers*.[155]

The year 2016, with a total number of 10 cartel cases, turned out to be a quiet year in terms of the CCI's activities vis-à-vis cartels. Out of five orders under Section 26 (2), two appeals were made to the tribunal, and both were dismissed. No appeal record was found with respect to the two orders of CCI under Section 26 (6). Only a couple of decisions under Section 27 were passed by the CCI in 2016. In *KCDA*, the CCI imposed a penalty on both the association and the drug manufacturing company for practising mandatory NOC requirement. The pharmaceutical company was held to be liable as it refused to supply drugs and demanded NOC. The tribunal in 2016 set aside the order against the pharmaceutical company as the association, and the pharmaceutical company could not have colluded to mandate NOC as they were not competitors, which is a requirement under Section 3. Further, there was no evidence from other distributors that there was a shortage of supply or that consumers suffered. NCLAT, in its 2017 order, clarified that the entire order would be treated as set aside. The review application filed to NCLAT was rejected in 2018.

The cement cartel case was decided afresh by the CCI after its previous decision of 2012 was set aside by COMPAT for violation of principles of natural justice. The CCI, in its 2016 order, largely retained the 2012 order. The appeal filed to NCLAT was dismissed in 2018.

In the year 2017, there is a record of just two appeals out of seven orders passed by the CCI. In the *DGHS* matter, the case was earlier remanded to CCI for fresh consideration after DGHS was held to be an "enterprise" under the Act. The CCI, like previously, came to the conclusion that there was no evidence to prove agreement and that "different rates prescribed by DGHS for NABH accredited hospitals would act as an incentive to non-accredited hospitals to secure such accreditation and provide quality health care services, which will ultimately benefit the patients". The tribunal dismissed the appeal in 2017. The appeal filed in *Applesoft*[156] was also dismissed for procedural defects in the filing. Only one decision was made by the CCI under Section 26 (6) in 2016.

The appeals from orders under Section 27 in 2017 have not yet culminated into final orders, and therefore, we restrict ourselves to the assessment of appeal cases till 2016 only.

4.7.8 *Profile of the CCI's orders that were set aside by the appellate forum*

Very clearly, the CCI has been struggling to protect the sanctity of its order before the appellate forum. If all the cases during the relevant observation period are taken into account, in more than 60% of the cases, the appellate forum questioned the use and adequacy of evidence by the CCI. It further set aside all these orders because of the wrong appreciation of evidence. The appellate forum seems to be asking for more concrete evidences to prove the allegation of collusion. Therefore, even if the cartel proceedings are civil in nature and the standard of proof required to prove a cartel is a preponderance of probabilities, appellate forums have kept a higher threshold for appreciation of evidence when compared to the CCI. Appellate forums have not really relied on the "but for" analysis done by CCI and are asking for unequivocal proof of cartelization. The benefit of the doubt has been given to parties alleged to be part of a cartel, and an opportunity has been provided in many cases to rebut the presumption of cartelization that arose from circumstantial evidence. Further, in 33% of successful appeal decisions, appellate forums have questioned the quantum of penalty imposed by the CCI. While the requirement to give reasons for the imposition of a penalty has been stressed in most of the cases, the tribunal has ended up reducing the penalty or setting aside the penalty due to the wrong basis of calculation in approximately 33% of successful appeal matters under Section 27 of the Act. The lack of penalty guidelines or any normative standard to fix the quantum of penalty has caused the two forums to jostle against each other. The tribunal has insisted on proper quantification of penalty by taking into account aggravating and mitigating factors. The CCI needs to urgently think of creating a proper methodology to quantify fines within the upper ceiling provided under Section 27.

Appeal orders can also be categorized on the basis of the type of cartel. Since a high percentage of the CCI's orders have been questioned on the lack of evidence, it is not surprising that 90% of orders concerning bid rigging, which are evidence-intensive, have been either set aside or modified in terms of quantum of penalty. The CCI's orders have been found to be lacking in the correct use of facts and evidence and unaccommodating of defences from the opposite parties. The tribunal has given more attention and importance to market factors leading to a particular conduct, something which was ignored by the CCI as it was more content with looking at the conduct of parties leading to attribution of *per se* illegality. Many of the cases related to price fixing and limiting production and involving trade associations have also been set aside because the CCI was unable to prove either the involvement of trade associations or the mandatory effect of their actions on market participants.

Notes

1 Emmanuel Combe, Constance Monnier and Renaud Legal, *Cartels: The Probability of Getting 360 Caught in the European Union* (2008) www.coleurope.eu/system/files_force/research-paper/beer12.pdf?download=1 (last accessed on Dec. 20, 2021).
2 *Ex officio cartel investigations and the use of screens to detect cartels*, Directorate for Financial and Enterprise Affairs, Competition Committee, OECD (2013), DAF/COMP (2013) 27. www.oecd.org/daf/competition/exofficio-cartel-investigation-2013.pdf (last accessed on Dec. 20, 2021).
3 Iuliana Zlatcu and Marta-Christina Suciu, *The Role of Economics in Cartel Detection. A Review of Cartel Screens*, 6 (3) Journal of Economic Development, Environment and People 16–26 (2017).
4 Kai Hüschelrath, *How Are Cartels Detected? The Increasing Use of Proactive Methods to Establish Antitrust Infringements*, 1 (6) Journal of European Competition Law & Practice 522 (2010).
5 *Ibid.*
6 *Supra note* 3. See, L. Petit, The Economic Detection Instruments of the Netherlands Competition Authority: The Competition Index, NMAWorking Papers, January 2012.
7 The OECD Guidelines for Fighting Bid Rigging in Public Procurement are now included in the 2012 OECD Recommendation on Fighting Bid Rigging in Public Procurement, www.oecd.org/competition/oecdrecommendationonfightingbidrigginginpublicprocurement.htm (last accessed on Dec. 20, 2021). *See also*, OECD Public Procurement Toolbox 2015, OECD www.oecd.org/governance/procurement/toolbox/principlestools/ (last accessed on Dec. 20, 2021).
8 *Ibid.*
9 *Supra note* 6.
10 Rosa Abrantes-Metz, Luke Froeb, John Geweke and Christopher Taylor, *A Variance Screen for Collusion*, 24 International Journal of Industrial Organisation 467–86 (2006).

11 Lorenz, *Screening Markets for Cartel Detection: Collusive Markers in the CFD Cartel Audit*, 26 European Journal of Law and Economics 213–232 (2008).

12 *Fighting Bid Rigging in Public Procurement* (OECD 2016) www.oecd.org/daf/competition/Fighting-bid-rigging-in-public-procurement-2016-implementation-report.pdf (last accessed on Dec. 20, 2021).

13 *The Impact of Cartels on the Poor*, Intergovernmental Group of Experts on Competition Law and Policy, Thirteenth session, Geneva, July 2013, TD/B/C.I/CLP/24/Rev.1 http://unctad.org/meetings/en/SessionalDocuments/ciclpd24rev1_en.pdf (last accessed on Dec. 20, 2021).

14 Luke Garrod and Matthew Olczak, *Explicit v. Tacit Collusion: The Effects of Firm Numbers and Asymmetries*, 56 International Journal of Industrial Organization 1–25 (2018).

15 S. Davies, M. Olczak, M. and H. Coles, *Tacit Collusion, Firm Asymmetries and Numbers: Evidence from EC Merger Cases*, 29 (2) International Journal of Industrial Organization 221–31 (2011).

16 *Ibid.*

17 John M. Connor, *Global Antitrust Prosecutions of International Cartels: Focus on Asia,* SSRN, https://papers.ssrn.com/sol3/papers.cfm?abstract_id=1027949 (last accessed on Dec. 20, 2021).

18 *Workload statistics*, Archives, Department of Justice, www.justice.gov/archives/doj/department-justice-archive (last accessed on Dec. 20, 2021). *Also see,* European Commission Statistics, EC, http://ec.europa.eu/competition/cartels/statistics/statistics.pdf (last accessed on Dec. 20, 2021).

19 *Workload Statistics*, Antitrust Division, FY 2008–17, Department of Justice, www.justice.gov/atr/file/788426/download (last accessed on Dec. 20, 2021). *See also*, John M. Connor, *The Private International Cartels (PIC) Data Set: Guide and Summary Statistics, 1990–2013*, Working Paper 2014, Research gate www.researchgate.net/publication/264898295_The_Private_International_Cartels_PIC_Data_Set_Guide_and_Summary_Statistics_1990-2013] (last accessed on Dec. 20, 2021).

20 *Cartel Statistics (1990–2019),* released by Directorate General – Competition, http://ec.europa.eu/competition/cartels/statistics/statistics.pdf (last accessed on Dec. 20, 2021).

21 *Supra note* 1.

22 *Global Competition Review, Rating enforcement*, 2015, Global Competition Rating (May 2019) https://globalcompetitionreview.com/series/rating-enforcement (last accessed on Dec. 20, 2021).

23 Scott D. *Hammond, Former Deputy Assistant Att'y Gen., Department of Justice, The Evolution of Criminal Antitrust Enforcement over the Last Two Decades, Speech* (25 Feb 2010) www.justice.gov/atr/speech/evolution-criminal-antitrust-enforcement-over-last-two-decades (last accessed on Dec. 20, 2021).

24 John M. Connor and Darren Bush, *How to Block Cartel Formation and Price Fixing: Using Extraterritorial Application of the Antitrust Laws as the Deterrent*, 122 Pennsylvania State University Law Review 813 (2008) cited in JM Connor, Anti-Cartel Enforcement by the DOJ: An Appraisal, 5 (1) The Competition Law Review 89 (2008).

25 Hazarika and Pratap Ranjan Jena, *Public Procurement in India: Assessment of Institutional Mechanism, Challenges, and Reforms*, 204 NIPFP Working Paper Series (2017), National Institute of Public Finance and Policy New Delhi, NIFPP (March 2019) www.nipfp.org.in/media/medialibrary/2017/07/WP_2017_204.pdf (last accessed on Dec. 20, 2021).

26 Sajjan Khaitan v. Eastern India Motion Pictures Association & Others, Case No. 16/201, order dated 9 August 2012.

27 In Re: Cartelization by broadcasting service providers by rigging the bids submitted in response to the tenders floated by Sports Broadcasters v. Essel Shyam Communication Limited & others, Suo moto Case No. 2/2013, order dated 11 July 2018. The Belgaum District Chemists and Druggists Association v. Abbott India Ltd. & Others, Case No. C-175/09/DGIR/27/28-MRTP, order dated 2 March 2017, has been excluded where although the final disposal took 93 months, the delay was caused not at the level of the Commission but due to filing of multiple writ petitions.

28 Reg. 20, Competition Commission of India (General) regulations 2009.

29 Michael Hellwig and Kai Huschelrath, *"Cartel Cases and the Cartel Enforcement Process in the European Union 2001–2015: A Quantitative Assessment"*, Discussion Papers, No. 16–063, Zentrum für Europäische Wirtschaftsforschung (ZEW), Mannheim, 2016, www.econstor.eu/bitstream/10419/146903/1/869752421.pdf (last accessed on Dec. 20, 2021).

30 Reg. 32, Competition Commission of India (General) regulations 2009.

31 Builders Association of India v. Cement Manufacturers' Association and Ors. 2012CompLR629 (CCI).

32 In Re: suo-motu case against LPG cylinder manufacturers, Suo-Moto Case No. 03/2011, order dated 24 February 2012 (CCI).

33 Kai Huschelrath, U. Laitenberger & F. Smuda, *Cartel Enforcement in the European Union: Determinants of the Duration of Investigations,* 34 (1) European Competition Law Review 33–39.

34 Annual Report 2016–17, Competition Commission of India (June 2019) www.cci.gov.in/sites/default/files/annual%20reports/CCI_AR-2016-17_English.pdf (last accessed on Dec. 20, 2021). *See also*, Deepali Gupta, CCI Verdicts Fail to Act as Deterrents to Malpractice, *Economic Times* (2 January 2018), economictimes.indiatimes.com/articleshow/62329440.cms?from=mdr&utm_source=contentofinterest&utm_medium=text&utm_campaign=cppst (last accessed on Dec. 20, 2021); AZB Partners, *The need for settlements and commitments under the Competition Act, Inter Alia Special Edition* – ' Competition Law – April 2019 (June 2019) www.azbpartners.com/bank/the-need-for-settlements-and-commitments-under-the-competition-act/ (last accessed on Dec. 20, 2021).

35 In Re: Cartelization in respect of zinc carbon dry cell batteries market in India, Suo moto Case No. 2/2016, order dated 19 April 2018 (CCI).

36 In re: Cartelization in Tender No. 59 of 2014 of Pune Municipal Corporation for Solid Waste Processing, Suo moto Case No. 4/2016, order dated 31 May 2018.

37 *Supra note* 1.

38 R.H. Porter and D. Zona, *Detection of Bid Rigging in Procurement Auctions*, 30 (2) The RAND Journal of Economics 263–288 (1999).

39 Abrantes-Metz, Rosa M. *Proactive vs Reactive Anti-Cartel Policy: The Role of Empirical Screens* (2013), SSRN https://papers.ssrn.com/sol3/papers.cfm?abstract_id=2284740 (last accessed on Dec. 20, 2021).

40 Market Research, *Competition Commission of India.* www.cci.gov.in/market-research (last accessed on Dec. 20, 2021).

41 Rosa Abrantes-Metz, *Roundtable on Ex-Officio Cartel Investigation and the Use of Screens to Detect Cartels*, Directorate for Financial and Enterprise Affairs Competition Committee, OECD, DAF/COMP (2013) www.oecd.org/daf/competition/exofficio-cartel-investigation-2013.pdf (last accessed on Dec. 20, 2021).

42 In Re: Alleged Cartelization in the Airlines Industry. (Suo Motu Case No. 03/2015) of 22 February 2021; XYZ v. Hindalco Industries Limited & Anr

(Case No. 18/2020); Arrdy Engineering Innovations Pvt. Ltd. v. Heraeus Technologies Pvt. Ltd. & Anr (Case No. 47/2020); Indian Laminate Manufacturers' Association/Sachin Chemicals & Ors. (Case No. 61 of 2016).

43 *Supra note* 42 (Indian Laminate Manufacturers case).

44 *Supra note* 42 (Airlines Industry case).

45 In Re: Alleged cartelization by steel producers, Case No.: RTPE No. 09 of 2008 (MRTP).

46 See also, Reg. 41, Competition Commission of India (General) Regulations, 2009.

47 ACF Chemiefarma v. Commission, 41/69, EU:C:1970:71.

48 Suiker Unie and Others v. Commission, EU:C:1975:174.

49 United Brands Company v. Commission, 27/76, EU:C:1978:22.

50 Aalborg Portland and Others v. Commission, C-403/04 P and C-404/04.

51 *Supra note* 50; Sumitomo Metal Industries and Nippon Steel v. Commission, EU:C:2007:52; Lafarge v. Commission, EU:T:2008:255, Siemens AG v. Commission, EU:T:2011:68; Solvay Solexis v. Commission, EU:T:2011:280.

52 Dresdner Bank and Others v. Commission, EU:T:2006:271

53 Intel v. Commission, EU:T:2014:547

54 *Prosecuting Cartels Without Direct Evidence*", OECD Policy Roundtables 2006, OECD (March 2019) www.oecd.org/daf/competition/prosecutionandlawenforcement/37391162.pdf (last accessed on Dec. 20, 2021). Also referred by the Supreme Court of India in the *LPG cartel* 2018.

55 *Ibid.*

56 In Re: Glass Manufacturers, MRTP Case No. 161/2008, order dated 24 February 2012; Consumer Online Foundation v. Tata Sky Ltd. &Others, Case No. 2/2009, order dated 24 March 2011 (CCI).

57 Para 69, Dissenting opinion, PN Parsahar, Neeraj Malhotra v. Deustche Post Bank Home Finance Ltd. & Ors., Case 5/2009, order dated 2 December 2010.

58 CCI placed reliance on both US [American Tobacco Co. v. United States, 328 US 781 (1946); US v. CHAS Pfizer Co., 217 F. Supp 199 (1963); US v. James P. Heffernan, No. 94–1080, US Courts of Appeals, Seventh Circuit] and Indian cases [Ghai Enterprises Pvt. Ltd. and Quality Ice creams (RTPE 18 of 1983); Bengal Tools Ltd. (1988) 63 Comp cas 468; In re Excel Industries Limited (1988) 64 Comp Cas 531].

59 M/s Excel Crop Care Ltd. v. CCI, Appeal No. 79 of 2012; M/s Sandhya Organic Chemicals Pvt. Ltd. v. CCI, Appeal No. 80/2012 (COMPAT); M/s United Phosphorus Ltd. v. CCI, Appeal No. 81/2012 (COMPAT).

60 Excel Crop Care Limited v. Competition Commission of India and Ors., 2017 (6) SCALE241.

61 M/s Pankaj Gas Cylinders Ltd. v. Indian Oil Corporation Ltd., Case 10 of 2010, decided on 22 June 2011 (CCI).

62 Para 14.12, *Ibid.*

63 *Fighting cartels in Public Procurement,* Policy brief, October 2008, OECD, (June 2019) www.oecd.org/daf/competition/cartels/41505296.pdf (last accessed on Dec. 20, 2021); OECD Recommendation on Fighting Bid Rigging in Public Procurement, 2012 (June 2019) www.oecd.org/daf/competition/oecdrecommendationonfightingbidrigginginpublicprocurement.htm (last accessed on Dec. 20, 2021).

64 Excel Crop Care Limited v. Competition Commission of India and Ors., 2017 (6) SCALE241.

65 Neeraj Malhotra v. Deustche Post Bank Home Finance Ltd. & Ors. 2/12/2010, Case 5/2009, order dated 7 March 2018 (CCI).

66 Imperial Chemical Industries Ltd. v. Commission of the European Communities, Final judgment, 48/69, (1972) ECR 619

67 In-house, *Top Court To Hear Cement Manufacturers Case Against Rs. 6,300 Crore Penalty,* 5 October 2018, NDTV, www.ndtv.com/india-news/supreme-court-to-hear-cement-manufacturers-case-against-rs-6–300-crore-penalty-1927596 (last accessed on Dec. 20, 2021).
68 Jute Packaging Materials (Compulsory Use in Packaging Commodities) Act, 1987.
69 Express Industry Council of India v. Jet Airways (India) ltd. & Ors., Case No. 30/2013, order dated 7 March 2018 (CCI).
70 *Supra note* 65.
71 *Supra note* 56 (Glass Manufacturers case).
72 *Supra note* 56 (Consumer Online Foundation case).
73 Indian Sugar Mills Association & Ors. v. Indian Jute Mills Association & Gunny Trade Association (GTA), order dated 31 October 2014 (CCI).
74 Builders Association of India v. Cement Manufacturers' Association & Ors., Case 29 of 2010 order dated 20 June 2012 (CCI).
75 Coal India Limited v. GOCL Hyderabad & Ors., Case No. 06/2011, order dated 16 April 2012 (CCI).
76 In Re: Aluminium Phosphide Tablets Manufacturers, Suo-Moto Case No. 02/2011, order dated 23 April 2012 (CCI).
77 Cyril Shroff and Nisha Kaur Uberoi, Cartel enforcement in India: Standard and burden of proof, 1 CPI Antitrust Chronicle, Feb 2015, http://awa2014.concurrences.com/IMG/pdf/india.pdf (last accessed on Dec. 20, 2021).
78 Steven Shavell, *The Appeals Process as a Means of Error Correction,* 24 (2) The Journal of Legal Studies 379–426 (1995).
79 Steven Shavell, *The Appeals Process and Adjudicator Incentives,* 35 (1) Journal of Legal Studies 1 (January 2006).
80 Florian Smuda, Patrice Bougette and Kai Huschelrath, *Determinants of the Duration of European Appellate Court Proceedings in cartel cases,* 25 GREDEG WP (2014), (March 2019) www.gredeg.cnrs.fr/working-papers.html (last accessed on Dec. 20, 2021).
81 Peter Ormosi, Tactical Dilatory Practice in Litigation: Evidence from EC Merger Proceedings, 32 (4) International Review of Law and Economics 370.
82 *Supra note* 80.
83 *Analysis and Recommendations, Vol. I, Report of the Financial Sector Legislative Reforms Commission, March 2013, FSLRC,* (June 2019) https://dea.gov.in/sites/default/files/fslrc_report_vol1_1.pdf (last accessed on Dec. 20, 2021).
84 Section 53B (2), The Competition Act, 2002.
85 Section 53B (3), The Competition Act, 2002.
86 Section 53B (5), The Competition Act, 2002.
87 Part XIV, Chapter VI, Finance Act, 2017.
88 See generally, Vedika Mittal Kumar et al., *Systematizing Fair Play: Key Issues in the Indian Competition Law Regime*, Vidhi Centre for legal policy, November 2017 https://static1.squarespace.com/static/551ea026e4b0adba21a8f9df/t/5a18f086ec212d9bd3c645f9/1511583896465/Systematizing+Fairplay+-+Key+Issues+in+the+Indian+Competition+Law+Regime.pdf (last accessed on Dec. 20, 2021).
89 Nisha Kaur, "India's evolving Competition regime: the big picture", Trilegal 2018.
90 Assessment of Statutory Frameworks of Tribunals, October 2017, PRS INDIA www.prsindia.org/report-summaries/assessment-statutory-frameworks-tribunals-india (last accessed on Dec. 20, 2021).
91 Michael R. Baye and Joshua D. Wright, *Is Antitrust Too Complicated for Generalist Judges? The Impact of Economic Complexity and Judicial Training on Appeals,* (2011) 54 (1) Journal of Law and Economics 1; OECD, Judicial Enforcement of Competition Law, (1996) OECD www.oecd.org/daf/

competition/prosecutionandlawenforcement/1919985.pdf (last accessed on Dec. 20, 2021).

92 PTI, Cabinet Clears Creation of More Posts for Judicial, Tech Members in NCLAT, *Business Standard* (March 28, 2019) www.business-standard.com/article/pti-stories/cabinet-clears-creation-of-additional-posts-in-nclat-119032700781_1.html (last accessed on Dec. 20, 2021).

93 Includes CCI v. Coordination Committee of Artists and Technicians of W.B. Film and television and Others, Civil Appeal No. 6691/2014, order dated 7 March 2017 (SC) where the Supreme Court in 2018 affirmed the order of the CCI.

94 Includes LPG cartel case where the COMPAT remanded the matter back to the CCI for reconsideration on penalty.

95 Amit Bansal, Shruti Gupta and Semanti Sengupta, Just 0.3% of CCI Penalties Recovered for Now, But Progress Made in Handling of Antitrust Cases, *Business Today* (23 October 2018) www.businesstoday.in/opinion/columns/just-0-per-cent-of-cci-penalties-recovered-for-now-but-progress-made-in-handling-of-antitrust-cases/story/286148.html (last accessed on Dec. 20, 2021).

96 Deepali Gupta, *CCI verdicts fail to act as deterrents to malpractice*, The Economic Times, 2 January 2018 https://economictimes.indiatimes.com/corporate/cci-verdicts-fail-to-act-as-deterrents-tomalpractice/articleshow/62329440.cms?from=mdr (last accessed on Dec. 20, 2021).

97 Pitambara Books Private Limited, Delhi v. Primary Education Department, Office of the Director, Andhra Pradesh Open School, Andhra Pradesh & Ors., Appeal No. 14/2012, order dated 21 November 2012 (COMPAT).

98 Consumer Online Foundation v. CCI, I.A. No. 7/2011 & I.A. No. 8/2011, order dated 14 July 2011 (COMPAT).

99 Travel Agents Association of India v. Lufthansa German Airlines. & Ors., Appeal No. 25/2011, order dated 7 December 2012 (COMPAT).

100 M/s Paper Merchants Association, Delhi & Ors. v. Vijay Gupta, Appeal No. 13/2013, order dated 16 May 2013 (COMPAT).

101 Dilip Thakkar v. Maharashtra Industrial Development Corporation (MIDC) & Ors., Case No. 19/2012, order dated 30 May 2012 (CCI).

102 M/S India Glycol Ltd. v. Indian Sugar Mills Association, Appeal No. 119/2012, order dated 9 December 2013 (COMPAT).

103 Exclusive Motors Pvt. Ltd. v. Automobili Lamborghini SPA, Appeal No. 1/2013, order dated 28 February 2014 (COMPAT).

104 All India Tyre Dealers Federation v. CCI, Appeal No. 2/2013, order dated 25 April 2013 (COMPAT).

105 *Supra note* 94.

106 Motion Pictures Association v. Reliance Big Entertainment Pvt. Ltd. & Ors., Appeal No. 66, 67, 69, 71, 73, 78, 96, 97, 102/2012, order dated 17 May 2013 (COMPAT).

107 Motion Picture Association v. Sunshine Pictures Pvt. Ltd., Appeal No. 19/2010, order dated 28 July 2011 (COMPAT).

108 Rajasthan Cylinders v. Union of India, Civil Appeal No. 3546/2014, order dated 1 October 2018 (SC).

109 PES Installations v. Foundation for common cause, Appeal No. 94,95/2012, order dated 25 February 2013 (COMPAT).

110 Excel Crop Care Ltd. v. CCI, Appeal No. 79/2012, order dated 29 October 2013 (COMPAT).

111 Excel Crop Care Ltd. v. CCI, Civil Appeal No. 2480/2014, order dated 8 May 2017 (SC).

112 *Ibid.*

113 Appeal No. 121/2012, order dated 11 December 2015 (COMPAT).
114 Cement Manufacturers Association v. CCI, Appeal No. 122/2012, order dated 11 December 2015 (COMPAT).
115 Chemist and Druggist Association, Baroda v. CCI, Appeal No. 140/2012, order dated 18 November 2016 (COMPAT).
116 Vedanta Bio Sciences, Vadodara v. Chemists and Druggists Association of Baroda, c-87/2009/DGIR, order dated 15 January 2019 (CCI)
117 Co-ordination Committee of Artist and Technicians of West Bengal v. EIMPA, Appeal No. 131/2012, order dated 3 April 2014 (COMPAT).
118 CCI v. Co-ordination Committee of Artist and Technicians of West Bengal, Civil Appeal No. 6691/2014, order dated 7 May 2018 (SC).
119 CCI v. Coordination Committee of Artist and Technicians of West Bengal and television industry, Civil Appeal No. 6691/2014, Misc Appli. No. 490/2017, order dated 7 May 2018 (SC).
120 N Sanjeeva Rao and Mrs. Fatima Tahir v. Andhra Pradesh Hire Purchase Association and 162 Others, Case 49/2012, order dated 7 February 2013 (CCI).
121 Surendra Prasad v. CCI, Appeal No. 43/2014, order dated 15 September 2015 (COMPAT).
122 (2006) 11 SCC 548.
123 Andhra Film Chamber of Commerce v. M/s Cinergy Independent Film Service Pvt. Ltd. & Ors., Appeal No. 15/2013, order dated 14 October 2015 (COMPAT).
124 Tamil Nadu Film Exhibitors Association v. Competition Commission of India Reliance Big Entertainment Private Limited & Ors., Appeal No. 14/2014, order dated 28 April 2015 (COMPAT).
125 All India Organization of Chemists & Druggists (AIOCD) v. CCI, Appeal No. 21/2013, order dated 9 December 2016 (COMPAT).
126 All India Organization of Chemists & Druggists (AIOCD) v. CCI, Appeal No. 7/2014, order dated 9 December 2016 (COMPAT).
127 All India Organization of Chemists & Druggists (AIOCD) v. CCI, Appeal No. 6/2014, order dated 9 December 2016 (COMPAT).
128 *Puja Enterprises v. CCI*, Appeal No. 8/2014, order dated 12 April 2016 (COMPAT).
129 Nagole Auto Drivers Welfare Association v. M/s. Abhinandan Motors (P) Ltd. & Ors., Appeal No. 35/2014, order dated 14 July 2014 (COMPAT); Muthoot Mercantile Limited v. CCI, Appeal No. 48/2015, order dated 6 April 2015 (COMPAT).
130 Wing Cdr. (Retd.) Dr. Biswanath Prasad Singh v. DGHS, Appeal No. 63/2014, order dated 1 March 2016 (COMPAT).
131 Ministry of Tourism v. Span Communications & Ors., Appeal No. 80/2015, order dated 16 July 2015 (COMPAT).
132 In Re: Alleged cartelization by steel producers, RTPE No. 9/2008, order dated 9 January 2014 (CCI).
133 In Re: Manufacturers of Asbestos Cement Products, Case 1/2012, order dated 11 February 2014 (CCI).
134 Chemist and Druggist Association v. Arora Medical Hall, Appeal No. 21/2014, order dated 30 October 2015 (COMPAT).
135 Bengal Chemist and Druggist Association v. CCI, Appeal No. 37/2014, order dated 10 May 2016 (COMPAT).
136 Alleged cartelization in the matter of supply of spares to Diesel Loco Modernization Works, Indian Railways, Patiala, Punjab v. M/s Stone India Limited & Ors., suo moto Case No. 03 of 2012, order dated 5 February 2014 (CCI).
137 *Ibid.*

138 Indian Jute Mills Association v. CCI, Appeal No. 73/2014, order dated 1 July 2016 (COMPAT).
139 M/s Kyal Agencies Pvt. Ltd. v. Utkal Chemists and Druggists Association (UCDA) & Ors., Case 79/2015 order dated 17 November 2015 (CCI).
140 Nitin Radheshyam Agarwal & Ors. v. CCI & Ors., Appeal No. 108/2015, order dated 14 December 2015 (COMPAT).
141 M/s. K. Sera Sera Digital Cinema Pvt. Limited v. Digital Cinema Initiatives, LLC & Ors., Appeal No. 42/2016, order dated 1 February 2017 (COMPAT).
142 *Ibid.*
143 In Re: Deputy Chief Materials Manager, Rail Coach Factory v. M/s Faiveley Transport India Limited & Others, Case 6/2013, order dated 8 September 2015 (CCI).
144 Deputy Chief Materials Manager, Rail Coach Factory, Kapurthala v. M/s. Faiveley Transport India Ltd., M/s. Knorr Bremse India Pvt. Ltd., Appeal No. 10/2016 order dated 17 February 2016 (COMPAT)
145 M/s Rohit Medical Store v. Macleods Pharmaceutical Limited & Ors., Case No. 78 of 2012, order dated 29 January 2015 (CCI).
146 Himachal Pradesh Society of Chemist & Druggist Alliance v. Rohit Medical Store, Appeal No. 58/2015, order dated 13 January 2016 (COMPAT).
147 Mr. P. K. Krishnan Proprietor, Vinayaka Pharma v. Mr. Paul Madavana, Divisional Sales Manager, M/s Alkem Laboratories Limited. & Others., Case No. 28 of 2014, order dated 1 December 2015 (CCI).
148 Alkem Laboratories Ltd. v. CCI, Appeal No. 9/206, order dated 10 May 2016 (COMPAT).
149 AIMTC v. CCI, Appeal No. 60/2015, order dated 18 April 2016 (COMPAT).
150 GlaxoSmithKline Pharmaceuticals Limited v. CCI, Appeal Nos. 85, 86/2015, order dated 8 November 2016 (COMPAT).
151 Sheth & Co. v. CCI, Appeal No. 102/2015, order dated 10 May 2016 (COMPAT).
152 Jet Airways Limited v. CCI, Appeal No. 102/2016, order dated 18 April 2016 (COMPAT).
153 M/s. National Insurance Company Ltd. v. CCI, Appeal Nos. 94, 96, 97/2015, order dated 9 December 2016 (COMPAT).
154 KFCC v. CCI, Appeal No. 13/2016, order dated 10 April 2017 (COMPAT).
155 M/s. Dumper Owners' Association v. CCI, Appeal No. 28/2016, order dated 12 April 2016 (COMPAT).
156 M/s Applesoft v. The Chief Secretary to the Government of Karnataka & others, Case 8/2017, order dated 5 May 2017 (CCI).

5 Sanctioning cartels

5.1 Introduction

There are primarily three elements of effective enforcement of competition law:[1] (i) clear and precise delineation of the law in terms of prohibited conduct; (ii) prevention of anti-competitive behaviour, including taking preemptive steps through active monitoring of markets, as well as advocacy efforts in order to disseminate the idea and ethos of competition in the market to build a normative commitment to competition law;[2] and (iii) an effective sanctioning mechanism in case such prohibited behaviour occurs. While there is a certain divergence of approach in the sanctioning mechanism for cartelization in different countries, they more or less agree on the broader objectives of such sanctions and aspire to achieve optimal sanctions.[3] The present chapter will examine the sanctions imposed by the CCI for cartelization on the touchstone of clarity, consistency and adequacy.

5.2 Theoretical underpinnings for antitrust sanctions

5.2.1 Regulatory punishment: application of theories of deterrence and desert

Regulatory law is different from criminal law. Criminal law, in contrast to regulatory law, does not entail behaviour that is valued by the community. Regulatory offences do not, therefore, entail the same moral condemnation that is attached to traditional crimes. Regulatory law underlines the collective goals envisaged in the regulation. They are still public laws as the regulations are generally enforced by the state. Market regulation not only entails advancing desired behaviour from market participants but also the mechanism to punish undesired or non-compliant behaviour. The second part requires an analysis of two basic questions. What is the role of regulatory punishment, and what should be the nature or quantum of such penalty? Although the theories of punishment have been advocated for traditional criminal offences involving moral improbity, they are relevant for regulatory offences, and both involve the application of power of the state to

DOI: 10.4324/9781003347651-5

intervene and punish. *Deterrence*, *rehabilitation*, *incapacitation*, *desert* and *reparation/restoration* are the five theoretical justifications for punishment. Three of these justifications – rehabilitation, incapacitation and reparation – have little application for regulatory offences.[4] This is because since the majority of offenders are firms, the rehabilitation theory is not very relevant, the incapacitation theory is mainly used for dangerous or career offenders, and the reparation theory is not used for determining penalty.

The deterrence theory of punishment, advocated by the renowned utilitarian philosopher J. Bentham, has the utilitarian goal of deterring future unlawful behaviour. Punishment of the offender (disutility) was justified to prevent others from committing the same offence (utility to society). Modern-day economists of law advocate punishment for offence as a means to minimize the costs (social) of the offence. The quantum of penalty, thus, is set at a point that eliminates or minimizes the costs to society to the maximum extent. Economics sees firms as rational beings who take rational decisions in their self-interest. If the benefits of violation outweigh the cost of committing an unlawful act, the firm will violate the law. Therefore, if penalties (as sanctions for costs to society due to an unlawful act) are kept at a level that, when added to the cost of the violation, outweighs the benefits of violation, firms would not break the law. A correct quantum of penalty thus can deter unlawful action. If, however, the benefit of any action on society outweighs the harmful effects, such action should be promoted. Considering both ideas regarding fixing of quantum of penalty, it can be said that penalty should be fixed at a level that will "deter unlawful conduct to efficient level".[5] If, therefore, unlawful conduct has only costs and no benefits to society or if the cost to society outweighs the loss to society, the quantum of penalty should be kept at the absolute deterrence level. If, however, there are net benefits to society, the quantum of penalty should be kept at the "optimal level" so as to not deter conducts which benefit society. Therefore, the theory of optimal deterrence advocates deterrence of only inefficient violations of law.[6]

The quantum of penalty premised on the theory of optimal deterrence is at a level equal to the total cost of harm caused due to unlawful conduct. The penalty also encompasses the externalities cost to others by the conduct in question. The theory of absolute deterrence, on the other hand, presumes that the alleged conduct has absolutely no social benefits and the benefits, if any, are hugely undermined because of the costs to society due to unlawful conduct. The quantum of penalty in such a situation is fixed at least to the level of net gains from unlawful conduct. The idea is to disgorge the ill-gotten profits in order to eliminate any incentive for unlawful conduct. The theory of absolute deterrence does not mind the possibility of over-deterrence due to excessive penalty because the penalty at the minimum is fixed at the gains derived from the unlawful act, thus removing all the incentive to violate the law.

The deterrence model has to be suited for practical reasons. It is folly to assume that there will be no cost of deterrence or that the rate of detection and punishment will be 100%. In the first model of deterrence, enforcement costs have to be added to the quantum of penalty. In the model of absolute deterrence, however, enforcement costs change the enforcement strategies rather than the quantum of penalty. Therefore, if the enforcement costs exceed the harms caused by the unlawful act, enforcement action need not be taken. Further, if the probability of detection is considered, the quantum of penalty, which, given the constraints at the agency level, cannot be 100%, will again have to be adjusted. A low detection rate lowers the expected cost of the offender.[7]

The desert theory of punishment differs substantially from the deterrence theory per which sanctions are commensurate to the wrongfulness of the sanctioned conduct, including state condemnation of the offender. The desert theory is backed by the philosophy of retributive justice, and its proponents[8] argue in favour of punishment as a mode of condemnation of the offender. Therefore, the quantum of penalty per the theory must be determined on the basis of the graveness of the offence. The principle of proportionality has been seen both as advancing the theory and also limiting the quantum of penalty. More serious offences, therefore, will invite a higher penalty. The graveness of the offence, in turn, will be determined through the harm caused by the unlawful act and also the degree of culpability (intent, motive and circumstances).

Choosing a theoretical model for determining the quantum of penalty is a bit tricky. The deterrence model assumes rationality of the offender where the offence is a rational choice after the *ex ante* assessment of costs and benefits. However, individuals or firms may be guided by factors other than profit maximization. Further, the use of this model throws in the challenge of data collection. Data on variables like costs and benefits, enforcement costs and probability of detection are extremely difficult to ascertain, making the whole process unviable. Since the probability of detection is used as a factor in quantifying penalty under the deterrence model, it runs the risk of making it excessively harsh. Further, the optimal deterrence approach reduces the penalty for recidivism as the detection of unlawful conduct in the first instance increases the probability of detection, making the approach counterproductive.[9] Even under the absolute deterrence model, which takes into account gains made by the offender, the penalty will be smaller when the gain to the offender is less, even if the harm caused to others is huge. On the other hand, the desert theory suffers from a lack of precision, inconsistency and arbitrariness. Under the deterrence model, the quantum of penalty is increased on the basis of the probability of detection. Therefore, if the probability of detection is low, the penalty increases. This method has the likelihood of increasing the penalty by multiple times, thus conflicting with the proportionality principle of the desert theory.[10]

5.2.2 Regulatory offences and choice of the theoretical model

The choice of a theoretical model to determine the quantum of penalty poses its own challenges. Regulatory offences are different from traditional crimes and do not involve a similar amount of moral condemnation. Since the regulatory laws are more concerned about advancing a collective objective, they tend to object to conduct that does not conform to such objective, and therefore, the deterrence model seems to be providing more suitable theoretical backings for a penalty. However, the quantum of penalty may take into account 'distinct and part conflicting' principles[11] to encapsulate different objectives. Therefore, issues of morality, fairness and proportionality are equally important when the level of punishment is determined. The model of punishment is generally hybrid in the form containing elements of both deterrence and desert theories.

5.2.3 Application of deterrence model to antitrust violations

The deterrence model of quantification of penalty can be adopted for antitrust violations in the manner as indicated earlier – optimal deterrence for conducts which may have societal benefits and absolute deterrence for conducts like hard-core cartels. Care has to be taken to avoid over-deterrence and deterrence of efficiency-enhancing actions. For instance, a vertical restraint from a market player having market power will be restrictive in nature. However, similar restrictions by a player not having market power may have positive effects. The same is true for efficiency-enhancing horizontal agreements and mergers.

5.2.4 Criminal sanctions for cartels

Criminal sanctions for cartel activities also derive legitimacy from the deterrence theory.[12] A criminal sanction is seen as a way to maximize utility, "to be employed only when the disutility of its imposition is less than the utility to society secured by its deterrent effect".[13] The justification for criminal sanctions comes from the fact that the penalty or fine is inadequate to deter cartel activity and that criminal sanction is the only way to club the gap. Per the classic deterrence theory, the administrative fine for cartelization should be at a level which increases the cost over the benefits of cartelization. Since cartels are presumed to be devoid of any redeeming virtues, fines are quantified, keeping in mind the expected gains divided by the probability of detection and prosecution. As discussed earlier, this methodology has the chance of excessively increasing the quantum of penalty,[14] which may also be in the range of 150% to 200% of annual turnover. Reliance on optimal fine, therefore, to bring deterrence is unjustified as such high penalties are never imposed because of arguments of proportionality and the need for survival of the firm in the market. Focus has shifted to individuals rather than firms.

Per the OECD, "as agents of corporations commit violations of competition law, it makes sense to prevent them from engaging in unlawful conduct by threatening them directly with sanctions and to impose such sanctions if they violate the law".[15] It has been argued that since there is a likelihood of indemnification by the firm, individual liability has to move from mere monetary penalty towards jail terms. The non-indemnifiable sanctions have been argued to have the potential to deter business executives from participating in cartel decisions.[16] The argument for criminalization, however, remains a normative one in response to an economic problem of under deterrence of cartel conduct. It has not been clearly established that cost of enforcement for criminal sanctions does not trump social welfare gains.[17] The debate on whether a jurisdiction should opt for the criminalization of cartel activities is still unresolved.

5.3 Sanctions for antitrust violations

Violation of antitrust law is generally a cost-benefit analysis. Assuming that business entities are rational beings, their decision to violate laws will depend upon whether the benefits of non-compliance exceed the benefits of compliance.[18] The benefits of non-compliance take into account the possibility of detection and the degree of sanctions. The higher the probability of detection or the severity of sanctions, the lesser the chance of violation. Different jurisdictions have attempted to increase the deterrence effect of their enforcement through the substantial increase in fines, the introduction of criminal sanctions for certain types of infringement like cartels, including jail terms for individuals or allowing treble damages in a private action. The introduction of amnesty and leniency programs have also added to the detection rate of antitrust violations. Deterrence forms the core behind sanctions for antitrust violations as they aim to both punish anti-competitive behaviour and prevent recidivism by creating fear that punishment from the alleged act will be more than their expected profit from the prohibited act. It is also not true that a regime of deterrence will prevent any sort of antitrust violation in future. The degree of prevention will always be less than 100% because of both economic and psychological reasons. Economic reasons include the possibility of errors in the form of unlawful sanctions on legitimate economic behaviour, and psychological reasons include the low traction of competition matters in the mind of the general public.

From an economic point of view, if an enforcement mechanism does not prevent unlawful conduct and only sanctions unlawful behaviour, it is a waste of resources as the process of enforcement incurs costs in detection and punishment. Such a system does not improve social welfare.[19] Therefore, a large part of the literature focuses on the means to achieve optimal deterrence in the form of optimal fines, criminal sanctions and private enforcement of competition laws. Hence, ideally, the crucial part of enforcement is deterrence of anti-competitive behaviour rather than punishment of anti-competitive behaviour. The idea is always to create an environment where businesses remain apprehensive of their engagement in anti-competitive behaviour and are also fearful of the consequences post-detection. The attempt is to minimize antitrust violations, if not to prevent them completely through an active and aggressive agency and an effective sanctioning protocol.

The level of deterrence will depend on both the probability of detection and the loss that will have to be suffered due to conviction. The expected loss, in turn, includes both monetary penalties and private damages. These again depend on the level of enforcement of competition law. The behaviour of the firms is guided by taking a sum total of all the costs that will be incurred on account of violation.

5.3.1 Fine as a sanction for the antitrust violation

Fines play a major role in the enforcement of competition laws and can be understood in two forms: one as a measure of compensation and the other as a means of restitution. The former is mostly covered under the domain of private enforcement of competition laws, whereas the latter is a form of corrective justice for which the enforcement agencies aim. The main purpose of fine or penalty is to punish the infringer (retributive factor) and cause deterrence. Fines for antitrust violations are seen as a tool for deterrence in many jurisdictions. The deterrence theory behind fines sees antitrust violation as an exercise of market power to extract wealth from consumers, something which needs to be prohibited and sanctioned.

However, any amount of fine will be able to create deterrence only if the business units know that the penalties would surpass the profit that they would make out of violation of competition laws.[20] It is also a fact that the parties generally take into account the expected fines while calculating expected profits. The expected fines would be further reduced by the probability of detection, which in turn will depend on the experience and sophistication of engagement of parties and the efficiency of enforcement agencies in detecting anomalies in the market. Per Bebchuk and Kaplow, “the minimum fine for deterrence to work equals the expected gain from the violation multiplied by the inverse of the probability of a fine being effectively imposed”.[21] Therefore, a strategy to increase the level of deterrence is to either increase fines or to improve the chances of detection.[22] The OECD Report of 2012[23] also stressed the need to take into account the probability of detection along with cartel gains to calculate the optimal fine.

Per Becker and Landes,[24] the optimal sanction for antitrust violation is premised on the fact that penalties should be sufficient to induce offenders to internalize the full social cost of their crimes. In any system where the detection of crime and enforcement is not perfect and costless, “optimal penalties must exceed the social cost of the crime so that the expected sanction facing each potential violator is equal to the harm his violation will cause”.[25]

The social costs in cartels or the harm caused to others in the form of total monopoly overcharges form a critical basis in calculating the optimal fines. However, social harms like allocative inefficiency, low rate of innovation or increase in prices of non-cartel members (umbrella effect) are generally ignored in calculating fines, which means that even if cartel overcharges are accurately calculated, it will be lesser than the optimal fines. Further, the rate of detection and enforcement in cartels is far lesser. Therefore, the optimal fine should be larger than the cartel's net harm to others.[26] The calculation of optimal fines for cartels presumes that cartels are always bad for society and that they do not have any benefits.[27] The optimal sanction must consist of a fine equal to the perpetrator's expected gain from the violation multiplied by the inverse of the probability of detection.

In most cases, however, the imposition of an optimal fine is marred by the firm's inability to pay. Therefore, the quantum of optimal fine can create a situation where many firms are pushed towards bankruptcy. Such an outcome is also not desirable as it will have social costs. Most of the jurisdictions take 'inability to pay' as a factor while imposing a penalty. This necessarily means that the fines are generally lower than that which is required for deterrence. Many scholars, therefore, advocate for jail terms for individuals rather than substantially increasing the fines for corporations that threaten their survival.[28]

While the goal of sanction is to deter future violations, there are concerns on the legal front with respect to proportionality and co-relativity. If we apply the principles of proportionality reflecting the retributive theory of punishment, fines will be further reduced. Courts may find penalties imposed by competition regulators conforming to the economic principles of deterrence and the implicit cost minimization approach to sanctions as disproportional. The theory of proportional punishment does not look at future deterrence of unlawful conduct as a source of punishment but rather towards the moral requirement to punish a person for an unlawful act in proportion to the degree of misconduct.[29] The law generally takes a middle path in combining the theory of deterrence with the idea of proportional punishment. While the retributive view does restrict the imposition of fines, proportional punishment helps strengthen the moral effect of the fines. A general threshold of the quantum of fine is generally prescribed for antitrust violations. This can be attributed to both the practical and economic aspects of the inability to pay and the aspect of proportional justice. The amount of fine imposed for anti-competitive practice thus runs the risk of being grossly lower than the sum required to reach optimal deterrence. The threshold of fine is considerably lower than the harm caused by offenders. Scholars like Maks, Shinkel and Bos argue that the capping of a fine in absolute value or on the basis of turnover has negative effects on deterrence and is generally economically unjustified.[30] The fines are calculated keeping in mind the principle of proportionality so that they are morally acceptable, as evident from the US and EU positions.

The quantification of optimal fines for antitrust violations is not that simple. While in some cases like price cartels, it is relatively easier to quantify damages to consumers or gain to the participants due to collusion, but it is extremely difficult to estimate the expected profits reduced by the expected probability of fines at the time of collusion. Further, in cartels, there is no unilateral action, thus making the estimate of gains for each cartelist nearly impossible. However, despite the difficulties in reaching a correct value of optimal fine, the theory of optimal fine is certainly helpful in the imposition of fines. To address some of the issues related to imposition of fines, including the unbridled discretion of the enforcement agency, many jurisdictions have formed fining guidelines. These guidelines have adopted similar methodologies where the ultimate fine is the result of the adjustment of base fine on account of factors like leniency, settlements and the gravity of offence. The base assessment may be done on the basis of profit, revenue or overcharge. The use of revenue as the basis to calculate the base fine is most common. It is more convenient and avoids the uncertainty or difficulty of calculating profit or overcharge. However, it does not address the issue of illegal gains and often faces allegations of discrimination when imposed within the upper ceiling provided within the statute.

5.3.2 Over- and under-deterrence

Over-deterrence may cause a loss in efficiency and increased enforcement costs. It may also deter and make market participants apprehensive of business practices that can cause enforcement action, thus reducing the overall welfare in the long run. Efficiency-enhancing horizontal agreements, for example, will take a beating. Further, it may cause the firms to spend large and disproportionate amounts of resources on preventing their individual officers from indulging in antitrust violations. Excessive fines, on the one hand, threaten the survival of the firm and, on the other hand, affect the innocent stakeholders of the firm, like employees, creditors and shareholders. Excessive fines have efficiency, welfare and social costs.

The question, however, is, is it excessive to impose sanctions for market behaviours like being in cartel which has no redeeming virtues? Many scholars examined the allegations of excessive fines in cartel cases in the EU and the US and found the monetary fines substantially low when compared to harms caused or illegal profits made by cartels, even when the detection rate was assumed as 100%.[31] The results do not change even if private action suits for damages are considered.[32]

The violation of the law can be attributed to both firm and individuals who were at the helm of affairs of the firm at the time of existence of anti-competitive behaviour. The application of optimal fine becomes a bit tricky in this scenario. The system of criminal sanctions on individuals is more effective when compared to system of fines for firms and managers. Mere imposition of fines on managers will fail to create an effect as individuals would be able to reimburse the fines from the firms for the benefit of which they took the decisions. Similarly, while fixing the quantum of fines for firms, the enforcement agency has to be mindful of the possibility of payment of damages by the firms in private suits. Further, a very high fine can affect the stability of the firm, which in turn affects the welfare maximization objective of the law. An upper ceiling in the imposition of fines can be justified on this basis. However, fear of bankruptcy of the firm should not lower the quantum of penalty to the extent that negatively impacts the deterrent value of fines. The exit of a few guilty firms because of high fines may be good for society as it may increase the level of competition in other industries through the *ex ante* general deterrence effect generated by these fines.

5.3.3 Civil penalties in competition matters

The mechanism of civil penalties lies somewhere between the traditional systems of criminal penalties of fine and imprisonment and civil damages. Civil penalties may be used for disgorgement, restitution or forfeiture of assets that were used to facilitate illegal acts. Although the nature of such action resembles the criminal judicial system, the usage of the term "civil" changes the dynamics of its enforcement. The thresholds of standard and burden of proof, the requirement of a mental element and double jeopardy, which are required for criminal cases, get relaxed. Civil penalties are in the form of monetary fines, which are imposed by the administrative agency through the application of civil procedure norms.[33]

The idea of deterrence remains behind the policy of imposition of civil penalties. The public enforcement of competition law with an idea of deterrence runs parallel to private enforcement of competition laws, which aims to compensate victims of competition law violations. While the idea of civil penalties aims at penalizing anti-competitive behaviour because of its economic effect through the imposition of fines to improve the overall compliance of competition laws, regulators tend to adjust penalties based on parameters like intent, cooperation and aggravating and mitigating circumstances, which take them slowly within the domain of criminal procedure.[34]

The real question with respect to civil penalties is on the sufficiency of penalties to deter anti-competitive conduct: can a system of civil penalties alone create deterrence, or is it necessary to club criminal sanctions and private enforcement along with it? Many countries felt the need to move to criminal sanctions for cartels when the system of civil penalties seemed inadequate.

5.4 Cartel sanctions

While there is no foolproof method to quantify the effects of cartels on society, it is widely accepted today that they are harmful, and sanctions must be imposed on firms and individuals participating in them.[35] The prime objective of sanctions, as discussed earlier, is to create some level of deterrence. Sanctions against cartels can be broadly divided into civil and criminal sanctions. Civil sanction comprises imposition of penalties on cartel participants. In some jurisdictions, penalties are also imposed on individuals who were the decision-makers in the involved firms. Criminal sanctions, on the other hand, involve monetary fines for firms and/or jail terms for individuals. The movement towards the criminalization of cartel conduct is gaining momentum due to the increasing understanding of the inadequacy of the existing sanctions to deter cartel activities.

5.4.1 Optimal fine for cartel deterrence

To achieve deterrence, it is not just essential that the fine is high enough but that it is equally important to increase the chances of detection and enforcement. The optimal fine has two reference points: the harm caused to society from the offence committed and the illicit profits made by the offender. The cost of enforcement is added to the cost to society. Fines in cases of cartels can follow two approaches. Per the first approach (the Becker[36] and Landes approach), which follows the idea of restitution, fines should be "equal to the harm that criminal activities have caused to society" plus the enforcement costs divided by the probability of detection and conviction. The second approach is dissuasive in nature rather than restitutive. Restitutive fines, which seek to recover the ill-gotten profits, may not be enough because some cartels might go undetected, or they could already break down. Dissuasive fines, on the other hand, disincentive the very participation in a cartel. If the firms come to realize the net profit on account of cartel participation is negative, they will not participate or continue to participate in the cartel. Therefore, per the second approach, fines should be high enough to deter participation. Harm-based penalties are generally preferred as the harm caused by cartels is greater than the benefits and has a higher likelihood of causing deterrence. They force the cartel firms to internalize harm rather than simply taking away the gains made, thereby pushing firms to invest in compliance and monitoring and prevention.[37]

5.4.1.1 Calculation of optimal fine

Calculation of optimal fine by combining cartel overcharge, deadweight loss, enforcement costs and probability of prosecution becomes difficult due to lack of precise data. While there have been some studies which estimate cartel overcharge and costs of enforcement, it is extremely difficult to correctly assess deadweight loss or probability of detection and punishment. Further, the formula ignores other effects of cartels like innovation costs or the umbrella effect, which add to the social costs, which in turn makes the final quantified fine less than optimal.[38] Further, the application of the principles of proportionality[39] and the fear of social costs on account of firms' inability to pay (multiplier is inverse of the probability of detection) reduces the fine even further. Multiple studies[40] have been done on the issue of adequacy of fines to cause optimal deterrence, and they all conclude that cartel fines are too low. Cartel fines sometimes have also been reported to be less than cartel overcharge.

The debate on the correct methodology, be it harm-based or gain-based, to calculate optimal fine is an ongoing debate. Huschelrath[41] argues that even though practical fines are lower than theoretical fines, they are still able to create deterrence and benefit the consumers and the economy. What is important is not the quantum of fines but the efficiency of fines.[42] Countries like the US and the UK have framed penalty guidelines for imposition of penalties which, on the basis of experiential data, uniformly assume certain figures to fit in the formula of optimal fine. The US Federal Sentencing Guidelines, for instance, fix a base fine equal to 20% of the volume of commerce (sales) affected by cartel decisions. The base fine assumes cartel overcharge proxy to be around 10% of the selling price. There are some scholars, however, who argue that a fixed methodology for calculating fines makes the fine predictable in nature which reduces its deterrence value. The predictability of fines, when added to the below-optimal-level quantum, may tempt undertakings that are otherwise law-abiding to assess the benefit of infringement. However, if the fines are high enough, they can aid the leniency regime of the jurisdiction.

5.5 Guidelines on the method of calculating fines for antitrust violations

Penalties for cartel conduct are determined keeping in mind the principles of economics and the requirements of law. Cartels cannot be equated with tortious conduct. Redressal, therefore, does not lie in creating a liability regime based on the harm caused. Cartels, considering their pernicious nature, have to be prohibited rather than taxed. Competition laws of the EU and the US have been the guiding light behind antitrust laws of many young jurisdictions, especially in Asia. Therefore, it is more than useful to examine the cartel sanctioning scheme of these two jurisdictions in order to then assess and evaluate the Indian regime of sanctions on cartels.

5.5.1 European Union

Unlike the US or even the UK, the European Commission (EC) sanctioning mechanism for competition law violations is restricted to the imposition of fines. Lack of transparency in the adjudication of fines leading to multiple court litigations marred the first half of the adjudication history of the EC.[43] Prior to 1998, the only restriction in the fixing the fine was the upper ceiling on the basis of turnover[44] (up to 10% of global sales) and the only guidance was a reference in the regulations to gravity and duration of the infringement.[45] The EC was also guided by the principles of equity, proportionality and non-discrimination. It started with caution in terms of imposing penalties in the 1960s[46] and 1970s but then soon switched to more severe and harsh sanctions in the later years.[47] It is mostly based on the calculation of penalty on the basis of relevant turnover multiplied by percentage with respect to gravity and duration of the infringement. Illegal gains made through the infringement were not particularly considered. The EC attempted, to a large extent, to prevent any presumption of infringement tariff as it affected the deterrent value of the fine because the offenders would then be able to carry out a cost-benefit assessment. Lack of transparency, therefore, was seen as a virtue.[48]

It was soon realized that the offenders anyhow do a cost-benefit assessment, and if there is a system which takes into account surrounding circumstances, fines can achieve the optimal level. The EC, however, made no public disclosure of the application of the percentage of turnover to calculate fine in order to maintain secrecy. Further, fines were reduced on an *ad hoc* basis. There used to be no scientific connection between the reasons provided by the EC and the final computed fine. The conversion of factors – like territorial extent, success of cartel, method of operation, sector affected, importance of product or service in question and level of individual participation into numbers to increase or decrease the final amount – was vague and incoherent and led to numerous appeals. The courts at the appellate stage, in the absence of any guidelines or reasons from the lower forum, reduced the penalties. The system enabled the offenders to both prolong and delay the entire enforcement process.[49] The criticism, associated with vague, arbitrary and inconsistent criteria to fix fines which made the entire system appear "like a lottery",[50] paved the way for the Guidelines on the Method of Setting Fines, 1998 (hereafter "1998 Guidelines").

The EC issued its first set of 1998 Guidelines to bring transparency and impartiality to its penalty decisions. The 1998 Guidelines, while retaining the upper ceiling for the quantum of penalty (10% of overall turnover),[51] underlined the need to bring transparency to the discretion of the EC to impose a penalty. The 1998 Guidelines set in motion a simple formula to reach an amount of fine. Starting with a base amount based on gravity and duration of infringement, the penalty was to be increased in light of aggravating and mitigating circumstances. It categorized infringements into three types based on their gravity, which in turn depended on the nature and size of the relevant geographic market and its effect on the market. *Minor infringements* related to trade restrictions, usually of a vertical nature, but with a limited market impact and affecting only a substantial but relatively limited part of the community market, attracting a fine of 1,000 to 1 million euros. *Serious infringements* related to horizontal or vertical restrictions with a wider market impact with possible abuse of a dominant position attracting fines between 1 million to 20 million euros. The third type is *very serious infringements*. Cartels and a clear abuse of dominance were categorized as very serious infringements with a likely fine of above 20 million euros. The 1998 Guidelines also permitted differential treatment to members of the same conduct based on the size and economic capacity of participants. The second component in the calculation of the base fine was the duration of the infringement. Infringements were again categorized as short (having a duration of less than one year with no increased amount), medium (having a duration of one to five years with a 50% increased amount per year) and long (having a duration of more than five years with a 10% increased amount per year) duration resulting in an increase in the fine. It listed aggravating and mitigating circumstances that would increase or decrease the base amount.

Interestingly, the 1998 Guidelines also envisaged penalties for trade associations. Therefore, ordinarily, the penalties, as far as possible, were addressed, and fines were imposed on the individual undertakings belonging to the association. If, however, there were a large number of members, a fine was to be imposed on the association per the principles of the 1998 Guidelines "but equivalent to the total of individual fines which might have been imposed on each of the members of the association".

Although the 1998 Guidelines were considered "a doctrinal shift of massive proportions",[52] they were also criticized for having retained the vague discretion of the EC. It was argued that the 1998 Guidelines provided no details on the quantification of factors, like the gravity of the infringement and aggravating and mitigating circumstances. Further, issues like the reading of base fine as a starting point or overall fine or the turnover[53] failed to bring the level of clarity which the 1998 Guidelines intended. The "lump sum" approach or the application of deterrence multiplier lacked transparency and was also alleged to be discriminatory. Calculation of starting fine on the basis of the nature of infringement (minor, serious and very serious) was creating troubles for the EC. For instance, it was only in 2005 that it was determined that all cartels would be treated as very serious infringements regardless of their territorial extent.[54] The 1998 Guidelines gave little importance to the duration of the cartel as the penalty for cartel participants increased only marginally with each year of continuation of the cartel.

The EC issued a new and revised set of Guidelines for Setting Fines, 2006 (hereafter "2006 Guidelines").[55] The 2006 Guidelines clearly underline the deterrence objective of the fines. While the basic methodology to calculate fines and the upper cap to penalties remains the same, the 2006 Guidelines use the value of sale as a reference to calculate the basic amount of fine.[56] Use of the value of sales to which the infringement directly or indirectly relates in the relevant geographic market along with the duration of infringement is considered as "an appropriate proxy to reflect the economic importance of the infringement as well as the relative weight of each undertaking in the infringement".[57] The basic amount, per the 2006 Guidelines, depending on the gravity and duration of the infringement, will be a proportion of the value of sales, pre-tax (up to 30%). The EC shall give due regard to factors like the nature of violations, the geographical scope of infringement and the combined market share in calculating the proportion of sales. Therefore, in the cases of cartels, the proportion of the value of sales will be kept at a higher scale. The amount will then be multiplied by the years of duration of the infringement. An additional amount based on the value of sales (between 15% and 25%) will be added to the basic amount in the case of cartels. This "entry fee" is imposed for hard-core cartels to act as a deterrence tool.

The 2006 Guidelines, similar to the earlier 1998 Guidelines, list out aggravating and mitigating factors to be used in the adjustment of fines. They prescribe an increase of basic amount up to 100% for recidivism. The EC has also been allowed to increase the quantum for bigger companies to create deterrence. The 2006 Guidelines, however, maintain the upper limit of fines for firms and trade associations, similar to the 1998 Guidelines. If the fine exceeds 10% of the firm's total turnover in the preceding business year, the EC applies a reduction so as to no longer exceed the maximum fine. The new set of guidelines also tries to reconcile the "inability to pay" and over-deterrence theory by granting power to the EC to reduce the penalty if the evidence is produced that the imposition of fines would "irretrievably jeopardize the economic viability of the undertaking concerned and cause its assets to lose all their value".[58] The 2009 Guidelines are not binding on the EC but have been used as a matter of practice which in turn will force the giving of reasons in cases of departure. The EC in *LRAF 1998 v. Commission*[59] observed that the guidelines determine, generally and abstractly, the method which EC has bound itself to use in assessing the fines imposed by the decision and, consequently, ensure legal certainty on the part of the undertakings.[60]

Per Article 31 of Regulation 1/2003, the Court of Justice has the power to review the penalty decisions of the EC where it may retain, alter, increase or decrease the fines imposed. The appellate court may employ different standards to check the appropriateness of the fines imposed in light of evidence, limitation period, incorrect methodology to calculate fine and so on.[61] Despite the efforts of the EC, there are still concerns about the unpredictable nature of the sanctions.[62] Similar concerns have been raised on the requirements of the application of a ceiling with respect to parental liability doctrine, absence of time limit for examining recidivism and non-separation of prosecutorial and decisional powers within the EC.[63]

5.5.2 United States of America

Sanctions for cartels (violation of Section 1 of the Sherman Act, 1890) involve both high fines (for firms and individuals) and jail terms for individuals. The maximum criminal fine was increased from $5,000 to $100 million, and the maximum jail term for individuals was raised from three years to ten years in 2004. In addition, the Alternative Fines Act, 2004,[64] allows crossing the statutory limit up to "twice the gross gain or twice the gross loss from the offence". The Department of Justice (DOJ) has to follow the prosecutorial system of antitrust enforcement, where it has to prove antitrust violations in the federal court or enter into a plea agreement to impose sanctions. Therefore, the fines are imposed by the courts which use the sentencing guidelines on the recommendations of the DOJ. The US sentencing guidelines are based on the Beckerian principles of optimal deterrence of crime, where the underlying idea is that the firms take rational decisions, and their engagement in crime is based on their perceived likelihood of detection and punishment. "The expected size of expected monetary penalties affects both the probability of detection and the rate of cartel formation".[65] Therefore, if the fines are high enough, it incentivizes defections and leniency applications.

The DOJ uses the Federal Sentencing Guidelines (hereafter "US Guidelines") to impose fines on individuals and firms. The US Guidelines, like that in the EU, are not binding but command respectful consideration.[66] While the Supreme Court of the US has ruled in favour of the discretion of federal judges in sentencing[67] and held the US Guidelines to be only of advisory character, the courts have been asked to consider the US Guidelines' ranges, which can then be tailored per the circumstances and facts of the case.[68] However, unlike the EU Guidelines, the US Guidelines only suggest a range of appropriate fines rather than an exact fine.

Per the US Guidelines, the fine is calculated by multiplying the base fine (i.e. 20% of the affected volume of commerce) by a culpability score (based on factors like previous record, cooperation with agency, antitrust compliance programme and self-reporting). The courts are also empowered to order for payment of restitution. The base fine is calculated on the basis of loss or harm caused due to infringement. Relying on empirical evidence of cartel overcharge being 10%, the Sentencing Commission doubled the figures to account for other losses, including "customers who were priced out of market" where the average cartel overcharge considered has been claimed to be low by some scholars.[69] Therefore, the base fine was calculated at 20% of the volume of affected commerce "over the entire duration of infringement". Calculation on the basis of affected commerce is intended to avoid the problem related to quantifying harm caused due to cartels. Further, the Alternative Fine Statute, 2004, provides pecuniary gain and loss to the firm on account of the offence as two additional measures for the base fine. The highest among the three listed earlier is taken by the DOJ. The third option is generally taken by the DOJ since the presumption of pecuniary loss is taken as 20% of affected commerce. The volume of commerce of each individual participant or his principal is taken into consideration. The US Guidelines are unclear on the issue of the determination of the value of commerce. However, per the practice followed, only US sales (domestic commerce) affected by the offence are considered. The question of what may be considered domestic commerce is also contentious. Some take the entire sales in the domestic market during the period of infringement as affected commerce,[70] while others only consider that amount of domestic sale which was done above the competitive price.[71]

5.5.2.1 *Culpability multipliers*

Once the base fine is fixed, it is multiplied with a culpability multiplier which is between 0.74 and 4; the quantum of a fine is between 15% and 80% of the volume of affected commerce. The multiplier is derived from the culpability score reached through the table provided in the Guidance Manual. The culpability score is used to determine a range of minimum and maximum culpability multipliers. The US Guidelines instruct the judges to start with a culpability score of 5 (ensuring a minimum fine of at least 15% of the affected volume of commerce) which is then adjusted based on a range of aggravating and mitigating factors.

The fine range (minimum and maximum) achieved after multiplying the base fine with the culpability multiplier range is then subject to the discretion of the court. The court may go outside the range due to factors like the risk presented by the offence to the integrity or continued existence of a market if the organization is a public entity or exceptional organizational culpability. The court also considers factors like the financial capacity of the firm, the impact of the fine on the firm, the order of restitution (if any), the ability of the firm to pass on the fine to the consumers, the size of the firm and the efforts made by the firm for antitrust compliance.

5.5.3 *Finding a common ground*[72]

A comparison of jurisdictions will help in identifying common and acceptable parameters to fix cartel sanctions.

5.5.4 *Upper capping/ceiling for cartel fines: "safeguard against disproportionality"*[73]

Most jurisdictions prescribe an upper limit of quantum of fine in case of the antitrust violation. "The existence of ceilings on sanctions in absolute value (as in USA) or in percentage of turnover (as in EU) can have perverse effects on deterrence. Such ceilings are, in most cases, economically unjustified".[74] Despite the criticism from the economic theorists, the idea of upper capping gets its legitimacy from the legal principle of "proportionality". Along with carrying the idea of proportional justice, the upper ceiling to the quantum of penalty also seems to answer the concern around the social and economic costs of astronomical fines.[75] It also protects the firms from going out of business due to their inability to pay. Some scholars have endeavoured to refute this presumption.[76] The upper ceiling also acts as a restraint on the possibility of the overzealous sanctioning authority. However, the insufficiency of the upper ceiling to deter cartels has also been argued by some scholars.[77]

Table 5.1 Comparative study of parameters to determine fine in the EU and the USA

Parameters to determine fines/ penalties	*EU fining guidelines, 2006*	*US sentencing guidelines and allied laws*
Statutory cap	*Firm:* 10% of total turnover in the preceding business year *Trade association:* 10% of the sum of the total turnover of each member that is active in the relevant market to which the infringement relates directly or indirectly	$100 million (application of Antitrust Criminal Penalty Enhancement & Reform Act, 2004, in special cases)
Base amount (basis)	Relevant sales in relevant geographic markets	20% of the volume of affected commerce (double the estimated cartel overcharge)
Undertaking	Undertaking that infringes competition law ("single economic entity" doctrine applicable)	Individual participant
Relevant sale	Sales made during the last full business year before taxes	Volume of commerce in the US affected over the entire duration of the cartel
Gravity of infringement	To determine the proportion of the value of sales to calculate fine; can be set up to 30% based on factors, like nature of the infringement, combined market share, geographical scope and implementation of the cartel	Culpability multiplier (between 0.75 and 4) based on culpability score
Duration	Percentage of the value of sales to be multiplied by the number of years	Affected volume of commerce takes into account the duration of the cartel
Entry fee	Additional amount (15–25% of the value of sales) added to the fine	Culpability multiplier of at least 0.75, leading to a fine of at least 15% of the affected volume of commerce in any circumstance
Aggravating circumstances	*Recidivism (can increase fine up to 100%) *Refusal to cooperate (alternatively, possible imposition of separate fines for procedural infringements of up to 1% of the relevant turnover under Article 23 [1] Regulation 1/2003) *Ringleader (increase in the fine for instigator or leader by 30–50%) *Continuation of infringement	Factors to determine culpability score: *Recidivism (addition of 1–2 points) *Refusal to cooperate (addition of 3 points) *Participation of high-level or substantial authority personnel of the firm in the infringement (addition of 1–5 points)

(*Continued*)

Table 5.1 (Continued)

Parameters to determine fines/ penalties	*EU fining guidelines, 2006*	*US sentencing guidelines and allied laws*
Mitigating circumstances	*Immediate termination of infringement *Effective cooperation beyond leniency (effective compliance programme not considered a mitigating factor)	*Effective compliance and ethics programme in place at the time of the offence (subtract 3 points) *Self-reporting, full cooperation in the investigation, and recognition and affirmative acceptance of responsibility for its conduct (subtract up to 5 points)
Specific increase in deterrence	Amount adjusted after mitigating and aggravating circumstances may be increased for large undertakings; fines may also increase to remove any improper gain due to infringement (where it is possible to estimate the amount).	Culpability multipliers take this into account.
Leniency discount	The final fine is reduced per the leniency notice. (Upper capping of fine is seen before leniency reduction.) Compliance with the settlement procedure may reduce the fine by 10%.	Reduction on the basis of type of leniency or amnesty plus application
Inability to pay	The EC may reduce the penalty under exceptional circumstances on the basis of objective evidence that the imposition of the fine would irretrievably jeopardize the economic viability of the undertaking concerned and cause its assets to lose all their value (Information Notice 2010).	Reduction in fine is possible.

5.5.5 Predictability of fines and optimal deterrence

Questions have been raised on fining guidelines on the issue of predictability of fines. There are divergent views on this. Wils argues that the fining guidelines reduce the deterrence effect.[78] While, on the one hand, they reduce the discretion of the competition authority in imposing fines, on the other hand, they allow individuals and firms to do a cost-benefit assessment of their actions. Firms would be able to identify areas and actions that will benefit them even if fines were to be imposed, thus raising questions on the deterrence value of fines. Even for law-abiding firms, the predictability of fines might tempt them to engage in anti-competitive behaviour. It is also argued that the uncertainty of fines clubbed with the possibility of different fines for different members of collusion affects the stability of the cartel as it tempts some members to cheat. Division of risk and reward becomes a contentious issue. Also, fines must not be easily foreseeable to the economic operators because if the method of calculation is indicated, incumbents would be able to predict such fines, which in turn undermines the deterrent value of fines.[79]

Others, however, argue that minimizing the discretion of the competition authority is a good thing as it minimizes enforcement and sanction bias.[80] Further, the fining mechanism clubbed with leniency scheme might nudge the offenders towards availing leniency.[81] Per the US DOJ, "If prospective cooperating parties cannot predict, with a high degree of certainty, their treatment following cooperation, then they are less likely to come forward".[82] In the US, predictability in the calculation of fines has been crucial for the success of the leniency program.[83] The presence of structured methodologies in the penalty guidelines ensures uniform treatment of firms and individuals for similar infringements and, in turn, also saves time and resources at the end of the adjudicating bodies. If the offenders know that the expected cost of infringement is substantial and which will trump the expected benefits, it will deter them from indulging in such actions.

Many countries today have come out with their own fining guidelines. However, they may differ on the level of detailing with the guidelines.[84] Countries like Japan and Korea have very detailed fining guidelines and do not leave much to the discretion of the judges. The US and the EU seem to have taken a middle path where they set out broad parameters backed with principles to fix fines. The competition authorities exercise a level of discretion and have the freedom (like in the EU) to deviate from the guidelines if there are sufficient reasons.

5.6 Aggravating circumstances and fining cartels

Per the dictionary meaning, aggravating circumstances are all those factors that increase the severity or culpability of a criminal act leading to tougher sanctions. The fining guidelines of both the US and the EU allow the use of aggravating and mitigating circumstances to adjust base fines. There is no definitive list for these factors, and it may differ from one jurisdiction to another.[85] The absence of aggravating circumstances is not a mitigating factor. Commonly used aggravating factors have been identified here, which will later be examined in context to Indian cartels.

5.6.1 Recidivism

Simply understood, recidivism means the "relapse of criminal behaviour",[86] after being previously prosecuted. It generally means that the offender who has suffered punishment for the crime has not been rehabilitated and falls back into former behaviour. Recidivism is seen as an indicator of committing future crimes. Although a term used in the criminal justice system, cartel recidivism has been loosely referred to situations when a cartelist who has been previously held guilty and punished for a particular cartel conduct is found to be involved in another cartel of a similar nature.

Some theorists equate individual criminal recidivism with psychopathy, where the individual derives a sense of gratification from the crime. Corporate culture is also guided by the minds that run the corporation. The indulgence of the corporation in crime repeatedly also indicates the corporate culture existing within the corporation. There are not many studies, however, which have gone into the question of determinants of corporate recidivism with respect to antitrust violations.[87] There are some who argue that recidivism should not be used as an aggravating factor for firms and should be restricted only to individual executives or managers of the firm.[88]

Instances of cartel recidivism are used as a parameter to assess the effectiveness of anti-cartel enforcement. If there are high instances of recidivism, it means that anti-cartel enforcement is not sufficient. Therefore, despite heavy sanctions, if market players are taking the risk of indulging in similar antitrust violations, it means that deterrence (more specifically, specific deterrence) that was supposed to be created through sanctions is not sufficient.[89] Since cartelists are taking the risk of indulging in a similar offence again, it also raises a question about the cartel detection mechanism of a jurisdiction. An increased rate of recidivism also means that the fines that are imposed on the cartelists are unable to disgorge the cartel profits, luring them to indulge in cartel activity again. Wils[90] identifies four reasons to impose higher fines for recidivists. Firstly, recidivism shows a higher-than-average propensity to commit a crime or, in this context, antitrust violation. This propensity may be based on a weak moral commitment of individuals to follow and respect the law. While it may not be possible to impose very high fines at the first instance of infringement, even if the regulator by some means identifies such propensity due to the application of principles of proportionality, there is no such restriction at the time of punishment for repeated infringement. Secondly, it is important for the law to express increased moral condemnation. Thirdly, high fines are required to compensate for the low rate of detection aggravated by the fact that old cartelists must have become better at cloaking their activities. Lastly, higher fines are required to reinforce deterrence.

Cartel recidivism is the most common and serious aggravating factor that has been used to impose sanctions. Both the EU and the US prescribe a substantial increase in fines in cases of recidivism. While the guidelines prescribe an increase in the base fine up to 100% for one prior infringement,[91] the EC has in practice increased the penalty up to 50% for one such infringement, 60% for two prior infringements and up to 100% where there were four prior violations. The 2006 Guidelines do not clarify any limitation period, and the EC is free to take old infringements into account while calculating the fine. Per the US Guidelines, the culpability score of an offender increases if he or she has a criminal history in the previous ten years.[92] Recidivism can raise the amount of fine, depending on the size of the company, up to 16%.

The idea of cartel recidivism becomes contentious when the paradigms of ownership, time and territory are added to it. Similarly, the nature of the offence has also been subject to interpretation. While some argue for the usage of a recidivism fine only for incidents of repeated infringement of the same type by the same cartelists, some interpret it broadly to use it for general cartel activity. Therefore, the penalty may be applied to a member of a price-fixing cartel that was previously fined for being a member of a market-sharing cartel. The EC has applied the former interpretation but has not been bound by the definition of market or time. Therefore, it has rejected the argument to consider the time gap between the previous infringement and the conduct in question or that the previous infringement was made in a different geographic market.[93] "Recidivism occurs when the same undertaking commits a similar antitrust infringement regardless of the product and geographic markets in which it takes place".[94]

Legally, recidivism has to be seen in a particular territory over a given period of time. Previously decided cases have to be used to see the similarity in the offence committed. Further, it may be possible that in a span of time, the name, management and ownership of a particular firm changes. The US Guidelines, for instance, use a time frame of ten years to check for recidivism. Simultaneous involvement in multiple cartels is taken as a repeated offence but not as recidivism. In the 2006 Guidelines, the EU does not prescribe a time frame for the use of recidivism as an aggravating factor in calculating fines. Therefore, the EC is free to consider past and historical involvement in cartels as a factor in calculating fines. Whether this violates the principle of proportionality is something that invites arguments from both sides. The discretion with the EC, however, also allows it to use a time-varying test instead of a mindless application.[95]

Similarly, the treatment of control and ownership of a particular firm may provide varying results on how we see recidivists. In the US, the involvement and punishment of a subsidiary company for involvement in a particular type of cartel previously will not make the parent company or a new acquirer a recidivist, if later the parent company is found to be involved in a similar cartel. The EC, however, has a different stance. In *Michelin v. Commission*,[96] the general court endorsed the parental liability presumption for assessing recidivism and held the subsidiary of the Michelin Group as recidivist because of an earlier indictment of another subsidiary company of the same group. The parent company was not addressed in the decision.

The general court in *Eni SpA v. Commission*,[97] however, laid out the rights of defence of the parent company. Accordingly, parent companies will be given the opportunity to rebut the parental liability presumption. Even prior knowledge of the parent company about a previous indictment of its wholly owned subsidiary in a case where it was not the party would not be sufficient to remedy the absence of a determination in the previous infringement. The EC's decision that the parent company and the subsidiary form a single economic unit means that the responsibility for the previous infringement is imputed to the parent company. The history of cartel punishment is carried forward by the parent company or a new acquirer.[98]

There are equally divergent views on the treatment of the paradigm of territory. The US Guidelines do not consider cartel punishment of the firm in a foreign jurisdiction for the determination of recidivism. The EC, on the other hand, considers at least the prior cartel conviction in the member states. The determination of recidivism, therefore, has been a very jurisdiction-specific exercise. The competition authorities exercise a wide sense of discretion in identifying and punishing recidivists.[99]

5.6.2 Refusal to cooperate

Refusal to cooperate or obstructing the investigation process of the competition authority has been commonly used as an aggravating factor. Both the EU[100] and US[101] guidelines consider refusal to cooperate as an aggravating circumstance. Non-cooperation includes "late provision of requested information, false or incomplete provision of information, lack of notice, lack of disclosure, obstruction of justice, destruction of evidence, challenging the validity of documents authorizing investigative measures, etc."[102] These may or may not be independently penalized irrespective of the decision on the substantive infringement.

5.6.3 Leadership role

Many jurisdictions, in order to create another level of deterrence, treat the cartel ring leaders differently from other cartel participants. It is understood that in most cartels, one (or a few in a big cartel) firm tends to take up the role of coordination and management of the entire scheme. They can act as initiators, instigators and even coercers in specific circumstances. Therefore, in a market with players of different sizes, cartel ring leaders might coerce or force the smaller players to join the cartel or face ostracization. Many cartels would not start or operate or break quickly but for these ring leaders. Therefore, to create some level of fear, competition law in many countries prescribes a higher penalty for ring leaders when compared to other cartel participants.

Leadership is taken as an aggravating factor in the calculation of a fine. In the 2006 Guidelines, the EU prescribes a higher penalty for leaders (undertaking with a significant driving force[103]) and instigators (one who persuades or encourages other business entities to establish or join a cartel) of a cartel.[104] However, not all founding members can be categorized as instigators. Instigators are only those undertakings that have taken the initiative for the cartel.[105] Further, in many cases, the benefit of leniency or amnesty is not extended to them. In the US, the benefit of amnesty is not extended to a leader or originator of a cartel or if the firm forced another firm to participate in the cartel.[106] The EC, under the 2006 Guidelines, may allow cartel ring leaders to apply for immunity on the fulfilment of certain conditions. Exclusion of ring leaders from the leniency scheme is expected to affect the very formation and, if formed, the operation of the cartel. No one would like to take the risk of being categorized as a ring leader and face the possibility of higher fines and no leniency. On a different footing, it would be problematic when a ring leader who established and ran the cartel and who has the best evidence to prove the cartel also applies for leniency and gets immunity, while others who were participants at the instance of the leader are penalized. The exclusion of ring leaders from leniency comes from this idea.[107] However, scholars like Aubert, Rey and Kovacic (2006), Spagnolo (2006) and Leslie (2006) argue in favour of extending leniency to ring leaders as that would cause distrust within the cartel, thus destabilizing it.[108] Leniency, as is argued, would incentivize ring leaders to report since if in case anyone else defects and reports, they would be penalized at a higher rate.

While the idea of leadership has been clearly marked as an aggravating circumstance, there is a general lethargy in the identification of leaders in cartel cases. This may also be due to a lack of an identification framework.[109] The low rate of identification of ring leaders in a jurisdiction with different schemes of penalty and leniency for cartel leaders might turn out to be counterproductive. If the detection rate is low, then it is better not to exclude the ring leaders as that might hinder them from confessing about the cartel and provide the best possible information that others cannot.[110]

5.7 Mitigating factors

The mitigating factor in law refers to any information or evidence regarding the offence or the defendant that may cause a reduction in sentence or fine. These are not legal defences and will not lead to the acquittal of the defendant. In the context of cartels, both the US Guidelines and the EU's 2006 Guidelines set out a non-exhaustive list of factors that may be taken into account to adjust the extent of fines.

5.7.1 Effective compliance programme as a mitigating factor

Compliance programs are voluntary codes accepted publicly by firms to ensure compliance with competition laws. It has both external signalling effect and internal disciplining benefits. These are designed in such a manner that they not only develop a culture of competition compliance but also detect acts of violation. Competition law risk identification, assessment, mitigation and review[111] are the core focus areas of competition compliance.

There is a certain divergence of opinion on whether an effective compliance program, which is a set of practical guidelines for the firm and employees to conduct themselves,[112] can be used as a mitigating circumstance or is it just a "natural obligation of all firms",[113] geared towards their own self-interest. For instance, the 2006 Guidelines of the EU do not consider an effective compliance programme as a mitigating factor while calculating fines. It is considered that the effectiveness of the compliance programme would have been the prevention of anti-competitive behaviour since the company is always in the best position to do that. The US Guidelines,[114] on the other hand, are not in favour of penalizing the corporation when certain employees or officers indulge in cartelization despite the corporation taking all the effort for competition law compliance.[115] The principle of good faith underlines the use of the compliance programme as a mitigating factor. This means it has to be shown by the defendant that it diligently enforced the programme and took all actions in good faith with the intent of complying with competition law.[116] Further, the benefit will not be advanced if senior executives were involved or if the company took no steps when it got to know about the violation or if there was an inordinate delay in reporting the violation. There is a growing trend in favour of using effective compliance programme as a mitigating factor as evidenced by countries like the UK, Brazil, Chile, Malaysia and Singapore.

Besides an effective compliance program, immediate terminations of infringement, self-reporting and full cooperation in the investigation are taken as mitigating factors.[117]

5.8 Cartel fines on trade associations

As has been discussed earlier, the activities of trade associations are not immune to competition law enforcement, and if their activities exceed the legitimate domain of functioning to promotion or coordination of anti-competitive practices, sanctions can be imposed. Competition authorities generally tend to go after actual participants of the cartel where the trade association did not have an actual involvement. However, in cases where the trade association played a central role in staging, coordinating and executing the cartel, the associations can be subject to separate fines. Calculation of fines in such cases cannot be based on the turnover of the trade association as they themselves are not engaged in economic activities and therefore do not have any revenue. The receipts/contributions from members are the only sources of revenue. Even when they are engaged in economic activity, the turnover is not big enough. Therefore, if the fines are calculated based on receipts or turnover of the trade association, they will not be enough to create any sort of deterrence, either specific or general, as it has no relation to the harm caused to society due to the illegal conduct. Recidivism among trade associations is the result of under deterrence of trade associations. Some jurisdictions allow fining of the board or executive members of the association. However, such a mechanism is marred with procedural issues. A large executive board will make the process lengthy and time-consuming, considering the amount of evidence that needs to be collected against the board members.

Some competition authorities, therefore, lift the "association veil" to impose sanctions based on the turnover of individual members. For instance, Article 23 allows the EC to impose a fine of up to 10% of "the sum of the total turnover of each member active on the market affected by the infringement of the association" provided that "the infringement of an association relates to the activities of its members".[118] The European courts have been clear on this aspect and have held that the impact of the trade association on the market is not determined by the turnover of the association but that of its individual members.[119] Further, the European regulations make it clear that if the trade association is unable to pay the enhanced fines due to its own financial limitations, it will be obliged to call for contributions from its members.[120] In case the trade association is unable to collect contributions from individual members, the EC has the power to recover the money directly from the members, but if the individual member is able to prove that it did not implement the anti-competitive decisions of the association and was not aware of such decision or it actively distanced from such action before the start of investigations, it can refuse payment to contribute for fine on the trade association.[121]

5.9 Review of the cartel-fining policy of the CCI

Similar to any competition jurisdiction, the prime objective of anti-cartel enforcement in India is deterrence.[122] An effective deterrence mechanism is assumed to also help in achieving rehabilitation as it causes market players to devise effective internal training and competition compliance programs to check anti-competitive action at any level in order to avoid high corporate sanctions. Corporate and individual penalties form the foundation of anti-cartel enforcement in India. The penalties are expected to be enough to deter any cartel activity.

As has been pointed out earlier, Indian law, unlike laws in the USA or the UK, does not envisage criminal sanctions for cartelization. Therefore, fines have become the primary tool of anti-cartel enforcement in India. This is more or less similar to the EU. Under Section 53N of the Competition Act, 2002, a claim for compensation can only be made to the appellate forum after a finding of contravention by the CCI on account of any loss or damage suffered by the applicant as a result of such contravention.

There are two ways to examine cartel fines. The first is to examine the quantum of fine, as a measure of seriousness of the CCI's actions, and the second is to inspect the very process of imposition of the fine. Since there are no penalty guidelines in India, it is imperative to analyze the parameters considered by the CCI to impose fines. The fining scheme should be clear and consistent. The determination of fine has to be guided by sound legal reasons and cannot be akin to a lottery, and even the EC's initial years' fining process has been criticized on these lines,[123] which was later revised by way of multiple measures in the form of Commission Guidelines on Fines, 1998 (revised in 2006), Leniency Scheme, 1998 (revised in 2002 and 2006) and Settlement Procedure, 2008. A transparent and consistent scheme of sanctions reduces the number of appeals, thus making the whole regime more robust and efficient. When it comes to the imposition of penalties on either enterprises or individuals, cartel decisions of the CCI do not present a very transparent or consistent picture. In a majority of cases, the CCI has imposed a penalty under Section 27 of the Act without giving any justification or reason, and it is not particularly clear whether the CCI did consider factors like type of cartel, area of operation, gravity of violation, duration of cartel, sector affected, the success of the cartel, participation level of each enterprise and so on. There is no apparent methodology that seems to have been used to compute penalty. The appellate forums have at multiple times questioned the rationale of the CCI to reach a particular fine and have sent the matter back to it for a reasoned order.

The quantum of fines can be examined from three aspects. The first is to look at overall fines on enterprises involved in cartelization over the years in order to form an idea of the general activity of the CCI vis-à-vis punishment for cartelization. The second is to examine the parameters used by the CCI to impose penalties or, in other words, examine the effect of aggravating and mitigating circumstances on the computation of fines. The third is to examine the leniency regime with respect to the imposition of a penalty.

5.9.1 Cartel sanctions under the Competition Act, 2002

Per Section 27 of the Act, if the CCI, after submission of an investigation report by the DG, comes to a conclusion that there is a violation of Section 3 of the Act, it can direct the entities involved in the anti-competitive action to discontinue or not to re-enter into such agreements (cease-and-desist orders). The CCI, by virtue of Section 27 (b), may also impose a penalty, but the same is not mandatory, as is evident from the usage of words such as "may", "all or any" and "as it deems fit". There are no rules, regulations or specific guidelines providing for the procedure for the manner in which the discretion with regard to the quantum of penalty is to be exercised.

Further, such discretion is expanded by the wordings of Section 27 (b). Within the upper limit fixed under Section 27 (b), the CCI has, under the proviso, the discretion, in cases of cartels, to impose a penalty either on the basis of profit or on the basis of turnover. The application of the proviso, although framed especially for cartel cases, has been read in a manner that leaves it to the discretion of the CCI. From a plain reading of the proviso as it stands today, particularly in light of amendments effected therein through the Competition (Amendment) Act, 2007, it is evident that the legislature has made an enabling provision whereby the CCI was conferred with the discretion to invoke the proviso in an appropriate case. The penalty under the proviso to Section 27 (b) requires the CCI to take into account the duration of the cartel. However, as discussed in the previous chapter, the CCI, apart from a handful of leniency cases, has rarely gone into the question of the duration of the cartel. This makes the very application of the cartel-specific proviso under Section 27 (b) uncertain.

The upper ceiling for the imposition of such a penalty has been prescribed, and therefore, any penalty cannot exceed "ten percent of the average of the turnover for the last three preceding financial years" of any entity found to be in violation of Section 3 of the Act. However, in the case of cartels, a penalty higher than three times the profit for each year of the continuance of the cartel or 10% of the turnover of each year of the cartel may be imposed. Penalty on the basis of actual profits will, apart from being always higher than one based on excess profits attributable to cartelization, also obviate the need to calculate the "but for" competitive price and the elasticity of demand for which data and econometric expertise may be lacking.

The CCI has made it clear that it has the discretion to impose a penalty in the case of cartels, either through the main text of Section 27 or by using the proviso to Section 27. There are no regulations or guidelines on the aspect of imposition of penalty. This necessarily means that the CCI has no readymade reference or a list of parameters to impose a penalty. Therefore, while it may take different factors into consideration, to what extent such factor should influence the imposition of a penalty (degree of application) is left to its discretion. The CCI may also not take any factor into consideration to impose the penalty. Therefore, for instance, while the quantum of penalty in the EU depends on factors like the duration of the cartel, the gravity of the offence, the type of infringement, the market share of the cartel and the turnover of the firm, the CCI in India is not obliged to take such considerations on board. It may be argued that the proviso to Section 27, designed especially for cartels, does take into account the duration of the cartel. However, questions can always be raised on the frequency of such usage. In the observation period, the CCI used the proviso only on a few occasions. Therefore, the imposition of the penalty in India has been largely based on turnover. The CCI, however, takes into account aggravating and mitigating circumstances, but that too per its discretion. In *Excel Crop Care Limited v. Competition Commission of India and Ors.*,[124] the Supreme Court interpreted "turnover" used in the main text of Section 27 (b) to mean "relevant turnover" for multi-product companies. It was influenced by the idea of "inability to pay" and over-deterrence if the provision was interpreted to mean total turnover. It has to be noted that the turnover prescribed under the main text of Section 27 (b) only prescribes an upper ceiling to the maximum quantum of penalty that can be imposed. The final penalty can be anything below the upper ceiling. The actual calculation of the fine has to be taken on affected relevant sales or relevant profits (as done in the US or the EU) applying the proviso to Section 27 (b). However, the application of proviso would then necessarily have to include a calculation based on the duration of the cartel. The Supreme Court made a reference to the South African case of *Southern Pipeline Contractors & Anr. v. The Competition Commission.*[125]

It is not clear under what circumstances the CCI will impose a penalty based on turnover or profit. There a very few cases where it has actually used the proviso. Usage of the proviso would mean that the CCI will have to make the comparison between turnover and profit during the relevant period (i.e. the period of cartelization) so as to determine the higher of the two. This essentially means that the duration of the cartel has to be ascertained with some level of clarity. Our experience has shown that due to a lack of sufficient evidence, the CCI does not go into a separate inquiry to ascertain the actual duration of the cartel. Further, the growth of the leniency regime, which was supposed to result in entities declaring all the relevant information to allow the CCI to make the necessary assessment has been slow. This is evidenced by the fact that in the last ten years, there are less than 15 cases that have been decided on the basis of leniency applications. The CCI, therefore, mostly uses the main text of Section 27 rather than the proviso included, especially for cartel cases. The idea of the proviso was to create a regime of higher penalties for violations that are of higher intensity (viz. cartels).

The second aspect of the fine structure can be seen on the touchstone of consistency and transparency. Even if the CCI has been using the main text of Section 27, has it been able to maintain a level of consistency in its approach? In India, the CCI has not passed any penalty guidelines, unlike other jurisdictions, to reach a fine. Section 27 only postulates an upper ceiling and does not lay out the factors on which the penalty has to be imposed. Therefore, there is a grey area as to whether factors like recidivism, aggravating and mitigating factors, duration of the cartel, number of entities and nature of violation play any part in the quantification of a penalty. While these factors have been taken as absolutely essential in jurisdictions like the EU, the CCI in India has not really, apart from aggravating and mitigating factors, used such parameters to quantify penalty. It has not really made an effort to explain the reasons of imposing a particular penalty within the upper ceiling of 10% turnover. This has raised questions about the consistency and even the transparency in the imposition of fines. For instance, while in some cases, the CCI has taken "gravity of violation" as an aggravating factor, the usage of this parameter is not consistent across all cases. Now, cartels are considered the most serious violations of competition law. This is the reason that none of the other jurisdictions that have come out with penalty guidelines uses the gravity of the offence as an aggravating factor. The very existence of the cartel is considered serious enough.

N. V. Ramana, J., in the case of the *Excel Crop Care* case,[126] aptly outlined the factors that have to be taken into consideration while calculating penalties for cartel participants, such as the nature, gravity and extent of the contravention, the role played by the infringer (ringleader/follower) and the duration of participation.[127] The question, however, is whether the CCI has given due weightage to the factors underlined earlier in its decisions in the last ten years of anti-cartel enforcement. As law abhors absolute power and arbitrary discretion, this discretion provided under Section 27 needs to be regulated and guided so that there is uniformity and stability with respect to the imposition of penalty. This discretion should be governed by the rule of law and not by arbitrary, vague or fanciful considerations.

The penalty structure for cartels in India does not envisage a base fine upon which the final penalty will be built based on different factors. Competition authorities in many countries have come to realize the under deterrent value of fines due to practical and legal difficulties in applying the Beckerian model of optimal fine, given the very low rate of cartel detection. They have, therefore, moved to enhanced methodologies to impose fines. The use of entry fees or specific increases for deterrence under the EU's 2006 Guidelines or culpability multiplier under the US Guidelines are examples of methods to increase the level of deterrence.

An optimal fine is inversely related to the rate of detection. Therefore, the lower the detection rate, the higher should be the quantum of fine. The rate of cartel detection in India, as discussed previously, is not very encouraging and raises the risk of under-deterrence. It has to be remembered here that penalties are the only sanctioning mechanism in India. There is, therefore, no possibility of creating a second line of deterrence through jail terms for executives involved in cartelization.

It is indeed surprising that while counterparts to the CCI have been engaged in making their penalty structure, both in terms of quantum and imposition, more robust and nuanced, the CCI has been satisfied with the present regime and its limited usage of aggravating and mitigating factors to calculate the quantum of penalty. The lack of consistency and reason in the imposition of sanctions has led to multiple appeals, where a number of original orders have been modified by the appellate forum. Apart from the less than the par value of the fine, the success of defendants at the appellate stage has contributed to under deterrence of cartel activities in India. If the cartelists know that there is a high possibility of a favourable order at the appeal stage, the number of appeals would also rise.

5.9.2 Use of aggravating and mitigating factors by the CCI

"The quantum of penalty imposed must correspond with the gravity of the offence and the same must be determined after having due regard to the

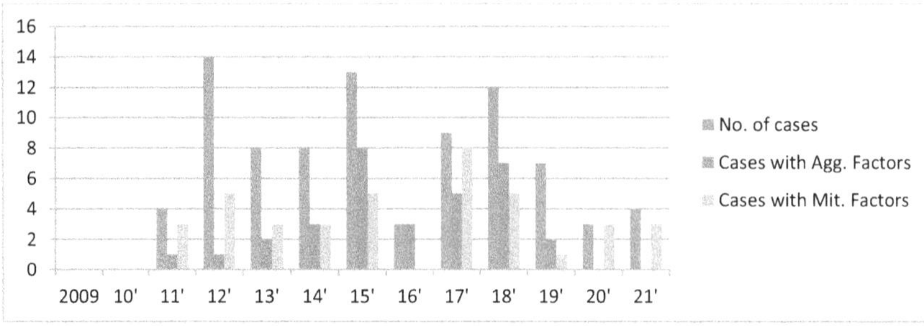

X axis: Years of enforcement; Y axis: Number of cases

Figure 5.1 Year-wise usage of aggravating and mitigating factors for the imposition of penalty.

mitigating and aggravating circumstances of the case".[128] These are the circumstances that tend to either increase the quantum of fine (aggravating factors) or reduce the quantum of fine (mitigating factors).

In the initial years, the CCI did not really get into the question of aggravating and mitigating circumstances and, therefore, their influence on the imposition of a fine was minimal. These factors are considered very important to differentiate cases of varying degrees. For instance, a naked price fixing in an important consumer-specific sector like health and pharmaceuticals must attract a larger penalty when compared to a minor violation of non-dealing done as a practice by a trade association. Non-segregation of cases into major and minor violations based on aggravating and mitigating factors fails to create an impression of seriousness from the CCI. A list of factors considered by the CCI during the observation period are illustrated in the following section.

5.9.2.1 Use of aggravating factors

5.9.2.1.1 LEADERSHIP ROLE

A leadership role is one of the most common aggravating factors taken into account for the imposition of fines in many jurisdictions.[129] A leadership role can be understood in the form of one who establishes the cartel or one who coordinates the cartel, and the various forms of such roles have been explained in Chapter 3 in detail. The identification of a ring leader may help in making a distinction in the award of penalties among various cartel members. It also sends a clear signal that the CCI will single out instigators and coordinators and deal with them in a sterner fashion. The EU's 2006 Guidelines or the US Guidelines, for instance, list leadership as an aggravating circumstance. Further, leniency benefits are not extended to cartel ring leaders by the DOJ in the US. The CCI in India has not actually made the effort to identify ring leaders. This may be because a high percentage of cases is centred on trade associations, and the final penalty is imposed only on the association or their executive members. Considering that membership of trade associations is composed of business undertakings, it would have been worthwhile to identify leader firms behind the decision-making of the association. Non-identification of ring leaders fails to create 'specific deterrence' for individual undertakings.

The leniency provision under Section 46 of the Act or the CCI (Lesser Penalty) Regulation of 2009 does not provide any clarity on the aspect of cartel ring leaders. India also does not have penalty guidelines which take into account different factors, including cartel leadership, in order to quantify fines for cartelization. It has to be mentioned here that nothing stops the CCI from taking into account cartel leadership as an aggravating factor to impose a penalty within the upper limit prescribed under Section 27 of the Act. However, the CCI in the last ten years has rarely considered the aspect of leadership as a relevant factor in imposing a penalty. While the idea of leadership has been clearly marked as an aggravating circumstance, there is a general lethargy in the identification of leaders in cartel cases. This may also be due to the lack of an identification framework. Through non-identification, the CCI has taken an easier route, sidestepping the requirement to collect evidence against one or more central actors. The CCI has, in the last ten years (2009–2019), attempted to identify such leaders in not more than six cases. Even in these six identified cases, while the evidence suggests that the cartel has key or central figures, there is no sign of any effect on the resultant penalty imposed. Since there is no attempt to identify ring leaders by the CCI, there is no fear of establishing or coordinating cartels.

In *Uniglobe*,[130] while the CCI identified three trade associations among six as taking the lead role and having a high degree of involvement, it did not reflect on the actual computation of fine. On the contrary, it acted as a mitigating factor for the other three associations who were left without any penalty. The three leader associations have imposed a penalty of one lakh each, something which was neither based on their turnover nor annual receipts. In *Nagrik Chetna Manch*,[131] while the managing director of one of the firms admitted to having established and operationalized the cartel of bid rigging, the CCI made no distinction in imposing a penalty, either individual or at the undertaking level.[132] A uniform penalty at the rate of 10% of average turnover and income was calculated for six firms and five individuals, including the ring leader. Interestingly, the CCI also granted leniency of a 25% reduction in penalty for the ring leader. Similarly, in the dry-cell batteries[133] case, even though the CCI observed that Panasonic played a key role in the cartel and "was in a position to influence and dictate the terms" of the anti-competitive arrangement to Godrej, it was granted a 100% reduction in penalty due to the leniency application. Non-appreciation of the fact that

Panasonic played the role of a ring leader made the outcome of the case a bit unfair.

The Apex Court in the *Excel Crop Care* case marked the importance of the role played by ring leaders in the determination of appropriate sanctions.

> *8. After such initial determination of relevant turnover, commission may consider appropriate percentage (of penalty), as the case may be, by taking into consideration nature, gravity, extent of the contravention,* ***role played by the infringer (ringleader? Follower?)****, the duration of participation, the intensity of participation, loss or damage suffered as a result of such contravention, market circumstances in which the contravention took place, nature of the product, market share of the entity, barriers to entry in the market, nature of involvement of the company, bona fides of the company, profit derived from the contravention etc. These factors are only illustrative for the tribunal to take into consideration while imposing appropriate percentage of penalty.*

Non-identification of ring leaders fails to create a specific deterrence for individual undertakings. The CCI may choose to exclude ring leaders from the leniency scheme. Even if the CCI follows a non-differentiated strategy for cartel ringleaders in terms of leniency, it has to start identifying leadership as an aggravating factor to impose higher sanctions on the leaders, which in turn might induce them to file for leniency. In the absence of penalty guidelines in India, there is no structural mechanism available to the CCI to take factors concerning the internal operation of the cartel into account while imposing sanctions.

5.9.2.1.2 DETRIMENTAL EFFECT ON INTERESTS OF CONSUMERS/CRITICAL NATURE OF THE PRODUCT OR SERVICE

Cartels are considered *per se* illegal because of their pernicious effects and lack of any redeeming virtue. The seriousness of enforcement and strength of sanctions are commensurate with the detrimental nature of cartels and the harm caused to the consumers. Therefore, it is not generally seen that harm caused to consumers, in general, is used as an aggravating factor. The CCI has, however, used harm to consumers as an aggravating circumstance.

In the cement cartel case,[134] the CCI noted the detrimental effect of cement cartels on consumers and the economy without clearly categorizing them as aggravating factors; and imposed a penalty at the rate of 0.5 times the profit during the period of violation without adducing any reason and the association was penalized at the rate of 10% of total receipts for the two years. The penalty was imposed under the proviso to Section 27 (b) on the basis of profits made during the period of violation. In the bid-rigging case concerning insurance companies,[135] the CCI acknowledged the effect of violations on consumers (poor families in the present case) as an aggravating factor. However, unlike the cement cartel case, the penalty was not imposed on the basis of profits but on the basis of turnover at the rate of 2% (of their average turnover of the last three financial years) using the main text of Section 27 (b). No reason was provided for the exercise of discretion or for the quantification of a penalty. Similarly, in *Western Coalfields*,[136] the CCI considered the criticality of services as an aggravating factor to impose a penalty on the firms and executives of the firms at the rate of 4% of average relevant turnover and 4% of their average income of the last three financial years respectively. Criticality of service for public health was also considered in *Delhi Jal Board*,[137] and it formed the basis of the penalty imposed at the rate of 8% of average relevant turnover. There is not much difference in the gravity of offence in the *Insurance*, *Western Coalfields* or *Delhi Jal Board* matters that commanded separate sanctions. The CCI switched back to the imposition of penalties on the basis of profits in the bid-rigging matter in the tender floated by *Maharashtra State Power Generation Co.*[138]

Similarly, in *Arora Medical Hall*,[139] the CCI, while acknowledging the principles of proportionality, imposed a penalty at the rate of 10% of average receipts of Chemist and Druggist Association of Firozabad (CDAF). It considered the harm caused and risk caused to the lives of consumers of drugs as aggravating factors. However, it ended up imposing similar penalties as in cases without aggravating factors. The office bearers of the associations were also penalized at the rate of 10% of their income during the relevant period. The CCI in the *AIMTC matter*[140] considered the cascading effect of fixing freight charges on the goods and services consumed by the common man to impose a penalty on AIMTC at the rate of 10% of the average turnover of the last three years.

5.9.2.1.3 HARM TO OVERALL PUBLIC EXCHEQUER/ECONOMY

Harm to the economy or exchequer has been considered by the CCI, not necessarily as a specific aggravating factor, to determine the quantum of penalty. In *Bio-Med*[141] and *Jet Airways*,[142] the CCI took note of the violation's harm caused to the economy and exchequer to impose a penalty at the rate of 3% of the average turnover in the last three preceding years. Harm to the economy, thus, has been seen as a lesser aggravating factor than the criticality of the product or service in question.[143] Therefore, when compared to *Delhi Jal Board* or *Western Coalfield*, the penalty imposed in *Bio-Med* and *Jet* matters were lesser.

5.9.2.1.4 IMPORTANT POSITION OF THE PLAYER

The position of power of the cartelists has been considered an aggravating factor. It is assumed that by virtue of the position of the cartelist, it is able to influence, instigate or force others to either join the cartel or continue with the cartel. Fear of ostracization prevents members of the cartel from defection. The CCI has used this factor only in the case of trade associations and that too only in pharmaceutical and entertainment sector associations. In *Santuka*,[144] the CCI noted that that AIOCD, by virtue of it being the apex body for chemists and druggists in India, was limiting and controlling the "supply and influencing the prices of the drugs and pharmaceutical products by insisting upon NOC for appointment of stockiest, fixation of trade margins" and so on. A similar stance was taken by the CCI for *Chemist and Druggist Association, Ferozepur*[145] and *Bengal and Chemist and Druggist Association*.[146] The CCI, in both cases, imposed a penalty at the rate of 10% of the average receipts of the associations. Listing of aggravating factors, as is evident, did not seem to have any effect on the quantum of penalty. The CCI had previously imposed a penalty on trade associations at the same rate where there were no aggravating factors. Interestingly, in *TG Vinaykumar*,[147] while the CCI did consider the importance and position of the association which contributed to the violation, a penalty was imposed at the rate of 5%. It is difficult to decipher a clear distinguishing feature in the cases listed previously.

5.9.2.1.5 NON-COOPERATION

Non-cooperation, or an attempt to tamper with an ongoing investigation, is seen as a serious aggravating factor. If the defendant, be it an individual or a trade association, causes hindrance to the investigative process directly or indirectly, it will be taken as a reason to increase fines.[148]

5.9.2.1.6 RECIDIVISM

Recidivism is one of the most serious aggravating factors and accounts for the maximum number of cases. The higher rate of recidivism raises a question about the deterrent effect of the previously imposed fine. "Recidivism is a circumstance which justifies a significant increase in the basic amount of fine. Recidivism constitutes proof that the sanction previously imposed was not sufficiently deterrent".[149] The EU's 2006 Guidelines on the methods to impose fine envisage a 100% jump to the quantum of penalty in case of recidivism. The US Guidelines also prescribe an increase in the culpability multiplier for repeated offences. In India, the CCI has dealt with two types of cases: first, where the same entity indulges in antitrust violation of the same type after being previously penalized for it, and second, where the entity indulges in violation similar to that of another entity known to have been penalized for it.[150] There is an abundance of cases of the second nature, with the first type not lagging much behind. All these cases are centred around sector-specific trade associations. This essentially means that the sanctions imposed by the CCI on trade associations have been unable to create either specific or general deterrence. This may be either due to the belief of trade associations of non-detection or the idea that even if they are detected, the resultant penalty will not cost them much. The CCI has, on multiple occasions, lamented the repeated nature of violations, especially among trade associations of the pharmaceutical sector. The irony is that it has not gone beyond penalizing trade associations at a rate which is similar to any ordinary case. In some cases, the CCI has imposed fines on office bearers of the association. For instance, it penalized the Chemist and Druggist Association (CDAG), Goa, in 2012[151] at the rate of 10% of average receipts. In 2014, the CCI, while referring to the 2014[152] order, noted that the CDAG continued with the anti-competitive behaviour with "utmost disrespect to the Commission's mandate" and imposed a penalty at the rate of 10% of the average receipts. Similarly, the CCI, in its 2015[153] order against Himachal Pradesh State Chemists and Druggists Association, noted the previous orders against the association by MRTPC in 2008. However, the CCI ended up penalizing the association at the same rate of 10%.[154] A similar scenario is seen in the matter of *Indian Foundation of Transport Research & Training*[155] and *Kerala Film Exhibitors Federation (KFEF)*.[156] Interestingly, the CCI in KFEF barred two office bearers from engaging with administration, management or governance of the trade association for two years because of their continued indulgence in anti-competitive activities. Such a measure (attribution of liability on individuals) has not been in other cases of recidivism. The CCI has imposed similar penalties even in cases of multiple counts of recidivism. In *Kannada Grahakara Koota*,[157] the Karnataka Film Chamber of Commerce (KFCC) was penalized at the rate of 10% of average income even after the CCI noted the prior sanctions imposed on it on two previous occasions.

Apart from the aggravating factors mentioned, there are other factors that, although very common in other jurisdictions, have failed to find a place in Indian decisions.[158] For instance, 'retaliatory or threatening measures' taken by cartel members against one or more entities, whether as a disciplining exercise for an insider who refused to toe the line of the leaders or against a cartel outsider. This is seen as a serious aggravating factor. In many cases in India, especially the trade association cases, the principal trade association used its market position to issue diktats to boycott or not to deal with entities refusing to follow their decisions. While the behaviour as such was brought under Section 3 (3) (b) of the Act, it was not used as an aggravating factor to impose higher penalties.

5.9.2.2 Use of mitigating factors

5.9.2.2.1 VIOLATION PRIOR TO NOTIFICATION OF SECTION 3

The CCI has considered the cause of action before the date of notification of Section 3 (i.e. May 2009) as a reason not to impose penalties. In the *FICCI Multiplex*[159] matter, the CCI traced the genesis of the dispute prior to the notification of Section 3 and used it as a mitigating factor even though the conduct had a continuing effect after May 2009. The CCI strangely imposed a uniform token fine of Rs. 1 lakh on all defendants despite there being clear identification of leaders. This was neither based on turnover nor profits, a trend that followed in all the cases in the year 2011. Similarly, the CCI in *Vipul Shah*[160] traced the history of the practice formally adopted by the association in the MOU in 2010 from 1966 as a factor not to impose penalties. The CCI also noted that some of the defendants were associations of daily wage earners, and hence, an order of cease and desist was sufficient to meet the ends of justice.

5.9.2.2.2 IMMEDIATE TERMINATION OR CORRECTION OF ANTI-COMPETITIVE CONDUCT OR VERY SHORT DURATION OF PRACTICE

Similar to the EU's 2006 Guidelines on fines, the CCI in India considers immediate termination or correction of anti-competitive action as a mitigating circumstance. Therefore, where there is no harm that was caused by an anti-competitive clause in the by-laws of the associations and which the association offered to correct immediately, the CCI chose not to impose any penalty.[161] Similarly, in *PV Basheer*,[162] when the new management of the association showed compliance with the CCI's orders and corrected the anti-competitive conduct by reinstating the informant as a member of the association, it was taken as a mitigating factor in the quantification of fines. The CCI in *Cochin Port Trust*[163] chose not to impose any penalty considering the short duration of the conduct in question, which was terminated even before the investigation started.

In *BCDA*[164] (2020), the CCI noted that the BCDA had been able to show that post the decision of CCI in *Santuka Associates Pvt. Ltd. V. AIOCD and Others*[165] in 2013, it had taken several steps in the direction of ending the practice of requiring NOC/SAI. In the CCI's view, taking such steps by the BCDA in the right direction, although not adequate, constitutes a mitigating factor for the BCDA. Therefore, no penalty in terms of Section 27 (b) of the Act was imposed.

5.9.2.2.3 NO HARM CAUSED DUE TO VIOLATION

In *Shree Cement*,[166] the CCI considered the harm caused in the form of cost to the exchequer and time loss. It then went on to make an artificial distinction between two terminologies, "causes" or "likely to cause an AAEC", to hold that the two need to be seen separately. In light of other factors, like the peculiar nature of the bid and the presence of a competition compliance program, the CCI imposed a penalty at the rate of 0.3% of their average turnover of the last three financial years. It is humbly submitted here that the CCI did not need to read a distinction or gradation in Section 3 when the statute does not envisage such a categorization. Cartels have been proved to cause anti-competitive effect, and "foreseeability of harm" is enough in such cases even when actual harm is not ascertainable.[167]

5.9.2.2.4 PENALIZED IN ANOTHER CASE WITH A SIMILAR PERIOD OF INVESTIGATION

Multiple cases[168] have been filed against trade associations in the last ten years for their alleged involvement in anti-competitive practice. Many such complaints relate to violations of a similar nature in a particular range of time, leading to investigations around similar periods of time. Therefore, if the CCI has already penalized a particular anti-competitive practice, it will not do it again for a violation of similar nature at the same time. These are not cases of recidivism or parallel violations. The CCI has chosen not to read such situations as different but one common violation and has erred in a few situations, though. In *Gulshan Verma*,[169] the CCI mistook two violations in the same time period having different subject matter as one common violation and chose not to impose a penalty on account of the previous sanction. The COMPAT later set aside the order as the CCI had also relied on evidence from the previous case.

5.9.2.2.5 LACK OF AWARENESS AND SMALL SIZE OF THE PLAYERS

The lack of awareness and small size of the defendants have been taken as a reason to reduce or exempt the parties from being penalized.[170] In *Sheth & Co.*,[171] the CCI noted that the defendants were small-scale units and reduced the quantum of penalty. In the dry-cell batteries[172] cartel, the CCI held that Geep Industries (India) Private Limited was only a dealer of the product with an insignificant market share. There was no negotiating power of Geep and Panasonic was in a position to dictate the terms of the anti-competitive agreement to it. In light of this, the CCI imposed a penalty at the rate of 4% of the turnover on Geep for each year of the continuance of the cartel. The CCI has recently, in a few cases,[173] refrained from imposing penalties despite there being a finding of contravention. In all these cases, the CCI considered the stressful situation of the micro, small and medium enterprises sector during the pandemic as an important factor. The CCI, however, before giving the exemption, did not look into the financial position of the parties involved in cartelization.

5.9.2.2.6 SMALL SIZE OF THE BID/TENDER

Small public procurements are not unimportant and cannot be ignored.

> The contravention of the competition law cannot be considered non-serious only because the amount of the bid was small. The size of tender in itself is not a decisive factor for taking a lenient view. However, it may be taken into consideration as one of the factors while imposing penalty.[174]

The CCI has considered the size of the bid as a factor in many cases related to bid rigging.[175]

5.9.2.2.7 PECULIAR OR WEAK POSITION OF THE SECTOR/INDUSTRY

The CCI has been mindful of the fact that certain sectors are in distress. Therefore, even though that in itself does not justify cartelization, it has taken a lenient view while imposing fines. For instance, in *Indian Sugar Mills*,[176] the CCI appreciated the fact that the jute industry was going through a rough financial phase and needed support. In light of this, a reduced penalty at the rate of 5% of the average turnover of the last three years was imposed on the IJMA and the GTA. The CCI, in the insurance matter, considered the peculiarities of the insurance sector, including the importance of the insurer's solvency for the consumers as a mitigating circumstance.[177] A similar stance was taken by the CCI in the aviation sector.[178]

It has, however, not entertained the argument of the weak economic position of the enterprise as a mitigating factor.[179] This is similar to the stand taken by other jurisdictions. The EC has maintained that treating weak economic conditions of enterprises as a mitigating factor would be akin to "conferring an unjustified competitive advantage on an undertaking". The CCI in India, however, in light of the weak economic condition of the market during the pandemic, has imposed only nominal penalties in some cases.[180]

5.9.2.2.8 COOPERATION AND COMPLIANCE

The CCI tends to treat defendants leniently when they cooperate in the proceedings.[181] In *Western Coalfields*,[182] it considered the cooperation of the defendants during the proceedings as a mitigating circumstance. Cooperation in leniency means admitting guilt and providing first-hand insider evidence, which is *quid pro quo* for a smaller fine or complete clemency. The reduction in fine is then based on the degree of cooperation vis-à-vis the significance of evidence and timing of disclosure. The CCI has, on different occasions, failed to retain the distinction between leniency and non-leniency applicants. For instance, in the CBB matter,[183] it did not impose any penalty on the cartelists after noting the cooperation and confession of the parties. Action on the part of the CCI to grant amnesty to cartelists even in non-leniency matters on the ground of cooperation seriously undermines the leniency regime.

Compliance and cooperation with CCI's orders and processes have also been considered reasons to reduce fines.[184] With respect to competition compliance programs, the CCI only tends to treat them as mitigating factors if they were undertaken before the investigation began.[185]

Many competition authorities are urging bigger corporations to adopt and adhere to competition compliance programs. These structures have two purposes: first, they would help prevent anti-competitive action, and second, they would help in the early detection of the cartel, which will enable the enterprise to apply and seek immunity on better terms.[186] While the existence of a competition compliance programme is taken as a mitigating factor in many jurisdictions, non-adherence to the self-set-up compliance programme is seen as an aggravating factor.

5.9.2.2.9 PECULIARITIES OF THE TENDER

In cases related to bid rigging, the CCI has sometimes attributed a given conduct of the parties on account of peculiar terms and conditions of the bids.[187] A tender design that created entry barriers and made collusion among the bidders conducive will be taken note of by the CCI.[188] Factors like "nature of the product procured, total volume of tender, involvement of small scale units, irregular requirement of product, single source of raw material and revenues generated from the product under consideration"[189] are considered when quantifying penalty.

5.9.2.2.10 SUCCUMBED TO THE PRESSURE OF THE LEADER

It is interesting to note that while the CCI does not spend any resources and time to ascertain ring leaders in the cartel to penalize them at a higher rate in comparison to others, it has used "undue influence" as a mitigating factor. Instead of focusing on the coercer, it has given benefits to the coerced entities. The EC, on the other hand, treats the passive role as a mitigating factor, but the threshold is quite high as the party claiming it needs to prove that it was "merely a follower" of the litigator. In *Kerala Film Exhibitors Federation*[190] (KFEF), the CCI reduced the penalty for Film Distributors Association (Kerala) as it acted under the pressure of KFEF. KFEF, on the other hand, was only penalized at the rate of 7% of average receipts, lesser than the general penalty at the rate of 10%. In *TG Vinay Kumar*,[191] even though it was noted that FEFKA Director's Union and FEFKA Production Executive's Union followed the diktats of the Film Employees Federation of Kerala, they were penalized at the same rate as that of the coercing entity. The acknowledgement of mitigating factors on account of being *coerced* did not result in the actual reduction of penalty when compared to that of the *coercer*. The resultant penalty for the FEFKA Director's Union was more than that of the Film Employees Federation of Kerala.

Another anomaly was seen in the dry-cell matter[192] where the CCI acknowledged the fact that Panasonic,

> being the manufacturer of dry-cell batteries and supplier of Geep, was in the position to influence and dictate the terms of the anti-competitive agreement to Geep, and Geep being a very small player having insignificant market share in the market for dry-cell batteries was not in a bargaining or negotiating position vis-a-vis Panasonic.

Ideally, therefore, Geep should have been penalized lesser than Pansonic. However, the CCI does not make the distinction between cartel leaders and others in terms of culpability and application for leniency, and Panasonic was able to claim 100% reduction in penalty, while Geep ended up paying more than nine crores.

In *BCDA (2020)*,[193] even though the CCI observed that the pharmaceutical companies who took the plea that they were indulging in the impugned conduct under threat/duress/directions from the BCDA would not escape liability under competition law, it decided, keeping in mind such circumstances, not to impose any monetary penalty on the companies.

Apart from the previously mentioned mitigating circumstances, the CCI has also considered factors like the nature of the product,[194] low amount of revenue generated[195] and level of participation in trade association decisions[196] as mitigating factors. In *Automotive Bearings*,[197] the CCI, after noting the peculiarity in facts and circumstances of the case, did not impose any penalty and only passed a cease-and-desist order. The reasons, however, were not particularly explained.

Clearly, the CCI has used a wide variety of mitigating factors when compared to aggravating factors. The numbers are more than most of the jurisdictions which have laid out a set of fining guidelines. Although the lists in these guidelines are not exhaustive, a definitive idea of circumstances that affect the quantum of penalty brings in both transparency and consistency.

5.9.3 Summarizing observations

The CCI has, without fail, underlined the objective behind the imposition of penalty as punishment, which is commensurate with violation and deterrence. The quantum of penalty, per the CCI, must correspond to the gravity of the offence after taking into account aggravating and mitigating circumstances. Cartels are considered the gravest form of antitrust violations. The CCI, unlike other jurisdictions, does not start from a minimum fine for hard-core cartels, which then gets amplified by the use of 'culpability multipliers'. Aggravating and mitigating factors to increase or decrease the penalty are only used after the quantum of penalty is finalized. The CCI does not employ any methodology to reach a penalty. Neither does it provide any reason for quantifying a penalty to be imposed. Moreover, the Supreme Court of India has now read turnover to mean "relevant turnover" and not "average turnover". This means that if the CCI applies turnover to calculate a fine, it is actually the turnover from the affected product or service. This causes a substantial reduction in the quantum of fine. Further, even if relevant turnover is used, it should be multiplied by the duration of the cartel so that penalty equivalent to the harm done by the cartel is imposed. However, in most cases, the CCI has used the average of the turnover as the base to impose a penalty, which further reduces the penalty.

Interestingly, in all cases concerning trade associations, no penalty has been imposed on individual participants, and despite having the presence of aggravating factors, the penalty has been imposed at a fixed percentage of average receipts. It seems that the CCI finds itself in a difficult position every time it has to impose penalties on trade associations. Since a penalty cannot exceed the prescribed limit under Section 27 (b), the penalties that have been imposed on trade associations are grossly inadequate. The CCI, unlike its counterparts in the US or EU, has not explored the possibility of imposing a penalty on the basis of the turnover of individual members and putting the onus on associations to collect the penalty from its members. The CCI has only gone to the extent of penalizing the executive or office bearers of the associations in the form of monetary penalties, which are again inconsequential.[198]

There has been no consistency in the exercise of discretion under Section 27 (b). Therefore, there is no uniformity of cases where the CCI chose to impose a penalty on the basis of profits or turnover multiplied by the duration of the cartel (i.e. use of proviso to Section 27 [b]) or where it imposed a penalty on the basis of the average (relevant) turnover in the preceding years. These cases cannot be categorized on the basis of the type or duration for which the cartel survived.

Ideally, the set of aggravating and mitigating factors should have an effect on the imposition of a penalty. One of the ways to go about it is to set the degree of influence these factors will have on the computation of fine. Therefore, a case with aggravating factors must show more penalty when compared with cases with no aggravating factors. Further, a case with a higher number of aggravating factors must reach a higher quantum of penalty when compared with cases with a lesser number of aggravating factors. The same goes for mitigating factors as well. Imposition of penalty without taking into account these factors will lead to a situation where every case of cartelization will be dealt with similarly, causing a serious dent to the overall deterrence value of such imposition of penalty. Even where these factors are taken on board, the competition regulator has to carefully balance aggravating and mitigating factors.

A regime without guidelines is like shooting in the dark, where it ultimately rests on the discretion of the CCI. This is evident from Indian cases where the CCI has nowhere given reasons as to why a particular penalty, whether in terms of a certain percentage of turnover or in terms of profit for the duration of the cartel or as a lump sum amount was imposed. In fact, even in cases where aggravating factors or mitigating factors were recorded, the CCI has not actually decided the quantum of penalty first and then, on the basis of the gravity of such factors, reduced the penalty by giving reasons. In fact, in many cases involving trade associations as the primary actor, the CCI has imposed a penalty at a flat rate of 10% of the average receipts or profits of the association for three years. Therefore, even when there were aggravating factors, the imposition of the penalty was still at the same rate. Most interesting are the cases of repeated violations. The CCI imposed a penalty of 10% of the average receipts for three years at the first instance of violation, but for repeated violations, there was no change in the imposition of penalty.

5.9.4 Trend analysis of the use of aggravating and mitigating factors by the CCI

As indicated earlier, we have divided the cartel cases into two categories: first, where the trade associations have played a primary role, and second, where the trade associations acted only as facilitators. However, it must be noted that only those cases have been taken into account where the penalty was imposed either on the basis of turnover or receipts or income, and these constitute 87% of total cartel cases under Section 27 of the Act.

In the year 2011, the CCI did not impose a fine on the basis of annual receipts. Fines were imposed on a lump sum basis, and it is not clear whether the presence of mitigating factors[199] or aggravating factors[200] had any impact on the overall fine imposed by the CCI. Even after 2011, the CCI took an easy route to impose a penalty on the trade associations on the basis of 10% of the average receipts for three years since most of these trade associations were not enterprises and were not doing an economic activity on their own. This also coincides with the language of Section 27 (b), where an upper limit of 10% "of the average of the turnover for the last three preceding financial years, upon each of such person or enterprise who are parties to the agreement", has been prescribed. The section, however, does not mention the term "receipts" and is silent on the imposition of fines on trade associations as entities in themselves. Imposition of fine at a flat rate of 10% meant that the CCI could not exceed the percentage even in cases where there were one or more aggravating factors. Cases against trade associations, as seen in matters of *Santuka,*[201] *Arora,*[202] *Reliance,*[203] *BCDA,*[204] *CDA*[205] and so on, are evidence of such a problem. There are also cases where, despite there being no mitigating factors, the CCI did not impose a penalty at the rate of 10%. Cases like *Cinemax*[206] and *Swastik Stevedores*[207] are evidence of such departure which has not been explained. This gets even more problematic when the existence of aggravating factors has not yielded in fines up to a mark fixed by the CCI itself.[208] Similarly, it has not been made clear as to what factor will be counted as a mitigating factor and to what degree it will have an impact on the calculation of fines. It is, therefore, not surprising that the list of mitigating factors consists of a whole range of factors, as indicated in the earlier part of the discussion. There are no cases where both aggravating and mitigating circumstances were considered which, of course, in all likelihood, would make the situation more problematic.

Similar inconsistency is noted in other cases as well. While the quantum of penalty has been calculated on the basis of a certain percentage of turnover, the application of aggravating and mitigating factors has not been consistent. The CCI has not provided any reason behind the imposition of fines or illustrated any methodology to increase or decrease the fine on the basis of aggravating and mitigating factors. Therefore, a similar number of factors in cases belonging to similar sectors have yielded different results. For instance, while the penalty in *Sheth*[209] with six mitigating factors was calculated as 3% of average turnover, a penalty at the rate of 0.3% of average turnover was imposed in *Shree Cement*,[210] which had a lesser number of mitigating factors and a higher number of aggravating factors. There have been multiple such examples. For instance, in *PES Installations*,[211] a penalty was imposed at the rate of 5% when compared with the aluminum phosphide[212] case, where a penalty was imposed at a rate of 9%, despite the fact that PES had one aggravating factor. Other examples are the cases of *Delhi Jal Board*[213] and the LPG cartel.[214] In the LPG cartel case, the absence of any aggravating or mitigating factor led to the imposition of fines at the rate of 7%, while in the *Delhi Jal Board*, the presence of four aggravating factors led to a fine being imposed only at the rate of 8%. Needless to say, had the CCI provided reasons to reach a particular percentage, it would have been more transparent and led to consistency.

5.9.5 Use of discretion by the CCI in the imposition of penalties

There are a total of six cases where the CCI has used the proviso to Section 27 (b) of the Act to impose a penalty on the basis of profit or turnover calculated for each year of the continuance of the violation. In all these cases, the initial assessment was done to compare penalties on the basis of turnover and profit (to ascertain the higher of three times the profit or 10% of turnover for each year of the continuance of such agreement). In the cement cartel case, fines were imposed on the basis of net profits – that is, at a rate of 0.5 times the net profit for each year of violation after it was calculated that three times the profit was higher than 10% of turnover. The rest of the cases where penalties were imposed using the proviso were leniency cases. In the zinc battery cartel case, a fine was imposed at a rate of 1.25 times the profit for eight years, while in the *DC Fans*[215] case, a fine was imposed at the rate equal to the profit of two of the three opposite parties. Interestingly, in the *Surendra Prasad*[216] bid-rigging case, the CCI did not even compare profits with turnover and decided to straight away fine the opposite parties at a rate of two times the profit for the period of violation. In the beer cartel case,[217] after comparing the quantum of penalty on the basis of profits and turnover, the penalty was imposed at a rate of 0.5 times on one party and at a rate of 2% of the turnover of two parties for each year of the continuance of cartel. The trade association was penalized at a rate of 3% of the average of its turnover for the last three preceding financial years of the cartel.

Again, there has been no consistency as to the cases where the CCI used the proviso or the main text of Section 27 of the Act. It is neither dependent on the duration of the cartel (for instance, the choice was made in the *DC Fans* case where the cartel existed for less than a year in comparison to the zinc battery case where the cartel existed for more than seven years) nor on the type of cartel (it has been used both for price fixing [zinc battery cartel] and bid rigging cases [DC fans]). The CCI, it seems, has gone by the amount of evidence it has at its disposal. Therefore, cases where the CCI has gone on to use the proviso are the cases where it is absolutely positive about the presence of a cartel in the form of evidence collected or through leniency applications. It is humbly submitted that this approach raises a lot of doubts about the decision-making of the CCI regarding the imposition of fines. Such an approach is neither correct nor practically sustainable.

5.9.6 Assessment of overall fines

Analysis of the sum of cartel fines is complementary to the number of cartel cases decided by CCI.

In the initial cartel cases, fines were not imposed in many cases, especially with respect to the trade associations in the media and entertainment sector and the wholesale and retail sector, because the trade association in question was already penalized for an act committed in the same investigation period in a previous case.[218] Therefore, finding anti-competitive behaviour was not followed with a fine. There are also cases where the CCI did not impose a penalty either due to the infancy of competition jurisprudence in the early years or because there were enough mitigating factors that prevented the imposition of a penalty. For instance, in the *Vijay Gupta*[219] case, no penalty was imposed after the CCI recorded cooperation from the opposite party and no damage done to the informant as mitigating factors. Similarly, in the *Sonipat*[220] case of 2015 or the *Cochin Port Trust*[221] case of 2017, the CCI did not impose any penalty due to the low gravity of the contravention and immediate termination of anti-competitive behaviour of the association. To date, there have been a few cases[222] where the CCI did not impose any penalty on the involved firms by taking factors like complete lack of awareness,

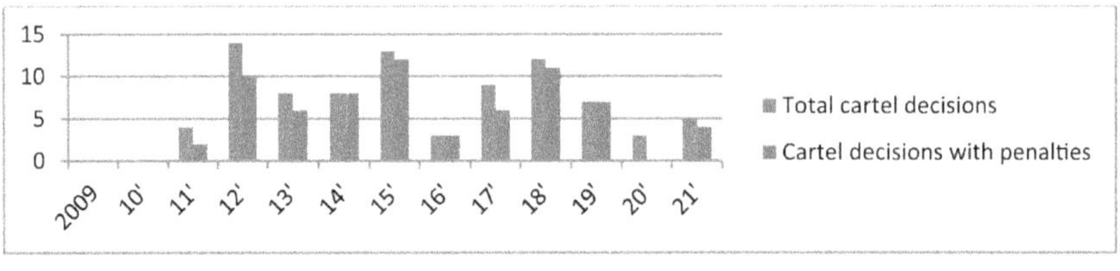

X Axis: Year of enforcement; Y Axis: Number of cases

Figure 5.2 The total number of cartel decisions vis-à-vis the number of cartel decisions with fines.

the small size of the enterprises and small size of the quote as mitigating factors. In *Automotive Bearings*,[223] the CCI, after noting the peculiarity in facts and circumstances of the case, did not impose any penalty and only passed a cease-and-desist order. The reasons, however, were not particularly explained. In the *CBB* matter,[224] the CCI did not impose any penalty on the cartelists after noting the cooperation and confession of the parties. Nonetheless, the number of cartel decisions with a fine has increased over the years. This may mean that there is a higher possibility of fines today for the discovery of cartels.

The final quantum of fines is achieved after factoring in the aggravating and mitigating factors to the base fines. In India, we have agreed on the concept of relevant turnover rather than overall turnover in the calculation of penalties for multi-product companies.[225] The Supreme Court of India affirmed the concept of relevant turnover, which was first devised by the then appellate tribunal (COMPAT). It has been held by the Supreme Court that the criterion of relevant turnover goes well "with the ethos of the Act and the legal principles which surround matters pertaining to imposition of penalties".[226] Although the CCI has adopted the concept of relevant turnover established and affirmed by the Supreme Court, it has differentiated cases by making a distinction between relevant turnover and restricted turnover. This essentially means that the CCI does not allow further breaking of a particular branch of an entity in terms of product or service into multiple activities within the same branch. Therefore, a contention by any party to consider the revenue from a particular activity of any product or service is likely to be rejected.[227] For instance, the CCI in the *Jet Airways*[228] case agreed that the penalty should be imposed on the basis of relevant turnover, but it rejected the contention that revenue generated only from the imposition of fuel surcharge (FSC) should be taken into account to impose a penalty instead of freight revenue from cargo handling services. Similarly, in *Western Coalfields*, the CCI took into account revenue generated from transportation services as a separate service in itself to calculate the fine.[229]

Therefore, any calculation of fine on the basis of either turnover or profit has to first determine the revenue being generated from the activity in question. Taking relevant turnover instead of total turnover causes a substantial decrease in the imposition of penalty due to two reasons. Reading the concept of relevant turnover into Section 27 (b) restricts the CCI from imposing a penalty within the new upper ceiling. This gets problematic when the final penalty does not take into account the duration of the cartel by using the proviso to Section 27 (b). The ultimate effect is on the quantum of penalty, which loses its deterrent value. The penalty neither satisfies the *Beckerian* principle of 'optimal deterrence' nor follows the legal principle of 'proportionality'. Penalty on the basis of 'relevant turnover' has to be multiplied by the duration of the cartel to make the penalty adequate. Further, unlike the EU, the CCI in India does not look at the group structure of enterprises to impose fines. Therefore, the turnover of the parent company is not considered for the imposition of a fine, even if the parent exercises decisive influence on the subsidiary company.

In sum, the absence of penalty guidelines prevents the CCI from taking relevant and important factors into consideration for the imposition of a fine. Apart from leniency and a set of ever-shifting aggravating and mitigating factors, the CCI does not concern itself with important details related to the character of the cartel itself.

The following chart presents figures for penalties (in absolute value) that have been imposed by the CCI during the observation period. It, however, does not capture heavy fluctuations but presents a sum total of fines imposed on different entities in a year after reductions, excluding fines imposed on individual office bearers of trade associations or executives of enterprises. It also does not take into account fines that were later reduced by appellate forums. The penalty has also been divided into penalties imposed on firms and penalties imposed on trade associations to give a wholesome picture. Examination of the total quantum of penalties across the years of enforcement will help in understanding the seriousness of the CCI in terms of its efforts to punish cartels. A higher quantum of penalty also proves the severity of punishment. Overall quantum of penalty has to be seen in the light of whether it is due to tackling the number of cartel cases or in terms of severity of punishments of large firms.

As is evident from the table, there is a heavy fluctuation in the total fines imposed per year on entities involved in cartelization. The sum of fines in a year is driven by a few large cartels involving high-revenue firms. The year 2009–2010 did not see a single cartel decision, and in the year 2011, a fine was imposed not on the basis of turnover or profit in either case involving individual firms[230] or on the basis of receipts for trade association cases[231]

Table 5.2 Quantum of penalty over the observation period

Year	*No. of cases*	*Total fine (in cr)*	*Fine imposed on trade associations (in cr)*	*Fine imposed on firms (in cr)*
2009	0	0	0	0
2010	0	0	0	0
2011	4	0.3	0.03	0.27
2012	14	7260.67	1.23	7259.43
2013	8	6.92	0.66	6.25
2014	8	62.6	0.36	62
2015	13	1070.64	0.46	1070.18
2016	3	0.86	0.86	0
2017	9	226.42	0.15	226.26
2018	12	525.32	0.84	524.5
2019	7	60.7	0.57	60.13
2020	3	0	0	0
2021	5	873.3	0.11	873.19

but as a lump sum amount. The year 2012 has recorded the maximum amount of penalty to date.[232] The high figure can be singlehandedly attributed to the cement cartel cases where a fine of Rs. 6,714.83 crores was imposed on cement companies and one trade association. Similarly, the high figures in 2015 can be attributed to two cases related to the insurance and aviation sectors, where a fine was imposed on the basis of turnover at the rate of 2% and 1%, respectively, but since the entities were big players in the market, the final penalty turned out to be high. It is emphasized here that the high quantum of fines across years is not attributable to the sustained action of the CCI in penalizing many cartels but is a result of a handful of big cases. For instance, the year following 2012 recorded a total fine of 6.92 crores, with 6.25 crores attributable to one case related to bid rigging in a railway tender. In the year 2014 again, the high amount of recorded fine is because fine at the rate of 2% of average turnover was imposed on three big firms in a matter related to bid rigging in spare parts supply to railways. This constituted 100% of the fines imposed on firms and 99% of the absolute fine for that year. In the year 2016, there were no new cases in which any firm was penalized. The same situation was repeated in 2017, where the fine imposed in the *Shree Cement*[233] case constituted roughly 91% of absolute fines for that year. The situation slightly improved in 2018, and the fines imposed were distributed across different cartels. The only case in 2016 related to anti-competitive behaviour by a pharmaceutical wholesale and retail trade association (the cement cartel case decision of 2012 was reiterated in the 2016 order). This is the reason that heavy fluctuations are seen in both absolute fines imposed across years and average fines per firm per cartel. The CCI dealt with three cartel cases in 2020. However, no penalty was imposed in any of the cases.

In comparison, the average fine per trade association across years is more uniform. One of the reasons for it is the similar rate at which these trade associations were penalized. Therefore, since most of the trade associations, as discussed earlier, belonged to a handful of sectors (media and entertainment, transport, and wholesale and retail) and were of similar size, the resultant fines imposed on these trade associations were similar. The years 2017 and 2018 saw a total of six leniency matters (one in 2017 and five in 2018). Therefore, the figures that have been taken into account are post-reduction figures.

5.9.7 Private claim for damages in India

Jurisdictions like the US have a very healthy record of private settlements. Private individuals and groups are able to recover damages equivalent to the fines imposed by the competition authority. This, in turn, may have the possibility of undervaluing the profits made or expected by the cartel even when the fine imposed by the competition authority is not sufficient. This is gaining momentum worldwide, and now, many countries allow for private settlements to act as supplementary deterrence. Suits for damages in the US[234] and Canada do not have to wait for a positive order from the competition authority to file a case. The combination of government fines and private damages, even though sub-optimal, improves the level of optimal sanctions.

In India, private action for compensation cannot be instituted before the CCI, which was originally allowed under Section 12B of the MRTP Act, 1969, but such power was taken away from CCI by the Competition (Amendment) Act, 2007. Per Section 53N of the Act, any person can file an application before the appellate tribunal for compensation from any enterprise for any loss or damage shown to be suffered by it. A claim for compensation can only be made after a finding of a violation of competition law has been made by the CCI or appellate tribunal on any appeal filed against the findings of the CCI, contravention of the orders of the CCI under Section 42A or contravention of orders of the tribunal under Section 53Q of the Act. The onus to prove loss or damage through oral or documentary evidence is on the applicant. There is no scope for treble damages, and the tribunal can, after inquiry, order the enterprise against whom the application is made to make good the loss suffered as a result of the violation of provisions of Chapter II of the Act.

Further, the term "compensation" is not defined under the Act. The term has been interpreted by Indian courts to include both actual and expected loss[235] and need not be restricted in terms of monetary sum.[236] The Apex Court in *Organo Chemical Industries*[237] laid down three essentials for claiming damages: (i) detriment to one by the wrongdoing of another, (ii) reparation awarded to the injured through legal remedies, and (iii) its quantum being determined by the dual components of pecuniary compensation for the loss suffered and often, not always, a punitive addition as a deterrent-cum-denunciation by the law. The Act is silent on both the standard of proof to prove harm and the quantification of damages. Considering the fact that applications for compensation are civil in nature, the standard of proof will be a balance of probabilities. Therefore, a connection between loss or injury and the infringement by the undertaking has to be shown. The quantification of damage is likely to be a contentious issue, and it is yet to be seen how the tribunal responds to the quantification of loss suffered as advanced by the petitioner. The CCI, although in a few limited cases has estimated the cartel overcharge,[238] in most of the cases, has not gone into the question of cartel overcharge, which will make the quantification issue more complicated.

Provision for compensation was aimed to have a salutary effect of preventing parties from indulging in anti-competitive practices. Remedy by way of damages was expected to act as a deterrent to prohibited activities right from incipiency and motivate the producers and suppliers themselves to desist from indulging in such practices. Further, class actions were hoped to become necessary tools in the hands of similarly placed persons who are unable to institute individual petitions to claim compensation due to a lack of resources. After more than ten years of enforcement of the Act in India, while public enforcement has resulted in the imposition of an aggregate penalty to the tune of more than Rs. 14,000 crores, private enforcement has largely remained underutilized. There has not been a single case where a final ruling on the compensation has been made, and currently, five such applications are pending before the tribunal.[239] In most competition active jurisdictions, private enforcement forms a formidable deterrent mechanism. A majority of the cases in India have not reached finality and are pending either before the NCLAT or the Supreme Court.

5.9.8 Sanctions on individuals

Per Section 48 (corresponding to Section 53 of the erstwhile MRTP Act, 1969) of the Act, when a violation of provisions of the Act is done by a company, individuals in charge and responsible for the business of the company shall be held responsible for the contravention and would be punished accordingly. There are two defences provided through proviso to Section 48: first, such individuals can plead the fact that they were unaware of the anti-competitive conduct and the same was done without their knowledge, and second, they had "exercised all due diligence to prevent the commission of such contravention". Only when this is established can the burden be shifted to the individual to prove the defence per the proviso to Section 48 (1).[240]

Further, per Section 48 (2), where the contravention has been committed by a company, the director (partner in case of firm), manager, secretary or officer of the company can be held responsible if it is proved that such contravention took place with their consent or approval or can be attributable to their connivance or negligence. "Section 48 (2) of the Act attributes liability on the basis of the de-facto involvement of an officer".[241] The primary burden of proof that a person was, at the time of the contravention, responsible to the company for the conduct of its business is on the informant or on the investigating officer.

The important distinction between clauses (1) and (2) of Section 48 of the Act is that clause (1) puts the onus only on the relevant individuals who were in charge and responsible for the conduct of the firms/associations at the time of contravention of the Act and also allows this presumption to be rebutted if the relevant individuals can demonstrate that the contravention has taken place without their knowledge or that they had tried their best to prevent such contravention. In contrast, the consent, connivance or neglect of the relevant individuals is established by their de facto involvement under clause (2) and is, therefore, not rebuttable. Moreover, clause (2) applies to any individual or person that has been involved with the contravention and is not limited to the individuals in charge.

There is no provision in the Act which deals specifically with individual responsibility in case of violation done by trade associations. Trade associations are seen as a combination of constituent enterprises, and penalty, if any, can be imposed on such constituents. Per the Act, liability, in case of trade associations, can be twofold. First, the association itself can be held responsible for its actions or decisions that violated Section 3 of the Act. Second, the constituent members or enterprises of such association can be held liable as the decision agreed between the members constitutes an agreement or a concerted practice. Further, per Section 48 and the explanation provided therein, which extends the definition of "company" to include "association of individuals", violation of Section 3 can also be attributed to the members/office bearers/executive committee members who were responsible for taking decisions on behalf of the association.[242]

The CCI, especially in the initial years, did not go beyond the trade associations, which were treated as "persons" in themselves. Later, however, when the nature of the violation was repeated, the CCI started imposing penalties not just on the associations but on the decision-makers of such associations, be it in the form of executive committees, governing bodies or office bearers. The CCI has neither imposed a penalty on the constituent members nor concerned itself with the mode of recovery of such penalty from constituent members by the trade associations.

In a few cases,[243] the CCI has also imposed a penalty on office bearers of the associations on a lump sum basis without going into the details of their income. In others, the CCI penalized the executive members at the same rate at which it penalized the trade associations, which generally is 10% of the average receipts. There seems to be no separate application of mind for the executive members in light of surrounding circumstances. In the *BCDA* case,[244] a distinction was made between office bearers and executive members, where office bearers were penalized at the same rate as the trade association (at the rate of 10%), and executive members were penalized at 7% of their annual income. No reason, however, was given as to how such figures were achieved. In the *Duper Owners* case,[245] office bearers were penalized at the rate of 5% of their average income, while the trade association was penalized at 8% of average annual receipts. A similar difference was seen in the cases of *Shivam Enterprises*[246] and *TG Vinay Kumar*.[247] In the cases against trade associations, the CCI has gone after the top executives of the associations –president, vice president, secretary, treasurer and so on – who are generally responsible for the decision-making on behalf of the association, issuance of directions, release of circulars, and if we speak in terms of decided cases, calls for boycotts against members who fail to follow the diktats of the association.

Even in other cases, where the trade association was not the leader, in the initial years, a penalty was imposed only on the companies or firms engaged in cartel activity. Therefore, not all cases where the guilty verdict was finally given did the CCI penalize the executives of such enterprises. It did not hold the executives at the helm of affairs responsible for the acts of their companies. This is somewhat surprising considering that the CCI was ordering massive penalties for companies found guilty of the violation of Section 3 of the Act.[248] Even in the biggest cartel cases to date – the cement cartel case or the LPG cartel case – there was no penalty that was imposed on the officers'/managers' entities. The CCI, as always, has not provided any reasons for leaving out the executives. Needless to say, all this has a major impact on the overall deterrence that the CCI seeks to bring. There are only a handful of cases where the executives were penalized by the CCI.[249] Even recently, while it did not impose any penalty on executives in the paper cartel case,[250] in the beer cartel case, the CCI decided to impose a penalty at the rate of 3% of the average of their incomes for the last three preceding financial years of the cartel. In the *Usha International* case,[251] a penalty of Rs. 10,000 was imposed upon each of the individuals of one of the opposite parties. It is evident that similar to trade association cases, the CCI has not been consistent in finalizing the amount of penalty on individuals. Similar to other jurisdictions, the CCI has recorded the involvement of top-level executives of the company.

While there is a positive trend in terms of holding individuals responsible under Section 48 of the Act for involvement in cartelization, individual fines and even the total individual fine are minuscule. Considering the affluence and high corporate positions that are held by the majority of these individuals taking decisions on anti-competitive behaviour, individual monetary fines provide an inconsequential potential source of deterrence. There are a couple of things that need to be considered here. First, corporate managers, as experience suggests, play a decisive role in the involvement of enterprises in cartelization. These managers draw huge amounts of money as salary or other perks. Second, there is no criminal liability for these individuals. Therefore, if the penalty is not high enough, it fails to create any level of deterrence for such individuals. Unlike Section 27 (b), there is nothing in Section 48 of the Act that prevents the CCI from imposing high penalties beyond a certain percentage. Can the CCI prevent a director or manager from managing the affairs of the company for a certain period of time as a penal measure? There is no clarity on this question. Section 48 only talks about enabling the CCI to proceed against individuals who were in charge of the company or body corporate or association of individuals. The CCI did, in the *KFEF* case, ban two individuals from associating with the administration, management and governance of the association for two years. It, however, has not used similar punishments for directors or executives of companies.[252]

5.10 Summarizing observations: too generous cartel sanctions

Sanctions are the most effective weapons to deter cartel activities. To reach to a level of optimal deterrence, it is required that the punishment envisaged under the law and one which is enforced is optimal or adequate. The seriousness of the competition authority to bust and deter cartels is also reflected in its eagerness to punish anti-competitive behaviour. Many jurisdictions in the world try and reach a level of optimal deterrence, considering the practical and legal limitations of the *Becker-Landes* methodology, through a mixture of civil and criminal sanctions, including jail terms for natural persons. Even jurisdictions where criminal sanctions are not imposed believe in heavy monetary penalties which are parallel to or more than the harm caused due to the cartel and, in order to do so, have developed their own methodologies to compute fines.

This chapter highlights the inadequate, inconsistent and opaque system of sanctions for cartel activities in India, which in turn negatively impacts the degree of optimal enforcement. It has been argued that the present system of cartel sanctions in India, considering the abysmal detection rate and absence of other means of punishment, is not adequate to cause any deterrence for future cartel activities. As has been discussed earlier, it often became difficult to decipher a coherent and consistent reasoning behind the sanctions imposed on cartelists. The chapter tries to build a case for both a set of definitive and robust guidelines to impose penalties in the case of cartels. A detailed and flexible tariff mechanism which will take into account surrounding circumstances, positions and differences between enterprises will render a pre-cost benefit analysis useless.[253] Bhattacharjea and De,[254] in their work, have appropriately summarized their observations on the cartel sanctions in India:

> It is certainly evident that penalties have been far lower than what were statutorily permissible, for several reasons: the use of the turnover rather than profit base (this is quite apart from the fact that theory shows that basing fines on turnover can be counterproductive); calculations based on an average of three years (with either base) rather than the actual duration of the cartel; penalties at much lower rates than the allowable maximum; imposition of penalties on the revenue of trade associations, which would be a tiny fraction of the turnover or profits of their members; failure to impose enhanced penalties on recidivists; imposition of penalties in only a single case when offences were established in multiple similar cases; and waiver of penalty on state-owned enterprises or MSMEs.

Notes

1 Wouter P. J. Wils, *Optimal Antitrust Fines: Theory and Practice*, 29 (2) World Competition 183 (2006).
2 Eva Lachnit, *Compliance Programmes in Competition Law: Improving the Approach of Competition Authorities*, 10 (5) Utrecht Law review 31–50 (2014).

3 E. Combe, C. Monnier and R. Legal, *Cartels: The Probability of Getting Caught in the European Union*, 12 Bruges European Economic Research Papers, European Economic Studies Department, College of Europe, (2008) www.coleurope.eu/system/files_force/research-paper/beer12.pdf?download=1. (last accessed on Dec. 23, 2021).

4 Karen Yeung, Quantifying Regulatory Penalties: Australian Competition Law Penalties in Perspective, 23 (2) *Melbourne University Law Review* 440 (1999).

5 *Ibid.*

6 *Ibid.*

7 Richard Posner, *Antitrust Law: An Economic Perspective* (University of Chicago Press, 1976).

8 Michael Moore, The Moral Worth of Retribution, Chapter IV in Andrew von Hirsch and Andrew Ashworth (eds), *Principled Sentencing Readings on Theory and Policy* 150 (Hart Publishing, 2009).

9 *Ibid.*

10 Richard Posner, *Retribution and Related Concepts of Punishment*, 9 (1) The Journal of Legal Studies 71–92 (1980).

11 Herbert L. A. Hart, *Punishment and Responsibility: Essays in Philosophy of Law*, 236 (Oxford University Press, 2008).

12 Dl Baker, The Use of Criminal Law Remedies to Deter and Punish Cartels and Bid-Rigging, 69 *George Washington Law Review* 693 (2001).

13 Peter Whelan, *Competition Law and Criminal Justice, The Intersections of Antitrust* (Galloway ed., Oxford University Press, 2017)

14 Wouter Wils, Is Criminalization of EU Competition Law the Answer? in Katalin Cseres, Maarten Schinkel and Floris Vogelaar (eds), *Criminalization of Competition Law Enforcement: Economic and Legal Implications for the EU Member States* (Edward Elgar Publishing, 2006). See also, Gregory Werden, *Sanctioning Cartel Activity: Let the Punishment Fit the Crime,* 5 (1) European Competition Journal 19, 24 (2009).

15 Cartels: Sanctions against Individuals, *Policy Roundtables, OECD Competition Committee*, OECD (2003) www.oecd.org/competition/cartels/34306028.pdf (last accessed on Dec. 23, 2021).

16 *Supra note* 14.

17 *Supra note* 15.

18 Mitchell Polinsky and Steven Shavell, *The Economic Theory of Public Enforcement Law*, NBER Working Paper, No. 6993, (1999) https://papers.ssrn.com/sol3/papers.cfm?abstract_id=226410 (last accessed on Dec. 23, 2021).

19 Paolo Buccirossi et al., *Deterrence in Competition Law*, WZB Working Paper SPII 2009–14 SSOAR (2009) www.ssoar.info/ssoar/handle/document/25821 (last accessed on Dec. 23, 2021).

20 Gary S. Becker, *Crime and Punishment: An Economic Approach,* 76 Journal of Political Economy 169 (1968). See also, William M. Landes, *Optimal Sanctions for Antitrust Violations,* 50 The University of Chicago Law Review 652 (1983).

21 Lucian A. Bebchuk and Louis Kaplow, *Optimal Sanctions and Differences in Individuals' Likelihood of Avoiding Detection,* 13 International Review of Law and Economics 217 (1993).

22 John M. Connor, Robert H. Lande, *Cartels as Rational Business Strategy: Crime Pays*, 34 Cardozo L. Rev. 427, 479 (2012) cited in Hwang Lee, *Sanctions in Antitrust Cases*, Global Forum on Competition, Session IV, Directorate for Financial and Enterprise Affairs Competition Committee, OECD (1–2/12/2016) https://one.oecd.org/document/DAF/COMP/GF (2016) 10/en/pdf (last accessed on Dec. 23, 2021).

23 Promoting Compliance with Competition Law, *Policy Roundtables, OECD* (2012) www.oecd.org/daf/competition/Promotingcompliancewithcompetition-law2011.pdf (last accessed on Dec. 23, 2021).
24 *Supra note* 22.
25 *Ibid.*
26 J. M. Connor and R. H. Lande, Cartel Overcharges and Optimal Cartel Fines, *Faculty Scholarship, University of Baltimore School of Law* (2008) https://scholarworks.law.ubalt.edu/cgi/viewcontent.cgi?article=1719&context=all_fac (last accessed on Dec. 23, 2021).
27 *Supra note* 14 (G. Werden).
28 Gregory Werden and Marylin Simon, *Why Price Fixers Should Go to Prison*, 32 The Antitrust Bulletin 917–937 (1987).
29 John Rawls, *Two Concepts of Rule,* 64 Philosophical Review 3 (1955).
30 Ioannis Lianos, *Competition Law Remedies in Europe: Which Limits for Remedial Discretion?,* in Iionnis Lianos and Damien Geradin (eds) *Handbook in EU Competition Law* 362–455 (Edward Elgar: Cheltenham 2013).
31 Emmanuel Combe and Constance Monnier, *Fines against Hard Core Cartels in Europe: The Myth of Over Enforcement*, 56 (2) The Antitrust Bulletin 235 (2011).
32 Andrea Renda et al., *Making Antitrust Damages Actions More Effective in the EU: Welfare Impact and Potential Scenarios* 109–110, Report prepared for the European Commission (2007) https://ec.europa.eu/competition/antitrust/actionsdamages/files_white_paper/impact_study.pdf (last accessed on Dec. 23, 2021).
33 Guidelines on the Method of Setting Fines Imposed Pursuant to Article 23 (2) (a) of European Commission Regulation No. 1/2003, 2006, (2006/C 210/02), Official Journal of the European Union, EU (2006) (March 2019) https://eur-lex.europa.eu/legal-content/EN/ALL/?uri=CELEX%3A52006XC0901%2801%29 (last accessed on Dec. 23, 2021).
34 Harry First, *The Case for Antitrust Civil Penalties*, 76 (1) Antitrust Law Journal 127–166 (2009).
35 *Report on the Nature and Impact of Hard-Core Cartels and Sanctions against Cartels under National Competition Laws*, OECD's Competition Committee, OECD (9 April 2002) www.oecd.org/competition/cartels/2081831.pdf (last accessed on Dec. 23, 2021).
36 *Supra note* 20.
37 Bruce H. Kobayashi, *Antitrust Agency and Amnesty: An Economic Analysis of the Criminal Enforcement of the Antitrust Laws Against Corporations*, 69 The George Washington Law Review 715–736 (2001).
38 *Supra note* 26.
39 *Supra note* 31.
40 Michael A. Utton, *Cartels and Economic Collusion: The Persistence of Corporate Conspiracies* (Edward Elgar Publications, 2011). *Also see*, *Supra note* 26.
41 Kai Huschelrath, *Detection of Anticompetitive Horizontal Mergers*, 5 (4) Competition Law & Economics, 683–721 (2009).
42 Jurgita Bruneckiene, Irena Pekarskiene, *Economic Efficiency of Fines Imposed on Cartels*, 26 (1) Inzinerine Ekonomika-Engineering Economics, 49–60 (2015) (May 2019) http://webcache.googleusercontent.com/search?q=cache:rCGjotkm1ewJ:inzeko.ktu.lt/index.php/EE/article/view/7763/4975+&cd=1&hl=en&ct=clnk&gl=in (last accessed on Dec. 23, 2021).
43 Prof. Damien Geradin and David Henry, The EC Fining Policy for Violations of Competition Law: An Empirical Review of the Commission Decisional Practice and the Community's Court Judgments, GCLC Working Paper 03/05, The Global Competition Law Center Working Paper Series, https://papers.ssrn.com/sol3/papers.cfm?abstract_id=671794 (last accessed on Dec. 23, 2021).

44 Pioneer, (1980) O.J. L 60/1).
45 Article 15 (2), Council Regulation 17/62 of 16 February 1962 implementing Articles 81 and 82 of the Treaty, (1962) O.J. L 13/204.
46 Quinine, (1969) O.J. L 192/5. Fine for all companies involved was a mere 500.000 units of account.
47 Pioneer Hi-Fi Equipment, (1980) O.J. L 60/28. Fines touched 4% of total turnover of the company.
48 S.B. Volcker, Rough Justice? An Analysis of the European Commission's New Fining Guidelines, 44 *Common Market Law Review* 1285 (2007)
49 R. Richardson, Guidance without Guidance – A European Revolution in Fining Policy? The Commission's new Guidelines on Fines, 20 E.C.L.R. 361 (1999) cited in Prof. Damien Geradin and David Henry, The EC Fining Policy for Violations of Competition Law: An Empirical Review of the Commission Decisional Practice and the Community's Court Judgments, GCLC Working Paper 03/05, The Global Competition Law Center Working Paper Series, https://papers.ssrn.com/sol3/papers.cfm?abstract_id=671794 (last accessed on Dec. 23, 2021).
50 Ivo Van Bael, *The Lottery of EU Competition Law*, 4 ECLR 237 (1995).
51 Case T-23/99, LR AF 1998 v. Commission, [2002] E.C.R. II-1705.
52 Julian Joshua, *EC Fining Policy Against Cartels After the Lysine Rulings: The Subtle Secrets of X*, Global Competition Review 5 (2004).
53 *Amino Acids,* (2001) O.J. L 152/24.
54 Joined Cases T-49 & 51/02, Brasserie nationale et al. v. Commission, [2005] ECR II3033, para 178.
55 *Guidelines on the method of setting fines imposed pursuant to Article 23 (2) (a) of Regulation No. 1/2003*, Official Journal of the European Union, (2006/C 210/02) (2006) (June 2019) https://eur-lex.europa.eu/legal-content/EN/ALL/?uri=CELEX:52006XC0901 (01) (last accessed on Dec. 23, 2021).
56 Damien Geradin and Katarzyna Sadrak, *The EU Competition Law Fining System: A Quantitative Review of the Commission Decisions between 2000 and 2017*, 18 TILEC Discussion Pape, Tiburg University (2017) (March 2019) www.competitionpolicyinternational.com/the-eu-competition-law-fining-system-a-quantitative-review-of-the-commission-decisions-between-2000-and-2017 (last accessed on Dec. 23, 2021).
57 Cl. 14, *Guidelines on the Method of Setting Fines*, 2006. "Where the infringement by an association of undertakings relates to the activities of its members, the value of sales will generally correspond to the sum of the value of sales by its members". See, Judgment of the Court (Third Chamber), 11 July 2013, Case C-444/11 P, *Team Relocations v. Commission*, [2013] ECR I-000 para 76.
58 Case COMP/38.344 – Prestressing Steel, 30.06.2010.
59 (T-23/99) [2002] 5 CMLR 10.
60 LRAF 1998 v. Commission, (T-23/99) [2002] 5 CMLR 10 at p. 27.
61 Case T-213/00 CMA CGM v. Commission, [2003] ECR II-913; Case T-67/01 JCB Service v. Commission, [2004] ECR II-00049; Case T- 224/00 Archer Daniels Midland and Archer Daniels Midland Ingredients v. Commission, [2003] ECR II- 2597.
62 *DG Competition Stakeholder Study*, Aggregate Report, p. 22, European Commission, (July 2010) https://ec.europa.eu/competition/publications/reports/surveys_en.html (last accessed on Dec. 23, 2021). See also, Damien Geradin, *The EU Competition Law Fining System: A Reassessment*, TILEC Discussion Paper No. 2011–052 (October 2011) https://ssrn.com/abstract=1937582 (last accessed on Dec. 23, 2021).
63 Ian Forrester, *Due Process in EC Competition Cases: A Distinguished Institution with Flawed Procedures*, 34 European Law Review 817 (2009).

64 18 USC 3571.
65 John M. Connor, Douglas J. Miller, *The Predictability of DoJ Cartel Fines*, unpublished, SSRN (2013) https://papers.ssrn.com/sol3/papers.cfm?abstract_id=2863327 (last accessed on Dec. 23, 2021).
66 United States v. Booker, 543 US 220 (2005); Pepper v. United States, 562 US 476, 501 (2011).
67 United States v. Blakely, 542 U.S. 296 (2004).
68 Carissa Byrne Hessick, *Critical Review of the Sentencing Commission's Recent Recommendations to Strengthen the Guidelines' System*, 51 (5) Houston L. Rev. 1335, 1337 (2014).
69 John Connor and R.H. Lande, *How High Do Cartels Raise Prices? Implications for Optimal Cartel Fines*, Tulane L. Rev 80, 513 (2005).
70 United States v. Hayter Oil CO., 51 F.3d 1265, 1273 (6th Cir. 1995); United States v. Andreas, 216 F.3d 645 (7th Cir. 1999).
71 United States v. SKW Metals & Alloys Inc., 195 F.3d 83, 91 (2d Cir. 1999).
72 Ioannis Lianos et al., *An Optimal and Just Financial Penalties System for Infringements of Competition Law: a Comparative Analysis*, CLES Research Paper Series 3/2014, Centre for Law, Economics and Society (2014) https://papers.ssrn.com/sol3/papers.cfm?abstract_id=2542991 (last accessed on Dec. 23, 2021).
73 Case C-397/03, Archer Daniel Midland v. Commission, [2006] ECR I-4429 at paras 100–106.
74 I. Bos and M. Schinkel, *On the Scope for the European Commission's 2006 Fining Guidelines under the Legal Maximum Fine*, 2 (4) Journal of Competition Law & Economics 673–82 (2006).
75 *Supra note* 1.
76 Paolo Buccirossi and Giancarlo Spagnolo, *Antitrust Sanctions in the Presence of Leniency Programs*, Concurrences, no. 4, 25–9 (2006). *See also,* Vasiliki Bageri, Yannis Katsoulacos and Giancarlo Spagnolo, *The Distortive Effects of Antitrust Fines Based on Revenue*, 123 The Economic Journal 545 (2013) www.eief.it/files/2014/02/spagnolo-e-altri_ej_2013.pdf (last accessed on Dec. 23, 2021).
77 Paulo Buccirossi and Giancarlo Spagnolo, *Optimal Fines in the Era of Whistleblowers – Should Price Fixers Still Go to Prison?*, 5 (1) Lear Research Paper (2005) (May 2019) www.learlab.it/Publications/Lear-RP-05-01.pdf (last accessed on Dec. 23, 2021); J. Harrington, *Comment on Antitrust Sanctions*, 6 Competition Policy International 41–51 (2010); Yannis Katsoulacos and David Ulph, *Antitrust Penalties and the Implications of Empirical Evidence on Cartel Overcharges*, 123 Economic Journal 558–581 (2013).
78 *Supra note* 1.
79 Case T-53/03, BPB PLC v. Commission, [2008] ECR II-1333, para 336.
80 *Pecuniary Penalties for Competition Law Infringements in Australia,* OECD Report (2018) www.oecd.org/daf/competition/Australia-Pecuniary-Penalties-OECD-Report-2018.pdf (last accessed on Dec. 23, 2021).
81 The OFT, *An Assessment of Discretionary Penalties Regimes* 22 (London Economics, 2009)
82 Makan Delrahim, Deputy Assistant Attorney General, Antitrust Division, Department of Justice, The Basis of Successful Anti-cartel Enforcement Program, *Speech, Seoul Competition Forum* (2004) www.justice.gov/atr/speech/basics-successful-anti-cartel-enforcement-program (last accessed on Dec. 23, 2021).
83 Massimo Motta, *On Cartel Deterrence and Fines in the European Union* (2008) ECLR 29 (4) 20 cited in Andreas Stephan, *The Direct Settlement of*

EC Cartel Cases, 58 (3) The International and Comparative Law Quarterly 627–654 (2009). See also, Caron B. Wells and Julie Clarke, *Deterrent Penalties for Corporate Colluders*, 37 (1) University of Queensland Law Journal 107–125.

84 Hwang Lee, *Sanctions in Antitrust Cases, Global Forum on Competition*, Session IV, Directorate for Financial and Enterprise Affairs, DAF/COMP/GF (2016) 10, OECD (22 Nov 2016) https://one.oecd.org/document/DAF/COMP/GF (2016) 14/en/pdf (last accessed on Dec. 23, 2021).

85 COMP/38.069, Copper Plumbing Tubes, 03.09.2004 [2006] OJ L192/21, para 740

86 *The Compact Oxford Dictionary*, 1525 (Oxford University Press, 2ndd ed., 1991).

87 Steven L. Friedlander, *Using Prior Corporate Convictions to Impeach*, 78 Cal. L. Rev. 1313 (October 1990) cited in John M. Connor, *Recidivism Revealed: Private International Cartels 1990–2009*, 6 (2) Competition Policy International 2010. www.competitionpolicyinternational.com/assets/0d358061e11f2708ad9d62634c6c40ad/Connor.pdf (last accessed on Dec. 23, 2021).

88 Jeremy Lever, Opinion: Whether and if so how, the EC Commission's 2006 guidelines on setting fines for infringements of Arts. 81 and 82 of the EC are fairly subject to serious criticism, BDI Law and Public Procurement, Berlin (2009) http://aei.pitt.edu/14570/1/Modernisation_Final_e-version.pdf (last accessed on Dec. 23, 2021).

89 Douglas H. Ginsberg and Joshua D. Wright, *Antitrust Sanctions*, Int'l J. Competition L. (2010).

90 Walter Wils, *Recidivism in EU Antitrust Enforcement: A Legal and Economic Analysis*, 35 (1) World Competition (March 2012) (June 2019) http://ssrn.com/author=456087 (last accessed on Dec. 23, 2021).

91 Para 28 (a), Fining Guidelines (2006). Also see, Case T-141/94 *Thyssen Stahl v. Commission,* [1999] ECR II-347.

92 USSG §8C2.5 I (–) - (2).

93 Case COMP/E-2/36.041/PO, Michelin, 20.06.2001 [2001] OJ L 143, 31.5.2002, p. 1–53. Also see, *Glass Containers*, (1984) O.J. L 212/13.

94 *Supra note* 56.

95 *Supra note* 90.

96 Case T-203/01.

97 T-558/08.

98 Case COMP/AT.39523, Slovak Telekom, 15.10.2014, C (2014) 7465.

99 John M. Connor, *Oceanic Disparities in Cartel Recidivism Attitudes and Penalties*, 12 (1) Cartel and Joint Conduct Review (2016).

100 Article 23 (1) of Regulation 1/2003 provides an alternative route to impose fine for procedural infringements up to 1% of the relevant turnover. This route is unrelated to the gravity of the infringement and is a more preferred route than using non-cooperation as an aggravating circumstance to calculate fine. In Case T384/06, IBP v. Commission (2011), it has been held that refusal to cooperate cannot be used as both a procedural infringement and an aggravating circumstance.

101 USSG §8C2.5 (e). Three points to the organization's culpability score is added also where the firm took no steps to remove obstruction even when it knew about it.

102 *Setting of Fines for Cartels in ICN Jurisdictions*, Report to the 7th ICN Annual Conference Kyoto, International Competition Network Cartels Working Group Subgroup 1 – general framework, ICN (April 2008) (June 2019) https://centrocedec.files.wordpress.com/2015/07/setting-of-fines-for-cartels-in-icn-jurisdictions-2008.pdf (last accessed on Dec. 23, 2021).

103 *See generally*, Case T-15/02, BASF v. Commission, Judgment of the Court of First Instance (Fourth Chamber), 15 March 2006 II – 516; Case T-410/03 Hoechst v. Commission, [2008] ECR II-881; Case T-224/00 Archer Daniels Midland and Archer Daniels Midland Ingredients v. Commission, [2003] ECR II-2597; [1983] ECR 3369, 96/82 to 102/82, 104/82, 105/82, 108/82 and 110/82 IAZ International Belgium and Others v. Commission; Commission decision of 30 October 2002, Nintendo/Video Games, (2003) O.J. L 253/33; Graphite Electrodes, (2002) O.J. L100/1).

104 *Supra note* 33, at para 28.

105 Case T-343/06, Shell Petroleum & Others v. Commission, [2012] ECR II-000 para 155.

106 United States Department of Justice (1993), Corporate Leniency Policy, para A6, B7.

107 Nicolo Zingales, *European and American Leniency Programs: Two Models Towards Convergence?*, 5 (1) The Competition Law Review 5–60 (2008).

108 Cecile Aubert, Patrick Rey and Walter E. Kovacic, *The Impact of Leniency and Whistleblowing Programs on Cartels,* 24 International Journal of Industrial Organization, 1241–1266 (2006); C.R. Leslie, Antitrust Amnesty, Game Theory, and Cartel Stability, 31 The Journal of Corporation Law 453–488 (2006); G. Spagnolo, *Leniency and Whistleblowers in Antitrust*, CEPR Discussion Paper No. 5794 (2004) (May 2019) https://econpapers.repec.org/paper/cprceprdp/5794.htm (last accessed on Dec. 23, 2021).

109 Eva van Leur, *Characteristics of Cartel Ringleaders: An Analysis of EU Commission Decisions*, Research in Business and Economics – MaRBLe Research Papers (2013). https://openjournals.maastrichtuniversity.nl/Marble/article/view/187 (last accessed on Dec. 23, 2021).

110 Iwan Bos and Frederick Wandschneider, *Cartel Ringleaders and the Corporate Leniency Program*, CCP Working Paper 11–13, CCP http://competition-policy.ac.uk/documents/8158338/8253131/CCP+Working+Paper+11-13.pdf/9bb116b7-0026-4e48-9bb2-48308f4dadc3 (last accessed on Dec. 23, 2021).

111 Case CE/9827/13 – *Property sales and lettings investigation*, Decision dated 8 May 2015.

112 T. Banks, N. Jalabert-Doury, *Competition Law Compliance Programs and Government Support or Indifference*, 2 Concurrences, Mayer Brown (2012) (March 2019) www.mayerbrown.com/en/perspectives-events/publications/2012/05/competition-law-compliance-programs-and-government (last accessed on Dec. 23, 2021).

113 J. Murphy and N. Jalabert-Doury, "*Cartel Prevention and Compliance Regimes: It is time for a smarter Approach*", 82 Business Compliance 03–04, Baltzer Science Publishers (2013) www.mayerbrown.com/-/media/files/news/2013/03/cartel-prevention-and-compliance-regimes-it-is-tim/files/cartel-prevention-and-compliance-regimes/fileattachment/cartel-prevention.pdf (last accessed on Dec. 23, 2021).

114 USSG §8C2.5 (f) (1–3).

115 Douglas H. Ginsburg and Joshua D. Wright, *Antitrust Sanctions*, 6 (2) Competition Policy International 3–39 (2010).

116 United States v. International Paper Co – Crim. Nos. 78-H-11, 78-H-12 (S.D. Tex. 1978).

117 USSG §8C2.5 (g) (1–3).

118 Regulation 1/2003 (OJ 2003 L1/1). Also see, *Supra note* 33 at para 14 and 33.

119 Case C-298/98 P, *Metsä-Serla Sales Oy v. Commission*, [2000] ECR I-10157, para 12, 62–74). See also Joined Cases T-39/92 and T-40/92, *CB and Europay v. Commission*, [1994] ECR II-49, and Case T-29/92, *SPO and Others v. Commission*, [1995] ECR II-289.

120 Regulation 1/2003, Article 23, para 4.
121 Regulation 1/2203.
122 *Defining Hard Core Cartel Conduct: Effective Institutions, Effective Penalties*, 1 Building Blocks for Effective Anti-Cartel Regimes, Report, ICN Working Group on Cartels, 4th Annual Conference, ICN, Germany (6–8 June 2005) (March 2019) http://old.internationalcompetitionnetwork.org/uploads/library/doc346.pdf (last accessed on Dec. 23, 2021).
123 *See*, Ian Van Bael, *The Lottery of EU Competition Law*, 4 ECLR 237 (1995).
124 AIR 2017 SC 2734.
125 Case No. 105/CAC/Dec 10) (106/CAC/Dec 10).
126 Excel Crop Care Limited v. Competition Commission of India and Ors., AIR2017SC2734.
127 Para 88, *Ibid*.
128 In Re: Builders Association of India Informant & Cement Manufacturers' Association, Case No. 29/2010, order dated 31 August 2016 (CCI).
129 *Supra note* 43.
130 Uniglobe Mod Travels Pvt. Ltd. v. Travel Agents Association of India & Ors., Case No. 3/2009, decided on 4 October 2011 (CCI).
131 Nagrik Chetna Manch v. Fortified Security Solutions & Others, Case No. 50 of 2015, decided on 1 May 2018 (CCI).
132 Nagrik Chetna Manch v. SAAR IT Resources Private Limited & Ors., Case No. 12/2017, decided on 9 August 2019 (CCI).
133 *In Re: Anticompetitive conduct in the Dry-Cell Batteries Market in India*, Suo-Motu Case No. 03/2017, decided on 15 January 2019 (CCI).
134 *Supra note* 128.
135 In Re: Cartelization by public sector insurance companies in rigging the bids submitted in response to the tenders floated by the Government of Kerala for selecting insurance service provider for Rashtriya Swasthya Bima Yojna, Suo moto Case No. 2/2014, Order dated 10 July 2015.
136 Western Coalfields Limited v. SSV Coal Carriers Private Limited & others, Case No. 34/2015, order dated 14 September 2017 (CCI).
137 Delhi Jal Board v. Grasim Industries Ltd. & others, Ref. Case Nos. 03 & 04 of 2013, order dated 5 October 2017 (CCI).
138 Surendra Prasad v. Maharashtra State Power Generation Co. Ltd. & Others, Case No. 61 of 2013, decided on 10 January 2018.
139 In re: M/s Arora Medical Hall, Ferozepur, Case No. 60/2012, order dated 5 February 2014 (CCI).
140 AIMTC v. CCI, Appeal No. 60/2015, decided on 18 April 2016 (COMPAT).
141 In Re: M/s Bio-Med Private Limited, Case No. 26/2013, decided on 4 June 2015 (CCI).
142 In Re: Express Industry Council of India, Case No. 30/2013, order dated 7 March 2018 (CCI).
143 In re: Alleged Cartelization in supply of LPG Cylinders procured through tenders by HPCL v. Allampally Brothers Ltd. & Ors., Suo moto Case No. 1/2014, decided on 9 August 2019 (CCI).
144 M/s Santuka Associates Pvt. Ltd. v. All India Organization of Chemists and Druggists, Case No. 20/2011, decided on 19 February 2013 (CCI).
145 *Supra note* 139.
146 In Re: Bengal Chemist and Druggist Association, Suo moto Case No. 02 of 2012, decided on 11 March 2014 (CCI).
147 Shri T. G. Vinayakumar v. Association of Malayalam Movie Artists & others, Case No. 98/2014, decided on 24 March 2017 (CCI).
148 M/s Rohit Medical Store v. Macleods Pharmaceutical Limited & Ors., Case No. Case No. 78 of 2012, order dated 29 January 2015 (CCI); Reliance Agency

v. Chemists and Druggists Association of Baroda (CDAB) & Others, Case No. 97 of 2013, decided on 4 January 2018 (CCI).

149 Judgment of the European Court of Justice, Case C-322/81, NV Nederlandsche Banden industrie Michelin v. Commission, [1983] ECR 3461.

150 *Supra note* 148 (Reliance Agency case); M/s Maruti & Company v. Karnataka Chemists & Druggists Association & Others, Case No. 71/2013, order dated 28 July 2016 (CCI); Sudeep P.M. & others v. All Kerala Chemists and Druggists Association, Case No. 54/2015, decided on 31 October 2017 (CCI).

151 Varca Druggist & Chemist & Ors. v. Chemists and Druggists Association, Goa, Case No. MRTP C-127/2009/DGIR4/28, decided on 11 June 2012 (CCI).

152 In re: Collective boycott/refusal to deal by the Chemists & Druggists Association, Goa (CDAG), M/s Glenmark Company and, M/s Wockhardt Ltd., Suo-Moto Case No. 05 of 2013, decided on 27 October 2014 (CCI).

153 *Supra note* 148.

154 Mr. P. K. Krishnan v. All Kerala Chemists and Druggist Association & Ors., Case No. 28 of 2014, decided on 1 December 2015; Madhya Pradesh Chemists and Distributors Federation (MPCDF) v. Madhya Pradesh Chemist and Druggist Association (MPCDA) & Ors., Case No. 64/2014, decided on 15 January 2019 (CCI).

155 Indian Foundation of Transport Research & Training v. Sh. Bal Malkait Singh, President and Ors., Case No. 61 of 2012, decided on 16 February 2015 (CCI).

156 M/s. Crown Theatre v. Kerala Film Exhibitors Federation (KFEF), Case No. 16 of 2014, decided on 8 September 2015 (CCI).

157 Kannada Grahakara Koota v. Karnataka Film Chamber of Commerce (KFCC) & Ors., Case No. 58 of 2012, order dated 27 July 2015 (CCI).

158 *Supra note* 43.

159 FICCI – Multiplex Association of India v. United Producers/Distributors Forum, Case No. 1/2009, order dated 25 May 2011 (CCI).

160 Shri Vipul v. All India Film Employee Confederation & Ors., Case No. 19/2014, order dated 31 October 2017 (CCI).

161 Mr Vijay Gupta v. M/s. Paper Merchants Association, Delhi, Case No. 7/2010, order dated 24 March 2011 (CCI). See also, Shri Ghanshyam Dass Vij v. M/s Bajaj Corp. Ltd. & Ors., Case No. 68/2013, order dated 12 October 2015 (CCI).

162 Shri P.V. Basheer Ahamed v. M/s Film Distributors Association, Kerala, Case No. 32/2013, order dated 23 December 2014 (CCI).

163 Cochin Port Trust v. Container Trailer Owners Coordination Committee, Ref. Case No. 06 of 2014, order dated 1 August 2017 (CCI).

164 Shri Suprabhat Roy, Proprietor, M/s Suman Distributors v. Shri Saiful Islam Biswas, District Secretary of Murshidabad District Committee of Bengal Chemists and Druggists Association & Others, Shri Sankar Saha, Branch Secretary, Pharmaceuticals Traders Welfare Association of Bengal v. Shri Hitesh Mehta, Depot Manager of Alkem Laboratories Limited & Others, Shri Joy Deb Das, Proprietor, M/s Maa Tara Medical Agency v. Shri Rajeev Mishra, authorized signatory of Macleods Pharmaceuticals Ltd. & Ors., Case Nos. 36/2015, 31/2016 & 58/2016, order dated 12 March 2020 (CCI).

165 2013 Comp.L.R. 223 (CCI).

166 Director, Supplies & Disposals, Haryana v. Shree Cement Limited & Ors., Ref. Case No. 05 of 2013, order dated 19 January 2017 (CCI).

167 *Supra note* 161.

168 M/s. FCM Travel Solutions (India) Ltd., New Delhi v. Travel Agents Federation of India & Ors., Case No. RTPE 09/2008 (C-31/2009/DGIR), order dated 17 November 2011 (CCI); Sunshine Pictures Private Limited & Eros International

Media Limited v. Central Circuit Cine Association, Indore & Ors., Case Nos. 52, 56/2010, order dated 16 February 2012 (CCI); Mrs. Manju Tharad & Ors. v. Eastern India Motion Picture Association (EIMPA), Kolkata & Ors., Case No. 17/2011, order dated 24 April 2012 (CCI); Mr. Sajjan Khaitan v. Eastern India Motion Picture Association & Ors., Case No. 16/2011, order dated 9 August 2012 (CCI); M/s Cinergy Independent Film Services Pvt. Ltd. v. Telangana Telugu Film Distribution Association & Ors., Case No. 56/2011, order dated 10 January 2013 (CCI); M/s Peeveear Medical Agencies, Kerala v. All India Organization of Chemists and Druggists and Ors., Case No. 30,41/2011, order dated 9 December 2013 (CCI); M/s Sandhya Drug Agency v. Assam Drug Dealers Association and Ors., Case No. 41/2011, order dated 9 January 2013 (CCI); The Belgaum District Chemists and Druggists Association v. Abbott India Ltd. & Others, Case No. C-175/09/DGIR/27/28-MRTP, order dated 2 March 2017 (CCI).

169 Shri Gulshan Verma v. Union of India, through Secretary, Ministry of Health and Family Welfare & Ors., Case No. 40/2010, order dated 25 April 2012 (CCI).

170 Re: Shri B P Khare, Principal Chief Engineer, South Eastern Railway, Ref. Case No. 05/2011, order dated 21 February 2013 (CCI); Shri Vipul v. All India Film Employee Confederation & Ors., Case No. 19/2014, order dated 31 October 2017 (CCI).

171 In Re: M/s Sheth & Co., Suo Moto Case No. 04.2013, order dated 10 June 2015 (CCI).

172 In Re: Anticompetitive conduct in the Dry-Cell Batteries Market in India, Suo Motu Case No. 02/2017, order dated 30 August 2018. See also, *Supra note* 133.

173 In Re: Food Corporation of India, Reference Case No. 07 of 2018, order dated 29 October 2021; In Re: Eastern Railway, Kolkata, Reference Case No. 02 of 2018, order dated 12 October 2021; In Re: Cartelization in Industrial and Automotive Bearings, Suo Motu Case No. 05 of 2017, order dated 5 June 2020; In Re: Chief Materials Manager, South Eastern Railway, Reference Case No. 03 of 2016, order dated 10 July 2020 (CCI).

174 Re: Alleged cartelization in the matter of supply of spares to Diesel Loco Modernization Works, Indian Railways, Patiala, Punjab, Suo Moto Case No. 03/2012, order dated 5 February 2014 (CCI).

175 In Re: M/s Bio-Med Private Limited, Case No. 26/2013, decided on 4 June 2015; Re: Shri B P Khare, Principal Chief Engineer, South Eastern Railway, Ref. Case No. 05/2011, order dated 21 February 2013 (CCI); In Re: M/s Sheth & Co., Suo Moto Case No. 04.2013, order dated 10 June 2015 (CCI).

176 Indian Sugar Mills Association & Ors. v. Indian Jute Mills Association & Gunny Trade Asso (GTA), Case No. 38/2011, order dated 31 October 2014.

177 *Supra note* 135.

178 *Supra note* 142.

179 Carbonless paper, (2004) OJL 115/1; NV IAZ International Belgium v. Commission, [1983] ECR 3369.

180 In Re: Anti-competitive conduct in the paper manufacturing industry, Suo Motu Case No. 05/2016, order dated 17 November 2021 (CCI).

181 *Supra note* 162.

182 *Supra note* 136.

183 In Re: Chief Materials Manager, South Eastern Railway, Reference Case Nos. 3/2016; 5/2016; 1/2018; 4/2018, order dated 10 July 2020.

184 *Ibid.*

185 Director, Supplies & Disposals, Haryana v. Shree Cement Limited & Ors. Ref. Case No. 05 of 2013, order dated 19 January 2017 (CCI).

186 James M. Griffin, An Inside Look at the Cartel at Work: Common Characteristics of International Cartels, in Fighting Cartels, Why and How?, *Swedish Competition Authority*, 2001 (March 2019) www.konkurrensverket.se/globalasseuropaish/publications-and-decisions/fighting-cartels.pdf (last accessed on Dec. 23, 2021).
187 Director, Supplies & Disposals, Haryana v. Shree Cement Limited & Ors. Ref. Case No. 05 of 2013, order dated 19 January 2017 (CCI).
188 *Supra note* 137.
189 *Supra note* 171, at para 45.
190 In Re: Kerala Cine Exhibitors Association, Case No. 45/2012, order dated 23 June 2015.
191 *Supra note* 147.
192 *Supra note* 172.
193 Case Nos. 36/2015, 31/2016 & 58/2016, order dated 12 March 2020.
194 *Supra note* 189.
195 In Re: M/s Bio-Med Private Limited, Case No. 26/2013, decided on 4 June 2015. Also see, People's All India Anti-Corruption and Crime Prevention Society v. Usha International Ltd. & Others, Case No. 90/2016, order dated 17 March 2021 (CCI).
196 XYZ – Informant v. Tamil Film Producers Council & Others, Case No. 07/2018, order dated 22 June 2021 (CCI).
197 In Re: Cartelization in Industrial and Automotive Bearings, order dated 5 June 2020 (CCI).
198 *Supra note* 142.
199 *Supra note* 161.
200 *Supra note* 130.
201 *Supra note* 144.
202 *Supra note* 139.
203 *Supra note* 148.
204 *Supra note* 146.
205 Suo-Moto Case No. 05 of 2013, decided on 27 October 2014.
206 M/s Cinemax India Limited (now known as M/s PVR Ltd.) v. M/s Film Distributors Association (Kerala), Case No. 62 of 2012, order dated 23 December 2014 (CCI).
207 M/s Swastik Stevedores Private Limited v. M/s Dumper Ow'er's Association & Ors., Case No. 42/2012, order dated 21 January 2015 (CCI).
208 M/s Rohit Medical Store v. Macleods Pharmaceutical Limited & Ors., Case No. 78 of 2012, order dated 29 January 2015 (CCI).
209 In Re: M/s Sheth & Co., Suo Moto Case No. 04.2013, order dated 10 June 2015 (CCI).
210 Director, Supplies & Disposals, Haryana v. Shree Cement Limited & Ors., Ref. Case No. 05 of 2013, order dated 19 January 2017 (CCI).
211 A Foundation for Common Cause & People Awareness v. PES Installations Pvt. Ltd. & Ors., Case No. 43/2010, order dated 16 April 2012 (CCI).
212 In Re: Aluminium Phosphide Tablets Manufacturers, Suo-Moto Case No. 02/2011, order dated 23 April 2012 (CCI).
213 *Supra note* 137.
214 In Re: Suo-moto case against LPG cylinder manufacturers, Suo Moto Case No. 03/2011, order dated 6 August 2014 (CCI).
215 Cartelization in respect of tenders floated by Indian Railways for supply of Brushless DC Fans and other electrical items, Suo Moto Case No. 03 of 2014, order dated 18 January 2017 (CCI).
216 *Supra note* 138.

217 In Re: Alleged anti-competitive conduct in the Beer Market in India; Suo-Motu Case No. 06 of 2017; decided on 24 September 2021 (CCI).
218 *Supra note* 168 (FCM case; Sunshine Pictures case; Sajjan Khaitan case; Cinergy Independent case, M/s Peeveear Medical case and Sandhya Drug Agency case). Also see, Shri Gulshan Verma v. Union of India, through Secretary, Ministry of Health and Family Welfare & Ors., Case No. 40/2010, order dated 25 April 2012 (CCI); UTV Software Communications Limited, Mumbai v. Motion Pictures Association, Delhi, Case No. 9/2011, order dated 8 May 2012; M/s Shri Ashtavinayak Cine Vision Limited v. PVR Picture Limited, New Delhi & Ors., Case No. 71/2011, order dated 10 January 2013 (CCI).
219 *Supra note* 161.
220 Shri Ghanshyam Dass Vij v. M/s Bajaj Corp. Ltd. & Ors., Case No. 68/2013, order dated 12 October 2015 (CCI).
221 Cochin Port Trust v. Container Trailer Owners Coordination Committee, Ref. Case No. 06 of 2014, order dated 1 August 2017 (CCI).
222 In Re: Shri B P Khare, Principal Chief Engineer, South Eastern Railway, Ref. Case No. 05/2011, order dated 21 February 2013 (CCI)
223 In Re: Cartelization in Industrial and Automotive Bearings, Case No. 5/2017, order dated 5 June 2020 (CCI).
224 In Re: Chief Materials Manager, South Eastern Railway, Reference Case Nos. 3/2016; 5/2016; 1/2018; 4/2018, order dated 10 July 2020.
225 *Supra note* 126.
226 *Ibid.*
227 *Supra note* 142.
228 *Ibid.*
229 *Supra note* 137; India Glycols Ltd. v. Indian Sugar Mills Association, Case Nos. 21, 29, 36, 47, 48 & 49 of 2013, decided on 18 September 2018 (CCI).
230 FICCI – Multiplex Association of India v. United Producers/Distributors Forum, Case No. 1/2009, order dated 25 May 2011 (CCI).
231 *Supra note* 161; Also see, *Supra note* 130.
232 Cement case was referred back to Commission which in 2016 passed the same order as in 2012. See, Builders Association of India v. Cement Manufacturers' Association, Case No. 29/2010, order dated 31 August 2016.
233 Director, Supplies & Disposals, Haryana v. Shree Cement Limited & Ors., Ref. Case No. 05 of 2013, order dated 19 January 2017 (CCI).
234 John M. Connor, *Anti-cartel enforcement by the DOJ: An Appraisal*, 5 (1) The Competition Law Review 89–121 (2008).
235 Ghaziabad Development Authority v. Balbir Singh, (2004) 5 SCC 65.
236 RC Cooper v. Union of India, (1970) 1 SCC 248.
237 Organo Chemical Industries v. Union of India, (1979) 4 SCC 573.
238 In Re: Cartelization in respect of zinc carbon dry cell batteries market in India, Suo Motu Case No. 02 of 2016, order dated 19 April 2018 (CCI).
239 MCX Stock Exchange Ltd. v. National Stock Exchange of India Ltd., compensation application No. 01/2014 (based upon the judgment dated 5 August 2014 in appeal No. 15/2011); Crown Theatre v. Kerala Film Exhibitors Federation, C.A. (AT) (COMPAT) No. 1 of 2017 in competition appeal (AT) No. 16 of 2017; Sai Wardha Power Ltd. v. Coal India Ltd. & Ors., Transfer C.A. (AT) (Compensation) No. 01/2017; Maharashtra State Power Generation Company Ltd. v. Nair Coal Services Pvt. Ltd. & Ors., compensation application (AT) No. 02/2018; Sateyendra Singh & Ors. v. Ghaziabad Development Authority, compensation application (AT) No. 02/2018. Another case related to abuse of dominant position in the real estate sector. But was later withdrawn. See, Amit Jain v. DLF Limited, CA No. 01/2015 in Appeal No. 20/2011.

240 *Shiv Shankar Nag Sarkar v. CCI*, Appeal No. 34/2014, order dated 10 May 2016 (COMPAT).
241 *Supra note* 147.
242 Varca Druggist & Chemist & Ors. v. Chemists and Druggists Association, Goa, Case No. MRTP C-127/2009/DGIR4/28, decided on 11 June 2012 (CCI).
243 M/s International Subscription Agency v. Federation of Publishers' and Booksellers' Associations in India, Case No. 33/2019, order dated 23 February 2021 (CCI).
244 *Supra note* 146.
245 *Supra note* 207.
246 M/s Shivam Enterprises v. Kiratpur Sahib Truck Operators Co-operative Transport Society Limited & Ors., Case 43/2013, order dated 4 February 2015 (CCI).
247 *Supra note* 147.
248 A Foundation for Common Cause & People Awareness v. PES Installations Pvt. Ltd. & Ors., Case No. 43/2010, order dated 16 April 2012 (CCI); In Re: Aluminium Phosphide Tablets Manufacturers, Suo-Moto Case No. 02/2011, order dated 23 April 2012 (CCI); Coal India Limited v. GOCL Hyderabad & Ors., Case No. 6/2011, order dated 16 April 2012 (CCI).
249 Cartelization in respect of tenders floated by Indian Railways for supply of Brushless DC Fans and other electrical items, Suo moto Case 3/2014, order dated 18 January 2017 (CCI); *Supra note* 136 (Western Coalfields case); *Supra note* 238 (Zinc dry cell battery case) and In re: Cartelization in Tender No. 59 of 2014 of Pune Municipal Corporation for Solid Waste Processing, Suo moto Case No. 4/2016, order dated 31 May 2018.
250 *Supra note* 180.
251 People's All India Anti-Corruption and Crime Prevention Society v. Usha International Ltd. & ors., Case No. 90/2016, decided on 17 March 2021 (CCI).
252 *Supra note* 89.
253 Wouter Wils, The Commission's New Method for Calculating Fines in Antitrust Cases, 23 ELR 255 (1998).
254 Aditya Bhattacharjea and Oindrila De, *India's Cartel Penalty Practices, Optimal Restitution and Deterrence*, IEG working paper no. 424, March 2021. http://iegindia.in/upload/profile_publication/doc-010421_162610WP424fc.pdf (last accessed on Dec. 23, 2021).

6 Organizational design and anti-cartel enforcement

6.1 Introduction

The effectiveness of a competition regulator can be assessed through its performance over the years as to whether it has been able to achieve the objectives for which it was created. The previous chapters took a non-welfarist approach to assess the performance of the competition enforcement in the context of cartels on the basis of output indicators, enforcement success and cost-efficiency activities. We tried to establish the sub-optimal enforcement of cartels through enforcement and punishment parameters. The test of efficiency, however, is not limited to the number of and visibility of cases pursued. There is also a need to evaluate an agency's commitments in light of its institutional capabilities.[1]

> In order to fulfil their role effectively, (competition policy) institutions must constantly assess and reassess their mission, objectives, structures, processes and performances. It is only through realizing and adapting to changes in their environment and through carrying out the corresponding improvement that their competences, powers, budget and ultimately existence can be justified before a wider public.[2]

Institutional or organizational design can be understood through enforcement and non-enforcement activities of the competition regulator. Enforcement activities include detection, sanctions and leniency. Detection and punishment of cartels have been mostly guided by the idea of optimal deterrence. Most scholars apply the Beckerian model of optimal deterrence to cartels through the interpretation provided by Landes. Intellectual shifts in time have also led to policy shifts in tackling cartels. While there has been a divergence of opinion among theorists on the issue of cartel sanctions, it is unanimously accepted that cartel enforcement has largely remained sub-optimal. In the US, for instance, while the Sherman Act was enacted in 1890, the shift to higher penalties or criminal sanctions only happened due to the low cartel detection rate.[3] The anti-cartel enforcement with the existing scheme of sanctions in the form of nominal penalties was sub-optimal

DOI: 10.4324/9781003347651-6

and inefficient to cause any sort of deterrence. By this time, the fact that cartels could survive for long durations of time,[4] leading to great harm to the economy, was empirically proven.[5] An increase in fines, the introduction of jail terms for individuals involved in cartelization and leniency constituted the bulk of response to cover for sub-optimal enforcement. Even though the framers of the Competition Act, 2002 of India (hereafter "Act") had both the experiential knowledge of the erstwhile MRTP Act, 1969, as well as the comparative scale of jurisdictions like the US and the UK, they chose to limit cartel sanctions to civil penalties. Private claims for damages under Section 53N of the Act also remained conditional.

The objective of this chapter is to examine the priorities and processes of the CCI in order to locate the deficiencies, if any, and see if they can be remedied. The aim is also to examine portfolio diversification within the competition agency. These performance indicators affect both the reputation and utility of the competition authority.[6]

6.2 *Choice of organizational design*

Organizational design for a competition authority aims to increase the effectiveness of its discharge of duties. The design of the competition enforcement depends on the social, political and economic environment and will vary from one country to other. However, there are certain parameters on which the effectiveness of the agency is tested. Kovavcic and Hyman[7] (2012) mention nine different institutional choices while designing an enforcement mechanism for competition law. The institutional choices include choosing between autonomy versus accountability, multi-member board versus unitary executive, stand-alone versus subsidiary, single- versus multiple-enforcement agency, single-purpose versus multiple-purpose, law enforcement versus competition policy, civil enforcement versus criminal enforcement, and procedural fairness versus institutional legitimacy and internal design. The parameters on which the institutional choices are based include the following:

a *Independence:*[8] it has been widely recognized and accepted that competition authorities should be kept away from political influence and be granted, as much as possible, administrative independence from the government. A number of jurisdictions have preferred a competition authority separate from the government department or ministries. Even where structural independence is not present, and the competition authority is linked to a ministry, a functionally independent body is strived for. Independence of the agency is commonly achieved through a separate statutory status, non-interference in decision-making, well-defined criteria for appointments and organizational autonomy in terms of internal processes and finances. Further, it has to be made sure that the removal of members of the agency is not at the discretion of the government but is guided by well-laid-out principles. Independence of the agency ensures that illegitimate goals do not interfere with the decision-making process. It also brings consistency in the treatment of cases.

b *Transparency*: Transparency in decision-making helps in strengthening the legitimacy of the competition agency as it prevents the assumption of bias, arbitrariness and discrimination. Publication of reasons for enforcement decisions is important not just for consistency but also to reinforce and establish principles on which such decisions are based. Transparency, however, has to be understood in light of the need for confidentiality of sensitive information.

c *Accountability*: Independent functioning of the competition agency has to be balanced with accountability. The agency must be held answerable for its decision-making and failures. It has to be ensured that the agency is responsive, unbiased and objective in its functioning. Competition law, therefore, must specify the role and duties of each component of the agency, which then must be geared towards the objectives of the agency itself. The decisions of the competition agency are subject to review by either courts or specially constituted appellate bodies. Further, the publication of competition decisions and annual reports is part of the system to ensure accountability.

Other essential parameters include assuring due process; being well funded in proportion to the mandate; being staffed by well-educated, well-trained and non-corrupt persons; and having an appellate process that itself is well structured and non-corrupt.[9] Additional components include the structure of leadership and the nature of agency. There are two common models of leadership structure: a multi-member board and a unitary executive. A majority of the competition jurisdictions have adopted a model of a diverse and heterogeneous multi-member board. The competition agency, on the other hand, can either be a stand-alone agency or part of a larger entity. For instance, the Antitrust Division in the US is one of the eight divisions of the Department of Justice (DOJ). The effectiveness of the competition authority is also influenced by its enforcement powers which include the power to effectively investigate and collect evidence, the power to impose sanctions for violations and non-compliance and the power to recover of penalties in a timely manner. Models of organizational design and the choice of structure are jurisdiction-specific, and there is no conclusive evidence to prove the superiority of one model over the other.

An administrative model is different from a prosecutorial model, where the competition agency fights the case that it brings in an adversarial proceeding in a court. There have been debates around the choice between the two models on the basis of risk of bias and transparency. However, an administrative model which separates adjudication from investigation and where each of the two tasks is performed by different staff, as in India, seems to be the response to minimize the risk highlighted. Further, it is not necessary that the prosecutorial model will yield better results. The lack of expertise of judges and lower priority given to competition matters plagues the prosecutorial model.[10] Trebilcock and Iacobucci[11] broadly categorized the institutional structures of competition regimes into three structural models:

a *Bifurcated judicial model:* In this structure, the competition authority has investigative powers and has to come before courts of general jurisdictions for enforcement actions. The right of appeal lies in general appellate courts. Australia is an example of this model.
b *Bifurcated agency model:* In this structure, the competition authority has investigative powers and has to come to specialized competition adjudicative authorities for enforcement actions. The right of appeal lies in general appellate courts or in specialized competition appellate bodies. South Africa and Canada are examples of this model.
c *Integrated agency model:* In this structure, the competition authority has both investigative and adjudicatory powers. The right of appeal lies in general or specialized appellate bodies. This model may be most efficient administratively, but there are serious concerns around due process. It has been adopted by countries, including the EU states, China, the US and Brazil.

The initial choice of design by any country is based on its own set of priorities and possibilities.[12] Jurisdictions differ on the issue of separation of investigative and adjudicatory functions within the competition authority. While it is desirable for the sake of upholding the principle of separation of powers to keep the two functions separate, many countries integrate the two through separate wings within the enforcement agency.[13] The structure of the competition authority also differs on the basis of purpose and composition. Single-purpose agencies have the sole role of enforcement of competition law. There is a growing trend to create multi-purpose agencies by combining competition and other regulatory functions. Jurisdictions like the UK, Spain, the Netherlands and Finland are some of the recent examples of merging of regulatory functions.[14] Similarly, many countries favour a multi-member board which allows for the appointment of individuals with different expertise or skills to be put together to examine a factual scenario. There are risks, however, of disagreements leading to inconsistency in decision-making.

When India adopted the Act, it was influenced by the idea of business in a liberalized economy. Lack of infrastructure, pervasive corruption and failures of the erstwhile MRTP Act, 1969, guided the design choice in the form of a specialized independent administrative body that would focus on just one area of concern (i.e. preserving competition in the market). In light of this, India chose an autonomous, stand-alone, single enforcer, single-purpose competition agency with a multi-member board. Further, the

CCI can be categorized as a middle-aged, medium-sized regulator. Here, "middle-aged" means India falls in the bracket of competition authorities which were established after 1992 but not later than 2003. "Medium-sized" denotes that the CCI has a strength of 50–200 full-time staff.[15]

The Competition Law Review Committee, 2019 (CLRC), highlights that the Competition Act, 2002 must dispense with two separate power centres: one for investigation and the other for adjudication. The CLRC discussed that formally adopting the integrated agency model may result in considerable administrative efficiency and reduce timelines. Merging the DG's office with the CCI may also result in improvement in the domain expertise of the DG as this model may lead to the appointment of the DG through means other than deputation. It was highlighted that since, currently, the appointment of the DG is through deputation, it can result in a lack of domain expertise and institutional memory. Consequently, the CLRC recommended that the office of the DG should be formally folded into the CCI as an investigation division. However, the CLRC was mindful that integration of the office of the DG within CCI would need to be accompanied by certain best practices to ensure adherence to due process. These include:

- i Functional autonomy for the office of the DG. The DG should report directly to the Chairperson of CCI;
- ii Meaningful internal division of investigation and adjudication functions (appointment of different personnel and maintenance of firewalls);
- iii Adequate right of representation to parties and the right to examine evidence;
- iv Strong appellate forum, staffed with persons with relevant expertise;
- v Issuance of guidance on issues like imposition of penalty to ensure certainty and reduce discretion.[16]

The debate on institutional or organizational design, at its core, involves questions of independence of the decision-making body, optimization of resources (including finances), safeguard from confirmation bias and the relationship with other non-competition sectoral regulators.[17]

6.2.1 Internal design features

The structure and functioning of the competition authority form the basis of organizational design. There is no set formula or a "one size fits all" approach to reach an optimal design. Every jurisdiction has to accept the environment in which it operates and then design its structure to reach the best possible result. Organizational design is understood in the form of independence of the agency, availability of resources to the agency and enforcement of competition law. The internal structure of the agency plays a huge role in the broad framework of organizational design. It is necessary to identify the reasons for sub-optimal performance to bring in necessary changes. For instance, if it is proven that the rate of cartel detection in the country is low, flaws in the internal structure (e.g. lack of resources or domain-specific knowledge) may be one of the reasons for the same. The effectiveness, efficiency and flexibility of the regulator can be tested on certain commonly used structural yardsticks.

6.2.1.1 Structural form of organization of enforcement staff

There has always been a debate on the choice of the regulator to develop sectoral (dealing with cases on the basis of the sector) or instrumental expertise (expertise from the investigation of certain types of infringement). It has been argued that allowing case units to deal with sector cases helps in screening and detection of infringement. Market knowledge ensures quick identification of issues and disposal of investigations. It also ensures consistency in competition enforcement. The development of sector-specific case units is, however, marred with a lack of personnel. It also creates a risk of developing fragmented expertise and inconsistency of competition enforcement across different sectors. There is also a possibility that merger investigations which have to adhere to a strict timeline will be prioritized over cartel and abuse of dominance investigations. Further, problems will arise in dealing with cross-sector behaviours. Instrumental expertise is, however, achieved at the cost of sector-specific knowledge.

The division can be based on the basis of function (enforcement, advocacy, consumer protection, sector regulation, etc.), professional service (legal, economic), industry (construction, electricity, telecom, etc.), area of law (cartels, abuse of dominance, mergers), hybrid (combination of functional and divisional structures) or division of staff. There is always a tussle between the choice of sectoral or instrumental expertise. Therefore, most of the advanced systems choose a hybrid system which allows the development of both. In small and young competition regulators, allocation of staff is done on an *ad hoc* basis and depends on the complexity of the case. Large and old agencies generally have hybrid structures. In India, the CCI has a hybrid model of organizational structure[18] where the work is divided into eleven functional divisions in addition to the Secretariat.

6.2.1.2 Specialized units

Most advanced regulators have specialized divisions for dealing with complex cases of competition. This expertise is leveraged across variables like legal and economic[19] expertise, industry or sector expertise, and compliance and policy development. It has to be seen whether the staff from the economic units form a part of the case teams during investigations, become part of case teams during complex investigations or get involved in specific economic issues that arise during cases, as and when needed. Economic staff may also act as performing the role of economic analysis of cases. Case teams are organized by including specialists who have a varied knowledge base and who can provide alternate inputs and perspectives. An aggregate expertise of the case team has to be considered before case allocation. Specialized units can also be created to look at post-decision compliance, settlement or remedies. Some advanced agencies have also created specialized international units for "bilateral and multilateral policy work". These units may also form part of cases involving international issues.

In the CCI, there are two divisions, one devoted to antitrust and one to combinations. Additionally, there are two specialized legal divisions and one economic division. However, there are no specialized divisions for post-decision compliance, settlement or remedies.

6.2.1.3 Division of cases on the basis of complexity

Resource allocation may be done on the basis of the requirement of the cases. Therefore, complex cases determined on the basis of scope, impact or nature of conduct require greater allocation of resources to achieve a timely outcome.

6.2.1.4 Financial and resource independence

The decision-making independence of the competition authority has to be seen along with financial and resource independence. It has to be seen that the budgetary allocation or appointment of resource personnel to the enforcement agency does not become a pressure point for the competition authority. Insufficient funding can endanger both the quality and integrity of the decision-making process. On the other hand, it has also to be seen that the competition agency does not have "a financial stake in the outcome of the cases it investigates" as it creates a risk of moral hazard. It raises a likely presumption that decisions of the agency are not entirely based on merits. The handling of the fines has to be, therefore, closely assessed. Competition agencies in certain countries are allowed to use the penalties or fines for funding their own budget. Some scholars argue that competition agencies may be allowed to use the fines imposed as it helps in correcting, to some extent, their under enforcement. Competition agencies tend to under-sanction undertakings to reduce the incentive to appeal. Low appeal rates can then be shown as a measure to prove the success of the competition agency. Even for cases involving large corporations where the fines, though appearing to be huge in absolute terms and bring a certain level of repute for the agency, are low in terms of percentage (fines are imposed on the basis of percentage of turnover), which makes the fine more acceptable. Given the fact that competition enforcement and the sanctions are sub-optimal, the agency may be allowed to utilize these fines in a manner to improve the quality of decisions.[20]

Per Section 47 of the Act, all sums realized by way of being credited to the Consolidated Fund of India. Therefore, it does not leave any scope for the CCI to utilize any portion of the sum realized through penalties. While there is no threat of a moral hazard due to the CCI's stake in the penalties imposed, it also prevents the CCI, in order to achieve larger acceptability, to impose a deterrence level sanction on the parties involved in violation of competition law. Allowing the CCI to utilize a portion of the fine imposed in the backdrop of fining guidelines could have been explored.

In India, budgetary support to the CCI is extended by the central government in the form of grants-in-aid, which can then be used for paying out salaries and other expenses of the CCI in the discharge of its functions and for the purposes of the Act.[21] The amount of grant-in-aid remains under the discretion of the government. Although the budgetary support has increased over the years (from 19 crores in 2009–2010 to 119 crores in 2017–2018), it has proven to be short on many occasions. Lack of adequate funding not just mars the activities of CCI but also raises concerns around the independence and autonomy of the regulator. The CCI also raises money from other sources like fees and income from interest. However, these additional sources form only a minor source of income for the CCI (constituting just over 12% of the total receipts in the financial year 2017–2018), just enough to cover the rent CCI had to incur for its previous office premises. The grant-in-aid provided by the government covers the institutional expenses of the CCI, and there is little flexibility in terms of expansion of work or workforce. Data shows that in many years, the expenses of the CCI that mainly comprised establishment costs, rent, professional charges, publicity charges and expenses of fixed assets were more than the allocated budget.

Financial independence allows a regulator to "have the required flexibility and human resources that are more difficult to achieve within a traditional government setup".[22] A regulator's independence on financial matters also allows it the "freedom to allocate the resources in the manner that it considers most appropriate to meet its regulatory objectives".[23] The CLRC noted that the CCI does have a ready base of regulated entities, and it only collects fees from filings in relation to combinations.

> Accordingly, the Committee recommended that CCI may be granted a one-time corpus fund. The Committee also recommended that CCI be empowered to charge an ad valorem fee for combination filings, with specification of slabs with upper limits. It was also discussed that since the ad valorem fee may have a significant impact on businesses, the Board of the CCI must ensure that an adequate cost/benefit analysis is conducted while formulating details of the proposed fee.[24]

6.2.1.5 *Internal composition of the competition authority and staffing issues*

The appointment of members of the competition authority has to be linked with the independence of the regulator. While some jurisdictions prescribe a fixed number for the members of the regulator, others have either left it open to be fixed by the government from time to time or have provided a range in which membership will lie at any point in time. Per Section 8 of the Act, CCI comprises a chairman and "not less than two and not more than six other members to be appointed by the Central Government". The size of the CCI was reduced from ten members to seven members vide Competition (Amendment) Act, 2007. The government in 2018 decided not to fill up vacancies and reduced the strength of the CCI again from seven to four. Per the government, this would result in faster disposal of cases. The idea that a greater number of members would bring a diversity of opinion and reasoning seems to have been discarded by the government. Section 7 (4) of the Act also allowed the establishment of benches across India, which could have decreased the workload and dealt with anti-competitive practices (especially cartels) at a more local level. However, there seems to be no effort on that front as well.

Presently, the DG is appointed by the central government and is, therefore, accountable to it. Although the DG is institutionally under the central government, in practice, it acts as a specialized investigative wing of the CCI,[25] and it is the CCI which monitors the activities of the DG. The CLRC has also recommended the alignment of divergence in the *de jure* and *de facto* position by formally merging the DG's office with that of CCI's. This will also improve the domain expertise and institutional memory of the DG as the appointment will then happen through means other than deputation.

6.2.1.6 *Staffing*

Another issue with the institutional framework relates to issues of staffing within the CCI. The current workforce is largely composed of civil servants or officers from other government departments who have worked on deputations for a certain number of years. The CCI suffers from both inadequate and non-expert staffing. The CCI currently has a sanctioned strength of 197 posts, including 124 posts for professionals from law, finance and economics and 73 posts for support staff. Out of 124 posts for professionals, 91 posts are reserved for the CCI and 33 posts are reserved for the DG office. Similarly, out of 73 posts of support staff, 65 are reserved for the CCI and 8 posts are reserved for the DG office. Even though the CCI has made an effort to recruit adequate staff, present data suggests a very high vacancy of posts, especially for professionals at both the CCI and DG offices. On average, across the years, only 48% of posts of professionals and 71% of posts of staff have been filled up in the CCI. The average number of posts

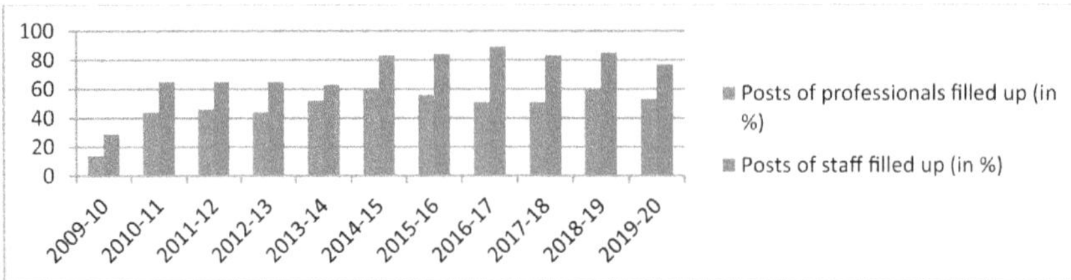

X Axis: Years of enforcement; Y Axis: Posts filled up (in %)

Figure 6.1 Posts of professionals and staff filled up in CCI (in %).

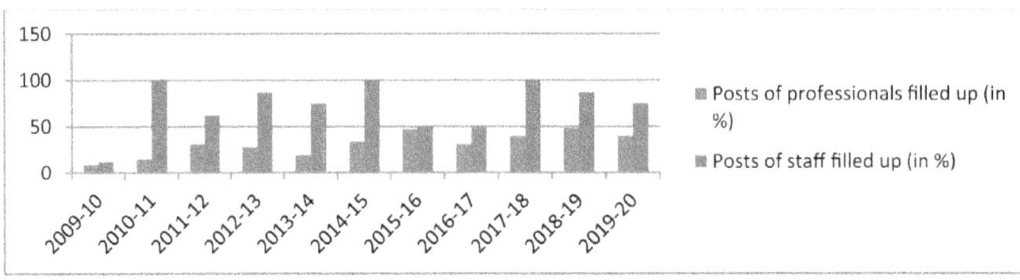

X Axis: Years of enforcement; Y Axis: Posts filled up (in %)

Figure 6.2 Posts of professionals and staff filled up in the DG office (in %)

of professionals at the DG office is at a worrying level of 31%. This might be the reason for high backlog of pending investigations by the DG. Year-wise data of staffing at the CCI and the DG has been shown in the following figures.

6.2.1.7 Qualification of persons appointed

Competition matters are complex in nature and, therefore, require a certain level of expertise and skill from the people involved in competition enforcement. A model competition law lists a broad range of skills, including "legal expertise, economic expertise, public administration skills, regulatory enforcement experience and specific industry knowledge"[26] for successful competition law enforcement. Per Section 8 (2) of the Act, all members of the CCI, including the chairperson, "shall be persons of ability and integrity" with a minimum of 15 years of professional experience in "international trade, economics, business, commerce, law, finance, accountancy, management, industry, public affairs or competition matters, including competition law and policy". Some jurisdictions prefer appointing representatives from the industry or trade associations as members of the authority. However, there is no such arrangement in India.

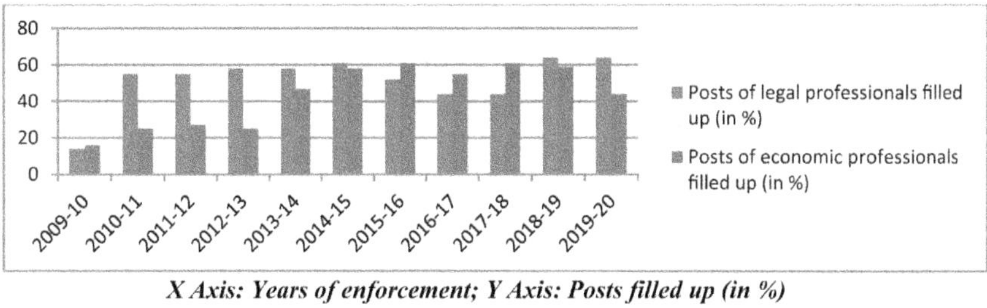

Figure 6.3 Posts of legal and economic professionals filled up in the commission (in %).

The data on recruitment of legal and economic professionals who are considered extremely important to appreciate the complexity of competition matters is also not very promising. Equal numbers of posts (36) have been created for legal and economic professionals. The average number of legal and economic professionals hired in the last ten years has been less than 50% of the earmarked posts. Interestingly, data suggests a clear shift in the hiring pattern of legal and economic professionals. Therefore, while in the first five years (2009–2014), the average hiring of economic professionals was close to around 28% of the earmarked posts, it jumped to almost 60% in the next five years. CCI has grown to realize the importance of economic assessment of competition matters, especially when quite a few of the cases have been set aside by the appellate forums on economic grounds.

The CLRC noted the need for 'generalist experts' at the senior level so that a big picture can be provided to further the CCI's advocacy efforts. In general, it also stated the need for the CCI to have seven to nine members with backgrounds of different expertise, as well as the need to embed two appropriately qualified and experienced persons at the state level so as to build expertise. Another area in which the Review Committee wants to incorporate experts is in the DG's investigative process. Accordingly, it recommended that the office of the DG could be strengthened with economics, analysts and competition law experts. The CCI may also enlist experts and government representatives in undertaking quasi-legislative work. This would reduce institutional costs that would otherwise go towards funding a separate governing board. These are the ways in which experts would help bolster the system of competition investigation and regulation in India.

Apart from these mentioned issues, the enforcement of competition law has suffered from the lack of guidelines from the CCI on various issues like imposition of penalty, understanding of turnover and use of economic evidence. The CCI's assessment often suffers from a general lack of reliable data on market conditions.

6.2.1.8 Market and sectoral studies

Market studies or sectoral inquiries are conducted by competition agencies to check for competition concerns. Market vetting is very important, especially in the case of cartels. It is proven that cartels breed and survive in a market with a certain set of features. It is, therefore, not very difficult to identify markets with features or characteristics which are conducive to cartelization, which can then be monitored by the competition agency to look for signs or patterns of cartelization. Suspicious market behaviours can then be investigated. The competition authorities generally have *suo moto* inquiry powers and do not have to wait for formal complaints to be filed to launch an investigation. The agency, therefore, can open an investigation if the market study leads to the identification of competition concerns. It can also undertake impact assessment studies to assess the effects of its enforcement. If there are positive outcomes in terms of consumer welfare or market efficiency, it can also be used as a reason to increase enforcement activities.

6.3 Procedural fairness in cartel investigations

6.3.1 Idea of procedural fairness

The idea of procedural fairness comes from the right of due process guaranteed to each individual and legal person. The idea is grounded in the fundamental principle of the rule of law. The OECD's competition committee concluded that "[t]he term 'due process' in competition proceedings does not have a clearly defined meaning and is generally understood in terms of 'procedural fairness".[27] Fairness of procedure in investigation and decision-making provides better results.[28]

Ginsburg J., in his keynote address at the International Competition Network roundtable, identified six facets of due process: "(i) delay; (ii) a hearing before the actual decision maker; (iii) a neutral decision maker; (iv) the right to confront evidence; (v) a reasoned decision based solely upon the evidence; and (vi) review by an independent tribunal".[29] Due process in competition matters largely includes acknowledgement of the principles of natural justice, neutrality of the decision-making body, certainty of application of legal and economic principles, transparency and consistency of decision-making, right of the defendant to have access to evidence and to challenge it, protection of confidential information and presence of an objective and independent appellate forum.[30] Fairness in procedure in competition cases has been a subject of debate for competition scholars around the world.[31]

Certain competition authorities have released best practice guidelines for competition proceedings to ensure transparency and due process. The European Commission's (EC) notice on best practices for the conduct of proceedings concerning Articles 101 and 102 Treaty on the Functioning of the European Union, 2011 (TFEU), "seeks to an understanding of the

Commission's investigation process and thereby enhance the efficiency of investigations and ensure a high degree of transparency and predictability in the process".[32]

Competition authorities around the world draw legitimacy for their actions from the fact that the process was transparent and due process was followed. Questions on the regulator's decision to act should be guided by merit and not on the procedure to reach such action. Transparency and due process forms the bedrock of procedural fairness and are considered vital to the rule of law. The idea of procedural fairness is not just for courts but also for administrative forums and quasi-judicial bodies. Fairness in procedure ensures that the discussion happens only on the merits of the case rather than the procedure to reach a decision. This also helps in establishing legitimacy for the competition policy and the activities of the competition agency,[33] benefitting both the businesses and consumers. Procedural fairness helps in reducing information asymmetries between parties and the competition agency, reducing procedural costs and reducing the number of appeals on procedural grounds. Different organizations have come out with broad themes or standards to assess procedural fairness.[34] The International Chamber of Commerce identified seven themes to recommend best practices for competition law enforcement: transparency, engagement, confidentiality, due process, non-discrimination, accountability and role of the courts.[35] Per OECD 2013, the US sees procedural fairness within seven components: (i) transparency on substantive standards and agency policies and procedures, (ii) open and frequent dialogue with parties under investigation, (iii) timeliness of information to the parties regarding allegations against them, (iv) opportunities that the agencies provide to the parties to respond to agency concerns, (v) opportunities that the agencies provide to parties to be heard before the agency makes an adverse decision, (vi) investigation length and (vii) publication of agency decisions.

The idea of procedural fairness ensures certain rights of defence to the parties against whom the competition enforcement has been initiated in terms of the right to be heard, the right to have access to incriminating evidence or the right to cross-examine witnesses.

6.3.2 Principles of natural justice and competition enforcement in India

Procedural fairness with respect to competition law is concerned with the process of making a decision which affects the rights of an individual or corporation or where a person has a legitimate expectation. A fair and transparent process is expected to result in a fair and reasonable decision, which protects both legal rights and legitimate expectations. The term "natural justice" is generally associated with court procedures, and the term "procedural fairness" is used in the context of administrative decision-making.

However, both these terms have a similar understanding and are interchangeably used.[36]

It is a settled position of administrative law in India that quasi-judicial bodies must adhere to the principles of natural justice. If the aim of both the quasi-decision function and administrative function is to reach a just decision, then the dividing line between the two functions in the context of the present issue is quite thin and blurred.[37] Therefore, an administrative body performing quasi-judicial functions must abide by the principles of natural justice.[38] The main objective of the principles of natural justice is to secure justice or, rather, to prevent miscarriage of justice. The idea, however, has changed and transformed over the years and is not limited to the twin pillars of *audi alteram partem* and *nemo debet esse judex in propria suo causa*. It may also differ per the constitution of quasi-judicial bodies and the statute under which they operate. Violation of principles of natural justice, therefore, has to be contextualized per *the* "nature of jurisdiction conferred upon the administrative authority, upon the character of the rights of the persons affected, the scheme and policy of the statute and other relevant circumstances disclosed in the particular case".[39] There is no particular formula for natural justice.[40]

Per Section 36 of the Act, the CCI is empowered to regulate its own procedure. The exercise of power and discharge of functions, per the said section, shall be guided by the principles of natural justice. Similar power has been given to the appellate tribunal under Section 53O where it can regulate its own procedure and is not bound by the procedure laid down in the Code of Civil Procedure, 1908, subject to adherence to principles of natural justice. The CCI and the appellate tribunal have been vested with powers of a civil court per Section 36 (2) and Section 53O (2) of the Act, respectively. Although CCI has powers similar to that of a civil court, it is not a court and is not bound by rules of evidence. The tribunal, on the other hand, per Section 53O (3), is deemed to be a civil court for the purposes of Section 195 and Chapter XXVI of the Code of Criminal Procedure, 1973 (hereafter "CrPC"). The Supreme Court in *SAIL*[41] has specifically held the CCI to be a quasi-judicial body bound by the principles of natural justice.

6.3.2.1 The hearing rule

Justice Wiles, in the famous case of *Cooper v. Wandsworth Board of Works*[42] (1863), remarked,

> a tribunal which is by law invested with power to affect the property of one Her Majesty's subjects, is bound to give such subject an opportunity of being heard before it proceeds: and that the rule is of universal application and founded on the plainest principles of justice.

There are two aspects of the hearing rule: (i) hear the other side (*audi alteram partem*) and (ii) no man should be condemned unheard (*audiatur et altera pars*). Both these versions essentially prevent quasi-judicial bodies from taking any action or passing any orders that affect the rights of the parties without giving them an effective opportunity to confront the grounds on which the decision or action is based. In simple terms, the rule implies giving an opportunity to the other side to put forward its case. This necessarily entails the right to know the case against it, receive all relevant information necessary to file a reply and a reasonable opportunity to rebut any evidence that has been used against it.[43] The principle of *audi alteram partem* requires furnishing of proper notice (one which is not vague) before decision-making. The Supreme Court has seen the requirement of notice under competition law as either statutory or where its non-issuance causes prejudice to any party.[44] Therefore, it did not read the requirement of prior notice for forming of prima facie opinion under Section 26 (1) of the Act.[45] There is no general guidance as to the stage at which notice ought to be given. The CCI may, per its discretion, call parties for the preliminary conference before passing an order to the DG to conduct an investigation. Otherwise, parties are generally made aware once an order under Section 26 (1) has been passed. This may not be done for cartel cases for confidentiality reasons. The DG is expected to publish the investigation order of the CCI under Section 26 (1) along with the report containing the investigation findings. Experience has shown that DG exercises discretion in sharing the copy of the order under Section 26 (1). It is required to share the investigation report with the parties to the proceeding and "invite any objections or suggestions including written and/or oral arguments before it".[46] It has been claimed that the DG's reports are often "not-comprehensive and at times do not include various annexures that are relied upon by the DG in the DG Report".[47] Regulation 20 (4) of the Competition Commission of India (General) Regulations, 2009, requires the DG to provide all information and evidence collected during the investigation.

The CCI must allow the opposite parties to refute any set of facts that can become the basis of the decision. This entitlement of hearing is similar to that in "judicial tribunals and body of persons invested with authority to adjudicate upon matters involving civil consequences".[48] Therefore, when CCI intends to rely on certain facts that do not form a part of the DG's report, it must be first disclosed to the opposite parties, and an opportunity to contest such fact or information must be provided. In the *BCCI* case,[49] the tribunal noted that the BCCI did not get an opportunity to contest the determination of the relevant market by the CCI, which was different from the one done by the DG. Further, the failure on the part of CCI to disclose the material on which it based its decision of abuse of dominance and the opportunity to contest it was held to be "failure of justice".

In *Interglobe Aviation*,[50] the failure of the CCI to give notice to the opposite parties of its reasons for disagreeing with the findings of the DG amounted to a violation of principles of natural justice. Per the tribunal, an effective opportunity has to be provided so that the parties could contest the allegation or finding of cartelization against them. In *Express Industry*,[51] the COMPAT noted that if the CCI disagrees with the findings of the DG, it must send a notice to the opposite parties and give them an opportunity to file a response. Failure on the part of the CCI to give reasons for the disagreement with DG's report and failure to give a reasonable opportunity to opposite parties to prove that there was no cartel to fix the price of fuel surcharge was held to be in violation of principles of natural justice.

6.3.2.2 Right to confront evidence and arguments[52]

It is an age-old principle[53] that an administrative body which is enshrined with both investigative and adjudicatory powers must comply with principles of natural justice and ensure that the defendants are given an opportunity to rebut the claims made against it. This includes a full appraisal of evidence submitted or to be considered, cross-examination of witnesses, inspection of documents and production of evidence to refute the claims made against it. The CCI has to make sure that the defendants are given access to evidence gathered during the investigation. Reliance by the DG on documents without giving an opportunity to cross-examine has been held to be a violation of principles of natural justice.[54] The COMPAT had to clarify that there is no requirement to specifically ask for cross-examination.[55]

The tribunal set aside the order of the CCI in *Bengal Chemist and Druggist Association (BCDA)*[56] for violation of the principles of natural justice as the defendants, including the office bearers of the association, were not provided with a copy of the main investigation report, which formed the basis of the adverse ruling against them.[57] Also, the penalty imposed on office bearers was set aside as the CCI failed to prove that they were personally responsible for the actions of the association. Further, the CCI failed to provide a reasonable opportunity to file objections to the investigation of office bearers. Similarly, in *Sunil Bansal*,[58] the tribunal set aside the order of CCI as it failed to provide an opportunity to the defendants to contest the findings of the investigation report. In *Vedant Bio Sciences*,[59] the COMPAT set aside the order of CCI because the DG relied on documents and affidavits without giving an opportunity to the defendants to cross-examine the deponents. In *Chemists & Druggists Association, Ferozepur*,[60] COMPAT set aside the penalty imposed on the association as the DG failed to objectively consider the objections raised by the association and "and did not advert to the unequivocal stand taken by the eight out of ten pharmaceutical companies that NOC/LOC was not mandatory for appointment of a distributor in district Ferozepur".

The CCI has to also balance applications of confidentiality in providing access to information. What information can be considered confidential that permits redaction is another issue that requires guidance from the CCI.

6.3.2.3 Decision by a person who has heard the case

The decision-maker should be the one who hears the case. Otherwise, the whole exercise becomes meaningless as the decision-maker has neither heard the witnesses nor examined the evidence. Divided responsibility is considered destructive to the adjudicatory process.[61] The process involving the DG while conducting an investigation and CCI in the course of taking a decision is similar to that of a civil court. COMPAT in *Lafarge India*[62] noted that the legislature consciously retained the adjudicatory powers with the CCI under the Competition (Amendment) Act, 2007. Therefore, even if the business of the CCI is transacted in meetings, it cannot be said that the CCI, while deciding the allegation made under Section 19 of the Act and passing orders, performs administrative functions. Thus, it was held that a situation where the Chairman authored the decision despite the fact that he was not part of the hearing would be a violation of principles of natural justice and such order would be a nullity.[63] Similarly, in *Sheth*[64] and *Indian Jute Mills Association*,[65] the participation of a member of the CCI who had not heard the matter in the decision-making was held to be a violation of principles of natural justice.[66] In *AIOCD*,[67] two of the members who signed the final order were not even members of the CCI on the date of the hearing. COMPAT held it to be in violation of principles of natural justice. The tribunal cited the Supreme Court ruling in *Union of India v. Shivraj*[68] to reiterate,

> personal hearing enables the authority concerned to watch the demeanor of the witnesses and clear up his doubts during the course of the arguments, and the party appearing to persuade the authority by reasoned argument to accept his point of view. If one person hears and another decides, then personal hearing becomes an empty formality.

6.3.2.4 Unbiased decision

6.3.2.4.1 INDIVIDUAL BIAS

A decision-maker has to be indifferent and neutral towards the parties and must decide the case on merits. This rule against bias is derived from the Latin maxim *nemo debet esse judex in propria suo causa*. The fact that he is himself a party or is interested as a party proves that he is not indifferent. Therefore, anyone who has an interest, whether pecuniary, personal or otherwise, in the outcome of the proceedings or the parties involved in the proceedings must not decide the case. Further, there is also a presumption of unfairness if the one who is deciding is the same person who investigated the case.[69] The test is whether a party can reasonably apprehend that a bias attributable to a member of the tribunal might have operated against him in the final decision of the tribunal.[70] In the case of a multi-member tribunal, proven bias on the part of even one member is enough to vitiate the order.[71]

6.3.2.4.2 INSTITUTIONAL BIAS

There is always a risk of confirmation bias[72] in systems that mix investigative and adjudicatory powers into one body. Confirmation bias means that when the competition agency first admits the case and recommends an investigation because it finds, on a *prima facie* level, a violation of the provisions of competition law, it is later compelled to confirm those prior positions in the final decision. In the cement cartel[73] case, the COMPAT noted that the chairperson who authored the decision of CCI, despite being absent during the oral hearings, had previously made his views public. This was held to indicate that CCI proceeded with the case with a predetermined objective.

6.3.2.5 Reasoned orders

Quasi-judicial bodies are required to give reasons for their orders.[74] The reasons so given must be fair and legitimate per reasonable man standards, and it should be enough to ward off any impression of bias. "Recording of reasons is the only visible safeguard against possible injustice and arbitrariness. Reasons, if given, substitute objectivity for subjectivity. Reasons, if recorded, indicate whether the adjudicatory or administrative authority has acted bona fide or otherwise".[75] The Supreme Court of India in *Rangi International*[76] noted that since the CCI and the appellate tribunal are exercising important quasi-judicial functions, it is imperative that they record reasons for their orders. The very fact that the decisions should be reasoned will force the adjudicating body to take precautions to prevent bias and arbitrariness. Unreasoned orders leave little scope for appellate forums to examine the case.[77]

As discussed in the previous chapter, while the CCI gives reasons in its decisions related to allegations of being in cartel, it has failed to provide reasons for fixing the quantum of penalty. Since Section 27 only prescribes an upper ceiling, in the absence of proper fining guidelines, CCI has been highly inconsistent in the imposition of penalties. Apart from the fact that the CCI takes into account certain aggravating and mitigating factors, it has rarely provided justification for the quantum of a penalty. The appellate forums, on multiple occasions, have questioned the rationale for the quantum of penalty and have either altered the quantum of fine or sent back the matter to the CCI for reconsideration. Similar problems lie at the heart of the imposition of individual liability. While CCI has taken a stand that investigation against the company and the concerned individuals can take place simultaneously, the COMPAT has held that the "proceedings against individuals cannot be initiated or combined with the prima facie view until contravention by the company is conclusively found on merit by the CCI".[78]

Despite the clear identification of the CCI as a quasi-judicial body[79] bound by the principles of natural justice, it has erred on multiple occasions and has violated the principles of natural justice, which led to the appellate tribunal overturning the decisions of the CCI. There have been numerous occasions where CCI failed to follow an ordinary process involving giving proper notice, denial of opportunity to cross-examine,[80] relying on statements of interested witnesses without giving an opportunity to the other side to contest it,[81] denying permission to lawyers to accompany parties at the time of deposition or investigation,[82] denial of the investigation report[83] and so on.

These decisions, especially those related to cartels, were overturned without going into the merits of the case and were remanded back to the CCI for fresh investigation, causing an unwarranted delay in the adjudication process. Setting aside the order leading to a fresh consideration of the case and passing of the order causes a minimum delay of three to four years. The effectiveness of cartel enforcement is analyzed through the speedy decision-making process and the magnitude of punishment. Both are affected because the CCI did not adhere to simple procedural requirements of adjudicatory processes. Far from creating a deterrent effect, such a scenario creates a situation wherein an appeal is incentivized, the finality of decisions is questionable, and recovery of penalty is delayed.

6.3.2.6 Dawn raids and the idea of fairness

The entire idea of dawn raids is based on the element of surprise, which means that raids are conducted at a time when the parties do not expect it to happen. This helps in preventing them from adversely affecting the search in any manner or to sanitize the place of search. Dawn raids have been used by competition agencies across the world, especially for cartel matters where gathering evidence is very difficult. Dawn raids are unannounced and are done without giving any notice to the entity in question. It would have been safe to assume that given the wide powers of the competition agency with respect to raids and investigations, there are proper checks to the exercise of such powers. However, there are no such checks or a proper methodology when it comes to the authorization or conduct of such raids. There is no known evidentiary standard that must be fulfilled that makes it necessary to conduct the raid. Dawn raids have also been questioned on the grounds of violation of the right to privacy of both natural persons (occupying positions of importance within the corporate entity) and legal entities; however, privacy protections do not extend to legal persons.[84] In the EU, prior authorization from the National Judicial Authority has to be obtained for inspection of premises other than business premises, but the necessity of such inspection cannot be questioned.[85]

The CCI derives the power of dawn raids from Section 41 (3) of the Act, which gives it a power similar to that of an inspector under Section 240A of the Companies Act, 1956, which empowers the inspector to do the acts as enumerated, namely – "(a) to enter, with such assistance, as may be required, the place or places where such books and papers are kept; (b) to search that place or those places in the manner specified in the order; and (c) to seize books and papers he considers necessary for the purposes of his investigation" – after a sanction from the Magistrate of First Class has been taken. However, the Companies Act, 1956, has now been replaced by the Companies Act, 2013, and the latter under Section 220 does away with the requirement of prior approval of the Magistrate of First Class and only contemplates compliance with the provisions of CrPC. Investigation under CrPC has been interpreted to mean both search and seizure. It is therefore required that the Act (Competition Act, 2002) is suitably amended to include the latest legal developments.

Under the present scheme of the Act, the DG cannot initiate an investigation unless an order of investigation is passed by the CCI under Section 26 (1). These investigation orders are supposed to be in the public domain. However, they are generally kept confidential for cartel cases. The Delhi High Court in *Google Inc.*[86] noted that the powers of the DG under Section 26 (1) of the Act are wider and more comprehensive when compared to the power of investigation of the police under CrPC. In light of this it held that the conduct of the investigation by the DG on the order of the CCI "is tantamount to the commencement of trial/inquiry on the basis of an ex-parte prima facie opinion".

Per Section 240A of the Companies Act, 1956, the DG exercising the powers of search and seizure akin to an inspector must have "reasonable ground of belief" that the "books and papers of, or relating to, any company or other body corporate may be destroyed, mutilated, altered, falsified or secreted". Although the expression "reason to belief" is supposed to act as a check, it is not open to scrutiny. Belief, however, has to be in good faith and must have nexus with the matter at hand. It cannot be unreasonable, arbitrary and irrational.[87] Interestingly, the Competition (Amendment) Bill, 2012 (hereafter "2012 Bill", now lapsed) sought to oust the authority of the magistrate and empower the chairman of the CCI to then empower the DG to conduct dawn raids. The necessity to conduct dawn raids was left to the discretion of the DG, which had to merely justify the fact that it had reasons to believe that the entity in question omitted to disclose or concealed any material document or such material document might be destroyed. The 2012 Bill also allowed the use of reasonable force with the help of local police authorities to conduct such raids. The 2012 Bill may be considered by some as an attempt to provide teeth to the investigative procedure. However, it raised serious concerns about procedural fairness and increased the risk of "fishing exercises".[88] The CCI has to date not come out with any guidelines on either the preconditions or the manner in which dawn raids would be conducted. The CCI may be guided by the decision of the European Court of Justice in *Nexans France SAS and Nexans SA v. European Commission*,[89] which cast an obligation on the EC to mention in its dawn raid orders "the essential characteristics of the suspected infringement, indicating inter alia the market thought to be affected". The EC must

> identify the sectors covered by the alleged infringement with which the investigation is concerned with a degree of precision sufficient to enable the undertaking in question to limit its cooperation to its activities in the sectors in respect of which the Commission has reasonable grounds for suspecting an infringement of the competition rules, justifying interference in the undertaking's sphere of private activity, and to make it possible for the Court of the European Union to determine, if necessary, whether or not those grounds are sufficiently reasonable for those purposes.

European courts, for instance, have made it clear that the inspection decisions must state the subject matter and purpose of inspection.[90] Further, in order to preserve business secrecy and the right to defence, the search has to be made only for those documents that come within the subject matter of investigation.[91]

The CCI conducted its first dawn raid in 2014, where it entered and searched the premises of *M/S JCB India Ltd.*,[92] in the matter related to abuse of dominance. Soon enough, the powers of the CCI for such raids were challenged before the court of law. The Delhi High Court, agreeing with the contention of JCB and reading the word "or" between search and seizure under Section 240A (4) of the Companies Act, 1956, to indicate mutual exclusivity of the two terms, restrained the CCI from using seized material because the search warrant from the Chief Metropolitan Magistrate only authorized the DG to search the premises. The Supreme Court in 2019 vacated the order of the Delhi High Court and affirmed the seizure proceedings of the CCI. Per the Apex Court, "provisions of Section 240A relating to search extend to authorization of seizure as well, because a search by itself will not be sufficient for the purposes of investigation". This was also held to go with the objective of Section 41 (3) of the Act, "which requires both search and seizure to allow the DG to reach to a conclusive finding". The whole episode is evidence of the stage at which the entire jurisprudence of dawn raids is.

6.4 Pendency of competition matters

6.4.1 Matters pending at the CCI and DG levels

Although competition matters are complex in nature, delay in the disposal and long pendency of cases can have a serious impact on the objective of achieving optimal enforcement. If we look at the track record of the CCI, there is no huge backlog of cases at the preliminary stage. However, the problem arises at the advanced stage. Per the Act, once the CCI forms a *prima facie* opinion that there exists a competition law violation, it orders the DG to conduct an investigation. The DG has to conduct the investigation in the stipulated time and submit the report back to the CCI. Data suggests a very low disposal rate at the DG level. One of the reasons cited for such a rate is the lack of adequate and professional resource personnel at the investigation level. The disposal rate of the DG has also gone down over the years with an increasing number of competition matters. Therefore, even if the matters pending at the level of CCI are low, it only means that CCI has formed a *prima facie* opinion on the competition law violation and either closed the matter under Section 26 (2) of the Act or directed the DG to conduct an investigation under Section 26 (1) of the Act. The final disposal of the cases is still delayed because the investigations have not been completed.[93]

6.4.2 Matters pending before the appellate tribunal

In the initial years, the COMPAT acted as the appeal forum under section 53A of the Act for orders passed by the CCI. Per Section 53B (5), appeals filed before the COMPAT have to be dealt with as expeditiously as possible and "an endeavour shall be made by it to dispose of appeals within six months from the date of receipt of the appeal". The average rate of pendency of cases (cases remaining unresolved over a year) has been reported to be around 46%, and the average disposal rate of appeals per year is around 40%.[94] This essentially means the appellate forum has not been able to adjudicate competition matters in a timely fashion. This position has to be read in light of Section 53T, which allows an appeal from the decision of the appellate forum before the Supreme Court of India. The Competition Commission of India (General) Regulations, 2009, do not provide an indicative timeline for the stage-wise disposal of cases. The Competition Appellate Tribunal (Form and Fee for Filing an Appeal and Fee for Filing Compensation Applications) Rules, 2009, and the Competition Appellate Tribunal (Procedure) Regulations, 2011, are silent in this regard.

The Finance Act, 2017, dissolved the COMPAT and vested all its powers in the National Company Law Appellate Tribunal (NCLAT). While the COMPAT was specifically created through the Competition (Amendment) Act, 2007, the NCLAT was originally created to deal with appeals from National Company Law Tribunal (NCLT) on matters related to company law. The NCLAT, apart from company law appeals, deals with appeals under the Insolvency and Bankruptcy Code, 2016, and the Competition Act, 2002. The disposal rate of competition appeals by the NCLAT is poorer than the erstwhile COMPAT. Per the data received from the NCLAT, a total of 328 appeals have been filed before the NCLAT from the decisions of the CCI up to 31 January 2021. Out of 328 cases, 80 cases have been decided, and 248 cases are pending.[95] As discussed earlier, a low success rate and a prolonged appellate procedure incentivize the filing of appeals. This is also evident from the increasing rate of appeals from the orders of the CCI. The rate of appeal shows a consistent increase in the number of appeals over the years.[96]

6.4.3 Recovery of penalty

As discussed previously, the prime objective for punishment for antitrust violations is deterrence. Penalties under the Act become all the more important in the absence of criminal sanctions for serious violations like cartels. The CCI notified the Competition Commission of India (Manner of Recovery of Monetary Penalty) Regulations, 2011 (2011 Regulations), in which it provides for an extension of time and grant of payment in instalments. To prevent delays, the CCI also provided that interest would be levied at an unspecified rate on the unpaid penalty amount.[97] This could be waived if the delay was due to circumstances beyond the control of the party. It also provides for a recovery officer who could issue a binding recovery certificate to an entity.[98] The 2011 Regulations were amended in 2014 to specify the rate of simple interest to be 1.5% for every month for which the party has delayed payment.

CCI, however, per the records, has managed to collect less than 1% of the total penalty imposed on enterprises and individuals held guilty of the violation of provisions of the Act. The main reason for this is the long pendency of appeals.[99] Most of the cases where the penalty was imposed by the CCI were appealed and are either stuck at the NCLAT or under challenge before the high courts or the Supreme Court. In some cases, parties were asked by the appellate forum to deposit a portion of the penalty at the appellate forum. No case to date has been referred to the Income Tax Department for recovery of penalty under Section 39 (2) of the Act.

Many cases, especially related to cartels, were remanded back to the CCI on procedural grounds, thereby delaying the entire process by a minimum of three to four years. The entire scenario seems to incentivize the appeal process where the parties against whom an order has been passed find it beneficial to file for the appeal because they know that it will take years before the case reaches its finality. It is possible that the enterprises try and delay the process so that they are able to recoup the penalty imposed on them through their business activities in the years post the decision of the CCI. The penalty in a system like this loses its deterrent value. By 2017, a value of up to approximately 11,000 crores in penalties imposed by the CCI were stayed by the appellate forums and approximately 3,000 crores in penalty orders were dismissed wherein, till March 2016, out of a total of 360 challenges, 114 matters were remanded to the CCI on technical grounds. This also raises concerns around the credibility of the CCI, which in turn increases the level of scrutiny that orders passed by it face in the appellate forums. The importance of the recovery of penalties has been emphasized by jurisdictions such as the EU, where the main objective of civil pecuniary penalties has been stated to be the prevention of cartelization and other offences.[100] The extent to which recovery of penalties has been prioritised for effective enforcement in the UK can also be seen through its provision allowing the competition authority to impose interest on the penalty right from the date of filing of the application for an appeal.[101]

Table 6.1 Comparative figures of the penalty imposed and realized by the CCI over the years[102]

Year	*No. of cases*	*Penalty imposed*	*Realised*	*Refunded*	*Being refunded*	*Net penalty realized as of 31 March 2020 (in crore)*		
						Realized without resorting to Section 39 (2)	*Referred to income tax authorities for realization*	*Realized by income tax authorities*
2011–2012	21	860.38	1.78	0.72	–	1.06	–	–
2012–2013	17	7,156.18	28.49	13.13	–	14.88	–	–
2013–2014	18	688.36	55.42	51.80	–	3.62	–	–
2014–2015	21	2,592.39	19.96	0.37	–	19.57	–	–
2015–2016	15	1,501.64	8.4	0.01	–	8.39	–	–
2016–2017	17	288.28	5.89	–	–	5.89	–	–
2017–2018	26	436.65	1.04	–	0.02	1.04	–	–
2018–2019	42	357.85	1.41		–	1.41		
2019–2020	16	450.89	17.89	–	–	17.89	–	–
Total	193	14,332.62	144.81	66.53	0.02	78.26	–	–

Note: Comprises all orders under Section 3 and Section 4 of the Act.

6.5 Cartels and leniency/amnesty

Cartels are secretive in nature, and a competition authority is required to devote substantial amounts of time and resources to unearth and punish them. Lack of sufficient evidence becomes a major hurdle in cartel prosecutions. Other tools to detect cartels like the use of market screens, economic assessment of collected data and dependence on complaints or information from consumers or competitors often prove to be inadequate for cartel detection. Competition authorities around the globe have therefore worked and evolved a system which enables them to detect cartels. Therefore, instead of externally looking for evidence, insider information is rooted in incentivizing defection. The leniency programme was first adopted by the US in 1978 and by the EC in 1996.

The leniency scheme is an official mechanism of the competition authority to offer immunity or lenient treatment vis-à-vis punishment to persons for their involvement in cartelization. The term "leniency" means a system of immunity and reduction of fines and sanctions (depending on the jurisdiction) that would otherwise be applicable to a cartel participant in exchange for reporting on illegal anti-competitive activities and supplying relevant information or evidence. The mechanism incentivizes coming forward with disclosures to assist the competition authority in busting cartels.[103] The idea of the leniency scheme is *to* "increase compliance with the competition rules by creating distrust between the cartelists and increasing the risk of detection".[104] The leniency scheme, therefore, increases the deterrence value of anti-cartel enforcement.

Per the scheme, a cartel member confesses voluntarily to its involvement in the cartel and provides relevant information related to cartel operation. The information provided must be relevant and crucial to the investigation process for the leniency applicant to claim a reduction of penalty. Leniency scheme also, as a long-term effect, reduces the duration of cartels, and it is also "effective in deterring the creation of cartels, or in reducing cartel overcharges, that is, constraining the prices set by those cartels that are not deterred".[105]

Leniency programs have been stated to be very effective at destabilising collusion as they incentivise cartel members to denounce the concerned cartel with reduced sanctions for their anti-competitive actions. In the US, the leniency programme is considered the most effective antitrust enforcement tool.[106] It has become one of the most important tools to detect cartels in many jurisdictions. While 45–55% of cartel cases in countries like Canada, Germany and Korea have been detected through leniency, the percentage goes up to 80% in the EU and over 90% in the USA.[107]

However, it can also be abused to generate adverse effects as it provides cartel members with a broader range of collusive strategies. Leniency may threaten punishment for any deviations from a collusive agreement, thereby increasing the sustainability of the cartel.[108] It is argued that allowing cartel members to pay a reduced fine may *ex ante* incentivise collusion (by increasing profitability)[109] and that the cartel members may find it more profitable to consensually report their behaviour if the leniency programme is suitably generous.[110] This "collude and report systematically" strategy then merely becomes a component of collusive agreements. Due to this, an optimal design for cartel enforcement would be a model which both destabilises collusion by incentivizing cartel members to report on the cartel while also ensuring that incentives are such that they do not allow for abuse of leniency programs.

In devising the optimal model, it is always advantageous to offer leniency. This is because the most effective way of detecting cartels is through incentivizing cartel members to report on the cartel themselves. There are two popular structures that have been advanced under the leniency scheme: the "first informant" rule and the ordered leniency.

Under the first scheme, the "first informant" rule, only the first informant who approaches the competition authority would be able to benefit (or benefit more) from leniency provisions. This is because allowing multiple firms to benefit from leniency would not affect normal collusion but would make "collude and report" more appealing, thereby reducing the efficacy of the enforcement mechanisms.[111] Further, under this scheme, it would be more beneficial to offer leniency before investigations. Leniency during investigations is provided when cartel members are patient, and investigations are unlikely to succeed. This would be the case where competition authorities do not have enough detection tools or powers of investigation.[112] Finally, they claim that leniency must not be restricted to first-time offenders. Under the '*ordered-leniency*' scheme, the degree of leniency is in relation to the order in which the cartel members have reported on the cartel.[113] It is argued that this facilitates greater deterrence and quicker detection by creating a "race to the courthouse". However, there would be lesser deterrence and reduced reporting in a setting where there is a low probability of detection.[114]

6.5.1 Indian experience

The CCI is empowered under Section 46 of the Act to impose lesser penalties than that prescribed under the law on any entity involved in the cartel if the entity makes full and true disclosure about the cartel and which turns out to be vital.[115] Per the Competition Commission of India (Lesser Penalty) Regulations, 2009 (Lesser Penalty Regulations), vital disclosure means full and true disclosure of information or evidence by the applicant to the CCI, which is sufficient to enable the CCI to form a *prima facie* opinion about the existence of a cartel or which helps to establish the contravention of the provisions of Section 3 of the Act. The provision, however, lays down four conditions for the imposition of a lesser penalty. First, the disclosure shall be made before the DG submits its investigation report to the CCI. Second, the disclosure has to be full, true and vital. Third, the person making the disclosure must continue to cooperate with the CCI till the completion of proceedings. Fourth, if the CCI is satisfied that such person during the course of proceedings did not comply with the condition on which leniency was granted or submitted false evidence or that the disclosure made was not vital, such person will be tried in a manner that leniency was not granted. The Competition (Amendment) Act, 2007, relaxed the earlier requirement of being the first applicant to claim leniency; as well as the previous position where no leniency was granted in case disclosures were made after the proceedings were instituted or any investigation was directed to be made under Section 26 of the Act. The Lesser Penalty Regulations, framed to streamline the process and grant leniency, adds another set of conditions for a lesser penalty. Accordingly, a leniency applicant must cease to have any further participation in the cartel from the time of disclosure. Further, the applicant must not "conceal, destroy, manipulate or remove the relevant documents in any manner that may contribute to the establishment of a cartel".[116]

There is a sliding scale of leniency from administrative penalties under the Lesser Penalty Regulations. The CCI can reduce the penalties of more than one leniency applicant. A 100% reduction in penalty may be granted if the applicant who is first to make a vital disclosure submits evidence of cartel, which enables the CCI to form a *prima facie* opinion about the existence of a cartel or where the evidence submitted by the applicant established the contravention in a matter under investigation for which and the DG/CCI do not have sufficient evidence. As a matter of practice, 100% reduction in penalty has generally not been granted in case a leniency application was filed after the investigation has started[117] but was granted[118] to the first applicant where the application brought a new cartel to the notice of the CCI. The second or third applicant in the priority status can also be granted the benefit of a reduction in a penalty up to 50% and 30% of the full leviable penalty, respectively, on disclosure by submitting evidence, providing a significant added value to the evidence already in possession of the CCI for establishing the existence of the cartel. The 2017 amendment to the Lesser Penalty Regulations now extends leniency to more than three applicants. All applicants subsequent to the third are eligible for a reduction in penalty up to 30% of the full leviable penalty.

The leniency scheme provides immunity or lenient treatment to cartel insiders for busting the cartel before CCI, and as clarified by the Competition Commission of India (Lesser Penalty) Amendment Regulations, 2017, even individuals involved in a cartel can file leniency applications which will have to disclose the names of other individuals involved in the cartel. Effective cartel detection procedures and a track record of enforcement with stringent punishment allow the leniency programme to grow and flourish. If the cartelists believe that the cartel will be detected by the competition authority and there is a credible threat of severe punishment, insiders to cartels will defect and approach the competition authority for lenient treatment. However, if the enforcement mechanism is not robust, the detection rate is poor and punishment is non-optimal, there is no fear created in the minds of the cartelists to then utilize the leniency provisions in order to save themselves from harsh punishment. It is safe to say that unless the cartel enforcement is optimal, the leniency scheme will not succeed. This is proven by the fact that in India, in an environment of sub-optimal enforcement, lengthy appeal process, the pendency of cases and ineffective punishment regime, the leniency scheme has not been very successful. In the last 12 years, there have been less than ten cases (the first case being in 2017) which have been decided through leniency applications. In contrast, more than 90% of cartel cases were decided by competition authorities in advanced jurisdictions like the US (with a rate of 60 filings per year) or the EU (investigations in 70% of cases in the period of 1998–2014 were based on leniency applications)[119] have been through leniency schemes.

Further, there are certain widely acknowledged prerequisites for a successful leniency program – high risk of detection and severity of punishment, predictability of procedures and consistency in decision-making, protection of identity and data of leniency applicants. If the cartelists do not fear detection or the punishment following detection, there is no incentive that they would see in the leniency scheme. Further, if there is no transparency or consistency in the grant of leniency, it would widen the trust deficit between the CCI and the enterprises and would prevent them from approaching the CCI.[120] Certain jurisdictions like the USA consider leniency as the most important investigation tool. In the USA, the Antitrust Division has collected more than $10 billion in fines and imprisoned more than 20 individuals in the period of 2008–2018.[121]

Predictability and consistency are the drivers of successful leniency programs. Even in the limited cases of leniency, inconsistencies have been seen in the treatment of factual scenarios. While in the *Brushless DC Fans* case,[122] the CCI read the cooperation with the CCI in conjunction with value addition through the leniency application, cooperation in itself was not seen as an independent factor to consider for leniency. However, in the zinc-carbon dry-cell batteries case,[123] even though CCI did not find the disclosure of the second and the third applicant to have significant value addition to the evidence collected, it granted a reduction in penalty based on the fact that they "cooperated and corroborated the available evidence". The CCI took into account depositions, admission of cartelization and market status for this purpose. The CCI altered its stand again in the *Pune Municipal Corporation (PMC)* case[124] decided merely a fortnight later, where it refused to extend any leniency reduction to two of the five applicants as there was no significant value addition to the evidence already in possession with the DG, despite the fact they cooperated fully with the CCI during the investigation. The metric adopted by the CCI seemed to oscillate between a "good value addition" and a "significant value addition". The reasoning provided was not only inconsistent with the Lesser Penalty Regulations but also with the approach of the CCI in the first leniency decision, where the CCI had granted a 75% reduction in penalty considering the cooperation extended in conjunction with and not independent of the value addition provided in establishing the existence of the cartel. There has also been an instance where the CCI has dismissed cartel allegations despite the same being raised by way of a leniency application on the basis that there was no evidence to show that the activities of the parties were implemented, thereby resulting in a cartel.

In the *PMC* case, even though the CCI recognized the role of one party as a ring leader of the cartel, it still extended the benefit of leniency to the enterprise. In the sports broadcasting case,[125] leniency was extended to both applicants. While the first applicant was awarded a 100% reduction in penalty even though there were instances of non-cooperation, the second applicant was only granted a 30% reduction in penalty despite adding value to the investigation.

The CCI has been giving greater significance to the stage at which the leniency application was filed. Therefore, if the application was filed before the CCI at a stage which aided the CCI in forming a *prima facie* opinion, a higher reduction is granted.[126] The Act and the Lesser Penalty Regulations do not provide any guidance as to the "nature and level of detail of the evidence that is required".[127] Confidentiality of identity of the applicant and disclosed details is another major concern around leniency in India.

6.5.2 Indian experience in comparison to the US and the EU

In the leniency programme formed by the Antitrust Division of the DOJ of the USA (post-1993[128]), full immunity is almost certain to any company, including the officers and employees of the company which comes forward to give information about cartel conduct of which either the DOJ is not aware or does not have enough evidence to pursue a conviction. The company will have to provide complete information and cooperate fully with the DOJ to claim leniency. Leniency includes immunity from criminal sanctions and a reduction in liability in cases of private actions. The US Antitrust Criminal Penalty Enhancement and Reform Act, 2004 (hereafter "2004 Act"), removes joint and several liabilities from firms granted immunity under the leniency programme and, in addition, reduces the liability of that firm to single damages. The 2004 Act, however, does not prevent the use of evidence contained in leniency statements for private claims.

Unlike in India, US leniency is only extended to the first applicant. Cooperation, if any, from subsequent applicants is only treated as a mitigating factor in the imposition of a penalty. As can be noticed, the DOJ works on the idea of "a carrot and a stick". It creates enough benefits under the leniency scheme to push cartel insiders to come forward. However, since this benefit is only extended to the first applicant, there is a high risk of facing the full rigour of sanctions. The combination of civil, criminal and private action against cartelists creates enough fear in the minds of the perpetrators to apply for leniency rather than risk detection or defection. The DOJ, in addition, also has a marker system where the reporting party who is unsure of the conduct or available evidence secures its position with the DOJ while the DOJ investigates further. The DOJ has also formulated two other extensions of the leniency program. One is the "amnesty plus" programme which allows subsequent applicants of leniency to help the DOJ to bust another cartel conduct outside the scope of the existing investigation. The applicant, if it satisfies the requirement of leniency in the second case, will get complete immunity from sanctions in the second case and also get a substantial reduction of fine in the existing case. In contrast, the "penalty plus" programme allows the DOJ to seek fines and jail terms at the highest range if the company, aware of the additional cartel conduct, chose to remain silent. These systems have not been currently developed by the CCI in India. Neither is there enough stick in the sanctions nor is there enough carrot in the leniency structure.

The leniency scheme in the EU (introduced in 1996 and later modified in 2002 and 2006), unlike in the US, does not follow the "only serve to first come" principle. It rather envisages a 100% reduction in the fine for the first applicant, up to 50% for the second applicant, 20–30% for the third applicant and up to 20% for others. Therefore, while it extends full immunity to the first applicant for providing evidence of cartel, it may also extend partial immunity to subsequent applicants.[129] Further, leniency applicants in the EU are not protected from liability in private actions. The EU Directive on Private Damages, 2014 (hereafter "2014 Directive") limits the liability of undertakings that have received immunity under the leniency programme of the EC or a national competition authority in follow-on actions for damages to their own direct or indirect purchasers or providers. This is different from the US, where the successful leniency applicants do not face joint and several liabilities in private action claims. However, while information made in leniency applications or statements are available for private claims in the US, it is kept a secret in the EU. Per the 2014 Directive, "national courts cannot at any time order a party or third party to disclose neither leniency statements, nor settlement submissions".

It has been argued by many scholars allowing multiple applicants to benefit from leniency may promote a "collude and report" strategy.[130] One of the reasons cited for the success of the leniency programme in the USA post-1993 is the "first informant" rule. The "first informant rule maximizes deterrence through strategic risk and the fear of being betrayed by somebody else".[131] "The rule generates a race to the courthouse effect in the case of investigations, which increases the expected sanctions inflicted on cartel members".[132] While scholars like Brenner[133] argue that the multi-applicant leniency scheme has failed to cause deterrence in Europe, there are also scholars who point to the benefits of the scheme in light of the absence of sufficient evidence with one cartel insider to prosecute other cartel members.[134]

There is a reason that leniency schemes are so much favoured and heavily relied upon. Leniency or amnesty programs are not resource-intensive. This means that the competition authority does not have to employ a large number of resource personnel in the collection of data which would then be required to be vetted by professionals to find any trace of cartel conduct. Further, leniency-application-led investigations have a very high success rate. While too much reliance on leniency schemes has also been questioned[135] and has been claimed to make the entire cartel enforcement passive, its success in many jurisdictions cannot be denied. This gets even more crucial in jurisdictions like India, where the detection rate is not very encouraging, and the sanctions do not have a deterrent value. The International Competition Network marks "a high risk of cartel detection based on vigorous public enforcement practice as well as sufficiently deterrent penalties" as preconditions for a leniency program.[136] The success of leniency programs is premised on the fact that the cartelists see a real risk of detection and that severe punishment will follow post-detection.

Additionally, any competition authority has to build trust through transparent and consistent decision-making.[137] A competition agency should, thus, ensure that its leniency policy is clear, comprehensive, regularly updated, well-publicized, coherently applied and sufficiently attractive for the applicants in terms of the rewards that may be granted.[138] The DOJ and the EC, in recent years, have worked towards increasing the predictability of the application of leniency provisions so that companies are not unsure about how their applications will be treated. The EC – in contrast with the previous EU Commission Leniency Notice, 1996, which required a supply of decisive evidence – offers to provide conditional immunity, immediately and in writing, to the first company to come forward with sufficient evidence to enable the EC to decide a dawn raid. The EC also allows anonymous informal guidance on hypothetical facts for entities to see whether the information provided will qualify for leniency. The EU Commission Leniency Notice, 2006, also lays down the kind of information or evidence required for availing immunity.

Sub-optimal fines allow firms to set higher prices than they would have otherwise fixed in the absence of enforcement. The expectation of a reduced fine through leniency may, in such a situation, influence *ex ante* collusion. Further, a scheme that allows multiple firms to claim leniency reduces the incentive to come out first. Multi-applicant structure with its concerns of deterrence has also been accepted due to litigation costs. This is because when many parties accept collusion, the requirement to do extensive investigation, including dawn raids, is reduced. However, it is also a fact that reduced fines on account of leniency for more than one cartel member reduces the deterrence value, which may allow more cartels to be formed, thereby increasing enforcement costs in the long run. Further, in a system where leniency statements are secreted, the multiple-applicant system does not leave anything to be utilized in private suits for damages. Buccirossi,

Marvao and Spagnolo argue that "protecting the information in leniency statements from being available for follow-on private damages actions is not necessary to preserve the effectiveness of a leniency program".[139]

As discussed earlier, the CCI has to work on all three pillars to achieve a successful leniency programme – effective enforcement, severe punishment and bridging the trust deficit between the agency and market participants through predictable and consistent decision-making. This is even more important considering the dismal rate of private action for damages, the absence of provisions that allow treble damages and non-criminalization of cartel activity for either corporations or individuals.[140] Many jurisdictions see the criminalization of cartel activity and leniency programme as mutually reinforcing. The threat of jail term is considered a vital inducement for confession. Further, the knowledge that one leniency applicant can get immunity from a jail term by becoming the whistle-blower negatively impacts the trust between cartel members, thus reducing the stability and duration of the cartel. On the other hand, criminal sanctions may dissuade applicants from applying for leniency if the system creates uncertainty in decision-making.

India does not also have a settlement or plea-bargaining mechanism for cartel cases. While a settlement mechanism is mostly seen as a procedural efficiency-enhancing tool and not as a detection tool like leniency, the experience in many countries shows that settlement structures can facilitate early inside information and cooperation.[141]

Notes

1 Timothy J. Muris, *Principles for a Successful Competition Agency*, 72 University of Chicago Law Review 165–181 (2005).

2 Philip Lowe, The design of Competition Policy Institutions for the 21st Century- The Experience of the European Commission and DG Competition, Competition Policy Newsletter (Nov 2008).

3 Alla Golub, Joshua Detre and John M. Connor, The Probability of Price Fixing: Have Stronger Antitrust Sanctions Deterred?, *Research Gate* (June 2019) www.researchgate.net/publication/255998787_The_Profitability_of_Price_Fixing_Have_Stronger_Antitrust_Sanctions_Deterred (last accessed on Dec. 28, 2021); Peter Ormosi, *How Big is a Tip of the Iceberg? A Parsimonious Way to Estimate Cartel Detection Rate*, 11 (6) Working Paper Series, Centre for Competition Policy, ESRC (2011) (June 2019) https://papers.ssrn.com/sol3/papers.cfm?abstract_id=1883448 (last accessed on Dec. 28, 2021).

4 Margaret C. Levenstein and Valerie Y. Suslow, *What Determines Cartel Success?,* 44 Journal of Economic Literature 43–74 (2006); Margaret C. Levenstein and Valerie Y. Suslow, *Breaking Up is Hard to Do: Determinants of Cartel Duration*, 54 The Journal of Law and Economics 455 (2011).

5 John M. Connor and Robert H. Lande, *The Size of Cartel Overcharges: Implications for US and EU Fining Policies*, 51 Antitrust Bull 983 (2006).

6 Maarten P. Schinkel, Lukáš Toth and J. Tuinstra, *Discretionary Authority and Prioritizing in Government Agencies*, Discussion Paper 15–058/VII, Tinbergen Institute (May 19, 2015), (June 2019) https://pdfs.semanticscholar.org/941c/430de3261309b55b6efc8d3193f8d14a4436.pdf (last accessed on Dec. 28, 2021).

7 William Kovacic and David A. Hyman, *Competition Agency Design: W'at's on the Menu?*, Paper 628, GW Law Faculty Publications & Other Works, GW Law (2012) (March 2019) https://scholarship.law.gwu.edu/faculty_publications/628/ (last accessed on Dec. 28, 2021).

8 Frederic Jenny, The Institutional Design of Competition Authorities: Debates and Trends, in Competition Law Enforcement in the BRICS and in Developing Countries-Legal and Economic Aspects, 1–57 (Springer, 2016). See also, William Kovacic and Marc Wineman, *The Federal Trade Commission as an Independent Agency: Autonomy, Legitimacy and Effectiveness*, 100 Iowa Law Review 2085.

9 *Foundations of an Effective Competition Agency*, Note by the UNCTAD Secretariat, Intergovernmental Group of Experts on Competition Law and Policy Eleventh session Geneva, UNCTAD (19–21 July 2011) (June 2019) https://unctad.org/en/Docs/ciclpd8_en.pdf (last accessed on Dec. 28, 2021).

10 Frederic Jenny, *The Institutional Design of Competition Authorities: Debates and Trends,* (June 2019) https://papers.ssrn.com/sol3/papers.cfm?abstract_id=2894893 (last accessed on Dec. 28, 2021).

11 Michael Trebilcock and Edward M. Iacobucci, *Designing Competition Law Institutions: Values, Structure and Mandate*, 41 Loyola University Chicago Law Journal 455 (2010) cited in Revised Chapter IX, Model Law on Competition (2010), *Consultations and Discussions regarding Peer Reviews on Competition Law and Policy*, Review of the Model Law, and Studies related to the provisions of the Set of Principles and Rules, Intergovernmental Group of Experts on Competition Law and Policy Eleventh session Geneva, 19–21 July 2011 (June 2019) https://unctad.org/en/Docs/ciclpL2_en.pdf (last accessed on Dec. 28, 2021).

12 Eleanor M. Fox, *Antitrust and Institutions: Design and Change*, 41 Loyola University Chicago Law Journal 473 (2010).

13 Indian Competition Act, 2002 faced a constitutional challenge on the issue of violation of principles of separation of power. See, *Brahm Dutt v. Union of India*, (2005) 2 SCC 431.

14 Annetje T. Ottow, *Erosion or Innovation? The Institutional Design of Competition Agencies – A Dutch Case Study*, 2 (1) Journal of Antitrust Enforcement 25–43 (2014).

15 Report on agency effectiveness through organizational design, 2019, Agency Effectiveness Working Group, International Competition Network (June 2019) www.internationalcompetitionnetwork.org/wp-content/uploads/2019/05/AEWG-Organisational-design-2019-report.pdf (last accessed on Dec. 28, 2021).

16 Report of Competition Law Review Committee, Ministry of Corporate Affairs, Government of India, July, 2019, p. 26.

17 Robert O'Donoghue and T. Johnston, *Notes From a Small Island: Natural Justice and the Institutional Design and Practice of Competition Authorities and Appellate Courts*, 10 (1) Competition Policy International 57 (2014).

18 The Competition Commission of India reviewed and modified its organizational structure vide an order dated 18 September 2015. See, Annual Report 2017–18, The Competition Commission of India (June 2019) www.cci.gov.in/sites/default/files/annual%20reports/AnnualReportEnglish2017-18.pdf (last accessed on Dec. 28, 2021).

19 *Supra note* 15.

20 Pierluigi Sabbatini, *Funding the Budget of a Competition Authority with the Fines it Imposes*, SSRN (October 22, 2009) (June 2019) http://dx.doi.org/10.2139/ssrn.1492666 (last accessed on Dec. 28, 2021).

21 Sec. 51, Competition Act, 2002.

22 Government of India, Report of the Financial Sector Legislative Reforms Commission (Vol 1, March 2013), para 3.5.
23 *Supra note* 22, Table of Recommendations 3.8.
24 *Supra note* 16 at p. 29.
25 CCI v. Steel Authority of India Ltd., (2010) 10 SCC 744, para 8.
26 Revised Chapter IX, Model Law on Competition (2010), Consultations and discussions regarding peer reviews on competition law and policy, review of the Model Law, and studies related to the provisions of the Set of Principles and Rules, Intergovernmental Group of Experts on Competition Law and Policy Eleventh session Geneva, 19–21 July 2011 (June 2019) https://unctad.org/en/Docs/ciclpL2_en.pdf (last accessed on Dec. 28, 2021).
27 OECD Competition Committee, *Procedural Fairness: Transparency Issues in Civil and Administrative Enforcement Proceedings*, Issues Paper, 11, DAF/COMP, OECD (2011) www.ftc.gov/system/files/attachments/key-speeches presentatiouropaien_procedural_fairness_convergence_in_process_cpi_11–18.pdf (last accessed on Dec. 28, 2021)
28 Paul O' Brien, *Procedural Fairness: Convergence in Process*, CPI Antitrust Chronicle November (2018) (June 2019) www.ftc.gov/system/files/attachments/key-speeches-presentatiouropaien_-_procedural_fairness_convergence_in_process_cpi_11-18.pdf (last accessed on Dec. 28, 2021).
29 Judge Douglas H. Ginsburg, *Due Process in Competition Proceedings*, Keynote Address, International Competition Network Roundtable on Investigative Process (March 25, 2014) Washington DC, (June 2019) www.internationalcompetitionnetwork.org/uploads/library/doc958.pdf (last accessed on Dec. 28, 2021).
30 Christopher B. Hockett, Antitrust and Due Process, 28 (2) ANTITRUST 2–5 (Spring 2014) cited in Paul Lugard, *Procedural Fairness and Transparency in Antitrust Cases: Work in Progress*, 1 CPI Antitrust Chronicle (June 2014).
31 D. Daniel Sokol, *The Case for Global Best Practices in Antitrust Procedural Fairness*, Competition Policy International (August 2018); D. Daniel Sokol, *Tensions between Antitrust and Industrial Policy*, 22 George Mason Law Review 1247 (2015); Ian Forrester, *Due Process in Competition Cases: A Distinguished Institution with Flawed Procedures*, 34 The European Law Review 817 (2009).
32 See also, DG Competition, Best Practices for the submission of economic evidence and data collection in cases concerning the application of Article 101 TFEU and in Merger cases, 2010 http://ec.europa.eu/competition/antitrust/legislation/best_practices_submission_en.pdf (last accessed on Dec. 28, 2021); European Commission guidance on function and terms of reference of the hearing officer in certain competition proceedings, 2011 (June 2019) https://eur-lex.europa.eu/legal-content/EN/ALL/?uri=CELEX:32011D0695 (last accessed on Dec. 28, 2021).
33 Daniel Sokol, *The Case for Global Best Practices in Antitrust Procedural Fairness*, Antitrust Procedural Fairness (June 26 2018); D. Daniel Sokol and Andrew T. Guzman editors, Oxford University Press, Forthcoming) (June 2019) https://papers.ssrn.com/sol3/papers.cfm?abstract_id=3220465 (last accessed on Dec. 28, 2021).
34 ICN Guidance on Investigative Process, International Competition Network, ICN (2014); Policy Roundtable on the Procedural Fairness: Transparency Issues in Civil and Administrative Enforcement Proceedings, OECD (2011); ASEAN Regional Guidelines on Competition Policy, ASEAN (2010); Best Practices for Anti-trust Procedures: the Section of Antitrust Offers its Model, American Bar Association (2015).

35 *Recommended Framework for International Best Practices in Competition Law Enforcement Proceedings, Policy Statement*, ICC Commission on Competition, Document No. 225/666, ICC (8 March 2010) https://iccwbo.org/content/uploads/sites/3/2017/06/ICC-International-Due-process-08-03–10.pdf (last accessed on Dec. 28, 2021). Also see, *Best Practices for Antitrust Procedure*, Report of the ABA Section of Antitrust Law International Task Force, American Bar Association (May 22, 2015) www.americanbar.org/content/dam/aba/publishing/antitrust_source/dec15_lipsky_tritell_12_11f.authcheckdam.pdf (last accessed on Dec. 28, 2021).

36 Guidelines Procedural Fairness (Natural Justice), *Ombudsman Western Australia, Government of Australia* (April 2019) (June 2019) www.ombudsman.wa.gov.au/Publications/Documents/guidelines/Procedural-fairness-guidelines.pdf.

37 AK Kraipak v. Union of India, AIR 1970 SC 150. See also, Rajesh Kumar v. CIT, (2007) 2 SCC 181 cited in The Board of Control for cricket in India (BCCI) v. CCI, 2015 CompLR 548 (COMPAT).

38 Maneka Gandhi v. Union of India, AIR 1978 SC 597.

39 Ramaswami, J., Union of India v. PK Roy, AIR 1968 SC 850.

40 MP Jain and SN Jain, *Principles of Administrative Law* (LexisNexis, 7th ed., 2011). See, CCI v. Steel Authority of India Ltd., 2010 Comp LR 61 (SC).

41 CCI v. Steel Authority of India Limited, (2010) 10 SCC 744.

42 Cooper v. Wandsworth Board of Works, (1863) 14 CB (NS) 180.

43 S.M. Dugar, 1 Guide to Competition Law (7th Ed., Sudhanshu Kumar, LexisNexis 2019).

44 CCI v. Steel Authority of India Ltd., 2010 Comp LR 61 (SC).

45 *Ibid.*

46 Board of Control for Cricket in India v. CCI, 2015 CompLR 548 (COMPAT).

47 Avirup Bose and Sagardeep Rathi, Procedural Fairness in India, in D. Daniel Sokol and A.T. Guzman, Procedural Fairness, 151 (Oxford Publications 2019).

48 State of Orissa v. D. Binapani Devi, AIR 1967 SC 1269.

49 The Board of Control for cricket in India (BCCI) v. CCI, 2015 CompLR 548 (COMPAT).

50 Interglobe Aviation Ltd. (IndiGo Airlines) v. CCI, Appeal No. 07/2016, order dated 18 April 2016 (COMPAT).

51 *Ibid.*

52 Douglas H. Ginsburg and T.M. Owings, *Due Process in Competition Proceedings*, 11 (1) Competition Law International 39 (April 2015).

53 Interstate Commerce Comm'n v. Louisville & Nashville RR Co, 227 US 88, 93 (1913).

54 Himachal Pradesh Society of Chemist & Druggist Alliance v. Rohit Medical Store, 2016 Comp LR 304 (COMPAT).

55 Schott Glass India Pvt. Ltd. v. CCI, (2014) Comp LR 295 (COMPAT).

56 Bengal Chemist & Druggist Association v. CCI, Appeal No. 37/2014, order dated 10 May 2016 (COMPAT).

57 See also, Alkem Laboratories Ltd. v. CCI, Appeal No. 9/2016 (COMPAT); Chemist & Druggist Association, Baroda v. CCI, Appeal No. 140/2012, order dated 18 November 2016 (COMPAT).

58 Sunil Bansal v. Jaiprakash Associates Ltd., Appeal No. 21/2016, order dated 28 September 2016 (COMPAT).

59 Chemists and Druggists Association of Baroda v. CCI, Case No. C-87/2009/DGIR, order dated 18 November 2016 (COMPAT).

60 Chemists & Druggists Association, Ferozepur v. CCI, Appeal Nos. 21/2014 to 28/2014 and IA Nos. 31/2014 to 46/2014, order dated 30 October 2015 (COMPAT).

61 Union of India v. Shiv Raj, (2014) 6 SCC 564.
62 Lafarge India Ltd. v. CCI, Appeal No. 105/2012 (COMPAT).
63 All India Organization of Chemists and Druggists v. CCI, III (2015) CPJ 4 (COMPAT).
64 Sheth & Co. v. CCI, Appeal No. 102/2015 (COMPAT).
65 Indian Jute Mills Association v. CCI, order dated 2 July 2016 (COMPAT). See also, Coal India Ltd. v. CCI, Appeal No. 1/2014 (COMPAT).
66 Chemists and Druggists Association of Baroda v. CCI, Case No. C-87/2009/DGIR, order dated 18 November 2016 (COMPAT).
67 All India Organization of Chemists and Druggists v. CCI, III (2015) CPJ 4 COMPAT.
68 (2014) 6 SCC 564.
69 Pieter Van Cleynenbreugel, Effectiveness through fairness? 'Due process' as Institutional Precondition for Effective Decentralised EU Competition Law Enforcement, 9th ASCOLA Conference Warsaw 2014 on Procedural Fairness in Competition Proceedings, Centre for Antitrust and Regulatory Studies, University of Warsaw (26–28 June 2014) www.ascola-conference-2014.wz.uw.edu.pl/conference_papers/VanCleynenbreugel.pdf (last accessed on Dec. 28, 2021).
70 Manaklal v. Prem Chand Singhvi, AIR 1957 SC 425.
71 Narayana v. State of Andhra Pradesh, AIR 1958 AP 636.
72 Ian Forrester, Due Process in EC Competition Cases: A Distinguished Institution With Flawed Procedures (2009) 34 E L Rev 817.
73 Builders Association of India v. Cement Manufacturers Association & Ors. Case No. 29/2010 (COMPAT).
74 Siemens Engineering and Manufacturing Co. Ltd. v. Union of India, AIR 1976 SC 1785.
75 Lord Denning, J, Breen v. Amalgamated Engineering Union, (1971) 1 All ER 1148. See, SN Mukherjee v. Union of India, AIR 1990 SC 1984; Raipur Development Authority v. Chokhamal Contractors, AIR 1990 SC 1426.
76 Rangi International Ltd. v. Nova scotia Bank, (2013) 7 SCC 160.
77 M/s DLF Limited v. Competition Commission of India & Ors., Appeal No. 20 of 2011 (COMPAT). See also, The Board of Control for cricket in India (BCCI) v. CCI, 2015 CompLR 548 (COMPAT).
78 Shib Sankar Nag Sarkar and another v. CCI and others; Appeal No. 42/2014 (COMPAT); Swapan Kumar Karak v. CCI and others; Appeal No. 09/2016 (COMPAT); Alkem Laboratories Limited v. CCI and others; Appeal No. 05/2016 (COMPAT); A. N. Mohana Kurup and another v. CCI and others; and Appeal No. 40 of 2016 (COMPAT).
79 CCI v. SAIL, (2010) 10 SCC 744.
80 *Supra note* 54.
81 Schott Glass India Private Limited v. The Competition Commission of India, (2014) CompLR. 295 (COMPAT).
82 Oriental Rubber Industries v. Competition Commission of India, (2016) CompLR 611 (Delhi).
83 Shib Sankar Nag Sarkar v. Competition Commission of India, (2016) SCC OnLine COMPAT 420.
84 Council Regulation No. 1/2003.
85 David Anderson and Rachel Cuff, *Cartels in the European Union: Procedural Fairness for Defendants and Claimants*, 34 (3) (1) Fordham International Law Journal 385 (2011). Also see, Implementation of the Rules on Competition Laid Down in Articles 81 and 82 of the Treaty Art. 21, Council Regulation No. 1/2003, 2003 O.J. L 1/1, OECD, https://eur-lex.europa.eu/legal-content/EN/ALL/?uri=celex%3A32003R0001 (last accessed on Dec. 28, 2021).

86 Google Inc. v. CCI, 2015 SCC OnLine Del 8992, cited in Vedika M. Kumar et al., *Systematizing Fair Play: Key Issues in the Indian Competition Law Regime,* Vidhi Centre for Legal Policy (2017) https://vidhilegalpolicy.in/wp-content/uploads/2019/05/SystematizingFairplay-KeyIssuesintheIndianCompetitionLawRegimeNovember2017.pdf (last accessed on Dec. 28, 2021).
87 Calcutta Discount Company Limited v. Income Tax Officer, 1961 *SCR (2) 241.*
88 Avirup Bose, Circumstantial Evidence and Dawn Raids: A New Era of Antitrust Investigation in India, *Competition Law Reports* (April 4, 2013), https://ssrn.com/abstract=2544832 (last accessed on Dec. 28, 2021).
89 Case T-135/09, Judgment of the General Court of 14 November 2012.
90 Para 4, Article 20, Council Regulation No. 1/2003, Implementation of the rules of competition.
91 Constanza Nicolosi, *No Fishing at Dawn (Raids) ! Defining the scope of the Commission's Inpection Power in Antitrust Proceedings*, 8 Queen Mary Law Journal (Special Conference Issue) 53 (2016). www.qmul.ac.uk/law/media/law/docs/undergrad/06-Nicolosi.pdf (last accessed on Dec. 28, 2021).
92 *M/s. Bull Machines Pvt. Ltd. v. M/s. JCB India Ltd. & Anr., Case No. 105 of 2013 (CCI).*
93 Annual Reports 2019–2020, Competition Commission of India (June 2019), www.cci.gov.in/annual-reports.
94 Vedika M. Kumar et al., *Systematizing Fairplay: Key Issues in the Indian Competition Law Regime*, Vidhi Centre for Legal Policy, 2017 https://vidhilegalpolicy.in/wp-content/uploads/2019/05/SystematizingFairplay-KeyIssuesintheIndianCompetitionLawRegimeNovember2017.pdf (last accessed on Dec. 28, 2021).
95 *Shri Anurag Singh Thakur, Union Minister of State for Finance & Corporate Affairs in a Written Reply to a Question in Lok Sabha.* See, https://pib.gov.in/PressReleaseIframePage.aspx?PRID=1696290 (last accessed on Dec. 28, 2021).
96 Annual Reports 2009–2018, Competition Commission of India www.cci.gov.in/annual-reports (last accessed on Dec. 28, 2021).
97 Clause 5, Competition Commission of India (Manner of Recovery of Monetary Penalty) Regulations, 2011.
98 *Supra note* 97 see Clause 9 (c).
99 Arun Jaitley, Former Minister of Corporate Affairs, *Answer to question on cases of cartelization,* Unstarred Question No. 6656, Lok Sabha, (Apr. 6 2018) www.mca.gov.in/Ministry/pdf/lu6656_18042018.pdf (last accessed on Dec. 28, 2021). See also, Amit Bansal, Shruti Gupta and Semanti Sengupta, Just 0.3% of CCI Penalties Recovered for Now, but Progress Made in Handling of Antitrust Cases, *Business Today*, (October 23, 2018) www.businesstoday.in/opinion/columns/just-0-per-cent-of-cci-penalties-recovered-for-now-but-progress-made-in-handling-of-antitrust-cases/story/286148.html (last accessed on Dec. 28, 2021).
100 OECD, *Pecuniary Penalties for Competition Law Infringements in Australia* (2018) p. 36 www.oecd.org/daf/competition/Australia-Pecuniary-Penalties-OECD-Report-2018.pdf (last accessed on Dec. 28, 2021).
101 Rule 27 of the Competition Appeal Tribunal Rules; *Napp Pharmaceutical Holdings Ltd. v. Director general of Fair Trading*, [2002] 4 All ER 376, para 542.
102 Annual Reports 2017–2018, Competition Commission of India. P. 21 (June 2019) www.cci.gov.in/annual-reports (last accessed on Dec. 28, 2021).
103 Anti Cartel Enforcement Manual Drafting and Implementing an Effective Leniency Policy, Chapter 2, ICN (June 2019) www.internationalcompetitionnetwork.org/uploads/library/doc1005.pdf (last accessed on Dec. 28, 2021).

104 Antonio Caruso, Leniency Programmes and Protection of Confidentiality: The Experience of the European Commission, 454 Journal of European Competition Law and Practice (2010).

105 Joan Brorrell et al., *25 Years of leniency programs: A Turning point in Cartel Investigations*, 1 (2) Antitrust Chronicle 12 Competition Policy International (Jan 2019) www.competitionpolicyinternational.com/wp-content/uploads/2019/01/AC_January_2019_2.pdf (last accessed on Dec. 28, 2021). *Also see,* James E. Harrington Jr and Myong H. Chang, *Modeling the Birth and Death of Cartels with an Application to Evaluating Competition Policy,* 7 (6) Journal of the European Economic Association 1400–1435 (2009); Iwan Bos, Stephen Davies, Joseph E. Harrington Jr. and Peter L. Ormosi, *Does Enforcement Deter Cartels? A Tale of Two Tails,* 59 International Journal of Industrial Organization 372–405 (2018).

106 Zhijun Chen and Patrick Rey, *On the Design of Leniency Programs*, 56 Journal of Law and Economics 917, 917 (2013).

107 *Challenges and Co-ordination of Leniency Programmes – Background Note by the Secretariat*, Working Party No. 3 on Co-operation and Enforcement, Directorate for Finance and Enterprise Affairs Competition Committee, DAF/COMP/WP3 (2018) 1, OECD, (June 1, 2018), https://one.oecd.org/document/DAF/COMP/WP3 (2018) 1/en/pdf (last accessed on Dec. 28, 2021).

108 *Supra note* 107 at p. 919.

109 Massimo Motta and Michele Polo, *Leniency Programs and Cartel Prosecution*, 21 International Journal of Industrial Organization 347, 349 (2003).

110 Giancarlo Spagnolo, Self-Defeating Antitrust Laws: How Leniency Programs Solve *Bertrand's Paradox and Enforce Collusion in Auctions*, Fondazione Eni Enrico Mattei [FEEM] Working Paper No. 52.2000 https://papers.ssrn.com/sol3/papers.cfm?abstract_id=236400 (last accessed on Dec. 28, 2021). *See also,* Jeroen Hinloopen and Adriaan Soetevent, *Laboratory Evidence on the Effectiveness of Corporate Leniency Programs*, 39 Rand Journal of Economics 607, 607–616 (2008).

111 *Supra note* 107 at p. 932.

112 *Supra note* 107 at p. 932.

113 Claudia M. Landeo and Kathryn E. Spier, *Optimal Law Enforcement with Ordered Leniency*, National Bureau of Economic Research [NBER] Working Paper 25095 (2018) p. 17.

114 *Supra note* 114 at p. 36.

115 Reg. 2 (g), the Competition Commission of India (Lesser Penalty) Regulations, 2009.

116 Reg. 3 (1), the Competition Commission of India (Lesser Penalty) Regulations, 2009.

117 In Re: Cartelization with respect to tenders floated by Pune Municipal Corporation for solid waste processing, Case No. 50/2015, Suo moto Case No. 3/2016 & Suo moto Case No. 4/2016, order dated 19 April 2018 (CCI).

118 In Re: Cartelization in respect of zinc carbon dry cell batteries market in India, Suo moto Case No. 2/2016; In Re: Cartelization by broadcasting service providers by rigging the bids submitted in response to the tenders floated by sports broadcasters, Case No. 2/2013 (CCI).

119 Joan Brorrell et al., *25 Years of Leniency Programs: A Turning Point in Cartel Investigations,* 1 (2) Antitrust Chronicle 12, Competition Policy International (Jan 2019) www.competitionpolicyinternational.com/wp content/uploads/2019/01/AC_January_2019_2.pdf (last accessed on Dec. 28, 2021).

120 Xavier Groussot, Justin Pierce, *Transparency and Liability in Leniency Programs: A Question of Balancing?*, SSRN (January 6, 2015) http://papers.ssrn.com/sol3/papers.cfm?abstract_id=2545011 (last accessed on Dec. 28, 2021).

121 Antitrust Division Workload, Statistics FY 2009–2018, DOJ www.justice.gov/atr/file/788426/download (last accessed on Dec. 28, 2021).
122 Cartelization in respect of tenders floated by Indian Railways for supply of Brushless DC Fans and other electrical items, Suo Moto Case No. 03 of 2014, order dated 18 January 2017 (CCI).
123 *Supra note* 119.
124 In re: Cartelization in Tender No. 59 of 2014 of Pune Municipal Corporation for Solid Waste Processing, Suo moto Case No. 4/2016, decided on 31 May 2018.
125 In Re: Cartelization by broadcasting service providers by rigging the bids submitted in response to the tenders floated by Sports Broadcasters, Suo Moto Case No. 02 of 2013, Order dated 11 July 2018 (CCI).
126 *Supra note* 126 *Supra note* 119 (Zinc carbon dry battery case); *In re: Anticompetitive conduct in the dry-cell batteries market in India,* Suo Motu Case No. 02 of 2017, order dated 30 August 2018 (CCI).
127 Farhad Sorabjee and Amitabh Kumar, *The Cartels and Leniency Review*, The Law Reviews (India), (Feb 2019) https://thelawreviews.co.uk/edition/the-cartels-and-leniency-review-edition-7/1179747/india (last accessed on Dec. 28, 2021).
128 The Antitrust Division first introduced the leniency scheme in 1978 and then later redesigned it in 1993. See, OECD Report, Fighting Hard-Core Cartels: Harm, Effective Sanctions and Leniency Programs (2002)
129 *Commission Notice on Immunity from Fines and Reduction of Fines in Cartel Cases, Official Journal of the European Commission*, C 45, 2002 OECD https://eur-lex.europa.eu/legal-content/EN/ALL/?uri=CELEX%3A52006XC1208%2804%29 (last accessed on Dec. 28, 2021).
130 Harold Houba, Evgenia Motchenkova and Quan Wen, *The Effects of Leniency on Cartel Pricing*, 15 (2) Journal of Theoretical Economics 351–389 (2015); Zhijun Chen and Patrick Rey, *On the Design of Leniency Programs,* 56 Journal of Law and Economics 917–957 (2013).
131 Giancarlo Spagnolo, *Optimal Leniency Programs*, Centre for Economic Policy Research, Discussion paper series, 4840, CPI, (2004) www.competitionpolicy-international.com/wp-content/uploads/2019/01/CPI-Motchenkova-Spagnolo.pdf (last accessed on Dec. 28, 2021).
132 Joseph Harrington, *Optimal Corporate Leniency Programs,* LVI (2) The Journal of Industrial Economics 215–246 (2008).
133 Steffen Brenner, *An Empirical Study of the European Corporate Leniency Program*, 27 (6) International Journal of Industrial Organization 639–45 (2009).
134 Marc Blatter, Winand Emons and Silvio Sticher, *Optimal Leniency Programs When Firms have Cumulative and Asymmetric Evidence*, 52 Review of Industrial Organization 403–427 (2018) and Konstantinos Charistos and Christos Constantatos, *On Leniency and Markers in Antitrust: How many Informants are Enough?,* Discussion Paper No. 2/2016, University of Macedonia (2016) www.competitionpolicyinternational.com/wp-content/uploads/2019/01/CPI-Motchenkova-Spagnolo.pdf (last accessed on Dec. 28, 2021).
135 Rosa M. Abrantes-Metz and Albert D. Metz, *The Future of Cartel Deterrence and Detection*, 1 (2) Antitrust Chronicle 12, Competition Policy International (CPI) (Jan 2019) www.competitionpolicyinternational.com/wp content/uploads/2019/01/AC_January_2019_2.pdf (last accessed on Dec. 28, 2021).
136 *Checklist for Efficient and Effective Leniency Programmes*, International Competition Network, ICN www.internationalcompetitionnetwork.org/wp-content/uploads/2018/09/CWG_LeniencyChecklist.pdf (last accessed on Dec. 28, 2021).

137 *Drafting and Implementing an Effective Leniency Policy*, Chapter 2, Anti-cartel Enforcement Manual, April 2014 www.internationalcompetitionnetwork.org/wp-content/uploads/2018/05/CWG_ACEMLeniency.pdf (last accessed on Dec. 28, 2021).

138 *Ibid.*

139 Paulo Buccirossi and Giancarlo Spagnolo, *Leniency and Damages*, CEPR Working Paper DP 10682 (2015) https://ideas.repec.org/p/hhs/hasite/0032.html (last accessed on Dec. 28, 2021).

140 Angus MacCulloch and Bruce Wardhaugh, The Baby and the Bathwater – The Relationship in Competition Law between Private Enforcement, Criminal Penalties, and Leniency Policy, *SSRN* (2012) https://papers.ssrn.com/sol3/papers.cfm?abstract_id=2089369 (last accessed on Dec. 28, 2021). See, Andreas Stephan, Four key challenges to the successful criminalization of cartel laws, 2 (2) Journal of Antitrust Enforcement 333–362 (2014).

141 The Implementation of the Council Recommendation concerning Effective Action against Hard Core Cartels, *Draft Report by the Secretariat, DAF/COMP/WP3 (2017) 2, OECD* (2017) (March 2019) www.oecd.org/daf/competition/recommendationconcerningeffectiveactionagainsthardcorecartels.htm (last accessed on Dec. 28, 2021).

7 Conclusion and planning ahead

Cartels remain the topmost priority of competition regulators across the globe. Realizing the pernicious effects of cartels on the market, the Indian competition law regime treats them on a *per se* basis, which means that such action or conduct cannot be justified on any grounds. Even though the law does not provide for criminal sanctions against the cartelists, the highest penalty has been envisaged for indulgence in cartel activities. As the Indian legislature mulls a reform in the regulatory regime, it is important to evaluate and assess the experiences of the Competition Commission of India (CCI) in dealing with cartel cases in India. Reforms, if any, have to be in light of previous experiences and challenges to the effective enforcement of anti-cartel laws. The present book aims to examine and assess the public enforcement of anti-cartel laws in India through an *ex post* evaluation of the decision-making and organizational design of the CCI. This enabled us to examine the efficiency of anti-cartel enforcement in India. Optimal enforcement leading to optimal deterrence formed the crux of the enquiry. Further, the exercise also presented anatomy of Indian cartels. A descriptive account of Indian cartels based on parameters like type of cartels, duration, number of involved entities (including trade associations), affected sectors and involvement of executives. was provided. A similar investigation was done to examine the investigative procedures of the CCI to depict assessment areas of anti-cartel enforcement like duration of investigation and disposal, nature of detection, yield ratio, use of evidence, standard of proof and cartel sanctions.

A majority of the CCI's orders under Section 27 of the Competition Act, 2002 ("Act") during the observation period belonged to just four sectors – manufacturing, transportation, media and entertainment, and wholesale and retail. The demography of cases is a telling story. It cannot be imagined that all the other areas of business apart from those highlighted earlier are purely competitive. Data suggested that there were essentially two types of anti-competitive behaviours that have happened in India across the observation period. The first involved the anti-competitive practices of trade associations, and the second was where trade associations had been involved as facilitators to advance a cartel. In a majority of cases where the practices of

DOI: 10.4324/9781003347651-7

trade associations were questioned, the behaviours were the result of collective decision-making or were taken by executive bodies (office bearers). Since most of the trade associations did not undertake any economic activity, a penalty, in the absence of identification of ring leaders, was imposed on the basis of annual receipts of the trade association which, in turn, was only nominal.

A high percentage of anti-competitive conduct ceased to operate due to the intervention of the CCI, and the role of economic and market factors in the breakdown of cartels has been minimal. Cartels displayed a high degree of stability and stayed active for long durations of time due to their all-inclusive nature and presence of strong trade associations.

As has been observed from the data set, anti-competitive conduct in India has been largely concentrated around the service sector with an aggregation of cases in the wholesale and retail, media and entertainment, and transportation sectors. These cases largely involved the primary action of sector-specific and powerful trade associations. A certain level of domino effect was seen in these sectors due to the decisions of the CCI in the initial years of enforcement. While Section 3 of the Act includes practices of trade associations within the ambit of anti-competitive agreements, it was not imagined that a majority of cartel activities would revolve around them. The problem of large trade associations, with membership running into hundreds indulging in anti-competitive practices, has become a unique problem for India. This gets even more concerning when effective sanctions cannot be imposed under Section 27 of the Act. The section has not been interpreted to meet the requirement of sanctioning associations, nor has the CCI attempted to lift the "association veil" to punish constituent members. Resultantly, there is a high incidence of recidivism among these associations, with many other cases dealing with a similar nature of violations. Sanctions imposed in these cases have failed to cause deterrence for other associations in the market. The CCI, in the majority of these cases, used direct evidence to arrive at its decision which essentially means that the activities were not actually secretive in nature or that they could be easily derived from the nature of decision-making.

The manufacturing sector, unlike other jurisdictions, does not show a concentration of cartel cases. Apart from a few matters, including leniency cases, CCI has not been able to unearth cartelization in different areas within the manufacturing sector. This is in stark contrast to the experience in other jurisdictions where cartels in the manufacturing sector form the bulk of the cases.

Indian cartels can be characterized as having a high market share and high duration with centralized decision-making. High membership has not seemed to weaken cartels over a long duration of time. The all-inclusive nature of most of these cartels has kept the cartel intact. The cartels involving trade associations have been able to survive in sectors that were not actually considered to be conducive to cartelization. Similarly, unlike the experience in other countries, most of the cartels have been localized in their operation and have not operated on a pan-India level. Limiting or controlling production or supply has been the most preferred conduct in the service sector, and even though market-sharing cartels are theoretically considered to be more stable, they are not really common in India. On the other hand, bid-rigging forms the bulk of cases in the manufacturing sector.

The Baker and Faulkner categorization technique was applied to the data set to examine the structural and organizational scheme of Indian cartels. Most of the cartels turned out to be centralized in their operation. The cartels involving trade associations were operationalized through decision-making at the level of executive committees or boards, and these decisions were accepted by all participants. In other matters, the CCI has not really felt the need to identify ring leaders, and even in cases where there were supporting facts to identify ring leaders, they were treated in the same manner as other cartelists. The CCI has not yet clarified its position on the treatment of ring leaders. Non-discrimination of ring leaders in terms of sanctions and leniency has been theoretically justified and empirically proven to have negative effects on the overall deterrence of anti-cartel enforcement. It also affects the rate of filing of leniency applications.

Data suggest that more than 90% of detected cartels in India ceased to exist due to the intervention of the CCI. The factors that play a role in the breakdown of cartels have not really played out that well in India. Therefore, there are only rare instances of cartels breaking down due to economic factors, changes in market dynamics, entry of new players or defection or cheating from the cartel. Most of these cartels are all-inclusive, which means that there is little possibility of outsiders undercutting cartels. Underlying determinants of cartel duration were mapped on the basis of sector of operation, type of infringement and number of involved firms.

After providing a descriptive account of anti-competitive behaviour in India during the observation period, an investigation of investigative procedures of the CCI was undertaken. The data was used both to analyze the priority areas of CCI and also to estimate the overall cartel infestation in the market. While the success ratio of investigations leading to indictments is good, it is marred by a dismal number of investigations. This gets even more troublesome when the data with respect to the nature of cases dealt with by the CCI is analyzed. The similarity in the nature of violations and the area of operation to which these matters are related shows some kind of domino effect of one or more penalty orders on the quantum of information filed. Therefore, clubbed with the fact that there is low information filed with CCI, the success ratio of investigations leading to indictments may give a false impression of the CCI winning the war against cartels. Most of the cartel cases show concentration in only certain regions of the country, which is also indicative of the level of percolation of competition awareness in all parts of India. Interestingly, the state governments have not really been proactive in reporting cases to CCI. Most of the cases have originated from information either from competitors in the market or from rival trade associations. References from statutory authorities have been limited to certain procurement agencies like railways and the coal sector in India. When the baton was passed from the MRTPC to the CCI, it was expected that the latter would proactively exercise its powers to vet and screen business sectors and launch inquiries wherever there was a suspicion of anti-competitive behaviour. The CCI, however, has been slow in vetting key industry areas like highways, education, health, manufacturing and so on, where even though the information is not forthcoming, the said sectors have cartel-conducive environments. Usage of screens by the CCI has been rudimentary. The CCI has been unable to develop, based on its experience, any country-specific screen which can then be applied to different subject matters. The usage of structural and behavioural screens by CCI has been used not to take pre-emptive action but only to build the case of cartelization, if any. The CCI has to move from passively applying cartel screens to taking proactive steps for detection.

Interestingly, information coming from consumers constitutes the least among all sources of information related to cartels filed with CCI. Also, they have the least success rate in terms of getting an indictment order. In a muted environment of private enforcement, consumers have not looked at competition law as a recourse to their consumer issues.

Duration of cartel enforcement has also been taken as a metric to evaluate the performance of the CCI. The duration of investigation or disposal of cases has a direct impact on the deterrence value of anti-cartel enforcement. A delayed procedure leading to deferred disposal of cases allows other cartelists to take preventive steps to avoid detection. The average duration of disposal of cases, the average duration of the investigation and the duration of decision from submission of investigation report have been mapped for both orders under Section 27 and orders under Section 26 (6) of the Act during the observation period. Data shows a consistent rise in the average duration of disposal of cases with a near constant number of matters decided in a year. The CCI has been taking a longer duration of time to deal with leniency applications when compared to ordinary matters. Delay in the disposal of leniency cases may be counterproductive to the very idea of leniency, which, in turn, reduces the trust of market players in the legal structure.

The administrative efficiency of a regulator can be assessed through its ability to churn out results that withstand scrutiny and the test of time. Chapter 4 examined the quality of decision-making by the CCI by first assessing its usage of evidence and then mapping the treatment of the CCI's decisions at the appellate stages. As pointed out earlier, in a majority of the cases concerning trade associations, the CCI did not have to make an effort to look for indirect or circumstantial evidence. The same was readily available, which was then applied to reach a verdict. In other cases, the usage of evidence by the CCI has been inconsistent, as shown through illustrative case studies. This also gets proven by the fact that the CCI's decisions have not fared well at the appellate stages. A very high percentage of orders of CCI has been contested in appeal.

The low success rate of the CCI's orders has hugely impacted the deterrence level it is trying to create. Successful anti-cartel regimes have been able to create deterrence through their tough decisions, which are able to withstand challenge and scrutiny at appellate forums. The high chances of detection clubbed with a high success rate of orders of the enforcement agencies have also contributed to the success of their leniency programs. If, however, the parties alleged to have been involved in anti-competitive behaviour know that they might fare well at the appeal stage, the chances of which are more than 50% in India, they would not take the CCI's order very seriously. Appellate forums generally grant stays to the recovery of penalty, if any, ordered by the CCI. Delay in the appeal process and the infinitesimal recovery of fines have also affected the recovery of damages by persons affected by anti-competitive conduct. Case-wise assessment of the CCI's orders was done for the entire observation period. Very clearly, the CCI has been struggling to protect the sanctity of its order at the appellate forums. If all the cases during the relevant observation period are taken into account, in more than 60% of cases, the appellate forums questioned the use and adequacy of evidence by the CCI. Appellate forums seem to be asking for more concrete evidence to prove the allegation of collusion. Since a high percentage of the CCI's orders have been questioned on the basis of a lack of evidence, it is not surprising that a high percentage of its orders concerning bid rigging, which are evidence-intensive, have been either set aside or modified in terms of quantum of penalty. The CCI's orders have been found to be lacking in the correct use of facts and evidence and being unaccommodating to defences from the opposite parties. Further, in one-third of successful appeal decisions, appellate forums have questioned the quantum of penalty imposed by CCI. While the requirement to give reasons for the imposition of penalties has been stressed in most of the cases, the tribunal has ended up reducing the penalty or setting aside the penalty due to the wrong basis of calculation in approximately 33% of successful appeal matters under Section 27 of the Act. The lack of penalty guidelines or any normative standard to fix the quantum of penalty has caused the two forums jostling against each other. The tribunal has insisted on proper quantification of penalty by taking into account aggravating and mitigating factors. The CCI needs to urgently think of creating a proper methodology to quantify fines within the upper ceiling provided under Section 27. The chapter on cartel sanctions showed that the sanctioning of cartels in India, in the absence of any fining guidelines, has largely been a mechanical exercise and has been imposed in disregard to the factors that should contribute to the quantification of penalty. A comparative assessment of sanctioning exercises in the US and UK was done to establish the lack of depth in the procedure adopted by the CCI. In light of inconsistent and inadequate decision-making, we have tried to establish the need for comprehensive penalty guidelines in India to club the issue of under-deterrence. The present work tried to argue that the current penalty structure for cartels is inadequate, inconsistent and is one of the reasons for excessive litigation. The present methodology fails to take into account important factors like duration of cartel, degree of involvement of firms, leadership role and harm caused because of cartels.

Many orders of the CCI were also set aside on procedural grounds as they failed to adhere to the principles of natural justice. This not only delays the entire enforcement process but also raises doubts about the ability of the CCI to perform adjudicatory functions. The essence of cartel enforcement is in the quickness of decision-making and the severity of punishments. A very low success rate of the CCI's decisions has had a major impact on the deterrence level.

Chapters 4 and Chapter 5 take a non-welfarist approach to assess the performance of the competition enforcement in the context of cartels on the basis of output indicators, enforcement success and cost-efficiency activities. Sub-optimal enforcement of cartels was established through enforcement and punishment parameters. Chapter 6 examines the institutional design of the CCI from the lens of dealing with the issue of cartelization in Indian markets. Issues related to understaffing, high pendency of cases and non-adherence to principles of procedural fairness were highlighted.

In the present book, we have tried to argue that despite the efforts to prosecute cartels, the CCI has been unable to reach a level of optimal enforcement and, thereby, fails to create the required level of deterrence in the market. In the absence of criminal sanctions for cartel activities, civil enforcement through monetary penalties is the only weapon in the hands of the CCI. This has to be necessarily used effectively and has to be clubbed with sanctions to match the gravity of the offence. The CCI has to switch from being a passive agency to becoming an active enforcer of the law.

7.1 Recommendations

In light of the discussion in the previous chapters, the following recommendations are proposed.

7.1.1 Suggestions to improve the situation of under-detection of cartels in India

a *Screening, at the end of day, is simply pattern matching.* The CCI should actively use cartel screens, collect market data and vet different markets and sectors to look for anomalies. It cannot entirely rely on information from competitors or leniency applications and has to develop its own detection tools to identify cartelized markets. It must actively screen markets through the use of reliable data and advanced algorithms.

b The CCI has to build innovative cartel detection methods, including whistle-blower incentive schemes, to increase the rate of cartel detection. Such incentive schemes may also include the protection of whistle-blowers from corporate backlash.
c Cartels are possible wherever business or economic activity takes place and, thus, are not limited to a particular region. Given that a majority of cartels are localized in nature, the CCI should explore the possibility of having local offices to attract more and more information.
d The CCI needs to design competition compliance programs so that everyone in the corporate setup understands that their conduct is being monitored and that they may be called to explain their decisions.

7.1.2 Suggestions to improve the situation of under-deterrence of cartels in India

a *Adoption of penalty guidelines to bring certainty to the scheme of fining*: The CCI should start from a base fine for hard-core cartels and then use multipliers based on factual scenarios.
b *Certainty to decision-making*: The CCI should bring clarity to the use of Section 27 (b) and proviso to Section 27 of the Act. There has to be some rationale and prescribed conditions to invoke the proviso to Section 27 (b) of the Act.
c *Aggravating and mitigating circumstances*: The use of a universally adopted set of aggravating and mitigating circumstances to minimize the use of discretion by CCI is also needed.
d *Increase in the severity of fines*: To increase the severity of fines, the calculation of a fine should be on the basis of global sales and not just on domestic sales. Further, the CCI should revisit the idea of the calculation of fines on the basis of a certain percentage of turnovers. It has been proven in many studies that cartel overcharges are much beyond 10% of affected sales, and therefore, penalizing corporations on the basis of earlier estimations may not be very wise. If the gains made from collusion exceed the penalty imposed, indulgence in cartel conduct, in fact, becomes profitable.
e *Linking corporate compliance with corporate governance*: Indian cases have shown that in a majority of cases pertaining to cartels, there is an involvement of top-level executives or directors. The decision to indulge in anti-competitive practices is taken by individuals who control the affairs of the company or the ones taking decisions on behalf of the company. While the Act does allow proceeding against individuals under Section 48, and the CCI has, on many occasions, imposed a penalty on executives quantified at a certain percentage of their income, the same has been found to be inadequate in causing any deterrence. The legislature has to think on lines of connecting competition violation

with corporate governance norms and provide for mandatory disqualification for such individuals to continue in office.

f *Increasing the severity of fines for trade associations*: A majority of cartel cases in India involve either the primary or secondary involvement of trade associations. Platforms of trade associations have been used to operate and sustain cartels for a long duration of time. The present scheme of penalizing trade associations has proven to be inadequate and is evident from the high incidence of recidivism in trade associations. There are quite a number of cases which were on similar subject matters. This essentially indicates that the penalty in one case failed to cause deterrence for the anti-competitive practices of other trade associations. This was attributable to both low detection rates and inadequacy of fines. Since most of these trade associations are not doing any economic activity, there is no turnover, and therefore, the penalty is based on income from receipts. The CCI has, in the last ten years, commonly imposed a penalty at a rate of 10% of the average income of the trade association in the last three preceding financial years. The final amount turns out to be so less that it rarely causes any trouble for them. The CCI has to start treating the association as a body involving economic units and then lift the veil of association to impose a penalty on the basis of the combined turnover of constituent members. Only when the associations or the constituent units start fearing the impact of high penalties will they consider the need for non-indulgence in anti-competitive practices.

g *Increasing the severity of fines for executive members of trade associations*: There is a need for a legal provision that disqualifies individuals holding positions in the executive committee of the association. The CCI did try initially to pass such orders but later refrained from passing orders of disqualifications for involved executive members, possibly in fear of a legal challenge.

h *Alternate routes:* The legislature also needs to ponder on measures to boost alternate routes to increase deterrence. While Section 53N of the Act does provide for a claim for compensation from the appellate tribunal, the same has not really been effectively utilized yet. A claim for compensation can only be made after a finding of contravention of the Act from the CCI or the appellate tribunal. The Act does not allow suits for treble damages and is limited to claims for compensation post proof of loss. There also remains a lack of clarity on the methodology to quantify loss suffered due to anti-competitive conduct. Since a majority of the competition matters have not reached finality and are stuck in a lengthy appeal process, not a single case to date related to a claim for compensation has been decided. On the other hand, private enforcement in advanced jurisdictions has been recognized as one of the pillars for achieving optimal deterrence.

7.1.3 Suggestions related to public information

a The CCI should release all information in the public domain related to the degree of involvement of different firms in the cartels, harm caused by cartels, figures of affected sales, cartels' duration and cartels' market share so that a correct estimation and empirical assessment can be done on cartels. This, in turn, would foster a better understanding of the operation and structure of Indian cartels. Only when we know what we are exactly dealing with can we take corrective and effective steps.

b The CCI should publish the reasons for imposing a particular penalty on the business units in a particular case. This will help to bring certainty and predictability to cartel decisions.

c The CCI should introduce and publish a post-decision compliance report, including information on price, production cost, sales and market share as submitted by the enterprises. This will also help to keep track of post-decisional effects on the market and check post-cartel tacit collusion.

Index

For Product Safety Concerns and Information please contact our EU
representative GPSR@taylorandfrancis.com
Taylor & Francis Verlag GmbH, Kaufingerstraße 24, 80331 München, Germany

www.ingramcontent.com/pod-product-compliance
Ingram Content Group UK Ltd.
Pitfield, Milton Keynes, MK11 3LW, UK
UKHW020316270926
475702UK00050B/919
* 9 7 8 1 0 3 2 1 8 7 3 1 0 *